Rhetoric in Tooth and Claw

RHETORIC IN TOOTH AND CLAW

ANIMALS, LANGUAGE, SENSATION

Debra Hawhee

The University of Chicago Press   CHICAGO & LONDON

The University of Chicago Press, Chicago 60637

The University of Chicago Press, Ltd., London

© 2017 by The University of Chicago

Published 2017

Paperback edition 2020

Printed in the United States of America

29 28 27 26 25 24 23 22 21 20   1 2 3 4 5

ISBN-13: 978-0-226-39817-4 (cloth)

ISBN-13: 978-0-226-70677-1 (paper)

ISBN-13: 978-0-226-39820-4 (e-book)

DOI: https://doi.org/10.7208/chicago/9780226398204.001.0001

Library of Congress Cataloging-in-Publication Data

Names: Hawhee, Debra, author.

Title: Rhetoric in tooth and claw : animals, language, sensation / Debra Hawhee.

Description: Chicago ; London : The University of Chicago Press, 2016. | Includes bibliographical references and index.

Identifiers: LCCN 2016011294 | ISBN 9780226398174 (cloth : alk. paper) | ISBN 9780226398204 (e-book)

Subjects: LCSH: Rhetoric, Ancient. | Rhetoric, Medieval. | Rhetoric, Renaissance. | Philosophy, Ancient. | Animals in literature.

Classification: LCC PA3265 .H35 2016 | DDC 808.009—dc23

LC record available at http://lccn.loc.gov/2016011294

♾ This paper meets the requirements of ANSI/NISO Z39.48–1992 (Permanence of Paper).

For Nora

CONTENTS

NOTE ON TRANSLATIONS
AND PRIMARY SOURCES

Sources for all translations are noted throughout, including the translations I completed myself. After checking the Greek or Latin, I frequently use other translations if I find them satisfactory or in need only of slight modifications, which I also note. I transliterate all Greek words except in a few cases when the diacritical marks matter for my interpretation or when I am citing the Greek-English lexicon. I have included a separate bibliography of primary sources, noting all editions consulted, including Greek and Latin editions as well as translations. All these decisions result from prioritizing accessibility, transparency, and artfulness.

ACKNOWLEDGMENTS

Time, the laboratory of the humanities, proved crucial for this book. Release time provided by Penn State's Institute for the Arts and Humanities helped me launch the study, and a yearlong fellowship from the National Endowment for the Humanities enabled me to complete it. Doug Mitchell's enthusiasm for the book has been enlivening; I am ever grateful to him for seeing it through publication. I also thank Alice Bennett for the editorial sensibilities she brought to the manuscript in its prepublication stage.

The Rhetoric Society of America's Summer Institute also offered book-beginning and book-sharing opportunities. In 2011, Diane Davis and I led a workshop called Nonrational Rhetorics. Over the course of the workshop, Davis persuaded me to reconsider the negative valence of its title. The resulting conversations sent me looking for the positive elements encompassed by the phrase nonrational rhetoric. That search for positive conceptions of the nonrational was immensely productive, and its results are documented throughout this book (especially in chapter 1). At the 2015 Institute, Vanessa Beasley and I led a weeklong seminar titled Rhetoric and Sensation, and some of that material sprang from the work on this book. During the seminar, Dean Beasley and I workshopped the book's conclusion. I deeply appreciate the conversations shared with Davis, Beasley, and the participants, and to the RSA for occasioning them.

My affiliation with Penn State's Center for Democratic Deliberation helped me notice and begin to identify some of the affective qualities deliberative rhetoric held for the ancients, especially in the chapter on fables.

It's too often forgotten that the discipline of rhetoric combines practices of oral and written communication, and nearly all the work in this book has been shared in formal talks. I am grateful to the following programs and departments for hosting me—their audiences helped me hone, affirm, and at times cast aside working parts: Penn State's Institute for the Arts and Humanities (twice); the University of Pittsburgh's Department of Communication (also twice); the Center for Humanities at Temple University, the Department of Speech Communication at the University of Georgia; the Department of Communication at the University of Kansas; the Department of Communication and Culture at Indiana University; the English Department at the University of South Carolina; the English Department at Temple University, the Humanities on the Edge Speaker Series at the University of Nebraska, Lincoln; and the UMass English Department.

The labor of recommending and reviewing ought not be so thankless. Gregory Clark, Manfred Kraus, Robert Markley, Jack Selzer, Michael Witmore, and reviewers whose names remain unknown to me all at various points lent their eyes, their time, and their names to this study, and I remain exceedingly grateful.

Several colleagues offered suggestions for my translations of particularly stubborn passages. Special thanks to Manfred Kraus, Zachary Lesser, Ryan McConnell, Vessela Valiavitcharska, and Jeffrey Walker for offering their eyes and ears to my working translations. Other colleagues who took time to read and offer feedback on chapters in progress include (again) Vanessa Beasley, Jeanne Fahnestock, Susan Jarratt, Michele Kennerly, Kellie Robertson, Susan Wells, and (again) Walker and Kraus.

Graduate students who took my 2014 Rhetoric and Sensation seminar at Penn State were important interlocutors for material that appears in the introduction. Research assistance was provided early on by John Belk and Connie Bubash. Theodore Chelis lent his remarkable scholarly acumen to all the chapters and helped me prepare the manuscript for readers. Curry "eagle eye" Kennedy helped inspect proofs. Advisees Sarah Adams, Jo Hsu, Kyle King, Kristopher Lotier, and David Maxson endured my research leave with patience and continued productivity.

Friends, colleagues, and family members offering encouragement, conversations, and support include Michael Bernard-Donals, Hester Blum, Dawn Bowers, Sarah Clark-Miller, Ebony Coletu, Brooke Conti, Anne Demo, Cara Finnegan, Chris Fowler, Lara Fowler, Richard Graff, my parents, Ed Hawhee and Mary Hawhee, John Jasso, Michele Kennerly, Janet Lyon, Carole Marsh, Kim Marsh, Elizabeth Mazzolini, Katrina McGinty, Roxanne Mountford,

Erin Murphy, Phaedra Pezzullo, Damien Pfister, Jenny Rice, Thomas Rickert, Jack Selzer, Kirt Wilson, Carly Woods, Marjorie Woods, Amy Young, and Courtney Young.

John Marsh read every page of this book in draft form, and most of them more than once. He had the nearness, the distance, and the poetic ear to solve the problem of the title, and for all of this care (and then some), I owe a debt of gratitude that I hope to repay in kind. The bulk of this book was written after the 2010 arrival of our daughter Nora, who proclaimed my writing about fables "cool" and helpfully shouted "BORING!" when she decided I needed to stop talking about them.

Feeling Animals

A dog walks into the middle of Aristotle's *Rhetoric*. It is not a specific dog—this is no Argos, Odysseus's gentle and loyal pet—but rather a generic dog, an example. In fact there is more than one dog, a pack, *hoi kunes*, generalized as a type. These dogs are calm, perceptive, responsive. They appear in Aristotle's discussion of calmness, defined as "a settling down and quieting of anger." "Even dogs," Aristotle writes, "show that anger ceases toward those who humble themselves, for they do not bite those sitting down."[1]

Both George Kennedy and J. H. Freese append notes to their translations of this passage, citing the scene from the *Odyssey* in which Odysseus "sank to the ground at once" on suddenly being charged by "snarling dogs . . . a shatter of barks." Odysseus, sings the poet, sat down knowingly and with characteristic *cunning*, for "he knew the trick."[2] Freese's note on the *Rhetoric* passage is largely contextual, verifying Aristotle's assertion as commonplace knowledge about canine behavior, but Kennedy's note is more overtly cautionary: "In *Odyssey* 14.29–38 Odysseus tries this strategy when attacked by dogs. As in that case, it probably should not be counted on to work unless the dog's master is nearby."[3] Apart from the dubious generalization about canines, what is this cross-species encounter doing at nearly the center of a treatise long considered foundational for rhetoric, an art thought by most to be distinctly human-to-human?

I believe it matters that dogs show up in this particular text, and in this particular part of the text, toward the beginning of the famous discussion on rhetoric and *pathos* (emotion, feeling). I would even hazard that the humans' strategically making themselves lowly before dogs behaving angrily also matters. This passage in the *Rhetoric*, that is, breaks with the hierarchy of humans over nonhumans so often attributed to Aristotle. But it does much more than complicate that presumed hierarchy: it shows humans and nonhumans mutually assessing dispositions and altering their own in response.

This brief passage contains at least two ways nonhuman animals functioned in premodern and early modern theories of rhetoric in the West: their responsive movements and energy, and their role as partners to humans in sensing and feeling. Aristotle's dogs illustrate the potentially calming effect of humility and submission. The dogs, in this case, vivify Aristotle's point because dogs were present in the everyday lives of the Greeks; an image of a dog becoming calm before a submissive animal—human or otherwise—is easily conjured out of that everyday familiarity.[4] Much as Aristotle's discussion of calmness depends for definitional contrast on his discussion of anger in the preceding section, this image of docile dogs depends on an image of dogs snarling, charging, and biting, not unlike the four ready to pounce on Odysseus, their "shatter of barks" announcing their disposition as neither settled nor quiet. The dogs in the passage *dēlousin*, they make visible, the principle that such a display of humility can quell rage, and that it can do so in an instant. In this way animals (especially nonhuman ones) and their noisy, kinetic movement fill the world with sensory material. That filling—simultaneously a performance and a performative extension of rhetorical theory into sensory interaction—fills out the art of rhetoric.

As I show in this book, nonhuman animals turn up in rhetoric's theoretical and instructional texts when sensation matters the most, thereby bringing rhetoric to its—or the—senses. Such will be the refrain of the history that follows, which notices convergences of rhetorical energies, human and nonhuman. It does so by pressing past the representational role of animals in texts to consider the constitutive work of nonhuman animals in the history of rhetoric and rhetorical education.

At times this book documents what classicist Mark Payne refers to as "the living flow of transactional energies between one animal and another" or what George Kennedy, also in work that began as a meditation on nonhuman animals, has called "rhetorical energy."[5] My point is not to argue that nonhuman animals *do rhetoric*—that argument has been made, at times convincingly.[6] The constitutive work I am finding is more than the work of the constitutive other, a story one might tell if one were to begin and end with contemporary theoretical approaches to animals following Jacques Derrida's late writings on the question of the animal.[7] The logic pressed into Kennedy's notion of rhetorical energy is that such energy, surging even between two human animals, exceeds verbal language, and the staging of human-nonhuman animal interactions keeps alive the extralingual dimensions of such energies. This book, then, seeks to account for the curious and contradictory role animals play in language theories and language training, and that accounting brings forth a decidedly sensuous, lively, and kinetic history of rhetoric and rhetorical education.

That, in a nutshell, is the argument of this book. But its engagement with animal and animality studies, its terminological choices, and its methods are more complicated matters.[8] I will treat those concerns in turn as a way of clarifying my contributions to the lively and ongoing conversations about animals, and as a prelude to a brief overview of the book's organization.

RHETORIC AND ANIMAL STUDIES

Rhetorical texts and traditions have been sidelined by scholars working in animal studies for various reasons, many of them involving habits and presumptions entrenched in disciplinary training. The greatest concentration of animal studies works can be found in literature and philosophy, two disciplines whose relation to rhetoric has long been complicated at best.[9] Such work on what Jacques Derrida famously termed "la question de l'animal" tends to focus on the enduring role animals play in writings about human identity, values, and ethics. Literary scholars working from a historical perspective follow Derrida in unraveling the narratives spun out of presumed hierarchies of beings.[10] It must be said that the most rigorous work in literary history expresses, explicitly or not, interdisciplinary commitments, for as medieval scholar Susan Crane puts it, "Animal studies often seek to reconfigure thinking about animals by turning interdisciplinary to skew and stretch each field's range of vision."[11] Yet rhetoric does not typically appear on the (often long) lists of disciplines informing these approaches.[12]

That omission may come at a cost. Including rhetoric in cross-disciplinary conversations about animals promises to do just the skewing and stretching Crane writes about by showing how rhetorical theory and rhetorical education have historically been the paths animals travel into other disciplinary traditions. These converging paths, ironically, may be partly why rhetoric is so easy to overlook in such contexts. In fact, as with so many other moments in its variegated histories, when it comes to nonhuman animals, the discipline of rhetoric may well stretch to the point of vanishing. The *progymnasmata*, for example, school exercises used to prepare for rhetorical study, teem with reptiles, mammals, insects, and birds, even as they blend rhetoric with poetics, with what would come to be called science, and with law. That blending occurs precisely because these exercises were for centuries the bedrock of education in the West.[13] Yet scholars who focused on animals and animality during periods when the *progymnasmata* flourished tend not to consider these exercises in their accounts of imaginative cross-species encounters.[14]

Language, or specifically speech (*logos*), long the core of rhetorical studies, is a constant sticking point in animal and animality studies, as initial forays into the question of the animal from the point of view of rhetorical studies have noted. John Muckelbauer follows the problem back to the Greeks when he observes, "Ever since the cicadas offered a sonic canvas on which Phaedrus and Socrates articulated their fetish for logos, rhetoric has made its way on the backs of animality."[15] Diane Davis, working in a posthuman vein with Derridean commitments to language and self/identity, sees it this way: "Without a representable sense of self, animals are not only without language, but also without thinking, understanding, reason, response (and so responsibility)." Such a construal, Davis continues, "leaves rhetorical studies free to continue ignoring animals—ignoring all of them, since it is this lack of language that defines what is called 'the animal' in general."[16]

Reigning presumptions about language and rhetorical capacities may also be challenged from within the texts and traditions thought to have fixed them. A meticulous look at premodern texts and traditions reveals that the relationships between humans and nonhumans are not straightforwardly one-sided. It may be tempting, for example, to follow those working in animal studies and to peg the pathos-ridden dog passage from the *Rhetoric* as yet another wince-inducing instance of anthropomorphism, offensive for casting nonhuman animals as having something like human feelings. Yet that approach seems a bit too easy, if not altogether insufficient. The dogs in the passage deserve, and receive, more credit than that. Animals return time and time again in rhetorical texts, carrying lessons, calling forth, engaging, and shaping humans' beastly sides, serving as partners in feeling. Aristotle's dogs split the difference—or better put, join and blend cross-species differences—serving as quick illustrations of changing dispositions, identifying a likeness. The picture we have here, then, is as much zoomorphic as it is anthropomorphic, and indeed, a useful point of exploration may well reside in the mingling of the two.

I do not, however, wish to gloss over the tension running from the calm dogs to their snarling counterparts, and the distinctly human will to control other species. The relationship between humans and beasts is often structured by fear, violence, or both—the swineherd's hurling rocks, after all, as Kennedy's note points out, ultimately prevented Odysseus's mauling.[17] Such is the caution I glean from animal studies, and contradictory impulses of respect and of control both show up, often in tandem, at the hand of rhetoric's most heeded teachers and theorists. The dogs in Aristotle's *Rhetoric*—like the nonhuman animals considered in this book—may begin in a metaphorical register, but they soon exceed it. After the time I have spent examining rhetorical texts from this angle, I am less inclined to see what's going on as beginning and ending with the human, a tale of strict, one-way co-optation. Instead, animals work their way into these texts, leading with lessons from their own worlds, inspiring in the theorists who write about them a profound sense of intermixed worlds. Animals are used (passive voice), yes, but they also in many cases *show* what then gets *told*. If for Derrida "thinking perhaps begins" with cross-species encounters, this history draws out the sensuous and feeling dimensions of such thinking.[18] And it does so by hovering at the very line thought to distinguish humans from other animals: language, the artful use of which forms the contours of rhetoric.

ANIMALS, SENSATION, AND RHETORIC

When I set out to make something of the veritable menagerie running (or flying, crawling, barking, cawing) through premodern rhetorical texts, I began to notice two things. First, nonhuman animals appear with some frequency in texts designed to delineate or teach the art of rhetoric, especially the *progymnasmata* and also those thought to have some relation to the training of aspiring rhetors, such as Aristotle's *Rhetoric* and treatises on style (Longinus, Demetrius, Dionysius of Halicarnassus). Second, I did not set out to prove anything about sensation. Instead, nonhuman animals led me to consider the role of sensation in rhetorical education, for cross-species encounters guided by imagination, whether by memory or by a creative conjuring, are frequently accompanied by attention to the most sense-able, energetic properties of rhetoric (rhythm, sound, expression, style, movement).

Sensation in the context of this research names the faculty of perceiving through the senses, and the related and fuzzier but no less useful term feeling stretches from pleasure and pain to what we nowadays tend to call emotions (anger, pity, happiness). Sensation and feeling—and their close Greek correspondents *aisthēsis* and *pathē*—have emerged as salient terms in this particular history, which is to say they align better with my findings than do affect and emotion. This deliberate terminological choice is not license to ignore important work on affect, the concept that scholars I discuss this study with think I must mean. Sensation and feeling are respectively both more and less specific than affect or emotion.

As scholars working in the realm of aesthetics like to point out, for the ancients *aisthēsis* meant sense perception or sensation.[19] And this is durably so, from the archaic Hippocratic corpus to Ptolemy and deep into the Byzantine period.[20] Sensation also—importantly—names the level of engagement with the world that, according to Aristotle, binds together all animals—human and nonhuman.[21] In *Posterior Analytics*, Aristotle points out that an "innate faculty of discrimination" subsists in all animals, and that the name for this innate faculty is *aisthēsis*.[22] Aristotle's attribution of *aisthēsis* to all living beings, as my first chapter will show, confounds his attempts to distinguish humans from other animals even as it makes nonhuman animals matter to rhetorical arts in ways this book will detail.

And so, while I find both helpful and compelling the now almost commonplace distinction between affect and emotion as riding a line of cognitive awareness (where knowable concepts of emotion organize otherwise inchoate though no less visceral affective intensities), I will refrain from imposing a contemporary account of that distinction on premodern and early modern thought where it may not have obtained.[23] As David Konstan puts it in his ranging account of ancient emotions, "We cannot take it for granted that the Greek words map neatly onto our own emotional vocabulary."[24] And as Daniel Heller-Roazen notes, "The ancients spoke little of consciousness and a great deal of sensing."[25] Like cultural theorist Ann Cvetkovich, I favor the imprecision of feeling, "retaining," as Cvetkovich puts it, "the ambiguity between feelings as embodied sensations and feelings as psychic or cognitive experiences."[26] For similar reasons, "feeling" could be a respectable translation of the Greek *pathos*, a word that indicates disposition or state as well as—and as formed by—experiences and incidents: *that which happens to a person or thing.*[27] Indeed, the line between sensation and feeling is slippery, especially in the haptic sense, in which one *feels* something through the sense of touch.[28] Perhaps for this reason, the Epicureans folded sensation into the *pathē*, especially pleasure and pain. And in counting pleasure and pain as sensations, they likely followed Aristotle.[29] Sensation preserves a "durational intensity," a phrase that political theorist Davide Panagia uses to describe a period, however brief, when a sensuous experience or feeling suffuses and disrupts, not yet making sense.[30] Though it often is, sensation needn't be confined to human animals. On Aristotle's reading, the dogs' perception of humility can disrupt an otherwise engulfing feeling of anger. Sensation therefore, for Panagia, has the ability to throw one's prevailing dispositions into disequilibrium. Or as Brian Massumi tantalizingly phrases it in *Parables for the Virtual*, "sensation is the direct registering of potential."[31] The moment of sensation, in other words, can disrupt feeling, and the durational intensity that follows a sensory encounter constitutes change. Such dispositional change is the very stuff of rhetoric, as the next chapter will show, and such change can happen in an instant. I suspect that ancient theorists of *pathē* knew what Massumi only recently observed: "The skin is faster than the word."[32]

A handful of rhetorical scholars are pursuing sensation and feeling in a variety of fascinating ways.[33] So a concern—or a returning concern—with sensation and feeling is, much like animal studies, having a moment (or beginning to have a moment) in the critical humanities generally and in rhetorical studies more specifically. Yet animals, sensation, and feeling have heretofore not (or at least not at this time) been brought together explicitly, and certainly not in the context of rhetorical studies. This book, then, and the animals it follows, returns again and again to the "undivided instant of sensation," to use a phrase of Heller-Roazen's, the intensities and capacities for dispositional transformation that moment entails.[34] And so sensation and rhetorical education are not my end points, but rather are one way to approach the overlapping and interactive life worlds of humans and nonhumans, especially as cross-species encounters result in mutual movement and interchange. Such an approach seeks to alter persisting conceptions of rhetoric, or at least to emphasize the importance of the other than rational to rhetoric and rhetorical processes. Sensation, feeling, and emotion, then, have emerged as the positive counterparts to rationality and reason—positive, that is, in comparison with the term nonrational.

PAN-HISTORIOGRAPHY

So much for the whats and whys of the book. At this point I will dwell briefly on the *hows*, the approaches I take. As I mentioned above, what started as a book about animals and rhetorical theory soon became a book about sensation and imagination in early rhetorical theory and education and the cultures in which those theories and educational practices were embedded. A focus on education therefore dictates the rather wide chronological span of this book, which tracks, generally, the life span of the *progymnasmata*, even though it neither explicitly begins nor ends there. The exercises known as *progymnasmata* lie at the core of this book, occupying the middle chapters.

The study does not end with instructional and instructive manuals, though, but tries to follow animal lessons into the cultures where they were taught and learned, looking for ways that attitudes toward nonhuman animals may have been shaped by a curriculum so attentive to them.

This approach has developed (and developed from) what Christa Olson and I call "pan-historiography," a method that offers an expansive view of a cultural/disciplinary trend.[35] This historiography takes a "time-slicing approach" in combination with a method that spans centuries, resulting in a focus on durability and also change. The effect of a pan-historiographic method in the context of this book is to make the small shifts in animal rhetoric over time more visible and the broader continuities more discernible, even remarkable. Such chronological and methodological range helps reveal the links between, on the one hand, animal-inflected rhetorical theory and school exercises and, on the other hand, broader cultural movements and moments (e.g., conceptions of memory, the culture of accumulation, visual depictions of rhetoric in the emblem tradition). The book follows that trajectory, with the first part focusing on texts that aim to teach their readers something about rhetoric, and the second part branching out to rhetoric's formative place in broader cultural phenomena such as the art of memory, natural history and the formation of scientific culture, and the world of emblems.

Of course the span of this book means I had to make choices. Readers may notice—as did one of the manuscript's reviewers—that Cicero and Quintilian, traditional rhetoric's Roman duo, do not show up as much as one would expect, especially given Quintilian's commitment to education. The reasons are twofold. First, when it comes to nonhuman animals, as chapter 1 makes clear, Aristotle had a good deal to say: what he said in the *Rhetoric* proves crucial for conceptions of rhetoric that get used and taught even today, and what he says in other texts (especially the *Politics*) has motivated—negatively—much work in animal studies. Examining a cross section of Aristotle's writings helps show the costs of leaving rhetoric out of the conversation so far in animal studies, and of leaving nonhuman animals out of the rhetorical theories derived from Aristotle. Second, new questions often draw out a different set of writers and artifacts. The third book on style in Aristotle's *Rhetoric* sets in motion a number of tendencies that recur in the Greek stylists who succeeded him, so for this particular investigation this cluster of writers proved more fruitful than did Cicero and Quintilian. Finally, nonhuman animals are by no means absent from the Roman treatises, but they do not show up with the same frequency and density as in the style manuals and the *progymnasmata*.

Perhaps this is because Cicero and Quintilian were concerned to give a comprehensive account of the art of rhetoric rather than zeroing in on style as did Demetrius, Longinus, or Dionysius; perhaps it is has something to do with the centrality of animal-dense Homeric writings for the latter set of authors. This is not to say that Cicero and Quintilian do not have a place in a sensuous history of rhetoric; their treatments of style offer all kinds of tantalizing evidence for their concern with sensation, and I hope to pursue that evidence in another book.[36]

When animals show up in treatises with an educational purpose—as they do with some frequency—they often function to activate sensation, whether through their own movement (think writhing or stamping), or through their sheer noise and at times stunning, or even frightening, imagery (think snarling or coiling for attack). At times they inspire a kind of kinetic mimicry, serving as dynamic teaching assistants, creatures at once mysterious, awe-inspiring, able to traverse long spans with grace and ease, and still to a great extent recognizable. This mix of wonder and recognition makes nonhuman animals invitational as creatures for learning.

To this end, the first and second chapters together tell a story of how animals keep the matter of sensation at the fore of rhetorical theory, beginning in chapter 1 with Aristotle's definition of man as the *logos*-having animal. In his attempt to distinguish humans from other animals, Aristotle pinpoints sensation (*aisthēsis*) as the common point of feeling, thereby making a place for nonhuman animals in his otherwise human-oriented rhetoric. Chapter 1, "Aristotle and *Zōa Aisthētika*," therefore lays the conceptual groundwork for this book, offering a reading of Aristotle's lines in the *Politics* next to significant passages from *History of Animals* and from the *Rhetoric*. Such a reading conceives of the relationship between nonhuman and human animals as, to borrow Derrida's phrase, "something other than a privation."[37] In such a view, the *alogos* of animals enables far more than it disables. Chapter 2 pursues that Aristotelian lineage into theoretical treatises on style, showing how animals repeatedly call attention to rhetoric's visual, aural, and tactile capacities. Nowhere are these lively, sensuous lessons more evident than in texts focused on rhetorical style, especially those in the Aristotelian tradition, such as book 3 of Aristotle's *Rhetoric*, Demetrius's *On Style*, and Longinus's *On the Sublime*. If Aristotle left the gate open for nonhuman animals to roam into the otherwise seemingly human-only realm of rhetoric, once there, they show how language can enliven the senses—especially vision and hearing, rhetoric's two leading senses according to Quintilian.[38] Aristotle enlists Homer to explain his conception of a vivified, energetic rhetorical style (*energeia*): "He makes everything move and live, and *energeia* is motion."[39] And Homer does this, repeatedly, by invoking the sights and sounds of animals, of living, moving things. The commentary from Aristotle, Demetrius, and Longinus therefore yields what I call a "zoostylistics," a vital, sensuous style energized by animals. If animals help to animate language, they also help style theorists convey how words get under the skin—how they sting or bite.

The next two chapters track the sensuous work of nonhuman animals into the *progymnasmata* tradition. Chapter 3, "Beast Fables, Deliberative Rhetoric, and the *Progymnasmata*," considers fable, a genre largely ignored by rhetorical scholars, owing (perhaps) to its association with children and trivial matters. But it is exactly that association, I contend, that makes the genre worth considering in the joint context of rhetoric's history and of animal studies. Fables exploit the liminal status of children and of storied animals vis-à-vis *logos* by depriving them of *logos* in the way Aristotle is thought to have done while at the same time conferring on them the capacities of *logos*. The chapter's survey of fable's role in the contexts of political oratory and early rhetorical education therefore continues to show the centrality of sensation to political imagination, this time in deliberative contexts.

Chapter 4, "Looking Beyond Belief: Paradoxical Encomia and Visual Inquiry," focuses on two interconnected exercises in the *progymnasmata* sequence where animals feature prominently: ekphrasis (description) and encomium (praise), especially mock or paradoxical encomia. The key texts here are Lucian's "The Fly" and Michael Psellos's "bug set," four previously untranslated encomia dating to the eleventh century, set pieces praising the tiniest of insects and written in the Lucianic vein. While Libanius's doxical (sincere, orthodox) encomia to the peacock and the ox feature in the chapter, they do so only to set the stage for those encomia that stretch beyond belief (the most literal meaning of paradox), of which Lucian's "The Fly" (second century CE) is the most famous example. Psellos carries on the tradition while further dramatizing its probing sense of wonder by describing and lavishing praise on bedbugs, fleas, and lice. Lucian is taken up and cited by the likes of Erasmus and even Robert Hooke, the seventeenth-century writer known for his vivid descriptions of what he saw through the newly invented microscope. That detail is not incidental to the story unwound by this chapter. The chapter, that is, culls from these paradoxical encomia a theory of magnified rhetorical vision—a kind of amplification through magnification—that cultivates an urge to bring the tiniest of animals up close, before the eyes, to press the senses into the realm of the wondrous because unknown. As such, the chapter provides an important backstory for early modern visual regimes discussed by Stuart Clark and Janice Neri from the points of view, respectively, of cultural history and art history.[40]

. Chapter 5, "Nonhuman Animals and Medieval Memory Arts," follows animal figures into arts of memory with particular attention to how those arts developed in medieval commentaries on Greek and Latin texts. Most intriguing are the places where commentators press together philosophical (Aristotelian) traditions of memory, which emphasize sense-based, imaginative conjurings of *phantasia*, and more technical, immediately usable advice offered by the author of the *Ad Herennium* and by Cicero and Quintilian. The result is a kind of performance-enhanced imagination, and the enhancing frequently happens with eye-widening (and hence memorable) animal bodies and body parts, be they charging, distended, or inflicting pain. As scholars Mary Carruthers and Francis Yates have shown, memorious images reached a height of potency in medieval Europe, and this chapter builds on those vibrant histories of memory by focusing on the nonhuman figures that often inspire that vibrancy.[41]

Chapter 6, "*Accumulatio*, Natural History, and Erasmus's *Copia*," examines Erasmus's treatise on *copia* or "abundance" in the context of and for its devotion to natural history, especially the elder Pliny's thirty-seven-volume *Natural History*, which shapes so much of Erasmus's commentary on animal relations (including human animals). The account that results here centers on a broad notion of *accumulatio*, of compiling and storing (words, animals, things), a trend that exhibits its own sensory features. And finally, the conclusion dips into the early modern emblem tradition, with a special focus on one early seventeenth-century portrayal of Rhetorica in which she holds a three-headed beast with a cord or leash. The beast has not yet been discussed by scholars in a satisfactory way, and my own discussion offers a reading that underscores the constitutive work of animals in rhetoric's Western history, setting up further concluding arguments about the need to include rhetoric in transdisciplinary inquiries into animal relations.

All told, this book yields an uncommon historical account of animals precisely because it brings a different educational/textual tradition to bear on "the question of the animal." At the same time, it offers a new perspective on rhetoric's history: rather than presuming, as most histories of rhetoric do, the centrality of *logos* as both reason and speech, this history stresses energy, bodies, sensation, feeling, and imagination. It's no coincidence that Aristotle turns to dogs when considering emotion and feeling in rhetoric. In my view, the dogs and other animals in the *Rhetoric* can shed light on his observations about human and nonhuman animals in other texts. In order to establish more firmly the importance of rhetoric to the animal question and of the animal question to rhetoric, the next chapter considers what, exactly, Aristotle says about many kinds of animals in relation to *logos*, rhetoric, and politics. The answers begin to show how animals kept sensation alive in rhetorical theory.

CHAPTER 1

Aristotle and *Zōa Aisthētika*

The first characteristic of an animal is sensation; for even those which do not move or change their place, but have sensation, we call living creatures.

ARISTOTLE, *De anima*[1]

The judgment is in perception.

ARISTOTLE, *Nicomachean Ethics*[2]

Since Aristotle. If animal studies has an opening gambit, this phrase may be it.[3] It was Aristotle, after all, who established the *logos/alogos*—the with- or without-*logos* (speech or reason)—distinction that so decisively cleaved humans from other animals. Even those who know that the *logos/alogos* distinction predates Aristotle acknowledge that he did something more emphatic: "With Aristotle," as classicist John Heath puts it, "the link between *logos* and humans, and the rejection of *logos* from the non-human, becomes explicit."[4] Usually the "since Aristotle" gambit is accompanied by a gesture to the famous passage in the first book of the *Politics* where Aristotle declares humans to be the animals that have *logos* (*zōon logon echon*).[5]

That passage may be worth another look, though, especially in conjunction with Aristotle's writings on other animals, on the soul, and on rhetoric, the artful use of language. Such a survey, as this chapter will show with more detail, helps to draw out a perceptive core of existence shared by all animals. This perceptive core is too often skipped over by scholars of Aristotle's rhetoric and politics, trained as they are to follow the path of *logos*.[6]

But leaving behind the *alogos*—the without-*logos*—as a category, or even presuming that Aristotle did so, comes at a cost. That cost is a more comprehensive, fully fleshed-out theory of rhetoric. The trick is to approach *alogos* as something other than an absence of *logos*, to identify in positive terms what takes the place of *logos*. In other words, the privative work of the alpha (α, *a*) in *alogos* needn't make it a deficiency or, as Jacques Derrida formulates it, a withholding.[7] *Alogos*, after all, names a part of the soul for Aristotle, a part that

operates without reference to rationality; it is nonrational (as opposed to *ir*rational).[8] *Alogos* may therefore usefully be approached as a capacity or set of capacities. Resources for approaching the term as a capacity or set of capacities
rather than a deficiency may be found in texts composed by Aristotle himself
and in the capacities exhibited by the nonhuman animals that appear there.

Richard Sorabji, a philosopher long preoccupied with Aristotle's writings
on nonhuman animals, models such an approach when he offers this observation: "If animals are to be denied reason (*logos*), and with it belief (*doxa*), then
their perceptual content must be compensatingly expanded, to enable them
to find their way around in the world."[9] This perceptual expansion occurs on
more than the content level where Sorabji leaves it. In the context of rhetorical theory, nonhuman animals expand into the role of proxy feelers and are
often carriers of sensation. In such a view, the implications of which I develop
in this chapter, an insistence on nonhuman animals' being *aloga* is as much
an *attribution* as it is a denial or rejection, and this attribution of expansive,
and oftentimes intense feeling to nonhuman animals helps account for their
constitutive role in the teaching and shaping of rhetorical theory, as chapter 3
on fables will help show. Such constitutive force is not, or not always, as one
might surmise, a simple constitutive outside—that which helps identify *logos*-
having by precisely and only not having *logos*. Instead, this constitutive role
works through instruction, illustration, and a persistent presumption of cross-
species likeness.

Nonhuman animals therefore do the work of sensation, folding back on the
logos they have been denied, lending it energetic life through sounds, shapes,
textures, and movements. This does not mean they are only or even mere
rhetorical objects or figures, but instead means that they infiltrate rhetorical
lifeworlds through encounters imaginative and real. In short, in premodern
rhetorical theory, and especially in Aristotle's key and formative texts, nonhuman animals exert a pull. And that pull is toward feeling.

As I will show, nonhuman animals frequently show up in passages where
sensation and feeling matter most; Aristotle thereby exploits their ambiguous
relation to categories of judgment and thought, but he consistently uses nonhuman animals to display feelings. Sensing, breathing, moving animals can at
times embody pure spirit (*thumos*). They show feelings ranging from pleasure
and pain to anger and friendliness. They can be especially confounding for
critics when they show up in discussions of cultural economies of honor and
shame so crucial for judgment, but less confounding if approached through
the category of *aisthēsis*, the ancient term for sense perception. For Aristotle,
nonhuman animals also act as sensible objects in that they are observable,

but they are also simultaneously sensing—on this Aristotle is completely un-ambiguous. This means that along with sensation, which is decidedly *alogos*, nonhuman animals often bring life, energy (*energeia*), to *logoi*, to speeches, to writings, or to words themselves. Such is the role they play in treatments of rhetorical style. Sensing, feeling animals help to fill out the parts of rhetoric that are *alogos*, but this does not mean that nonhuman animals remain far removed from the domain of *logos*. As this chapter's last section and the next chapter will show, nonhuman animals as lively, energetic, sensible beings in-habit discussions of rhetorical style, filling *logos* with life.

Nonhuman animals have capacities to be uniquely instructive for politi-cal life and for rhetorical theory. Aristotle does not underestimate those ca-pacities, nor should we. To show how this constitutive force plays out, I will begin by reexamining the passage in the *Politics* that inspires all those "since Aristotles," putting it next to passages that draw out a more dynamic and lively version of *alogos*. I will then follow *aloga zōa* into the *Rhetoric*, showing how a zoocentric approach to rhetoric and to rhetorical theory stresses with specificity the components of rhetoric that are themselves *alogos*, outside the bounds of both verbal language and rationality, but nevertheless crucial for a comprehensive account of the art.

ARISTOTLE'S POLITICS OF *AISTHĒSIS*

Here, then, is the passage where Aristotle famously denies *logos* to all animals except human ones:

> That man is much more a political animal than any kind of bee or any herd animal is clear. For, as we assert, nature does nothing in vain; and *man alone of the animals has speech*. The voice indeed indicates the painful or pleas-ant, and hence is present in other animals as well; for their nature has come this far, that they have a perception [*aisthēsin*] of the painful and pleasant and signal these things to each other. But speech [*ho de logos*] serves to make visible [*dēloun*] the advantageous and the harmful, and hence also the just and the unjust. For it is peculiar to man as compared with the other animals that he alone has a perception [*aisthēsin*] of good and bad and just and unjust and the other things of this sort; and community [*koinōnia*] in these things is what makes a household and a city.[10]

In placing *logos* at the polis's center, Aristotle twice asserts a distinction be-tween human and nonhuman animals. The first and more famous of these two assertions has to do with exclusivity: *logos* is that which man alone of the animals possesses.[11] This assertion is too often where scholars stop. But the rest of the passage, the part that contains the second assertion, deserves attention as well. In elaborating the *zōon logon echon* doctrine, the passage moves from *logos* to sense perception (*aisthēsis*) and—curiously—not back again. In remaining with *aisthēsis*, the passage introduces the capacity that binds together all animals (human and nonhuman) in Aristotle's writings on the soul, on zoology, on ethics, and even—as I will show—on rhetoric.

In the *Politics*, the *zōon logon echon* distinction supports Aristotle's assertion that it is clear (*dēlon*) why "man is a much more political animal than any kind of bee or any herd animal."[12] The comparative word rendered as "much more" is *mallon*, and the implication is that other animals are also political, just not as intensely so as *anthrōpos*.[13] Supporting this reading is Aristotle's characterization of *politika* in *History of Animals* as "those which have some one common activity," a characterization he supports with a list of examples: "humans, bees, wasps, ants, cranes."[14] Without the connection to the *History of Animals* it might be easy to overlook the centrality of *aisthēsis* in the *Politics* passage. Indeed, even those scholars who insist on the connection between the two treatises stress the indicative work of *logos* over the perceptive work of *aisthēsis*.[15]

But the link across the two treatises—and the nonhuman animals prompting the link—ought to alert readers to the cross-species comparison happening here as much as to the differentiation.[16] When the *Politics* passage unravels the claim about *logos* to a core of perception, that unraveling is enabled and shared by the nonhuman animals considered *alogos* in this scheme. Reading this passage as a gloss on the *phōnē*/*logos* (sound/speech) distinction rather than the *logos*/*alogos* distinction returns more forcefully to a base of *aisthēsis* or sensation. *Phōnē*, in this passage, names the way animals signal "a perception of the painful and pleasant," while *logos* "serves to make visible (*dēloun*) the advantageous and the harmful, and hence also the just and the unjust."[17] That difference repeats in the second distinction, where Aristotle ascribes to *anthrōpos* alone "a *perception* of good and bad and just and unjust and the other things of this sort." Read in this way, the *Politics* passage places *logos* at a perceptual remove from the polis, for *logos* "serves to make visible" (*epi tō dēloun*) a perception of a just world, to, in a way, hand it over to or share it with other perceiving humans, thereby creating (or in some cases maintaining) an associative bond. That handing over of a perception, at least in this passage, constitutes a polis. This emphasis on sharing perceptions matters because it places all animals on the same plane in the way they participate in their world. On such a reading, the differences between sound and words seem smaller inasmuch as both are deemed the means by which animals exchange perceptions. But what humans are deemed to perceive and to make visible to others bears more of the cross-species difference than *logos* itself.

A similar emphasis on sharing perceptions or *aisthēsis* constitutes friendship for Aristotle, and the relevant passage in the *Nicomachean Ethics* also distinguishes such perception sharing from the associative activity of nonhuman animals:

> Existing is, as we saw, a choiceworthy thing because of a person's perception [*aisthanesthai*] that he is good, and this sort of perception [*aisthēsis*] is pleasant on its own account. Accordingly, one ought to share in the friend's perception [*sunaisthanesthai*] that he exists, and this would come to pass by living together and taking part together in word and thought—for this is what living together would seem to mean in the case of human beings, and not as with cattle, merely feeding in the same place.[18]

Here again, *logos* is presented as the means by which the perception of good is shared with others.[19] The last line above sidesteps the point made in the *Politics* about animals signaling feelings of pleasure and pain to each other, thereby reaching for a sharper contrast between friendly humans chatting together and cattle grazing in the same field.[20] In the *Politics*, though, *logos* and the shared perception it enables parallel the process nonhuman animals use to signal (*sēmanein*) perception, or *aisthēsis*, of pleasure and pain. In both passages, according to Aristotle, political behavior—the associational gathering endemic to *politika* and communal sense making—depends on rhetorically assisted sense perception. *Logos* facilitates shared perception, *sunaisthanesthai*.[21] At stake in the role of *logos* here is a making common, a sharing, of perceived lifeworlds, which could well operate as a general definition of rhetoric. The sensation at the heart of such a conception matters a good deal for the way rhetoric meets the problem of individuation.[22] As philosopher Jill Frank notes in her commentary on the *Nicomachean Ethics* passage:

> Aristotle's choice of the word *aisthesis*, perception, to describe what friends share is key. We perceive with our senses, and what we sense we perceive in its particularity or differences. Because we perceive in this way, one person cannot have another person's perception. To share a perception thus

requires that the friend whose perception it is communicate it or make it common.[23]

Later in this book I will have more to say about *logos*'s perceptive capacity and how it works in the context of rhetoric. For now it is crucial to note that the process of making visible through *logos* abstract principles such as goodness or justice is embedded in the very definition of *politika*, but this does not mean that more direct sensations of pleasure and pain (the capacities of all animals) are excluded from that definition. Indeed, as Sorabji points out, and as Jessica Moss elaborates with considerable depth, *De anima* points the *aisthēsis* of pleasure and pain toward good and bad as such, further softening the distinction in the *Politics*.[24] Taking this *aisthēsis* emphasis of *politika* and of political friendship back to the *History of Animals* helps to make better sense of the cross-species distinctions Aristotle asserts rather emphatically in that treatise: "Of all animals, the only deliberative one is *anthrōpos*. Many animals have the power of memory and can be trained; but the only one which can recall past events at will is *anthrōpos*."[25] When temporality—the preservation of past perceptions through memory and the future-oriented, projective work of deliberation—is added to the mix, what results is a highly circumstantial, contingent, *rhetorical* account of *aisthēsis*, one that Aristotle in other texts does not restrict to humans. Nonhuman animals, as creatures of the now, help to clarify this contingency precisely because they embody it. Any sense of the character of an action requires perception, or as Aristotle phrases it in the excerpt used as the epigraph to this chapter, "The judgment is in the perception."[26] Embedded in this phrasing is the centrality and immediacy of *aisthēsis*—a link between circumstance and perception—that needs to be drawn out and theorized in the context of rhetoric, and the most sensible place to begin is Aristotle's treatise on that subject. But first I want to consider more carefully three kinds of *aisthēsis* Aristotle puts forth.

THREE KINDS OF *AISTHĒSIS*

The handful of passages on human exceptionalism considered above form something of a self-referential loop: (human) perception of the just and good constitutes a *polis*, and participation in the *polis* by means of *logos* that works to vivify perception binds and distinguishes humans in the context of politics and friendship. Aristotle's conception of *politika* therefore depends at every turn on habits of perceiving and conveying perceptions, habits not necessarily restricted to humans in the Aristotelian corpus. On this reading, two kinds of *aisthēsis* may be discerned in these passages, the division between which more accurately distinguishes humans from other animals in Aristotle's scheme: *aisthēsis* as sensing pain and pleasure through touch and a host of other senses,[27] a cross-species *aisthēsis* that I will call "feeling *aisthēsis*"; and the *aisthēsis* of discerning the good or right, which Aristotle presents as a higher-order, justice-oriented, *logos*-dependent perception that I term "deliberative *aisthēsis*."[28]

To this pair I would add a third kind of *aisthēsis* not mentioned in these passages but discernible in the *Politics* passage's passing-on of perceptions, and in passages where Aristotle wrestles with conceptions of memory, of calculation, of *phronēsis*, of deliberation. This third kind of perception, called *phantasia*, Aristotle describes in the *Rhetoric* as "a kind of weak perception."[29] *Phantasia* works indirectly as a mode of sensation, which is to say at a remove from a sensible object, and is often translated as imagination, though controversially so (I prefer to leave it untranslated).

Neither is it uncontroversial to call *phantasia* a kind of *aisthēsis*. Indeed, working against the "weak *aisthēsis*" line in the *Rhetoric* is the assertion in the *De anima* that "*phantasia* is different from both sensation [*aisthēseōs*] and thought [*dianoias*]," yet he equivocates even here, noting that still, *phantasia* "does not come about without sensation, and without it there is no conceiving that something is the case." The passage continues:

> But *phantasia* and judgment are different modes of thought, clearly. For the former is an affection [*pathos*] lying in our power whenever we want, *hotan boulōmetha* (it is possible to bring before the eyes as for instance those who form mental images placing them into mnemonic systems), but it is not in our power to form opinions, since those must be true or false. Still, whenever we decide that something is terrible or frightening, we immediately feel the same way, and similarly when we think something inspires courage. But in *phantasia* we have the likeness of spectators beholding something terrible or courageous in a picture.[30]

Phantasia, then, is "not sensation" (*ouk estin aisthēsis*).[31] This is the case for two reasons. First, *phantasia* can occur without, for example, the kind of sight or seeing that happens with the organ of sight, as Aristotle notes a few lines later: "visions appear to us even when our eyes are shut."[32] Second, sensation is a presumed constant, but *phantasia* is not. So while *phantasia* and *aisthēsis* are not identical, they are connected: where one stops the other often begins. This complementary relation between *phantasia* and *aisthēsis* helps to account for why in the *Rhetoric* Aristotle calls *phantasia* a "kind of weak perception," because *phantasia* steps in when direct forms of *aisthēsis* for whatever reason are not possible. Examples include looking at one's reflection in water; straining to see someone in fog; searching with one's outstretched hands in the dark; or other conditions of inhibited or obscured sight. *Phantasia* is, as Moss puts it, "quasi-perceptual."[33] It approximates *aisthēsis* and works on a similar register.

Phantasia and *aisthēsis* are therefore similar, *homoiōs*, and they perform similar functions of engaging with and moving through the world, but they arise in distinct situations. As Aristotle writes in *De anima*, "because *phantasiai* abide in us and resemble sensations, living creatures frequently act in accordance with them, some, *viz.*, brutes, because they have no mind, and some, *viz.*, men, because the mind is temporarily obscured by emotion, or sickness, or sleep."[34] Note here the correspondence between *pathos* and *phantasia*: a disturbed state of feeling can inhibit perception as much as a feverish state or even deep slumber. This association of *pathē* with *phantasia* will become more evident later in this chapter when I discuss Aristotle's famous treatment of the *pathē* in book 2 of the *Rhetoric*. For now I want to focus on the way this passage emphasizes the circumstantial nature of *phantasia*. The contingency of *phantasia* on temporary states (anger, sleep, fever), and the fact that they "abide in us," lends a portability, as well as a temporality, to feeling *aisthēsis*.[35] As a result, sensations, which are more usually immediate, bound to the undivided instant of the now, are carried forward (in the case of planning for the future)[36] and backward (e.g., with memory) in relation to time.[37] *Phantasia* therefore works somewhere between feeling *aisthēsis* and deliberative *aisthēsis*, which is more concerned with goodness and justice. Indeed, in *De anima* Aristotle carves out a special category of *phantasia*, which he names "deliberative phantasia," *phantasia bouleutikē*,[38] and which involves "calculative weighing of multiple *phantasic* images."[39] What makes things interesting, then, is that these three kinds of *aisthēsis* rarely operate independently of each other; far from it. In fact, as I will attempt to show, in Aristotle's scheme the rhetorical processes that happen on registers without recourse or reference to *logos* (which is to say *alogos*)—surges of highly complex feelings, snap judgments, changes of heart, *transformation*—happen in the connective tissue among feeling *aisthēsis*, deliberative *aisthēsis*, and *phantasia*. These connections are not difficult to find in Aristotle's work; one need only follow animals other than humans.

"OTHER ANIMALS": PLEASURE, HONOR,
AND THE LOGIC OF LIKENESS

For all the talk of Aristotle's exclusion of nonhuman animals from modes of reason, a notable and mostly consistent logic of cross-species likeness pervades his writings. When his biological and metaphysical treatises are considered, few capacities that draw on perception and something like reason exclude other animals—neither knowledge (*gnōsis*), nor critical acumen, nor prudence (*phronēsis*); definitely not *thumos*, and not even *phantasia* or imagination. While restricting the amount of *gnōsis* for some animals in *Generation of Animals*, Aristotle nevertheless asserts that "sensation is, of course, a sort of knowledge."[40] In *De anima* Aristotle observes that "the soul in living creatures is distinguished by two functions, the judging capacity [*tō te kritikō*] which is a function of the intellect [*dianoias*] and sensation combined [*aisthēseōs*], and the capacity for exciting movement in space."[41] In the *Metaphysics*, Aristotle allows *phantasia* and memory to some animals and therefore explicitly opens the door to some nonhumans' capability of being *phronima*, intelligent, or at the very least "capable of learning," *manthanei*.[42] And in the *Nicomachean Ethics*, Aristotle acknowledges the flexibility of *phronēsis* or prudence such that "even some of the lower animals are said to be prudent, namely those which display a capacity for forethought as regard their own lives."[43] In *Parts of Animals* Aristotle forwards a seemingly Hippocratic spectrum of animal qualities based on thickness and warmth of blood, where thin, cold blood "is conducive to sensation and intelligence, *aisthētikōteron de kai noerōteron*," whereas thick, warm blood "makes for strength."[44] This logic of likeness is particularly striking in the discussion of *thumos* (spirited inclination, or just plain spirit) and courage in the *Nicomachean Ethics*, where Aristotle asserts that *thumos* emboldens humans, "like wild beasts which rush upon a hunter that has wounded them,"[45] but courage adds to *thumos* a layer of deliberate choice, *proairesis*.[46] At the end of the discussion, Aristotle reasserts the similarity: "Still, they [viz. *thumos* and courage] have some similarity."[47] Aristotle exploits the similarities across animal species at least as much as—if not more than—he can be found distinguishing humans from other animals. This logic of likeness therefore courses through his considerations of humans and other animals, especially in the context of rhetoric and language.

More often than not in the *Rhetoric* nonhumans appear as specific kinds of animals—e.g., dogs, horses, birds. But Aristotle does mention nonhumans generally—he speaks of *allōn zōōn*, of other animals—a few times in the treatise.[48] The first mention of *allōn zōōn* appears in a discussion of topics for epideictic rhetoric. Here is that passage from the beginning of the chapter:

> Let us speak of virtue and vice and honorable and shameful; for these are the points of reference for one praising or blaming. . . . Since it often happens, both seriously and in jest, that not only a man or a god is praised but inanimate objects and any random one of the other animals, propositions on these subjects must be grasped in the same way.[49]

This passage's questioning of people's sincerity when praising "other animals" deserves full attention, as does Aristotle's grudging neutrality, and I have more to say on these matters (and on this passage) in chapter 4's discussion of paradoxical encomia. For now, and in support of the current chapter's assessment of the line Aristotle draws between human and nonhuman animals, I want to tease out the logic in this passage. Regardless of their sincerity, and regardless of their object, Aristotle seems to be suggesting, propositions of praise can—ought to—be treated in the same way.[50] In other words, no matter what rhetors are praising, the values remain constant. The passage therefore sets forth a logic of cross-species likeness, a logic that persists in the example drawn from book 2 of the *Rhetoric* and noted in this book's introduction, whereby calm dogs illustrate the calm disposition under discussion.[51]

Likeness, albeit an intraspecies likeness, in fact is the explicit focus when a flurry of nonhuman examples turns up in the *Rhetoric* two chapters later (in chapter 11). Here Aristotle is cataloging topics about pleasure useful in the context of judicial rhetoric. Note that this chapter is a remarkable contribution to Aristotelian theories of sensation, and the conceptual work he does here is important background to book 2's delineation of the *pathē*. If read with the *Politics* passage in mind, where Aristotle notes that all animals share the voice's indication of pleasure and pain, his discussion of pleasure and pain in the *Rhetoric* also offers insight into how Aristotle believes sensation works for all animals, and at the same time how it matters for rhetoric.

The chapter begins by defining pleasure (*hēdonē*) as "a certain movement [*kinē*sis] of the soul, a sudden and perceptible settling down into its natural state"; "pain [*lupē*]," he continues, "is the opposite."[52] This definition presents pleasure and pain not as themselves states of feeling, but as soul movements (*kinēsis*), one (pain) pulling toward disequilibrium, and the other (pleasure) toward equilibrium.[53] As the subsequent discussion in the chapter on pleasure makes clear, three things follow from this definition: (1) Soul movement contains the possibility for more movement into durable states, that is, for state change, or rhetorical transformation. (2) Pleasure stems from appetite, *epithumia*, and can be rational or nonrational (as Aristotle writes a few lines later, "Everything is pleasurable for which there is longing").[54] (3) Where there is pleasure there is also sensation and *pathē*; indeed, at times Aristotle treats pleasure and pain as themselves sensation, though this matter is up for debate.[55] When leading up to his definition of *phantasia* or indirect perception, Aristotle offers that "to be pleased consists in perceiving a certain emotion."[56] Pleasure inheres in the perception of *pathos*.

Indeed, in contrast to the picture of antisocial cattle in the *Nicomachean Ethics*, the *Rhetoric*'s discussion of pleasure presents something like non-human community:

> And since what accords with nature is pleasurable and kindred things are by nature related to one another, all things that are related and similar are, for the most part, pleasant; for example, human being to human being, horse to horse, and youth to youth. This is the source of proverbs "coeval delights coeval," "Always like together," "beast knows beast," "jackdaw by jackdaw," and other such things.[57]

No fewer than three direct mentions of nonhuman animals occur in this passage. This is of course not surprising, since nature (*phusis*) is the topic, and animals were—and are—presumed to be guided by nature. But considered in light of what sociologists now call the homophily principle, which accounts for a greater frequency of affinity between beings perceived to be similar, the move from humans to horses and back again is not simply a naturalizing move.[58] Take the proverb "jackdaw by jackdaw," the ancient Greek version of "birds of a feather flock together,"[59] a proverb that Aristotle mentions again in *Nicomachean Ethics* when noting varied opinions on whether friendship stems from similarity or difference.[60] According to the logic of these proverbs, the feeling of pleasure through similarity is shared across species, and so humans and nonhumans alike are presented as capable of experiencing pleasure through association. When Aristotle offers these proverbs about animals, he has it both ways: birds that hang out with birds like themselves illustrate the workings of human filiation; but the proverbs themselves do not consider human-nonhuman association, clumping as they do members of a species with members of a same species.

Yet a looser association may persist in the very act of observing, another point implicit in the flocking proverbs: the horses, beasts, and jackdaws in these proverbs are sensible objects—that is, they exhibit observable behaviors structurally analogous to observable human behavior, but they are sensible objects that also themselves sense. This sensible sensation, in my view, along with the shared and oftentimes analogous lifeworlds, is what makes non-human animals so readily available as examples in Aristotle's views on human behavior.[61] And it is their ability to flexibly and at times simultaneously perform both roles—at once to be analogous to humans and to intensify feelings—that accounts for the persistence of nonhumans in theories of rhetoric and language.

BUT FOR SHAME

The examples above considered the logic of likeness that puts forward non-human animals as subjects for speeches and as sensing, sensible objects, binding them with humans by analogy. Yet while other animals may receive honor, beasts are deemed profoundly deficient in the ability to confer—or, in the case of shame, remove—honor. This exclusionary move is particularly revealing for where Aristotle in fact draws a line between humans and other animals. I discussed these two passages earlier in the context of *phantasia*, and *phantasia* remains crucial for the link between feeling *aisthēsis* and deliberative *aisthēsis*. The latter two kinds of *aisthēsis* make better sense of the passages in question.

It is helpful to approach the question of honor and shame with beasts at the fore. *Zōa* (animals) are mentioned by Aristotle rather inexplicably, even parenthetically, at the end of both passages, but as I hope to show, the three kinds of *aisthēsis* (feeling *aisthēsis*, deliberative *aisthēsis*, and *phantasia*) help to make sense of them. Here is the first passage:

> And honor and reputation are among the pleasantest things, through each person's imagining that he has the qualities of an important person; and all the more [so] when others say so who, he thinks, tell the truth. Such ones are neighbors (rather than those living at a distance) and his intimates and fellow citizens (rather than those from afar) and contemporaries (rather than posterity) and the practical (rather than the foolish) and many (rather than few); for those named are more likely to tell the truth than their opposites, [who are disregarded] since no one pays attention to honor or reputation accorded by those he much looks down on, such as children or small animals, at least not for the sake of reputation; and if he does, it is for some other reason.[62]

The passage in book 2 makes a nearly identical point but in the context of honor's inverse, shame. Book 2's discussion of "those before whom people feel shame" helpfully elaborates the same points in the discussion of honor, similarly framing this *pathos* in terms of *phantasia*: "Since shame is *phantasia* about a loss of reputation for its own sake . . ."[63] There, Aristotle also returns to sensation by offering the proverb "shame is in the eyes," with the implication that shame inheres in—is conferred by—the eyes of the witnesses to the shameful act.[64] Toward the end of this discussion of shame, Aristotle again invokes those pesky children and animals with this line: "But on the whole they [people] are not ashamed before those whose reputation of telling the truth they much look down on (no one feels shame before children and animals)."[65] In both these passages, Aristotle uses *paidia* and *thēria*, common nouns for children and beasts.[66] These creatures, though capable of feeling *aisthēsis*, according to Aristotle, have no capacity for the discerning, deliberative *aisthēsis* discussed earlier; that is, they are not, in this scheme, capable of distinguishing honorable actions from shameful. Nor (in this scheme) does Aristotle deem them particularly good at sharing those perceptions even if they had that capacity, so Kennedy's interpretation in the second edition that it comes down to the ability to speak isn't wrong per se. Still, recalling from the *Politics* that the role of *logos* in a *polis* is to convey the perceptions of good and bad, right and wrong, a satisfactory interpretation of these mentions of beasts needs at least two kinds of *aisthēsis* (feeling *aisthēsis* and deliberative *aisthēsis*), though the third (*phantasia*) remains prominent as well.

The beasts and children round out what is mostly a catalog of opposites designed to privilege the reliability of esteem holders, and that reliability is indexed mainly by opportunities for solid observation. Yet the category exemplified by children and beasts stands alone, grouping together these unreliable narrators. George Kennedy's note on the passage corroborates such a reading. He writes, "This parenthesis really applies to those who cannot speak at all, infants and animals."[67] In the first edition, Kennedy interprets the diminutive form of beasts as small animals kept indoors and therefore retroactively posits a witnessing of acts meant to be private, while his second edition opts for the inability to speak or to judge an action as shameful: that is, children and animals are unreliable narrators, often because they cannot (or cannot yet) narrate.[68] So children and beasts, in this passage at least, are distanced if not excluded from economies of honor and reputation. But to stop with the exclusion point or to lean on Kennedy's readings (as I myself have done in previous publications) misses a finer point about perception, one that finally helps these instances make sense: these matched parentheticals depend on the distinction between feeling *aisthēsis* and deliberative *aisthēsis*, because the passages turn on a distinction between sheer perception and sheer perception intermingled with perception of right and wrong. Aristotle is using children and beasts as creatures possessing one but not the other; they are capable of sensing, yes, but not in the morally discerning way indicated by deliberative *aisthēsis*.

Aristotle's mention of children and beasts in book 6 of the *Nicomachean Ethics* supports my account even as it helps draw out the implications of deliberative *aisthēsis*, showing them at work in the sphere of virtue. There Aristotle is discussing the ways that "virtues in the true sense," instead of naturally existing in one's soul, "come to belong to us in another way."[69] Here, as with the *Rhetoric*, Aristotle turns to children and beasts, using the same words: "The natural states [*phusikai*] are already in the dispositions of children and beasts too, but manifestly harmful without discerning intelligence [*aneu nou*]."[70] Moss, referring to the children and beasts here as "proto-virtuous," helpfully draws out the implications for the use of *nous* by tying it to the *phronimos*, the figure of prudence and discernment.[71] But the very next line is worth considering as well because it invokes sense perception explicitly by comparing those *aneu nou*—without discerning intelligence—to an animate being without the sense of sight: "At any rate, this much would seem to be clear: Just as a heavy body moving around unable to see suffers a heavy fall because it has no sight, so it is with virtue."[72] At stake in this analogy—of the being whose sight has been removed—is the importance of a particular kind of perception in the moral sphere. The risk of mishap increases.[73] The word *sphallesthai*, here translated as "suffers a heavy fall," does double duty in the text, though, because it indicates tripping up or being overthrown, falling (as in from fortunes), or simply failing or being led astray. What is noteworthy about this analogy is the absence of judgment on Aristotle's part. Things will get in the way of a large creature moving through the world without the means to perceive those things, thereby making hard falls more likely; similarly, those without the ability to discern good and bad—also things in the world—are more likely to be led astray. Sense perception—here figured as literal eyesight—guides both. The analogy points back to the near certainty of manifest harm in the children and beasts line and thereby simultaneously draws together feeling *aisthēsis* and deliberative *aisthēsis* in order to sharpen the distinction: they are parallel and work similarly but not identically.

The distinction made in the *Nicomachean Ethics* helps to clarify the tandem asides in the *Rhetoric* by "showing the work"; Aristotle is compelled to assert a kind of exceptionalism in the area of moral discernment or deliberative *aisthēsis*. Beasts, along with children, their associative partners,[74] are stamped as nonparticipants in the most complex and other-dependent, abstract, perceptive feelings of honor and shame. And in a separate passage, this time in the discussion of hatred, Aristotle even casts abstract notions as less graspable because he deems them less perceivable: "Painful things [*lupēra*] are all perceivable [*aisthēta panta*], but most exceedingly bad, injustice [*adikia*] and thoughtlessness [*aphrosunē*], are least perceptible [*hēkista aisthēta*]."[75] This passage effectively replaces Aristotle's nonsighted person, discussed above, with obstacles that are themselves difficult to see. Danger may inhere in both of his scenarios. Read in terms of Richard Sorabji's hypothesis, by which, recall, perception is expanded in a compensatory way, this set of exclusions also releases nonhuman animals (and children as well) into the realm of pure sensation, feeling *aisthēsis*, where they are able to illustrate, teach, and move through this still important category of feeling in the context of rhetorical theory.

Rhetoric, after all, as Aristotle teaches in book 2, has everything to do with the workings—the routings and reroutings—of feelings. In order to sort through the implications of feeling *aisthēsis*, how it feeds and bends deliberative *aisthēsis* in Aristotle's rhetorical theory, and further what *phantasia* does in the context of this circuitry, it is crucial to revisit those famous chapters on feeling with nonhumans at the fore.

TURBULENT *AISTHĒSIS*:
THE DISTURBANCE OF FEELING

In book 16 of the *Iliad*, one of the most spirited, *thumos*-laden scenes, the one where Achilles goads his men, the Myrmidons, into attacking the Trojans, Homer suspends Achilles outside his hut momentarily and devotes six lines to an extended metaphor:

> Boys will sometimes disturb a wasps' nest
> By the roadside, jabbing at it and infuriating
> The hive—the little fools—
> Until the insects become a menace to all
> And attack any traveler who happens by,
> Swarming out in defense of their brood.[76]

The kinetic fury of this scene-within-a-scene effectively dramatizes the coming action. It is less a departure from the account of the charging troops than a layering of intensity. The Myrmidons, who "filed out and swarmed up to the Trojans," were moving deliberately, with fervor. The image of the wasps vivifies their collective temperament: they were *bent*. The passage also suitably frames Aristotle's take on sensation and temperamental shifts, and it is of course convenient for me—and not coincidental either—that Homer renders those shifts by invoking the directed movement of wasps, a species Aristotle acknowledged to be capable of the kind of gathering necessary for *politikē*. The key verbs here are *eridmainōsin* and *kinēsē*, verbs of provocation and disturbance. The cascade of motions—the provoked ire, the transformative gathering of a calm nest into a charging "menace," the resulting swarm—all follow directly and suddenly from the initial provocation by the stick-bearing boys. Such immediate, sudden, turbulent responses cut across species, binding together humans and nonhumans, as indicated by the elegant simplicity of the line returning readers to the action in the epic: "so too the Myrmidons."[77] Even confined within the swarm scene, though, the stirred wasps, almost absorbing the disturbance, themselves become a disturbing force. The disturbance tears through the scene, showing how suddenly disturbance can move. A transferal of feeling, much like the feeling moving through the frenzied wasps, courses through Aristotle's *Rhetoric* in ways that have not been fully theorized.

With this remarkable scene as a backdrop, then, I want to loosen the tangle of terms with which Aristotle knots feeling *aisthēsis* in the first half of book 2 in the *Rhetoric* and elsewhere: desire or appetite, pleasure and pain, the *pathē*, and *phantasia* or indirect *aisthēsis*.[78] When we begin with *aisthēsis*, especially with the charged, feeling *aisthēsis* not limited to human animals, what emerges is an account of *pathē* that is not so much psychological or cognitive as commentators have long thought, but one that allows for direct, sudden transformation that does not necessarily, or at least not primarily, traffic through cognition per se.[79]

Helpful for such an account is *De anima*, Aristotle's famous work on the soul (*psychē*), breath, the vital principle or animating force, the treatise that classical scholar Charles Kahn characterizes as "primarily a treatise on Sensation."[80] In *De anima*, as noted in this chapter's epigraph, Aristotle identifies sensation (*aisthēsis*) as "the first characteristic of an animal."[81] Still, *aisthēsis* also, according to Aristotle, entails imagination and appetite, *phantasian kai orexin*, "for where sensation is there is also pain and pleasure, and where these are there must also be desire [*epithumia*]."[82] In the next section, Aristotle reiterates this statement with a bit more detail when he offers *aisthēsis* as the capacity distinguishing all other living things from plants. He then hastily adds:

> But if for sensation then also for appetite; for appetite consists of desire, inclination, and wish, and all animals have at least one of the senses, that of touch; and that which has sensation knows pleasure and pain, the pleasant and the painful, and that which knows these has also desire for desire is an appetite for what is pleasant.[83]

The relation among pleasure, pain, and sensation in Aristotle is murky at best, but it matters. In his book on ancient Greek emotions, David Konstan argues that pleasure and pain are themselves sensations in Aristotle's scheme, while commentator E. M. Cope prefers a more associative reading—where there is sensation there is pain or pleasure or both.[84] Two things, though, are clear from this passage: pleasure and pain are impossible without sensation; and pleasure works as the positive driver of desire, which is to say all ensouled beings seek it.

A bit later in *De anima*, Aristotle further develops his conception of *aisthēsis*, this time by naming its transformative effects rather than its associated states. That definition rests on two infinitives, *kineisthai* and *paschein*, "a kind of being moved upon and being affected."[85] Aristotle then offers a justification, "for it [that is, sensation] is believed to be a certain alteration."[86] The Greek here rendered as alteration, *alloiōsis*, joins the difference indicator (*allos*) with *ōsis*, condition or state. Change of state is therefore at the heart of sensation. *Paschein*, of course, "to be affected," is the verb that yields *pathos* and the *pathē*, states of feeling central to rhetoric and in the *Rhetoric*.[87] A verb form of *alloiōsis—alloiousi*—appears in *Movement of Animals* with a triple subject: *phantasia*, *aisthēsis*, and *ennoiai*, "thought." All three cause state alterations, as follows:

> For sensations are from the first a kind of alteration, and *phantasia* and thought have the effect of the objects which they present; for in a way the idea conceived—of hot or cold or pleasant or terrible—is really of the same kind as an object possessing one of these qualities, and so we shudder and feel fear simply by conceiving an idea; and *all these affections are alterations*.[88]

Note the use of the term affections to gather together the sources of alteration. The Greek here of course is *pathē*, the condition of change in Aristotle's
Rhetoric.

Indeed, when Aristotle introduces the *pathē* in the *Rhetoric*, he uses the
term *metaballontes*, which might be described as high-speed *alloiōsis*, for it
combines *meta* (in this case, changed) with *ballontes*, a throwing or even a
hurling, as in to hit with a missile.[89] *Metaballontes*, then, names a throwing
into a notably different position, a sudden or quick turning. It has yielded
our contemporary notion of metabolism, which in biology indicates struc-
tural change in tissue or chemical composition of a living being.[90] And so sensation and *pathē* both have transformation and movement at their core, and
the transformation of *pathē* speeds things up. In *De anima*, Aristotle invests
phantasia too—one of the three kinds of *aisthēsis* considered here—with the
idea of movement, *kinēsis*.[91] Reading with these points at the fore—the importance of imagination, of desire and appetite, of the affecting, transformative
work of sensation and the *pathē*, and of the motivating pleasures and jolting
pains attending all these states of the soul—helps to show how such levels of
agitation, of disturbance, feed Aristotle's account of *pathē* in the *Rhetoric*.[92]
There Aristotle ascribes to emotion a fairly potent role in the transformation
of dispositions, and that transformative process lines up with the deliberative,
morally discerning *aisthēsis* mentioned in the *Politics*.[93]

At the opening of book 2, Aristotle reminds his own audience that rhetoric
"is concerned with making a judgment,"[94] thereby tacitly placing rhetoric in
the land of deliberative *aisthēsis*, since such a judgment would presumably
turn on abstract ideas of justice or goodness. Underlying that discernment is a
process of judgment that I have elsewhere characterized as a "layering of dispositions on dispositions" and "a meeting of appearances."[95] The subsequent
discussion in the *Rhetoric*, teeming with verbs of perception, clears the way to
the treatise's famous discussion of the *pathē*, or feelings, which Aristotle defines as "those things through which, by undergoing change [*metaballontes*],
people come to differ [*diapherousi*] in their judgments and which follow pain
and pleasure."[96] This definition of *pathē* is remarkable for any number of reasons, not least of which is the layers of transformation Aristotle ascribes to the
pathē, as I have already considered. For this discussion, though, Aristotle's
conception of rhetorical *pathē* contains both kinds of *aisthēsis* delineated in
the passages from the *Politics* and in *History of Animals* as well as the third
kind, *phantasia*. The feeling *aisthēsis* of the *pathē* set up the transformative
work of rhetoric for the polity, or deliberative *aisthēsis*, and *phantasia*—the

"weak" perception that indicates how something seems to someone at a moment—results, looping back into the other two.

The relation between sensation and *pathē* is in fact more direct than it is tangential: things appear (*phainetai*) different to those who are friendly than to those who are hostile.[97] As philosopher Stephen R. Leighton puts it in a gloss on this passage, "Emotions may move one to a particular judgment, may alter the severity of the judgment, or may change a judgment entirely."[98] And they do so by altering appearances and perceptions themselves. To return to Homer's disturbed wasps: the boys' agitation of the nest altered the wasps' disposition such that mere passersby were pursued as threats.[99] Aristotle's definition of anger shows the layers of perception necessary to produce it: "Desire, accompanied by pain, for apparent retaliation because of an apparent slight that was directed, without justification, against oneself or those near to one."[100] The words translated as apparent here derive from *phantasia*—these are perceived slights, and they depend on perceptions of existing hierarchies; in the context one replays *what just happened*, trying to make sense out of sense. But before sense in the cognitive way can be made, the body knows: heat is already building, cheeks flush, *lupē* (pain or distress) has made itself felt; there has been a disturbance. "The judgment is in the perception," indeed.

Such a sensuous account of the *pathē* offsets overly cognitive conceptions of them.[101] The kinetic disturbance of pleasure, pain, and the *pathē*, bundled as Aristotle thinks they are into sensory parts of the soul, is crucial for the multiple roles animals end up playing in his theory of rhetoric, the central question of this chapter—to which I will now return.

ZŌA ALOGA AND/AS THE LIFEBLOOD OF STYLE

That Aristotle has it both (or several) ways when it comes to nonhuman animals—that he puts forward and exploits their difference from and their likeness to human animals—becomes most apparent in the part of the *Rhetoric* where he explicitly theorizes rhetoric itself in relation to sense perception, the treatment of *lexis* or style in book 3. In other words, the energy and feeling of nonhuman animals are enabled by the very feature Aristotle attributes to them, their status as *zōa aloga*. My reading so far presumes that the *aloga*—being without *logos*—is not a deficiency but rather signals capacities that in a perhaps surprising twist feed into practices around *logos* (as both word and reason).[102] Animals, familiar yet varied and captivating, hold a unique and felt charge, and they bind rhetoric most notably to poetic and mythical traditions. Ancient style theorists, for example, discerned a zoopoetic phenomenon realized by Homer and Aesop: the way animals can be pithily but vividly (and memorably) captured by and imagined through words, their lively wildness retained and replicated—revived—by *logos* itself, as with the swarming wasps or a pack of wolves moving along a riverbank, their mouths dripping blood.[103]

The logic of likeness found throughout the treatise is unsurprisingly but still tellingly pressed into book 3's discussion of similes. The discussion in fact elaborates the logic of likeness with its treatment of *eikōn*, the Greek word for likeness or image (think icon).[104] Nonhuman animals show up immediately in the discussion of *eikōn*; at the outset Aristotle uses a lion comparison to illustrate the slim difference between *eikōn* (likeness, comparison, image, simile) and metaphor:

> A simile is also a metaphor; for there is little difference: when the poet says "He rushed as a lion," it is a simile, but "The lion rushed" [with "lion" referring to a man] would be a metaphor; for since both are brave, he used a metaphor and spoke of Achilles as a lion.[105]

Aristotle then offers two more animal-based examples:

> Examples of similes are what Androtion said to Idreus, that he was "like puppies that have been chained"; for they jump to bite, and Idreus, freed from prison, was vicious. . . . And the one in the *Republic* of Plato, that those who strip the dead [on the battlefield] are like curs that snap at stones but do not bite the throwers.[106]

Aristotle also includes similes featuring children, those reliable partners of beasts, pointing as he does to "Pericles' simile for the Samians, that they are like children who accept the candy but keep crying . . . and the way Democritus likened orators to nannies who, after swallowing the pabulum, moisten the baby's lips with their spit."[107] The barrage of examples, of course, contains instances of similes to ideas or nonliving objects or even adult humans as well: Pericles also compares the Boeotians to oak trees knocking down other oak trees, presumably in a storm; Theodamas calls Archidamus "'a Euxenus that does not know geometry'";[108] Plato likens citizens to "a ship's captain who is strong but deaf," and the verses of poets to "youths without beauty."[109] When lined up, the two kinds of examples—on one hand, those likenesses featuring beasts and babies, creatures deemed, for the most part, *aloga*, and on the other hand, those featuring objects or adult humans—the former exist to draw out feeling, while the others focus on different likenesses. The snapping curs, the crying children, the rushing lion, the leaping puppies, are all doing something with intensity of feeling; they embody and convey *pathos*, and that embodiment constitutes their likeness to the human animals being described.

It would be easy enough to credit Homer with the persistence of non-human animals in Aristotle's treatment of style; as Steven Lonsdale's study of creaturely similes in Homer shows, more than half the similes in the *Iliad* feature animals other than humans.[110] Yet animals themselves, not Homer, deserve the credit here; as Lonsdale puts it:

> Animals, like their human counterparts, are animate and mobile creatures. . . . They are more similar to human beings than, for example, trees or bodies of water, even though these inanimate subjects may share forces with human beings in the Homeric cosmology. The greater similarity and *sympatheia* between people and animals sharpen the portrayal of pathos.[111]

What Lonsdale refers to as a "theriomorphic urge," an inclination to compare humans and other animals, rests on a distinct logic of likeness, and that logic appears throughout Aristotle's *Rhetoric*.[112] It is a pointed logic, one that itself gestures toward—and conjures—feeling.

Lively feeling is most intensely conjured by the visual work of two more concepts Aristotle discusses in the *Rhetoric*: "bringing before the eyes" and *energeia*. Here, he offers "bringing before the eyes" as something of an intensified, hypersensuous version of metaphor, and his discussion helps to elaborate the role nonhuman animals play in matters of style. First, Aristotle specifies that he calls "those things 'before-the-eyes' that signify things engaged in activity" (*hosa energounta sēmainei*). He then helpfully elaborates on the *energeia* at the center of "bringing before the eyes," the activity at the root of sensation:

> For example, to say that a good man is "foursquare" is a metaphor, for both are "complete"; but it does not signify activity [*energeia*]. On the other hand, the phrase "having his prime of life in full bloom" is *energeia*, as is "you, like a free-ranging animal" and "now then the Greeks darting forward on their feet." *Darting* is actualization and metaphor; for he means "quickly." And [*energeia*], as Homer often uses it, is making the lifeless living through metaphor.[113]

The three examples of *energeia* stand in contrast to the geometric metaphor of "foursquare," which Aristotle draws from Simonides.[114] Put simply, in contrast to the still abstraction of the *tetragōnos*, the other examples *move*. The first metaphor, a floral one, implies the height (*akmēn*) of growth, the most vigorous phase of life. And the last one moves through the use of a (hyper) active verb, *axantes*, which means darting or shooting. The metaphor in the middle, of course, features a nonspecific animal—the word *apheton* (here translated as free-ranging animal) especially applied to "sacred flocks that were free from work"—and zeroes in on how the animal lives through its freedom of movement.[115] The phrase's source is Isocrates's speech "To Philip" in which Isocrates exhorts Philip to initiate war against Persia. The passage, offered by scholars as an accurate snapshot of Isocrates's political views on the Macedonian king, contrasts Philip with leaders throughout Greece who are bound to their more local government and laws and who "cleave fondly to that state in which they happen to dwell."[116] Those other leaders, in other words, are like animals in captivity. Philip, in contrast, lives as he moves, unfenced and unfettered.

Aristotle repeatedly stresses *energeia* as the quality that elevates metaphor to "bringing before the eyes." The word names a kind of vivification, what lexicographers call in this context "vigorous style."[117] In Aristotle's philosophy, *energeia* is actualization, the counterpart to—and fulfillment of—*dunamis*.[118] In *De anima*, Aristotle pairs *energeia* with *dunamis* in the context of sensations: "The term sensation [*aisthēsis*] must be used in two senses, as potential and as actual. Similarly to perceive [*aisthanesthai*] means both to possess the faculty and to exercise it [*energeia*]."[119] But of course *energeia* cannot be exercised without *psychē*, as Aristotle makes clear in the same treatise: "Soul is the cause and first principle of the living creaturely body";[120] "nothing feels [*aisthaneitai*] which does not have a soul."[121] Reading these terms back into Aristotle's theory of style in book 3 stresses the ability of language to confer life, to render images that are brimming with energy, both in the perceiver (first as potential and then as actual sensation) and in the perceived, the sense-able images conjured by words. A style that features *energeia* brings life to meet life. After a litany of examples drawn from Homer, Aristotle makes this quality just about as plain as he can when he observes that Homer "makes everything move and live, and *energeia* is motion."[122]

The idea of rhetorical vision helps stress the stylistic notion of *energeia* as sensation mingling with sensation, life meeting life. This act of bringing life to life (through lively word images and in the sensations of hearers or readers), a process of *vivification*, is often exemplified in ancient discussions of style through a kind of zoostylistics. Animals, after all, as the line from *De anima* indicates, were thought to possess souls, and their movement—their ability to roam freely or even to buck, pace, or writhe in captivity—counts as the most graspable manifestation of *energeia*. If Aristotle's discussion of "bringing before the eyes" is meant to guide his students or readers to liven up their style, the observation that Homer "makes everything move and live" might take on a more literal cast. The implicit command of the passage would be something like this: make your words live.

GORGIAS AND THE SWALLOW

Finally, there is the passage from book 3 in the *Rhetoric* that helpfully encompasses many of the tendencies I have identified so far: the passage returns to shame and the nonhuman in the context of style; it exploits a likeness; and it invokes a myth well known to Athenians. The second chapter of book 3 introduces the two-pronged virtue of style: clarity (*saphēs*) and propriety (*prepon*). Aristotle's treatment here is a nimble one; he repeatedly edges up to situations in which principles of clarity may be successfully violated.[123] In this context he shares an interjection purportedly delivered by the famous sophist Gorgias who, in mid-speech, pauses to address a swallow that had "let go her droppings on him."[124] The account, which characteristically (for Gorgias) turns on the audience's knowledge of myth, in this case refers to the violent mythical story of Philomela, whom the gods ultimately turned into a swallow as retribution for reporting the rape of her sister.[125] Here is Aristotle's interpretive account of Gorgias's words: "He said, 'Shame on you, Philomela'; for if a bird did it there was no shame, but [it would have been shameful] for a maiden. He thus rebuked the bird well by calling it what it once had been rather than what it now was."[126] Unlike the other Gorgias-based examples in Aristotle's discussion of inappropriate metaphors, this one wins Aristotle's admiration, for he calls it "the best tragic manner," which is to say neither "laughable" nor "too lofty and tragic"—in fact, this instance is obviously both. Aristotle later refers back to the instance as appropriate emotional style because it is used in mockery (*eirōneias*).[127] Perhaps the reason Aristotle finds the anecdotal interjection successful is because it exploits the very division that Aristotle has alluded to parenthetically in discussions of honor and shame earlier in the treatise: Philomela the woman may be placed in a shame economy, while her alternate form, the swallow, may not. The deflection onto the bird itself of Gorgias's own annoyance, if not embarrassment, at the excremental interruption, in Aristotle's book is worthy of admiration. This anecdote illustrates vivification and *energeia* even as it depends on the supposed inability of a bird to move in the realm of deliberative *aisthēsis*. It therefore displays nicely the circuitry of *aisthēsis* and feeling I have so far delineated by exploiting humans' ability to shame an animal (that is, to confer or remove honor) and the inability of that nonhuman animal to recognize shame, unless of course the addressee is a human encased in bird form by mythology.

The Philomela-sparrow might therefore serve as something of an absurd symbol (Gorgias was no stranger to absurdity) of the surprising variety of ways nonhumans turn—and turn up in—rhetorical theory. Undermining Aristotle's attempt to demarcate humans as *zōa politika*, that is, is the condition that binds together all animals, *zōa aisthētika*. This chapter has drawn out the capacities of the condition known as *aloga*, without speech or reason. In doing so, I hope to have shown how for Aristotle nonhuman animals were not so easy to shake, and neither, in the end, did he seem particularly eager to shake them. Such are the conditions by which nonhuman animals began to take their place in ancient rhetorical theory. They would persist in ancient theories of style following Aristotle, especially when those theories tended toward *energeia*, be it in discussions of grandeur, charm, or compactness. Elaborating the zoostylistics that would develop will be the work of the next chapter.

CHAPTER 2

Zoostylistics after Aristotle

In book 3 of the *Iliad*, Homer depicts the elders of Troy perched on the city's wall, too old to fight but not too old to speak. "They were good speakers," in fact, sings the poet, "like cicadas that in a forest sit on a tree and pour out their lily-like voice."[1] From their vantage point, the Trojan elders witnessed the stunning approach of a tearful Helen, followed by two handmaids, "Aethra, daughter of Pittheus, and ox-eyed Clymene."[2] As the elders watched the trio approach, "softly they spoke winged words to one another."[3] This passage exemplifies Homer's remarkable capacity for activating sensation through words, and in this case he achieves that by rousing emotion through vivid, sensory depiction. The framing portrayal of Helen is really a depiction of the elders, compared to cicadas for their "lily-like" voices, a synesthetic description simultaneously invoking delicate texture and harmonious color to characterize sound.[4] The passage's cicada sound image is buttressed by two additional sensory references to beings other than human: the description of Clymene as "ox-eyed," and probably one of the most common images in the epic, presenting the elders' words themselves as birds bearing wings, taking flight.

The phrase *epea pteroenta*, "winged words," appears no fewer than 124 times in the *Iliad* and the *Odyssey*; its meaning has received careful consideration from commentators and philologists over the past century and a half.[5] The most common interpretation of the noun-epithet combination is that words fly from the speaker's mouth to the listener's ear. And while scholars disagree on the root and status of the metaphor, what matters here is the way the phrase focuses on words' capacity to flutter and flap, to erupt like a disturbed covey, to traverse a distance.

Homer scholars Paolo Vivante and Richard P. Martin both seek to revive W. E. Gladstone's 1874 interpretation of the phrase as a "carrying force."[6] Both Vivante and Martin tacitly invoke the flushing quality of the phrase— Vivante by stressing the suddenness and surprise of the occasions where the phrase appears, and Martin by associating it with a density and urgency of the words spoken.[7] The phrase, in Vivante's account, marks a "quickening of the senses" at the moment when sensations and feelings "are touched off into voice and made articulate into winged words."[8] Vivante's examination of winged-word passages in Homer leads him to this conclusion:

> Winged words thus mostly come when the mind is free, quick, receptive, sympathetic; they are neither aggressive nor self-conscious but naturally effusive. What the phrase points out is, therefore, the inherent spontaneity of speech: sense-perception instantly transformed into the airy substance of words . . . it presents the wonder of voice made suddenly articulate—the vocal element rather than the message, the distinction of significant sounds rather than the speaker's tone.[9]

Martin's reading complements Vivante's for its stress on the sonic properties of wings flapping: "It is the aural quality resulting from the flight of birds that is the primary association in the phrase 'winged words.'"[10] Martin reads the phrase as marking "the enduring physical quality of the epos" and an intensifying of the "tautness, power, and movement that makes [words] whir and beat, like the motion of a wing."[11] Like birds, words can fly, flutter about, or hover in the air.

At stake in these accounts of winged words is the vitality and energy of rhetorical language, its *energeia*. Those stakes are made clear by Gladstone, who notes a contrast between the "extraordinary" instances of "debating oratory" and the translations of said addresses, which, as Gladstone grumbles, "seem to plod or gallop," not fly.[12] As Walter J. Ong puts it in a passing reflection on Homer's winging of words: "Words fly, which means that they not only move but do so energetically."[13]

Ancient writers on rhetorical language and style, captivated by the energetic force of words, often focused on their material properties and their ability to enliven the senses, to invigorate a speech or a piece of writing and, by extension, an audience. This chapter begins where the previous chapter left off, with Aristotle's treatments of style, moving to the tradition of book-length style manuals *On Style* and *On the Sublime*, attributed, respectively, to Demetrius and Longinus and probably dating to the beginning of the Hellenistic period and to the later edge of antiquity.[14] Occasionally it is necessary to return to Aristotle, especially his *Poetics* and *Rhetoric*, the two Aristotelian treatises most explicitly concerned with language, for discussions of pertinent concepts such as magnitude and *mimēsis*. All together, this group of texts offers unique access to nonhuman animals' roles in compositional pedagogies and philosophies of language and as such can be more revealing than the exemplary texts themselves. In these theoretical accounts, animals serve distinctive stylistic functions, many of which elaborate the principle of vivification contained in Aristotelian *energeia* discussed in the previous chapter. Such an investigation shows how animals, by enlivening theoretical discussions of style, helped make explicit the importance of using words to activate sensation.

I chose to focus on this strain of texts because of their devotion to matters of style (*lexis*), the main emphasis in book 3 of Aristotle's *Rhetoric*. Demetrius's place in what Kathy Eden calls a "family tree of literary theorists," "flourishing first in antiquity and then again in full flower by the beginning of the seventeenth century," is worth noting, for as Eden observes, this very group "places front and center the question of style."[15] This is not to say that Roman theorists and pedagogues of rhetoric such as Cicero and Quintilian do not focus on style or don't have something to say about animals—they do. In fact, in Cicero's dialogue *De oratore*, the character Crassus invokes nonhuman animals in a tantalizing treatment of delivery: "By action the body talks, so it is all the more necessary to make it agree with thought; and nature has given us eyes, and the horse and the lion their mane and tail and ears, to indicate the movement of feeling (*motus animorum*)."[16] In this analogy, tails and manes vivify feeling's motion that Crassus contends shows in the eyes of humans.

As I discussed in the introduction, my reason for following the distinctly Aristotelian line of style theorists instead of, say, Cicero and Quintilian is that they allow me to bear down on matters of style, on the place where rhetoric and poetics converge, and where rhetoric's sensuous properties matter the most. Demetrius, Longinus, and Dionysius of Halicarnassus devote their treatises to style, and as such they stand in contradistinction to Cicero and Quintilian, whose treatises elaborate the art of rhetoric in toto. Focusing on the treatises of these three thinkers together with the third book of Aristotle's *Rhetoric*, with special scrutiny of the places animals crawl through, fly by, or otherwise appear in, helps to reveal a working theory of zoostylistics, which names a theory of style that uses animal images—sonic, visual, tactile—to vivify words.

Put simply, when Aristotle, Demetrius, Longinus, or Dionysius of Halicarnassus focuses on sensation, nonhuman animals are very often nearby, drawing out language's sensuous properties, making words whir and weigh. Presenting trends culled from this particular selection of texts risks introducing its own potential confusion, given that they may span from three to six centuries, depending on which date hypotheses are to be believed.[17] As I began working with these style manuals, the mentions of nonhuman animals started to clump in a variety of distinctive thematic categories or stylistic properties ranging from grandeur to charm to weight. Considering those properties in turn helps us more precisely document what nonhuman animals are doing there in relation to language, and the resulting focus on language's elasticity means that Longinus often leads the charge. That's a deliberate choice, but one that should be mentioned as such, since the discussion often moves back in time to Demetrius's text. This chapter is therefore arranged according to those properties—an organizational choice that offers more critical salience than would an arrangement that heeds, say, authorship or chronology—and offers up this insight: nonhuman animals animated ancient thinking about how words, while also traversing distance, can reduce distance between interlocutors, even getting under the skin. Words, in effect, as the chapter's last section shows, sting and bite.

STAKES OF ZOOSTYLISTICS FOR ANIMAL STUDIES

An examination of zoostylistics hones the argument laid out in the previous chapter that animals carry the sense-able weight of language's less than rational features. Zoostylistics, then, both is and is not limited to an examination of animal imagery. Animal symbols in rhetorical treatises provide a starting point, but merely cataloging them does not go far enough. For starters, the idea of symbol is too static to capture what animals are doing in, for, and to these passages. The zoostylistics set forth in ancient rhetorical style texts refuses the assertion made most recently by cultural theorist Rosi Braidotti that metaphor (in general) is dead, that the era of looking at animals as signs needs to end. "The main point," in Braidotti's words, "is for us to move on, beyond the empire of the sign, toward a neoliteral relation to animals, anomalies, and inorganic others."[18] Before so swiftly turning away metaphor as a dead end, or a road leading away from "neoliteralism," we might do well to scrutinize what animals are in fact doing in these texts. What emerges from this analysis is an animal pedagogy in which stylists learn from animal acts and movements and repeatedly invoke those acts and movements to teach principles of rhetorical style. Representation is not at stake here, but movement and feeling, through words, are.

Acknowledging the sensuous dimension animals lend to language honors the life they bring to ancient theories of style. Until we honor that life, it's all too easy to accept Braidotti's distinction, to leave vitality, affinity, and life on one side and metaphor, ownership, and death on the other. Zoostylistics reminds us that animal metaphors, like most ancient metaphors, are in fact underwritten by the kind of neoliteralism that Braidotti seeks in opposing the idea of animal signs, but that admittedly is difficult to fathom from the point of view of the twenty-first century. G. E. R. Lloyd, writing about the function of animals in ancient texts, contends that if we think of animals as metaphors, "we should not suppose that the metaphors were translatable back, without remainder, into any single univocal literal message. It would be better to think of them as an alternative language, radically indeterminate in its translation into literal terms."[19] The classicist Donald Lateiner's tantalizing foray into nonverbal behavior complements Lloyd's observations about animal metaphors. Meditating on the strategies of ancient writers in the face of literature's "severe curtailment" of affective expression, Lateiner notices the work of animals to close that gap: "The similes drawn from nature, from speechless animals and elements echo the pathos of a world in which words don't work."[20] Lateiner's phrasing "a world in which words don't work" and Lloyd's "alternative language" both refer to a profoundly sensuous mode of interaction, one that seeps into words, calling attention to their ability to move and work *as if they were alive*. Words about—and in some cases originating with—animals draw out sensuous elements of a scene. They cut to the chase of feeling. Nonhuman animals, time and again, bring rhetoric to its senses.

Detailing how they do so undoes the usual anthropomorphic presumptions about what happens when words meet animals. Zoostylistics instead, and again, following the trend set by Aristotle discussed in the previous chapter, shows strong theriomorphic leanings (*thērios* is Greek for beast) whereby nonhuman animals set the terms and either stand on their own or draw out the bestial qualities of humans or—as this chapter's final section will show—of words themselves. Such a view tacitly assumes that charges of anthropomorphism are themselves presumptuously anthropocentric and strategically leaves open the idea that ancient attitudes toward animals may have been a bit more complicated than contemporary animal studies would have us presume. In short, zoostylistics turns anthropomorphism inside out and works in a liminal space between *logos* and *alogos*.

In the context of zoostylistics, animals for the most part do not emote in a strictly human way, which is precisely why they become touchstones for style. Instead, through their vivid, weighty, kinetic presence, and through movements that lie outside human capacity, they draw out the nonrational features of *logos*. Further, it matters a great deal that these style texts are often guided by animals as they overtake the senses, drowning out *logos* as we (think we) know it. Instead of just standing against *logos* as both speech and reason, zoostylistics breaks apart these two meanings of *logos*, emphasizing the nonrational features of words, their animated materiality, their ability to intensify visual effects through sounds that are not—or not quite—speech per se. Such sounds challenge the linguistic principle of arbitrariness and emphasize the role of bodies, sensation, and nonhumans in forming words. In doing so, zoostylistics offers another way to theorize what Kennedy calls, in the field's first contemporary articulation of an animal rhetoric, "rhetorical energy." Kennedy, inspired by the sights and sounds of unsubtle crows on his campus in North Carolina, decided to focus on rhetoric's communicative properties, whereby communication is figured as a transmission of energy. Kennedy's wish to articulate a "universal" rhetoric, one that encompasses communicative sounds and movements made by animals, led him to define rhetoric "as an energy existing in life."[21]

Kennedy also, and I believe not coincidentally, stresses the energy of *energeia* in his popular translation of the *Rhetoric*.[22] And so while Kennedy's notion of rhetorical energy owes explicitly to his engagement with studies of animal communication and to the flocks of crows cawing over his head, it could just as well be theorized from the text and tradition with which Kennedy has likely spent more time than any other. In linking this central Aristotelian term *energeia* to nonhuman animals, I do not aim to glean a universal rhetoric from the animal kingdom as Kennedy does. Rather, I aim to draw out a more specific (and more modest) zoostylistics from theories of rhetorical style. Again, it is a rhetoric that leans away from *logos* as rationality and toward the nonrational work of language. Or put more positively, in deference to the problems of negation inhering in the term nonrational, zoostylistics emphasizes less how words make sense (in a logical way) and more how they pile up to activate the senses.

EMOTIONS, SENSATION

Much has been written about Aristotle's notion of *phantasia*, which, as chapter 1 details, names a kind of mental picturing, and while the *Rhetoric* features an ambient concern for the concept, later authors focus more overtly on what the concept means for rhetorical style. Quintilian, another common source for scholars of *phantasia*, draws a direct line from *phantasia* to the emotions:

> What the Greeks call *phantasiai* (let us call them *visiones*), it is through these that images of absent things are represented to the mind in such a way that we seem to see them with our eyes and to be in their presence. Whoever has mastery of them will have the most powerful effect on the emotions [*adfectibus potentissimus*]. Some people say that this type of man who can imagine in himself things, words, and deeds well and in accordance with truth is *euphantasiōtatos* (most skilled in summoning up *phantasia*).[23]

The "mastery" of *phantasiai* matters the most, or has the most powerful effect (*potentissimus*) for the emotions, *adfectibus*. Simon Goldhill puts it succinctly in his reflection on this passage: "Vivid language penetrates the emotions."[24]

Longinus, too, stresses the emotional force of *phantasia* by offering a brief history of the term:

> For the term *phantasia* is applied in general to an idea which enters the mind from any source and engenders speech, but the word has now come to be used predominantly of passages where, inspired by strong emotion [*pathous*], you seem to see what you describe and bring it vividly before the eyes of your audience. That *phantasia* means one thing in rhetoric [*rhetorikē*] and another in poetry you will yourself detect, and also that the object of the poetical form of it is to enthrall, and that of the prose form to present things vividly [*enargeia*], though both indeed aim at the emotional and the excited.[25]

This passage roots *phantasia* in intense emotion—the strength of the phrase "inspired by strong emotion" almost tilts toward frenzy—and follows the Aristotelian tradition by locating vividness through words (*enargeia*) in the realm of rhetoric.[26] Also noteworthy, though, is how the distinction between the phantasic work done by oratory and poetry gets raised only to then be swallowed by the twin forces of emotion and excitement, and the word for excitement, *synkekinēmenon*, features kinetic movement. The passage itself tracks *phantasia* from enthusiastic, frenzied emotion (of the speaker or writer) through words and to the ears, minds, and bodies of the listeners or readers. *Pathos* is both the source and rhetorical effect of *phantasia*, wordy material its means of transport.[27]

Animal *Phantasia*

Emotions transmit sensuously, as Longinus indicates rather pithily else-where in the treatise with the phrase *pathos phainētai*, "whole congeries of emotion."[28] In chapter 15, Longinus's observations about the movement of *phantasia* play out in a set of nine exemplary phantasic passages the author comments on. Seven of the nine achieve "the emotional and the excited" (*pathētikon kai to sugkekinēmenon*) by means of animal-assisted vivification. Nonhuman animals dominate these examples of *phantasia* for a reason be-yond the simple fact that they figured into nearly every part of ancient life. This section will consider more exactly how animals operate in these exam-ples in order to further develop a theory of ancient zoostylistics.

First there is Orestes's mad vision of his mother unleashing the Furies:

> Mother, I beg you, do not shake at me
> These snake-like women with blood-stained eyes
> See there! See there! [They are] so close to attacking me.[29]

The Furies, here depicted as snakes, come vividly into view, virtually spring-ing on Orestes. Reflecting on this passage, Longinus reiterates the transfer that happens, only this time in terms of sense perception rather than emotion: "The poet himself saw [*ephantasthē*] the Furies and compelled the hearers [*akaouontos*] to see [*theasthai*] what he saw."[30] The compulsion here is driven by the vivid liveliness of the serpentine Furies, their eyes glowing red, poised to spring, then probably striking the air right in front of Orestes. Longinus offers this passage as one of Euripides's display of "the greatest laborious-ness in presenting these two feelings—madness and love—tragically."[31] Mad-ness—*manias* is the Greek—is probably the emotion most vivified by the bloody-eyed, springing figures. After a brief reflection on how brilliantly this vivification is accomplished, followed by a touch of damning by faint praise that amounts to "hey, that's pretty good for Euripides," Longinus recruits a passage from Homer's *Iliad* to characterize the style in Euripides's "great pas-sages."[32] The passage describes a wounded lion:

> His tail at his ribs and his haunches whips from one side to the other,
> He stirs himself to fight.[33]

Here the lion's tail continues to embody the animal's brave and fighting spirit, offering a double commentary on *phantasia*. First, it tosses on the pile another example of vivification by which the charged movement of the tail accomplishes a lot through a little. The vivid, energetic description of the switching tail mobilizes the animal's (or really, Achilles's) complex *pathē*, the strong desire to keep fighting—"his mighty spirit groans within"—despite the debilitating wound.[34] Second, Longinus's passage metaphorizes Euripides himself, subtly comparing his *phantasia*, his vision, with that of the lion. The subject of the preceding sentence, Euripides, carries into—and blends with—the lion such that it is Euripides brushed over Achilles, lying on his side, energetically aspiring to overcome the fact that, at least according to Longinus, "his natural genius is certainly not sublime."[35]

To illustrate Euripidean yearning textually, Longinus offers two passages from Euripides's *Phaethon* in which a messenger details the title character's harrowing (and ultimately deadly) ride in the sun god's chariot. Here is the second of those passages, after Helios hands the reins to Phaethon with a caution not to drive to the sky and melt his wheels:

> "But on the seven Pleiades hold your course."
> Having heard this, the boy seized the reins,
> Slashed at the flanks of his winged horses,
> And set them loose to fly upon the folds of clouds.[36]

Longinus's commentary on the more extended passage is in the form of question and amazed answer: "Would you not say that the soul of the writer is aboard the chariot and [that it] takes wing to become the horse's partner in danger? Never could it have visualized [*ephantasthē*] such things, had it not run beside those heavenly phenomena."[37] What is remarkable to Longinus is the stark vividness, the lively *energeia*, produced in this passage. *Energeia* is accomplished through flickers of sensation: the words "slashed at the flanks" effectively zoom in on the point where whip meets hindquarters as quickly as the distant cloudy hills pull back the view for the frenetic launch. Longinus then compares Euripides's phantasic capacity with the *phantasiais . . . hērōikōtatais*, the "heroic imaginings" of Aeschylus, offering as support a passage from *Seven against Thebes*. In this passage the captains

> Black-bound with hide have slit a bull's throat,
> And touched the bull's blood with their hands,
> Took an oath by Ares and Enyo
> And Panic, friend of blood—[38]

The *phantasiai* in this passage, much like the Euripidean and Homeric ones just preceding it, depend on the vivid actions performed with the body and blood of a bull. Words about animals in action are themselves stirred to life: animation begets animation. Their near constant presence in discussions of vivified style is owed in part, of course, to their constant presence in the daily lives of the ancients. As I will discuss in the next section, animals' distinctive colors and forms—the shank of a horse is a sight most Greeks can easily conjure—make for a highly efficient *energeia*. Words about animal bodies can almost function like modern-day binoculars, bringing forth the crispest of animal sightings. The strong, switching tail of the Homeric lion, the snaky, red-eyed Furies, the flinching flanks of horses all serve up images so vivid as to carry with them, according to Longinus, traces of the emotional state that first gave them form. Animals move through words with ease, and vividly, with something that might be called character.

Beyond Persuasion

Such images also move rhetoric beyond persuasion. One of the chief features of Longinus's approach to style is his emphasis on what Ned O'Gorman calls the "extraordinary."[39] Extraordinary style is achieved by taking rhetoric beyond the limits of persuasion. This drive to excess can be seen in the animal passages in book 15, and those passages inform the book's long, conclusive discussion of *phantasia* in which Longinus folds poetic *phantasia* into rhetorical situations. After worrying about the "exaggeration" (*huperekptōsin*) of poetry compared with the need for rhetoric's *phantasia* to accord with truth (*enalēthes*), Longinus articulates a rhetoric-friendly theory of *phantasia*:

> What then can *phantasia* do in rhetoric? It may be said generally to introduce a great deal of excitement and emotion [*empathē*] into one's speeches, but when combined with factual arguments it not only convinces the audience, it enslaves [*douloutai*] them.[40]

A few lines later, the writer points out that the combination of facts plus *phantasia* "far exceeds the limits of mere persuasion" by a kind of overtaking:

> The stronger element seems naturally to catch our ears, so that our attention is drawn from the reasoning to the enthralling effect of the imagination, and the reality is concealed in a brilliant light. And this effect on us is

natural enough; set two forces side by side and the stronger always absorbs the virtues of the other.[41]

The concealing accomplished by *phantasia*—the word *egkryptetai* yields the English word encrypt—is more like a drowning out, an overtaking. *Phantasia*, for Longinus, helps rhetoric past reason and the real, which are by contrast rather dull. The play of sound and light images in this passage stands out as well—the *phantasic* element "seems naturally to catch our ears," *akouomen*. The synesthesia implied here—a kind of seeing through hearing—is the rhetorical work of *phantasia*. Sounds enrich, enliven, and even conjure images on their own.

Vivid Sounds

Discussions of sound also mark an important entry point of animals into rhetorical theory, for nonhuman animals dominate particularly the discussion of sound that achieves intensity by less than rational means. At times sounds associated with animals create a harsh or ugly cacophony that can fill out a scene; at others they appear to assist or even overtake meaning with a stress on the physical contours of words.

Words that conjure vivid sound sensations inhabit a special place in Longinus's and Demetrius's notions of *phantasia*, for they fill out the sensory picture. What is more, the vividness of sound, far from committing the truth transgressions that preoccupy Longinus, actually brightens what he figures as "the real." Demetrius has a good deal to say about vivid sound, and as with Longinus's discussion of visual *phantasia*, animals bolster his discussion. Demetrius's *On Style* includes a lengthy account of the plain style, which ought to privilege clarity (*saphē*) without sacrificing *energeia* and persuasiveness (*pithanotētos*). The discussion of *energeia* is tethered to a sound image—the regularized noisy clip-clop of horses' hooves:

> *Energeia* also comes from the use of circumstantial detail, as in someone's description of a country man walking along, "the clatter of his feet was heard from far away as he approached," just as if he were not just walking along but virtually stamping the ground.[42]

Both words, *ktupos* and *laktizontos*—here translated as clatter and stamping—were frequently used to describe the sound of horses' hooves. The sound

image is meant to simultaneously capture noise and render distance, and it invokes the precedence that sound can take over sight in certain situations—that
is, when a noisy subject has not yet come into view. As I have noted elsewhere,
Aristotelian *phantasia* designates precisely the kinds of images blurred by
distance, by degrees of separation (e.g., dreams or imagination).[43] In this passage, sound lends clarity, *saphēs*, to an otherwise blurred picture. In this case
a character is at the center, and the countryman's stamping feet approximate
the horse's, drawing out the man's beastly movements.

While animals appear in the most striking of visual images in Longinus's
text, they show up more frequently in what Demetrius calls "harsh" or "ugly"
sounds (*dysphōnia*). When Aristotle observes in the *Rhetoric*, citing Licym-
nius, that "verbal beauty is in the sound or in the sense,"[44] he quickly un-
derlines the importance of sensuous effect when he enumerates the "sources
from which metaphors should be taken from the beautiful either in sound
or in meaning or in visualization or in some other form of sense perception
[*aisthēsei*]."[45] Demetrius's treatment of *dysphōnia* keeps with the spirit if not
the letter of this passage from the *Rhetoric* by bracketing beauty and espous-
ing the notion that sound—even ugly sound—can produce stylistic force.
Sometimes this observation remains at the level of word order, or the harsh
sounds produced by violating meter, as in this passage:

> Occasionally cacophony produces vigor, especially if the nature of the sub-
> ject calls for it, as in Homer's line "the Trojans shuddered, when they saw
> the writhing serpent." It would have been possible for him to construct the
> line more euphoniously, without violating the meter, "the Trojans shud-
> dered, when they saw the serpent writhing," but then neither the speaker
> nor the serpent itself would have been thought forceful.[46]

The "nature of the subject" that Demetrius refers to is in this case the visual
image of the serpent just dropped to the ground by an eagle after turning and
biting its predator. The cacophony of the passage is attributable wholly to
word order, but the writhing serpent (as opposed to the serpent writhing)
further vivifies the critical point itself. In the example that Demetrius believes
opts for cacophony, the visual focus and grammatical emphasis both land on
the snake, which is important because the serpent is what the onlooking Trojans take to be an omen. The sound works with sensation here, disrupting the
rhythm, producing a metric shudder. At other times, *dusphōnia* centers on
the word itself, which can issue from the very mouths of animals.

Words and/as Sensation: The Case of Onomatopoeia

Demetrius's discussion of cacophony moves from syntax (word order) to the formation of words themselves, all the while attending to the sonic dimensions of *phantasia*—how the sound of a passage supports its sense (or sensuousness). According to Demetrius, *phantasia* produced by a gathering of harsh sounds, *dusphonia syntheseōs*, can happen at the level of composition, as with the writhing snake discussed above, or it can happen at the level of a word: "Harsh composition creates grandeur, just as a harsh word does."[47] Demetrius continues: "Instances of harsh words are 'shrieking' instead of 'crying out' and 'bursting out' instead of 'charging.'"[48] The more dysphonic words of the pairs are more frenetic than their counterparts. The first pair is interesting, for *kekragōs* (shrieking) is a noisy croaking sound often attributed to crows, while the less harsh alternative (*boōn*, from *bazō*) entails a sharp means of address. The three gutturals and rising short alpha in *kegragōs* exemplify onomatopoeia, the trope that marks not a shift (as most tropes do) but an inceptive moment crediting those Quintilian refers to as "the originators of that language, who suited sound to sensation":[49] that is, nonhuman animals.

Onomatopoeia, as might be intuited from memories of high-school English, stands as the most obviously zoostylistic and most notably sonic trope, associated as it is with the hissing of snakes and the cawing of crows. Jeanne Fahnestock notes that Giambattista Vico denies onomatopoeia's very status as a trope, presenting it instead as "that activity by which the most fitting terms are formed having been fashioned after the sounds themselves of things."[50] The idea of word making as an activity begins to capture the energy of the naming itself. I would take Vico a step further and say that *onomatopoeia*—a word widely known to combine the Greek verb for making and the noun for name—leaves open exactly where the making happens. Onomatopoeia, that is, roots itself at the source of the sound, and as such it fashions users of onomatopoeic terms as mere copyists. What's more, the copied utterance usually comes from nonhumans, and often nonhuman animals.

Onomatopoeia receives special consideration in the treatise on composition written by Dionysius of Halicarnassus, the first-century BCE Roman writer who stands between Demetrius and Longinus, following in the Aristotelian footsteps of the former and in some ways anticipating the latter,[51] whose *On Composition* focuses on the material sounds of words.[52, 53] Dionysius's often-cited passage on onomatopoeia is nested in a discussion of words and their component parts and follows the quotation of exemplary lines from

Homer in which syllables are drawn out or compressed, or words appear to have been selected for the physical contours of their vowels or consonants in accordance with the feeling of the passage. Here is the passage leading up to that discussion:

> Countless such lines are to be found in Homer, representing length of time, bodily size, extremity of emotion, immobility of position, or some similar effect, by nothing more than the artistic arrangements of the syllables; while other lines are wrought in the opposite way to portray brevity, speed, urgency, and the like.[54]

Dionysius then settles on two examples from those "countless such lines," both of which use foreshortened words to render emotional states—the breathless anguish of Andromache on seeing Hector's body being dragged in front of the gates of Troy, and the sudden terror charioteers experience when a fire blazes up in front of them. Dionysius concludes the analysis this way: "Thus the poets and prose authors, on their own account, look to the subject they are treating and furnish it with words which suit and illustrate it."[55] The words for "suit" and "illustrate" here—*oikeia* and *dēlōtika*—underscore the art of choosing words that fit the context (related to a familial or household sort of belonging, *oikeia*) by visibly performing or showing (the root here is *dēlos*, which marks a conspicuousness). The spirit of this passage captures Aristotle's firm insistence on the importance of "proper and appropriate words and metaphors" in prose style.[56] Dionysius's pursuit of what is fitting depends on the ability of words and their component parts to do things. Words, that is, can stretch and chop, howl and moan. The most vivid example of howling and moaning appears in Dionysius's account of the Cyclops's bellows on having a stake plunged into his eye.[57] The words Homer uses in the line, "The Cyclops utters groan on groan in throes of anguish sore" feature, as Dionysius's translator notes, "a preponderance of *o, ō, u,* in a manner befitting the anguished groans themselves."[58]

With the physical, mimetic qualities of words at the fore, Dionysius turns, unsurprisingly, to *onomatopoeia*, words that are imitations of things (*mimētika tōn pragmatōn*) in the sense of concrete or material reality. Here Dionysius offers in rapid succession four examples, all from Homer, the second and fourth of which invoke sounds of animals. The one that is actually attributed to an animal comes from the "serpent writhing" passage Demetrius uses to discuss the cacophony of word order. Dionysius, though, tilts his head upward, focusing on the shrill shriek of the eagle, which carries in its talons a blood-red, huge snake, still alive and struggling, nor was it yet forgetful of combat; for it writhed backward, and struck him who held it on the chest beside the neck, and the eagle stung with pain, cast it from him to the ground and let it fall in the midst of the throng, and himself with a loud cry [*klanxas*] sped away down the blasts of the wind.[59]

Energeia, like the eagle itself, soars in this passage, with the close-up image of the snake's color, the direction of its writhing, its combative spirit, and the precise location of its strike (on the eagle's chest beside the neck). The sonic *mimēsis* of *klanxas*, a "sharp piercing sound" elevates the *energeia* even further, intensifying the bird's pain, heightening the fear felt by the Trojan soldiers who, on witnessing this scene, stop to deliberate its status as an omen.[60] Dionysius continues:

The great source and teacher [*archē kai didaskalos*] in matters of names is nature, *hē phusis*, which makes them mimetic and fitting and coins words which show things according to certain resemblances [*homoiotētas*] that appeal to sensibility and movement of thought.[61]

Dionysius's conception of *phusis* is helpfully illuminated by Walker's very literal translation of a passage in Dionysius's *Lysias*, in which Dionysius holds that grace can be learned "by extended practice and nonlogical felt experience to discipline one's nonlogical sense perception."[62] By *phusis*, continues Dionysius, "we have been taught to speak of the roars of bulls, the neighs of horses, the bleats of goats, the crackle of fire . . . and many other similar imitations of sound, shape, deed, feeling, movement, stillness, and really anything else."[63] Dionysius's discussion of onomatopoeia is fascinating on a number of levels. First, it attributes to *phusis*, natural inclination, the double role of source and of teacher, about which a few words may be in order.

While it may be tempting to view this *phusis* as something like Nature, capital *N*, as in Usher's translation of *On Composition*, which makes Nature into a gendered subject and converts the verbs from passive to active ("It is she who has taught us to speak"),[64] it is more likely that Dionysius is talking about something like "human nature," which is to say a composer follows his (or her) ears.[65] These are ears that, of course, as Walker's treatment of Dionysean *phusis* suggests, have been made ready by a fine-tuning of perception.[66] And the voice, too, was thought to be naturally mimetic, as Aristotle observes in the *Rhetoric*'s ambivalent account of delivery: "The poets were naturally the first to set in motion [study of verbal expression]; for words are imitations, and the voice, the most mimetic of all our parts, was there to start with."[67] In turn, as de Jonge puts it in the context of Dionysius, "A mimetic word triggers a certain image in the mind, thus stimulating our thinking."[68] Extending these accounts, onomatopoeic words develop out of the four-way encounter between the sensation of hearing, the sound itself, the attuned awareness of language's power to mime and to evoke, and the voice, which Aristotle called that "most mimetic of all our parts."[69] Onomatopoeia, especially those words that imitate sounds of animals by reproducing the sound as closely as possible, enfolds signifier into signified, materializing the sense (as in meaning) via the sensation of hearing. Onomatopoeia, the most beastly of tropes, repeatedly stresses the sheer physicality of words; indeed, this might be the trope's primary lesson. Dionysius calls attention to this physicality when he enumerates the kinds of imitations similar to bleating goats. The list goes from sound to shape to deed, then to feeling, movement, and stillness. The net effect is sound so vivid that it very nearly conjures its "original" source.

Demetrius's discussion of *onomatopoeia* further delineates the sonic dimensions of *phantasia*. As Demetrius reflects on it, the sound imitated is either an emotion or an action:

> Onomatopoeic words are defined as those uttered in imitation of an emotion or action, for example "hissed" and "lapping." They create grandeur by their resemblance to inarticulate sounds, and above all by their novelty.[70]

The hissing and lapping examples are both taken from Homer, and both invoke animals. The first occurs in the description of Odysseus plunging a flaming stake into the Cyclops's eye and embeds onomatopoeia within a smithing metaphor: "And as when a smith dips a great axe or an adze in cold water to temper it and it makes a great hissing—for from this comes the strength of iron—so did his eye hiss around the stake of olivewood."[71] The Greek word translated as hiss, *size*, fills out the cringe-inducing, multisensory passage detailing the whirling of the stake in the eyeball, the mingling of blood and heat, the singeing of his eyebrows, the crackling of the eye's root in the flame. The snaky hiss passage appears between the crackling and the Cyclops's bellow, further vivifying the sound of the gruesome scene. The passage, that is, issues a cacophony of noises, none of them speech-based, but all of them presented through words.

The second onomatopoeic example, lapping, Demetrius also draws from Homer, this time from the *Iliad*. There the word *lapsontes* appears in an extended metaphor likening the Myrmidon warriors to a pack of wolves. The passage in the *Iliad* is remarkable—and remarkably vivid:

> They rushed out like ravening wolves in whose hearts is fury unspeakable—wolves that have slain in the hills a great horned stag, and rend him, and the jaws of all are red with gore; and in a pack they go to lap with their slender tongues the surface of the black water from a dusky spring, belching forth blood and gore, the heart in their breasts unflinching, and their bellies gorged full; so did the leaders and rulers of the Myrmidons speed out around the noble attendant of the swift-footed grandson of Aeacus.[72]

This passage follows exactly the sort of pattern laid out by Longinus, wherein the intense, unspeakable (*aspetos*) emotion is rendered sensuously by means of *phantasia*, in this case a scenic, *energeic* and extended wolf metaphor. This passage counts as an extraordinary example of Aristotelian bringing before the eyes for its combination of vivid images—the up-close visible and audible mouths spilling over with kill, "red" and "belching" with gore, that then lap up the water. Demetrius returns to this passage, and specifically to the use of "lapping," later in his treatise in a discussion of sound's vividness and the role of *mimēsis* in making things vivid:

> Onomatopoeic formations also produce vividness, since they are coined to suggest an imitation, as in "lapping" [*laptontes*]. If Homer had said "drinking" he would not have imitated the sound of the dogs drinking, and there would have been no vividness [*oute enargeia*]; and the addition "with their tongues" [*glōssēisi*] after "lapping" makes the passage still more vivid.[73]

Lapping's second onomatopoeic appearance in *On Style* counts as more than a passing reference. While the first mention of Homer's word choice is meant to illustrate the figuring of an action (rather than an emotion) through sound, the second mention captures the difference between mere description and *mimēsis*. *Laptontes*, like its English offspring "lapping," is doubly mimetic, for it achieves the *sound* of lapping by mimicking the very *action* of bestial lapping with the oral-gestural movement from the alveolar *l* to the labial *p*. As Demetrius points out, this mimetic action is not performed by the word drinking, *pinontes*, the verb that applies more readily and less mimetically to a cup-raising human. The choice of *pinontes* would have pulled the picture back to mere description rather than vivid description, here *enargeia*. Demetrius's observation that the descriptor "with their tongues" serves to add still more *enargeia* (*enargesteron*) calls attention to the combinatory power of the senses: "lapping" captures the gestural and sonic *mimēsis*, and the focus on the tongues turns up the visual. Interestingly, the powerful *enargeia* of "lapping with their tongues" seems to have caused Demetrius to forget that the animals in the *Iliad* passage are wolves (*lukoi*), not dogs (*kunas*).

Demetrius's reading is all the more interesting when placed next to Aristotle's observation in the *Rhetoric* that the voice is "the most mimetic of all our parts,"[74] given the difficulty of separating voice—sound emitted from the vocal chords—from oral gesture such as that described with detail in Longinus's *On the Sublime*. When Longinus notes that the letter *l* is smooth, he ascribes to words perceptible texture in addition to visuality (*phantasia*), thereby filling out the picture and even subtly appealing to a sense of touch.[75]

Words derived from animal sounds also stand as a kind of common denominator between beasts and humans, further troubling, or at least clarifying, the widespread ancient belief articulated by Aristotle and discussed at length in chapter 1 that humans alone possess *logos*. In fact, careful scrutiny of that claim in the *Politics* shows Aristotle almost immediately hedging along the lines of voice, *phōnē*. The division in the *Politics* passage between voice and speech, a pair of words that, as I showed in chapter 1, encompasses pleasure and sensation on the one hand and justice and morality on the other, helps to account for why animals keep sensation alive in rhetorical theories of style as they do in political life: bodily sensation—even voiced bodily sensation—is a domain that some animals expressly share with humans. It is in this broad, shared faculty of *phōnē*, voice, that onomatopoeic words materialize. While their properties remain sensuous and often do accompany descriptions involving pleasure or pain (as with the *klazos* of Homer's eagle), they nevertheless attain the status of a word (*logos*) and can be incorporated into all manner of discourse. Onomatopoeic words therefore serve as sensuous, subtle reminders of language's bestial qualities, even as they fill out the sonic dimensions of zoostylistics.

Weighty Words

The materiality of sound—voice breathed into words by animals—helps to create *energeia*, expressly vivifying a particular passage, as in the case of lapping wolves. Words also pronounce their own materiality through a stylistic feature the ancients call weight, or *onkos*, which relates to *megethos*, another size-related word usually translated as either grandeur or magnitude. Both terms are central to the notion of *phantasia* put forth in *On the Sublime*. Book 15 opens with this observation:

> Weight, grandeur, and urgency in writing are very largely produced, dear young friend, by the use of "visualizations" [*phantasiai*]. That at least is what I call them; others call them "image productions" [*eidōlopoiias*].[76]

Wordy images, then, create and bear weight—here the word is *onkos*, which indicates the bulk or mass of a body. Aristotle used the term to suggest the space filled by a body,[77] and Euripides applied it to the heavy bulk of fetus in the womb.[78] *Onkos*, in short, captures the way words clump and weigh.

A weighty style, as elaborated by Demetrius, could be achieved through repetition, *anadiplōsis*. To illustrate this idea, he quotes a passage ostensibly from Herodotus:[79] "There were serpents in the Caucasus, [vast] in size, yes in size and number."[80] It helps Demetrius's argument about size that the snakes themselves are weighty: in fact, the word repeated (*megethos*) is identical to the word he uses in introducing the passage: *anadiplōsis d'epous eirgasato megethos*, "repetition of a word is also imposing."[81] After he shares the line, Demetrius brings it back to weight, *onkos*: "The repetition of the word 'size' adds weight to the style."[82] The stylistic weight bears down through the repetition of the word "size" (*megethos*), emphasizing the weight of the snakes themselves. Illustrating *megethos* or magnitude/greatness with a passage that repeats the very word in relation to a serpent could almost be seen as cheating.

But Demetrius is not the only theorist who invokes animal passages to think about magnitude. Aristotle before him does it rather famously in the *Poetics* on the topic of tragedy: "Tragedy is *mimēsis* of an action that is complete, whole, and of magnitude, *megethos*."[83] To discuss magnitude, he invokes a nonspecific animal object, *zōon*:

> A beautiful object, whether an animal or anything else with a structure of parts, should have not only its parts ordered but also an appropriate magnitude: beauty consists in magnitude and order, which is why there could not be a beautiful animal which was either minuscule (as contemplation of it, occurring in an almost imperceptible moment, has no distinctness) or gigantic (as contemplation of it has no cohesion, but those who contemplate it lose a sense of unity and wholeness, say an animal a thousand miles long). So just as with our bodies and with animals beauty requires magnitude, but magnitude that allows coherent perception, likewise plots require length, but length that can be coherently remembered.[84]

It is tempting to read this passage as yet another instance of Aristotle playing Goldilocks, calling for something to be just the right size. And while that is largely the case, this passage is even more interesting than that, because it scales magnitude to perceptive capacities.

As rhetorical scholar Thomas B. Farrell points out, the *Poetics* is not the only place where Aristotle discusses *megethos*.[85] As Farrell notes in one of the rare treatments of the concept in rhetorical studies, in Aristotle's *Rhetoric* "the single most frequently recurring commonplace is that of quantity, degree, largess, magnitude."[86] He continues: "Magnitude has to do with the gravity, the enormity, the weightiness of what is enacted, a sense of significance that may be glimpsed and recognized by others."[87] Farrell's characterization of *megethos* nicely captures the way the concept works with multiple sensations: the notion packs a sense of weight, which could be metaphorical, as in grave, important subject matter such as war, or it can be material weight, as with the snakes. It indicates a significance, as Farrell puts it, "that may be glimpsed and recognized by others."[88] In order to be glimpsed or recognized, though, *megethos* must first be depicted through words. Discussing the *Poetics* passage quoted above, Farrell believes that Aristotle

> also has in mind, given the frequency with which the word for magnitude pops up in the *Poetics*, a sort of inventional logic for what sort of perspective is needed to size up and take in actions and events of a certain magnitude . . . there is also something that is recognizably "right" about this intuition. It is an ocular-centered aesthetic of what can properly be taken in.[89]

Farrell's detection of an Aristotelian inventional logic around the idea of *megethos* has been woefully underappreciated. *Megethos* is one of the concepts that adds to rhetoric a crucial aesthetic dimension, in the ancient sense of sense perception (*aesthēsis*). For Farrell, such is "the point of magnitude": "It is something important enough to be recognized, beheld, and reflected upon—presumably in one encompassing vision."[90]

But what can be made of the fact that Aristotle illustrates *megethos* with a discussion of animal bodies too small, excessive, and just right? A clue is provided by the subject of the passage that directly precedes the example: *to kalon*, here translated as beautiful object, "whether an animal [*zōon*] or anything else with a structure of parts."[91] More to the point of this chapter (and this book), Aristotle shows just how useful animal bodies can be as gauges of something like magnitude: as exemplary percepts, visible, coherent, ordered (*tachei*) objects in this case, animals fill *phantasia*, but they are not able to overfill it: no one would try to render an animal "a thousand miles long." In other words, there are mimetic limits to poetic description, and those limits are set by the idea of coherent perception as well as coherent memory. As Farrell puts it, "In between the microbe and the gargantuan are the many truths of human scale, density, amplitude, weight, and proportion for poetic and rhetoric to invent, recover, depict, and judge."[92] Nonhuman animals, with their just-right size (there *is* no animal a thousand miles long on earth), offer up those points. The variety of animal species—furred or feathered, differently mobile, and multicolored—also offers the possibility of endless depictive variations. Those implied variations inform Aristotle's analogy as the discussion returns to plot as *mimēsis*:

> A limit of length referring to competitions and powers of attention is extrinsic to the art: for if it were necessary for a hundred tragedies to compete, they would perform them by water clocks, as they say happened once before. But the limit that conforms to the actual nature [*autēn tēn phusin*] is that greater size, provided clear coherence remains, means finer beauty of magnitude.[93]

Here Aristotle eschews some sort of existing standard of plot size for attention to the nature of the tragedy itself. The observation fits perfectly back onto the exemplary animal body, the *mimēsis* of which ought to suit the size: such a limit, this passage implies, is intrinsic to mimetic arts.

The discussion of *megethos* and *mimēsis* also entails a point Aristotle makes earlier in the *Poetics* about pleasure and *mimēsis*, tying them both back to sensation and *aisthēsis*. In the famous discussion of how naturally enjoyable and instructive humans (young and old) find mimetic objects, the sweet spot of mimetic pleasure results from the precision of the *mimēsis* under contemplation, but it is a precision without the real thing: "We enjoy contemplating the most precise images of things whose actual sight is painful to us, such as the forms of the vilest animals and of corpses."[94] *Mimēsis* therefore produces pleasure by providing an occasion for contemplating (*theōrountes*) as a means of understanding. As with the *megethos* passage in book 7, Aristotle here has located another outer limit of *mimēsis*, this time not in size or perceptibility, but in the squirmy discomfort of the real. A human actor in a bull costume is one thing, but an actual bull on stage would be just too much.[95]

Yet an incomprehensibly large animal, specifically a horse as depicted by Homer, is upheld centuries later in *On the Sublime* as an instance of supreme (*hyperbolēn*) *megethous*. In offering for consideration a passage from the *Iliad* that depicts the goddess Hera guiding her horses from earth to sky, Longinus calls attention to how Homer "magnifies the divine":

> Far as a man sees with his eyes into the shadowy distance, keeping his watch on a hilltop, agaze over the wine-dark ocean, so far leap at a bound the loud-neighing horses of gods.[96]

Longinus points out matter-of-factly and with his own signature elegance that the poet "uses a cosmic interval to measure their stride."[97] He continues, "one might well say that if the horses take two consecutive strides there will then be no place found for them in the world."[98] In effect, Homer depicts the horses with a magnitude so great that their strides take them beyond the perceptive limits to which Aristotle binds *megethos*. Even so, given that Longinus's exemplar text is dealing with the deities, the grandeur here is appropriately incomprehensible. The cosmic strides are awe-inspiring precisely because they bear reference to—and radically outpace—the comprehensible, earth-bound strides of human-guided horses. Such extreme magnitude can be very gratifying for humans, as Longinus puts it later in his treatise: "The whole universe is not enough to satisfy the speculative intelligence of human thought; our ideas often pass beyond the limits that confine us."[99]

Demetrius, too, invokes animals in relation to grandeur (here the word is *megaloprepon*), this time on the grandeur inherent in subject matter. In so doing, he provides pointed insight on the question of animals as subjects: in other words, why the horses, rather than Hera herself, bear the weight of magnitude in the previous example. Demetrius locates force, *deinous*, in the subject matter rather than the style: "Some writers like Theopompus are said to be forceful [*deinous*], but it is their subject, not their style that is forceful."[100] He then turns to painting and invokes an observation attributed to Nicias, the famous painter of animals, to illustrate his point:

> The *zōographos* Nicias used to maintain that no small part of the painter's skill was the choice at the outset to paint an imposing subject, and instead of frittering away his skill on minor subjects, such as little birds or flowers, he should paint naval battles and cavalry charges where he could represent horses in many different poses, charging, or rearing up, or crouching low, and many riders hurling javelins or being thrown. He held that the theme itself was part of the painter's skill, just as plot was part of the poet's. So it is no surprise that in prose similarly grandeur comes from grandeur in the subject.[101]

This passage reveals exactly what animals—as subject matter—might lend to the quality of writing. Demetrius comes closer than anyone, that is, to theorizing a kind of zoostylistics. Note the sheer variety of images one can derive from a single animal. Charging, rearing up, crouching low, the figure of the horse in this passage illustrates a bounty of *energeia*; when Demetrius mentions riders, the horses are still very much in the picture, bucking and throwing them off. The variety of positions, which themselves make movement visible, produces a kind of frenetic *kinēsis*, thereby elevating the writing. With Aristotle, Longinus, and Demetrius as critical guides, it would be safe to claim that magnificent animal subjects are exactly how Homer achieves magnitude. These subjects, themselves kinetic, powerful, and often beautiful, inspire just that sort of style.

Charm

All this talk of magnitude and weight centered on serpents and horses raises the question, What of those smaller animals—Nicias's maligned "little birds," bees, and other insects? These nonhuman animals are by no means absent from exemplary passages on style. But their domain, in keeping with their material form and manner of moving, is a lighter, airier charm or delight (*charis*) rather than the robust *megethos*. In a discussion of elegant style, which he describes as "speech with charm and a graceful lightness,"[102] Demetrius again invokes Homer to illustrate charm already inherent in the subject but played up by diction. He quotes these lines from the *Odyssey*:

> Just as Pandareus' daughter, the pale nightingale,
> Sings beautifully at the beginning of spring[103]

And then Demetrius offers this commentary on the passage:

> This passage refers to the nightingale, which is a delightful little bird, and to spring, which is of its nature a delightful season of the year, but the style has made it much more beautiful, and the whole has added charm from "pale" and the rendering [*kourē*] of the bird as Pandareus' daughter. Both these touches are the poet's own.[104]

As with the energy and magnitude inherent in the matter of horses, the subject here—the nightingale, "a delightful little bird"—exudes charm. The charm, of course, must be supported by style, as it is here by Demetrius's reading, with the slender but vivid descriptor pale. Demetrius's attention to the bird's delight smooths over the simile's complexity as it appears in the poem: the nightingale a distraught Penelope refers to "sits perched amid the thick leafage of the trees, and with many trilling notes pours out her rich voice in wailing for her child."[105] The nightingale was considered a bird of mourning by the ancient Greeks, and this particular nightingale had "in a previous life been a woman who suffered the ultimate grief of 'inadvertently' killing her own child."[106] The airiness of the bird's song is counterbalanced by gravity of context and of character; the song's analogue in the passage is Penelope's heart, "stirred to and fro in doubt."[107] In Gregory Nagy's reading, what matters in this passage is the quality of "variance" indicated by the word *poludeukea* at line 521, and its attendant movement.[108] After discussing how Homer accomplishes charm—through the simple word pale and by presenting the nightingale as Pandareus's daughter—Demetrius turns to the need for a writer to use a "lighter tone" for subjects that are otherwise unattractive or somber. That topic follows quite obviously from the "charming" presentation of the nightingale, which, together with spring, offsets Penelope's deep despair.

The rest of Demetrius's discussion of charm is densely populated by birds and other winged creatures. He shares lines of uncertain origin (perhaps from Alcaeus) to illustrate how charm can be produced by the use of a single word, for example from metaphor, as in the passage about the cicada:

> from under his wings
> he pours out a stream of piercing song, as
> in the blazing heat of summer he flies and flutes.[109]

The charm in this passage stems from the metaphorical verb "flutes," which intensifies the charm already inherent in the cicada's song. That possibility is made explicit by Demetrius's observation that many words owe their charm to their application to a particular object, for example: "This bird is a flatterer [*kolax*] and a rogue [*kobalos*]."[110] Demetrius explains why the words *kolax* and *kobalos* (flatterer and rogue) exude charm: "Here there is charm because the author mocked the bird as though it were a person, and applied words not usually applied to a bird."[111] Of course, the story is more complicated than this. Demetrius's translator here points readers to Aristotle's *History of Animals*, which figures the eared owl as a rogue or trickster (*kobalos*) and a mimic (*mimētēs*).[112] While Demetrius claims the charm of the descriptors "flatterer" and "rogue" inheres in words that present the bird as if it were human, *kathaper anthrōpon*, the owl in question is also easily caught, according to the similar passage in Aristotle, because of its tendency to mimic a human: "It is a trickster and a mimic, and is caught when dancing in response to a hunter dancing while the second hunter goes round behind it."[113]

Demetrius's discussion of charm repeatedly invokes birds and other animals. Particularly charming, *eucharis*, is the opportune or fitting (the word here is *kairiōs*) use of a fable. The example he gives of one option, a traditional, established fable, again comes from "Aristotle's fable of the eagle: 'It dies of hunger, when its beak grows more and more curved. It suffers this fate because once upon a time when it was human it wronged a guest.'"[114] The eagle, like all the other animals, was thought to have been human in what was deemed by ancients the Golden Age. Demetrius, it should be noted, knew the fable genre well; he is thought by the most central Aesop scholars to have been the first to compile an anthology of fables for the use of oratory.[115] I will talk about fables in the next chapter, but the discussion of fable in *On Style* reveals Demetrius's stance toward fable as a charm-filled source of rhetorical invention. His Aristotle example shows how one can draw a fable from existing fables, told and retold so that they are familiar. But his next example contrasts explicitly with the earlier one:

> But we can often also invent fables which fit closely and match the context, for example one writer on the topic of cats said that they thrive and pine in phase with the moon, and then added his own invention, "and this is the origin of the fable that the moon gave birth to the cat." Not only will the new fiction in itself be attractive, but the actual fable is charming in making the cat the child of the moon.[116]

Here the novelty of the story doubles the charm inherent in the fable form, and fable, as is commonly known, is the genre of animals.

This cluster of charming examples—from the nightingale to the cat—all locate charm in the animal subjects' proximity to the human: the nightingale is made a "daughter," the cat a "child [*paida*] of the moon." The owl is figured as a rogue and by association becomes humanlike, and the eagle fable reads into the curved beak a remnant of the species' earlier status as human. This feature stands in contrast to the examples of *megethos*, where the animals—the snake-eyed Furies, the lion as Achilles—serve to draw out the bestial qualities of humans. Indeed, their status as nonhuman animals is what achieves grandeur.

After the discussion of fables, Demetrius mentions three more ways to achieve charm—release from fear, comparison, and hyperbole—and each approach is accompanied by at least one animal example. The first describes a moment of comic relief: "a man needlessly afraid, mistaking a strip of leather for a snake";[117] the second compares "a cock to a Persian because it holds its crest up, or to the Persian king because of its purple plumage;"[118] and the third quotes an unknown author describing the Thracians by saying "'their king Medoces would carry a whole ox in his jaws.'"[119] Each of these examples, presented in quick succession, connects an emotion or value to an animal image and receives little commentary from Demetrius; their charm, it seems, is self-evident.

Charm is also like magnitude in that it needs to be kept in check. Much as a single word (e.g., pale, or rogue, or fluted) in relation to an already charming animal can intensify delight, the wrong word or words can compromise the entire effort. Demetrius's example—and the one that ends his treatise as we have it—is drawn from the historian Clitarchus. Demetrius uses Clitarchus to illustrate the observation that "the choice of words often makes even subjects which are themselves charming lose their attractiveness."[120] The offending, overreaching passage is described by Demetrius as follows:

> Clitarchus, for instance, gives this description of the wasp, an insect like a bee: "It lays waste the hillsides and rushes into the hollow oaks." It is as if he described some wild bull, or the Erymanthian boar, rather than a kind of bee. The result is that the passage is both repulsive and frigid.[121]

The Erymanthian boar, itself a kind of hyperbole on Demetrius's part, was famous for wreaking havoc and generally inspiring fear. Only Heracles could capture him; others trembled at the sight of the beast. In his complaints against Clitarchus, one can almost see Demetrius shaking his head at the description of an otherwise charming (at least by Demetrius's account) insect.

Certain animals, then, can yield magnitude, while others inspire charm. It is no coincidence that most of Demetrius's examples of charm feature smaller animals such as cats, or winged ones, with the exception of the ox, used appropriately to charm with hyperbole. The lesson is clear: descriptors should match up with an animal's qualities, and that zoostylistic matching will become so important that it will, as I will show in the next two chapters, feature centrally in the school exercises of fable and *ekphrasis*. That nonhuman animals—and so many different kinds of them—appear so frequently in style theorists' discussions of magnitude and charm is owed, I argue, to visual and sonic familiarity, the ease with which they can be conjured through the senses even as they conjure multiple sensations.

Countenance

That Demetrius notes Clitarchus's inability to match his prose to a bee's disposition and movement indicates an awareness of the range of style and manner different kinds of animals can bring to the matter of style. His criticism centers on something like countenance or attitude. Implicit in the discussions of magnitude and charm is the idea that some animals lend one quality, others lend another. Had Penelope compared herself to a bleating goat rather than a nightingale, the passage's charm would have been compromised. In this way animals provide something like a metaphor palette, to go with the comparison to Nicias the painter. Or a metaphor of a sculptor's unmolded material might work, as it does for Demetrius's discussion of the different shapes words can help form, the way style can convey countenance: "In general," he observes, "language is wax, from which one man will mold a dog, another an ox, another a horse."[122] In addition to stressing the unformed mass of language-one translation emphasizes this mass by rendering *kuron* as "a lump of wax"[123]— the wax metaphor points to the softness and pliability of words. The gesture to softness is assisted by the verb here (*eplasen*), which usually applies to artists working with earth, clay, wax, or some other soft substance.[124] But the animal figures push the analogy even further into the realm of style as attitude, a crucial element of zoostylistics.

The three examples—dog, ox, horse—are animals Greeks would have encountered regularly, for they were three of the species most often domesticated in ancient Greece.[125] These are not just animals selected at random for their varied physical forms. Rather, the hulky, straining shoulder of an ox contrasts with the high head and flowing mane of a horse to invoke each species' capabilities and countenances. This sculpting passage is worth dwelling on, because the animals persist by countenance (though not by name) in Demetrius's illustrative explanation in the subsequent passage. He maintains the same order (dog, ox, horse), and I have annotated each example to indicate the corresponding animal characters. Each style in this passage is its own animal.

The same subject will be treated by one person in the form of direct statement and accusation [dog], for example: "men leave property to their chil-

dren, but they do not leave it with the knowledge of how to use the legacy."
This is the type used by Aristippus.

Another will, as Xenophon frequently does, put the same idea in the form
of a precept [ox], for example, "men ought to leave not only property to
their children, but also the knowledge of how to use it."

What is specifically called the Socratic manner—the type which Aeschines
and Plato in particular are considered to emulate—would redraft the same
idea in the form of questions, in this sort of way: "'My boy, how much property did your father leave you? Was it a lot and not easily assessed?' 'It was a
lot, Socrates.' 'Well now, did he also leave you the knowledge of how to use
it?'" Socrates unobtrusively drives the boy into a corner; he reminds him
that he does not have knowledge and encourages him to find instruction.
All this is done with characterization and in perfect taste [horse], far from
the proverbial Scythian bluntness.[126]

The first approach, the most direct version, is likened to the kind of statement that might be uttered by someone like Aristippus, the fifth-century
philosopher whose grandson (by the same name) built the Cyreniac school
on the principle of hedonism. Aristippus was "celebrated as a defender and
exemplar of a life of sensual pleasure" who advocated a focus on the present
without regard for the past or future.[127] As W. Rhys Roberts points out, Demetrius's is not a statement attributed to Aristippus, but it is his attempt to
capture a *manner* of stating. The bare, cut to the chase quality of the example
corresponds with a dog—say, Odysseus's tick-ridden, abandoned dog Argos
who, even in misery and just before dying, lowered his ears and wagged his
tail on recognizing his owner.[128]

The character of the ox, the toiling, strong-shouldered drawer of the plow,
inheres in the precept form Demetrius associates with Xenophon. Here the
ox's status as one of the most useful ancient animals entwines with the sentiment of the observation itself—that knowledge of what to do with material
wealth ought to accompany the wealth. As is well known, oxen were a standard unit of currency in the archaic period.[129]

It is no surprise that the horse corresponds to the style Demetrius deems
superior to the previous two. He goes on to discuss the final approach as, like
the horse, the most noble: "This type of speech was very successful at the
time it was first invented, or rather it stunned everyone by the verisimilitude,

the vividness, and the nobility of the ethical advice. Let this be enough on how to mold and configure speech."[130] The last sentence here informs readers of the passage's aim—to consider how words can be molded and shaped. The word for "configure" here, *schēmatismōn*, a genitive form of *schēmatismos*, can bear meanings of shape, formation, and more suggestively, of bearing or attitude. Dionysius of Halicarnassus uses the word in this sense in his critical essay on Demosthenes, in a discussion of how the tone and manner of delivery ought to suit the subject matter at hand. So, for example, a city's "complete destruction . . . demands an overwhelmingly angry and tragic manner of delivery."[131] My sense is that Demetrius's use of the word pulls in the direction of attitude, with the help of the dog, the ox, and the horse, all animals exhibiting distinctive bearings. That is, this lengthy three-part passage on qualities of characterization (*ēthika*) is underwritten by forms and characters of animals, the types of which help make visible the varied manner conveyed by how one says something, what form the mass of words is made to take. Demetrius therefore brings my argument full circle, through magnitude and charm, to attitude and density, or *onkos*. Another sort of density is achieved through compactness, the final stylistic feature enabled by animals, or better, by their sensuous efficiency.

Efficiency

The idea that animals as subjects inspire—or even dictate—certain styles of depiction points to an important feature of zoostylistics: the ability of animal images to render feeling with compact brevity. Because animals pack more sensory punch—because they are familiar enough to be conjured through words that activate sight, sound, or touch—they can be relied on to activate sensation with few words. A good instance of animals' capacity to minimize words by maximizing sensation is offered in Longinus's exasperated revision of a passage by Theopompus, whose description of the Persian king Artaxerxes Ochus's "descent into Egypt" is sullied by a kind of overdescription: Longinus's lengthy excerpt of the offending passage features a catalog of the emissary's entourage:

> Besides there were countless myriads of weapons, some Greek, some barbarian; baggage animals beyond number, and victims fatted for slaughter; many bushels of spice, and many bags and sacks and pots of papyrus and of all other things needful; and such a store of salted meat of every kind that it

lay in heaps so large that those who approached from a distance took them for mounds and hills confronting them.[132]

Longinus's criticism centers on this passage, for it is here that Longinus believes Theopompus "descends from the sublime to the trivial" by giving "the effect of a cook shop."[133] Instead, Longinus thinks the passage ought to be cast as follows:

> He might have given a comprehensive description both of what he calls the heaped-up mounds and of the rest of the equipage by altering his description thus: "Camels and a multitude of baggage animals laden with all that serves the luxury and pleasure of the table."[134]

Longinus tightens Theopompus's prose by specifying one kind of baggage animal—camels—thereby sharpening the image and rendering volume not by item but by number of animals and the weight they can bear. The switch to camels from "baggage animals beyond number" shows how familiar animals can in fact bear the visual load of an unwieldy list, brightening the style by trimming the bulk of the passage.

The need for keeping prose as trim as possible concerns Demetrius as well. Twice he uses an example from Xenophon of a metaphor turned simile, "like a gallant hound which recklessly charges a boar,"[135] which he offers as a risky poeticizing of a metaphor. In the first mention of this line, Demetrius is addressing the need to aim at conciseness in the realm of simile—to "do no more than prefix 'like'" or to run the risk of creating "a poetic comparison instead of a simile."[136] In addition to the boar-charging hound example, Demetrius offers Homer-style simile, "'like a horse let loose, kicking and proudly prancing over the plain,'" followed swiftly by a caution: "Such descriptions no longer seem similes but poetic comparisons, and poetic comparisons should not be used freely in prose nor without the greatest caution."[137] The second occurrence of Xenophon's charging hound sheds more light on how the line violates a Demetrian sensibility. This time it appears in a discussion of forceful style, a style that is not suited by "detailed comparisons."[138] Again, Demetrius focuses on the line's level of detail, which he deems too excessive for the passage to have force: "There is an element of beauty and precise detail about this sentence, whereas forcefulness needs to be short and sharp, like a close exchange of blows."[139] The details Demetrius deemed extraneous come with the added descriptions. A sparer description—say, a hound charging a boar—might have more force. Likewise

with the horse line. In the context of prose, such a line might be successfully trimmed to just the first part—"like a horse let loose," an image still
vivid enough to stir the imagination, yet concise enough to have force. As
Longinus implies with his revision of the Theopompus passage, the name
of an animal can achieve *energeia* without sacrificing the force of concision.
Demetrius specifies one reason such efficiency is desirable: "The compression of a lot of meaning into a small space shows more skill."[140] Compression
is accomplished through a stress on the depictive, visual force of rhetoric.
As rhetorical theorist Michael Osborn puts it in his treatment of "rhetorical
depiction," "Depiction . . . is characteristically more a compression than a
reflection";[141] it "is a key to synchronic, multiple, simultaneous meanings in
rhetoric,"[142] and it can result in what Osborn aptly characterizes as a kind of
intensification of response,[143] not unlike the intensity of response elicited by
a tragedy's moment of dramatic recognition.

Compactness, variability, attitude, charm, and magnitude: all these stylistic
features depend on the sensuous impact of phantasic animals. The teachers of
style realized this, for as this chapter's concluding discussion will show, they
also at times figured words themselves as animals.

WORDS *AS* ANIMALS

The animal metaphors in the Demetrius passage discussed above go even
deeper than just the point of variability, providing another important hint
about why nonhuman animals populate these style texts in particular places.
What emerges from thinking about animals with words is an animated theory
of style that views words themselves *as animals*. Such a view continues to
draw on the visual and sonic *energeia* of animals, but it goes even further to
the more startling encounters with both animals and words: words don't just
buzz or fly, they also sting and bite. Demetrius's discussion of playfulness offers a delightful case in point.

That discussion begins with a straightforward observation: "Mixing in an
element of playfulness often produces a kind of vigor, for example in comedy;
and the whole Cynic manner is like this."[144] He then mentions a story about
the Cynic philosopher Diogenes:

> At Olympia, when after the race between men in armor he ran forward
> and personally proclaimed himself victor in nobility of character. This an-
> nouncement raises simultaneous laughter and applause, and unobtrusively
> it also somehow gently bites as it is being said.[145]

He then gives another instance of a charged quip Diogenes made to a "handsome youth" with whom he was wrestling. When Diogenes "somehow experienced an erection and the boy became afraid and jumped away," Diogenes is reported to have said: "Never fear my boy, I am not like you in *that* way."[146] As Demetrius reads it, the quip contains both wit and, "hidden beneath," force. "Generally speaking," concludes Demetrius, "the whole character of Cynic sayings suggests a dog that fawns as it bites."[147] Of course, Diogenes is best known as Diogenes the Dog, and the dog (*kuōn*) is famously the namesake of Diogenes's philosophical school, the Cynics. The "dog that fawns as it bites" assumes a vivid posture—front paws forward, rear in the air, tail wagging—demonstrating an attitude of playfulness, and that attitude dominates even though the playful biting can sometimes, seemingly by accident, inflict pain.

Another passage likens speech to an animal posture, this in the context of force and impact (*deinos*), which Demetrius contends comes from short statements. To describe the effect of such statements he again turns to animal postures, this time a generic "wild beasts," *ta thēria*: "Just as wild beasts gather themselves together to fight, speech should similarly gather itself together as if in a coil to increase its force."[148] The image of compression gathers energy for the burst of action that is to come, capturing the coil even as it activates the spring.

Longinus sees a similar compressed effect when one removes connectors from a sentence, resulting in a speedy concision. In a discussion of the force of repetition and asyndeta in Demosthenes's speech against Meidias, Longinus notes how Demosthenes uses these figures

> to prevent the speech from coming to a halt by running over the same ground—for immobility expresses inertia, while emotion, being a violent movement of the soul, demands disorder—he leaps at once into further asyndeta and anaphoras.[149]

Leap here translates a verb derived from *methallomai*, which can apply to warriors as much as to lions pouncing on prey. Longinus goes on to further praise the "continual variation" created by repetition and asyndeta[150] and then suggests that readers adopt "the style of Isocrates and his school" by paraphrasing the lines and inserting connecting particles. Here is what would happen:

> If you thus paraphrase it sentence by sentence you will see that if the rush and the ruggedness of the emotion [*pathous*] is leveled and smoothed out

by the use of connecting particles, it loses its sting and its fire is quickly put out.[151]

The word for the resulting loss of sting, *akentron*, is taken, of course, from the tails of bees, wasps, and scorpions: *kentron* (sting) names just about anything that pierces the skin, even the quill of the porcupine. It is also frequently used to describe a spur or goad used to propel a horse.[152] "In Praise of Demosthenes," questionably attributed to Lucian, notes the qualities of Demosthenes's oratory, "known to us by tradition," namely "his thunderings and lightenings and his 'sting of persuasion,' *pathous ti kentron*."[153]

But Demosthenes's style is not the only one that stings. A fragment from the fifth-century writer of comedies Eupolis attributes an oratorical *kentron* to Pericles: "Persuasion perched upon his lips, and that's how he enchanted; and he alone of the speakers left a sting in his audience."[154] Centuries after Eupolis, when the poet Babrius set Aesop's fables to verse, in the second of two prologues he describes his own style by combining metaphors of stings and teeth: "I do not sharpen the teeth [*odontas*] of the iambs, but I test them and refine them as it were in the fire, and I am careful to soften their sting."[155] Here the word *kentra* occurs once again, this time in reference to the effects of the style in which the words are arranged.[156]

Words therefore bite, and they can sting. To voice the nearly mad Orestes, like the snake-eyed Furies, they "leap upon me close," and in doing so, they snap shut any remaining distance between action or thing and hearer or reader, by activating sensation through *phantasia*.

Ancient zoostylistics reveals how animals assist visually, aurally, and sensuously with an almost instantaneous process of vivification, *energeia*. In this way, nonhuman animals helped to remind the discipline of rhetoric of the importance of sensation. From the physical sounds of *onomatopoeia* to the variable compression of sense into word images, animals helped writers achieve a lively style, be it in the form of magnitude or of charm. Which is perhaps why Homer, who, as Aristotle reminds us, knew best of all how to make "everything live and move," equipped his words with wings.

CHAPTER 3

Beast Fables, Deliberative Rhetoric, and the *Progymnasmata*

The political situation in 335 BCE Athens was this: Thebes had been destroyed in a ruthless and bloody battle waged by Alexander of Macedonia in 335, a part of his plan to intimidate Greek city-states into declaring allegiance.[1] In the ensuing chaos, Athens sent the famous orator Demosthenes as an ambassador to the king, but he turned back out of fear. Alexander, in turn, commanded the extradition of Demosthenes and seven other Athenian orators. If Plutarch is to be believed, on this occasion, his freedom and life at stake, Demosthenes shared with the people of Athens a version of the following fable:

> The sheep and the wolves were at war with one another, but the sheep could not be defeated because the dogs' protection kept them safe. The wolves sent ambassadors to the sheep, pretending to offer an end to the hostilities if the sheep would surrender the dogs and let the wolves serve as their guardians. Hoping this would establish an accord once and for all, the sheep agreed to all the wolves' demands. Afterward the wolves broke the treaty and were able to devour the sheep now that they no longer had anyone to protect them.[2]

Demosthenes, in the example above, might be hard pressed to find a historical correlative for the situation in Athens, but the dog-wolf-sheep triumvirate "as a (triple) metaphor for politicians protecting, or demagogues pretending to protect, the people against enemies" would have been familiar at the time.[3]

This instance of beast fable operates on a logic of comparison or similitude, by bringing the comparates up close. In the case of beast fable, the creaturely situation and the political situation at hand are compared to each other; the Demosthenes instance typifies such comparison.[4] Demosthenes's fable lays before the eyes a transmutation: Alexander morphs into a "singularly fierce wolf," the eight orators into dogs (loyal, protective), and the people into sheep (unthinking and bleating).[5] By Plutarch's account, this fable worked, at least indirectly. For as "the Athenians were deliberating [*bouleuomenōn*] on [Alexander's] demand" and found themselves at a loss for what to do, Demades, an orator whose name was not on Alexander's list, stepped forward and for a fee offered to visit Macedonia on what would turn out to be a successful mission to have the command retracted and ultimately to keep Athens from suffering a Thebes-scale loss.[6]

Plutarch's telling implicitly argues for the usefulness of fable in the context of deliberative rhetoric, but Demades himself features in a short fable that counters such an argument:

> The orator Demades, trying to address his Athenian audience [and] holding very little of their attention, asked if he might tell them an Aesopian fable. The audience agreed, so Demades began his story. "Demeter, a swallow, and an eel were walking down the road. When they reached a river, the swallow flew up in the air and the eel jumped into the water." Having said these things, he fell silent. They asked him, "And what happened to Demeter?" He replied, "She is angry at all of you for holding a fable by Aesop above matters of the polis!"[7]

This anecdote positions fable as antithetical to politics, trading on the genre's reputation as overly simple, a trifle. In spirit at least, Demades's shaming proclamation is not unlike prevailing sentiments toward fables in contemporary critical animal studies, where they are deemed all too human and are indicted for their profound and seemingly insurmountable anthropocentrism. As Derrida puts it in the long essay *The Animal That Therefore I Am (More to Follow)*:

> Above all, it was necessary to avoid fables. We know the history of fabulization and how it remains an anthropomorphic taming, a moralizing subjection, a domestication. Always a discourse *of* man, on man, indeed on the animality of man, but for and in man.[8]

Derrida is mostly right, yet scholars working in critical animal studies seem to have taken "avoid fables" as a general command rather than as Derrida's specific pledge in this specific lecture,[9] thereby allowing a sweeping and dismissive characterization of a genre to spell the end of the story. Derrida's passing observations about fable are not reason enough to avoid the genre, nor are they the measure of what fables always or only do. As Susan Crane's treatment of medieval fable demonstrates, the animals in fable can in fact invite reflection across species other than human, and they can exceed the bounds of and turn back on language.[10] Crane's findings support Jeremy Lefkowitz's recent observation that "our notions of what the ancient fable *is* and *does* have undergone radical revision over the past several decades, making it increasingly difficult to characterize the genre's attitude towards animals in simple terms."[11]

A book about what animals are doing in premodern and early modern rhetorical theory can hardly avoid fable. Fables, after all, featured prominently in ancient oratory: Aristotle assigned them a specific and vital role in deliberative rhetoric, and the writers of *progymnasmata* manuals, those school exercises that prepared students for rhetoric, placed fable early in their sequence. John of Sardis, writing in the eighth century CE, declared that fable was placed first in the *progymnasmata* because it included "the seeds of all the art," which is to say it prepared students early on for a comprehensive rhetorical education.[12] It seems, then, that fable must not be avoided.

In the context of rhetoric, fables exploit a privative version of *alogos* shared by nonhuman animals and human children, which is to say that children and animals were thought not to possess language. The privative version of *alogos* is interestingly confirmed by the "fiction" of fable, which is that beasts are granted *logos*, for in fable characters of all species famously talk among themselves. At the same time, fables enact the nonprivative version of *alogos* that chapters 1 and 2 culled from Aristotle and from ancient treatments of style, which means they bring energy, movement, and sensation to the fore. Yet fables foreground sensation in a different way from the animals in those chapters, in part because of their specific roles in oratory and rhetorical education. In those contexts, the sensible qualities of fable vary from suffering to sweetness, transmitted via the "picturing" work of fable and its ability to tap the faculty of *phantasia*. And so despite Demades's separation, and as suggested by the Demosthenes anecdote, fable was seen as a useful mode for deliberative rhetoric, the most overtly political of rhetoric's three branches.[13]

Careful scrutiny of the link between the flexible form of fable and the often urgent context of deliberative rhetoric reveals the centrality of *phantasia* and the ability of all kinds of animals to activate the political imagination in the

divergent contexts of oratory and of early rhetorical education. Fables, characterized by more than one *progymnasmata* author as *psychagōgia* (enchantment, a leading of the soul), exemplify, sometimes in startling ways, the sensory work of deliberative *phantasia*.[14] Through their sensuous engagement
with and development of the faculty of *phantasia* early in the lives of children,
fables establish a partnership grounded in the *aloga*—the without-logos—
qualities delineated in the previous two chapters. Examining that partnership
reopens the question of what fables do and resituates them in the context of
rhetorical theory and rhetorical education.

To present that view, this chapter first positions fable in relation to deliberative *phantasia*, then takes that working theory into Aristotle's treatment of
fable in book 2 of the *Rhetoric*. From there, I consider the curious insistence,
found in later *progymnasmata* manuals, of counting the fable as deliberative
rhetoric and examine that in the context of the "picturing" work those authors instilled into their definition of fable. Finally, I inspect the partnership
between children and animals structured by their shared status as *aloga*, a
bond that dictates the prime place of fable in the *progymnasmata* exercises.
Examining in tandem these two seemingly disparate traditions—Aristotelian
deliberative rhetoric and early fable teaching—keeps animals and deliberation
at the fore in an incongruous perspective, unsettling prevailing presumptions
about the fable genre, specifying what else it is that fables, and specifically
beast fables, do in the context of rhetoric.

FABLE AND DELIBERATIVE *PHANTASIA*

Pertinent to this account of fable is the special category of *phantasia* considered in chapter 1, deliberative *phantasia* (*phantasia bouleutikē*),[15] which
involves "calculative weighing of multiple *phantasic* images."[16] Elsewhere I
have drawn from Aristotle a notion of deliberative *phantasia* as composite
imagination—that is, a bundling together of several images—and that feature
of deliberative *phantasia* informs what follows. Fables, after all, are themselves composite pictures that both draw on and activate sensuous imagination. And they lay bare the paradox inherent in the very notion of deliberative
phantasia: the push of the rational toward the calculative mode inherent in
the act of deliberation, and *phantasia*'s pull of the nonrational toward feeling.
When brought into harmony, though—and this is the explicit aim of fable
in the context of rhetoric, as I will show—deliberation and *phantasia* work
together, pushing and pulling powerfully in the same direction. In the Demosthenes example that opens this chapter, the composite picture is formed

by interspecies interaction, and that interaction is governed in the context of fable by the perceivable differences among animal species.

The importance of sensation and feeling in deliberation is made clear by two interconnected passages in Aristotle's *De anima*, the treatise on the soul that lays out a theory of *phantasia*, of which deliberative *phantasia* is a part. As Ned O'Gorman has demonstrated, Aristotle places *phantasia* squarely in the province of deliberation, "designating deliberation as entailing the combination of mental images."[17] For Aristotle, the process of judgment resulting from direct sensation is very similar to the process of movement resulting from *phantasia*:

> Just as those [imaginings] marked out what is to be pursued and avoided, even apart from sensation, [the thinking faculty] is moved when it is occupied with imaginings [*tōn phantasmatōn*]. For instance, in sensing a torch one recognizes that it is fire; then observing by what is common to the senses that it is moving, that it signifies an enemy.[18]

At stake in Aristotle's account of *phantasia* here is the relation between sensation and future action. That relation, and the interpretive judgment that facilitates it, depends on the composite picture, which itself accumulates details: that is fire, and the fire is moving. The relation between composite sensations and future action, the straining to discern that which is not, or not yet, certain, and acting accordingly, constitutes the world of rhetoric.

A *De anima* passage I discussed in chapter 1 is relevant here for the way Aristotle places feeling at a slight remove in the context of imagination: "When we form an opinion that something is threatening or frightening, we are immediately affected by it, and the same is true of our opinion of something that inspires courage; but in imagination we are like spectators looking at something dreadful or encouraging in a picture."[19] The immediacy of feeling's arrival upon forming an opinion about something is slowed down a little and given distance—or at least a vaguely contoured blurriness—in the context of imagination. The most useful and feeling-laden description along these lines is the one I discussed in chapter 2 in the context of *mimēsis*, where Aristotle considers the pleasure of such spectatorship: "We enjoy contemplating the most precise images of things whose actual sight is painful to us, such as the forms of the vilest animals and of corpses."[20] When used in the context of deliberative oratory—that is, in an attempt to shape prevailing opinion and encourage a particular action—fable exploits both the pleasure of spectatorship and the pain of imagining an undesirable future. Operating in the somewhat safely distanced mode of *phantasia*, the fictitious narrative of fable can create a dreadful or encouraging picture, brimming with violence, pain, and gore. Then, when the likeness between the fable scenario and the deliberative situation comes into view, the difference between animal characters and the situation of the auditors slips away, so that Alexander's wolflike characteristics linger, the blood of the sheep mingles with imagined blood of Athenians, and the composite picture, however blurry-edged, can suddenly be eye-widening.[21] Such a theory of the deliberative work of fable, suffused by example with pain, violence, and blood, is put forth in Aristotle's *Rhetoric*.

DELIBERATIVE FABLES IN ARISTOTLE'S *RHETORIC*

Consider the first of two fables Aristotle offers as exemplars of example, the first drawn from the sixth-century poet Stesichorus, the second attributed to Aesop:

> When the people of Himera had chosen Phalaris as dictator and were about to give him a bodyguard, after saying other things at some length, Stesichorus told them a fable about how a horse had a meadow to himself. When a stag came and quite damaged the pasture, the horse, wanting to avenge himself on the stag, asked a man if he could help him get vengeance on the stag. The man said he could if the horse were to submit to a bit and he himself were to mount on him, holding javelins. When the horse agreed and the man mounted, instead of getting vengeance the horse found himself a slave to the man. "Thus you too," said Stesichorus, "look out, lest while wishing vengeance on your enemies you suffer the same thing as the horse. You already have the bit [in your mouth], having appointed a general with absolute power; if you give him a bodyguard and allow him to mount, you will immediately be slaves to Phalaris."[22]

As with the fable Demosthenes reported about the wolf-sheep-dog triumvirate, this fable features a political bargain gone bad. Aristotle offers little direct commentary on this anecdote, deferring any rhetorical lesson until after he relays the second fable. But the framing of the fable hints at the circumstances in which Stesichorus chose to tell the fable—he did so after going on at some length.[23] The intimation of duration emphasizes by implied contrast the compactness and argumentative efficiency of fable. That efficiency is enabled by the vividness of the animals' physical, material situation and by the brevity of the genre. The image of the bit has the potential to activate multiple senses simultaneously: the shiny clanking metal, a noisy reminder of forced submission, and the horse, in his very nonhumanness, keeps the situation at a safe distance until the explicit comparison draws it close: one can almost feel the audience stiffen at the felt image of their own bit.

The second exemplary fable in this discussion, which Aristotle attributes to Aesop, even more vividly presents pain—this time of the body politic—through the pitiable, tick-ridden body of a trapped fox:

> Aesop, when speaking on behalf of a demagogue who was on trial for his life in Samos, told how a fox, while crossing a river, was carried into a hole in the bank. Not being able to get out, she was in misery for some time and many dog-ticks attacked her. A hedgehog came wandering along and, when he saw her, took pity and asked if he could remove the ticks. She would not let him and, when asked why, [said,] "These are already full of me and draw little blood, but if you remove these, other hungry ones will come and drink what blood I have left." "In your case too, O Samians, said [Aesop], "this man will no longer harm you; for he is rich. But if you kill him, other poor ones will come who will steal and spend your public funds."[24]

Like the Stesichorus fable, the fox and hedgehog fable analogizes the situation at hand with a vivid and efficient image, this time of the scrawny fox, its body covered with engorged parasites. The fox's pitiable suffering is conveyed through the hedgehog's concern, but in the end the fox knows what is good for it. Both of Aristotle's paradigmatic fables are likely to have functioned as something like concluding arguments—in his introduction of Stesichorus's fable, Aristotle practically states that outright—and the conclusive force of paradigm as a logical means of argument receives the most stress in Aristotle's subsequent discussion.

In that discussion, Aristotle first notes the suitability of fables to deliberative oratory.[25] While the second example (the Aesop anecdote) occurs in an explicitly forensic context, it has a deliberative cast inasmuch as Aesop uses the fable to turn to questions of the future—that is, to what could happen were the demagogue in question convicted and removed from power. In a deliberative context, then, according to Aristotle, fables "have this advantage, that while it is difficult to find [*heurein*] similar historical incidents that have actually happened, it is rather easy with fables. They should be made in the same way as comparisons, provided one can see the likenesses."[26] Aristotle's remarks hint at two related features of fables: the ease with which the beast fable can be adapted to a particular situation compared with factual historical events, which are harder to find (*heurein*), and the fable's dependence on the audience's ability to see the likeness.[27]

For the first feature, the adaptability of fable, I want to reflect for a moment on Aristotle's comparison of fable with historical events. Because fables provide a bare scenario, without reference to a specific time other than at one point in the past (the genre of fables is often marked by the term "once"), they are more customizable. Orators may rely on the current exigency to supply the specific analogy, leaving the audience members to work it out for themselves, or they can more explicitly coax the comparison with the verbal equivalent of an "after fable" (*epimythion*) composed specifically to relate the fable's lesson to the Samians in the case of Stesichorus, to the demagogue's trial in the instance of Aesop, or to the future of Athens in the case of Demosthenes. By contrast, historical events the audience is familiar with contain their own sets of circumstances, their own human characters with their particular flaws, and the risk is that the circumstances of the past would cloud the analogy, distracting from the positive points of comparison. As Aristotle notes, perfectly comparable historical incidents, while preferable, would in fact be very difficult to find. But beast fables, as fictions residing mostly in the oral tradition, are malleable, the animal characters fungible, their situations tweakable, their lessons adaptable to circumstance. Indeed, stripping fable away from such circumstantial telling in deliberative rhetoric transforms the genre into primarily a mode of what Derrida characterizes as "moralizing subjection."

Yet despite the advantage of their freedom from the fetters of prior circumstance and the resulting adaptability to present circumstance, to guarantee their success fables need to be seen as a likeness. Thanks in large part to the animal characters, beast fables retain their vividness. When Aristotle discusses this ability to see the likeness, he uses *horan*, from *horaō*, the visual verb most closely related to the physical sense of sight, to the eyes, rather than *theōrein*, the more abstract term he uses in his famous definition of rhetoric (the ability to see the available means of persuasion in each case).[28] In fact, *theōrein* is the term Aristotle uses in book 3 to describe a similar capacity of metaphor to make a likeness apparent. This passage refers back to the discussion of grasping likeness in fable when it too invokes those trained in philosophy: "As in philosophy, too, it is characteristic of a well-directed mind to observe [*theōrein*] the likeness [*to homoion*] even in things very different."[29] Indeed, the likeness of the two passages suggests that Aristotle may have been laying the groundwork for his famous treatment of metaphor in his discussion of fable. Certainly fables operate very broadly on the level of metaphor, as argued by Gert-Jan van Dijk and by classicist Arti Mehta.[30] They make an inferential argument through transferential trope. Indeed, reading as a pair the two discussions of vision created through language—one (fable) through vivid comparison and the other (metaphor) through recognition of the likeness—doubly stresses the visual element of fable: audience members are able to *see* the likeness of the present situation to the scenario vividly depicted in the animal world. Hence the in*sight* fable allows.

Yet it would be a mistake to let the visual verbs—no matter how pronounced—overshadow other sensations activated by fables, especially felt pain. Recall from chapter 1 the felt pain (*lupē*) that accompanies nearly every treatment of feeling (*pathē*) in book 2 of the *Rhetoric*. So fear (*phobos*), the operative *pathē* in the three main instances of oratorical fable discussed so far, is defined in the *Rhetoric* as "a sort of pain and agitation derived from the *phantasia* of a future destructive or painful evil."[31] The word conjoined to *lupē* here, *tarachē*, names disorder, disturbance, *upheaval*. Together the two words aptly characterize the feltness of fear. For many, fear itself can bring on a physiological aporia, the temporary paralysis by which the body seems to discern no obvious way out. And that feeling can arrive with the glimpse of a possible future as furnished by *phantasia*. In this way *phantasia* all but carries with it the pain and the disturbance. Sensation-wise, it is therefore difficult to limit *phantasia* to the sense of sight, though perhaps the feeling begins there, with the straining to see of *phantasia*—in this case, straining to see an uncertain future that depends on a deliberative outcome.

Sight also underwrites the work of fables much as it does for metaphor (as considered in the previous chapter). In his discussion of fable, Aristotle specifies that philosophical study boosts the capacity to see likeness, and the animals' vivification of future evil helps to ensure that audience members—trained or untrained in philosophy—are able to see, *horein*, the comparison or the likeness between the animal scenario and the present occasion as presented by the orator. If placed in a scenario that emphasizes their vulnerability (Aesop's fox was carried into its hole by a rushing river), animal characters can efficiently and vividly bring before the eyes pain and torment. Fable provides the perfect narrative stage for zoostylistics, detailed in the previous chapter; the recognizable styles of movements and distinctive physical characteristics of animals rely on and promote the feelings of *phantasia*. Pain, in other words, is carried by the animals of fable. They serve as its bodily witness and conjure *pathos* as a result.

The witnessing connection is made by Aristotle. As the discussion of fable in book 2 continues and he considers paradigm in relation to enthymeme, he notes that if the orator has enthymemes at his disposal—those signature quick twists of logic that cut right to listeners' hearts—then paradigms such as fable ought to be used "as witnesses [i.e., as] a supplement to the enthymeme."[32] He then repeats this reinforcing function, "when [paradigms] are put at the end they become witnesses, and a witness is everywhere persuasive. Thus too," he adds, "when they are mentioned at the end, one is sufficient; for even a single trustworthy witness is useful."[33] The witnessing performed by fables, then, is the kind that is both "everywhere persuasive" and singularly useful.[34] Following directly on the heels of Aristotle's discussion of fable, this passage captures the effective work of paradigms by using four forms of the word *martus*, witness, from which derives the English word martyr, one who singularly (and often visibly and painfully) bears witness.

For a discussion of *martus* in rhetoric, one need only flip back to book 1's treatment of witnesses in the context of *topoi*. Most helpful for seeing how fables work as witnesses in deliberative rhetoric is Aristotle's concluding point about the witness *topos*, in which he distributes what would later become known as the stasis question of fact and quality across a spectrum of witnesses. Here Aristotle ascribes questions of fact to recent witnesses, reserving matters of quality for ancient ones. Those, he says, are "the most credible; for they are incorruptible."[35] Book 1's discussion of ancient *marturos* highlights a third feature of fables that makes them "everywhere persuasive": they help to make arguments not about fact, but about the quality or value of an action, and they do so because they carry enduring forms of wisdom—Aristotle also offers proverb as a category of witness.[36] It is worth reiterating too that those forms of witness reside in the physical, material situations in which the animal characters act: the composite images created out of them. The beasts in these fables, that is, endure the suffering of a latter-day martyr, bearing physical witness to the causes or effects of certain kinds of decisions. The fictional enslavement of Simonides's horse, the tick-ridden body of Aesop's fox, and even the slaughter of Demosthenes's unfortunate sheep make them paradigmatic sufferers, their predicaments visible and felt—and therefore more present—in pools of imagined blood or the clanking of a bit.

The specific witness that fable provides serves Aristotle as an example in the context of deliberative rhetoric. And the idea that fables are useful for deliberating about the future repeats in the other place where beast fables show up in rhetoric's history in the West, the *progymnasmata* manuals.

DELIBERATIVE FABLES IN THE
PROGYMNASMATA TRADITION

The *progymnasmata* writers were well aware of the tradition of using fables in deliberative oratory. The manual attributed to Hermogenes appends exactly that observation to its treatment of fable: "Orators too seem (sometimes) to have used a fable in place of an example," and Aphthonius leads with it.[37] The fifth-century *progymnasmata* manual written by Nicolaus the Sophist makes explicit the deliberative function of fables at the beginning and end of a discussion on the genre of fable, the first in Nicolaus's list of exercises. On the matter of categorization he is emphatic: "Fable clearly belongs to the deliberative kind; for we are exhorting to good deeds or dissuading from errors."[38] This logic ties together fable's moral and rhetorical force. But it is the second statement on fable's value for deliberative rhetoric that reveals more about how it was thought to work and, further, why it was ultimately placed first in the *progymnasmata* sequence:

> But that it clearly belongs to the deliberative part, no one should doubt; for in addition to its power of enchantment, it benefits those who are persuaded, dissuading them from bad things, advising them to desire good things, and together with its sweetness accustoming them to taking advantage of its benefits.[39]

Rich with purpose, tinged with sweetness, the desiderative quality of fable—the ostensible pull toward good things—stands out here. Indeed, sweetness is presented in this passage as that which habituates hearers; setting up something like a modern-day sugar addiction, the pleasures of sweetness draw them in and keep them coming back.[40] But without leaving sweetness behind, I want to linger on the word in this passage that Kennedy translates as enchantment, *psychagōgia*, soul leading. It is possible, I think, to tie this "soul leading" quality of fable to the sensory work of deliberative *phantasia*, which for Aristotle arises in particular instances:

> But sometimes by means of the images or thoughts in the soul, just as if it were seeing, it calculates and plans for the future in view of the present; and when it makes a statement, as in sensation it asserts that an object is pleasant or unpleasant, in this case it avoids or pursues; and so generally in action.[41]

Here, as with the definition of fear considered above, the soul needs to con-jure images of the future in order to make a decision. In the case of Demos-thenes, the Athenians had one set of images put there by Alexander, and De-mosthenes used the violence and wiliness made possible by fable to supplant the existing images.

The act of picturing in the soul that Aristotle ascribed to deliberative *phan-tasia* inheres in the definition of fable put forth by Theon, as a fictitious story picturing truth.[42] It is, according to one of the most authoritative scholars of Aesop, "a perfect and complete definition" of fable.[43] Of the four remain-ing *progymnasmata* authors from antiquity, three repeat Theon's definition verbatim.[44]

The word for "picturing" in the definition, *eikonizōn*, returns to the Aristo-telian realm of *phantasia*, of appearances, especially those imagined or other-wise conjured. Theon helpfully specifies the direction of the picturing in the next clause: "But one should know that the present consideration is not about all fables but about those in which, after stating the fable, we add the mean-ing of which it is an image [*eikōn*]."[45] Fable in the *progymnasmata* tradition is presented as a perfect instance of words conjuring images, which operates by way of the capacity of *phantasia*. Theon discusses *phantasia* briefly when he mentions the usefulness of paraphrase, one of the many exercises Theon suggested ought to be done with fable: "Thought is not moved [*kinoumenēs*] by any one thing in only one way so as to express the idea [*phantasia*] that has occurred to it in a similar form, but it is stirred in a number of different ways."[46] Reading the "picturing" work of fable in the context of *phantasia* stresses the sensuous movements of fabulous beasts while still preserving the transferential work they do, as discussed above in the context of Aristotle. The fictional scenario relates metaphorically to the current situation by means of the easily visualized, lively animal characters, whose kinetic movements stir the senses. The fable's truth—*alētheia*—is both heightened by and abstracted from the powerful images conjured by the story. Mehta describes fable on her way to (also) arguing for fable as a mode of visualization:

> What the fable needs to make possible for the speaker's audience is the ability to see the problem within a different situation or context, in particu-lar one slightly removed from the immediacy or the danger or the dilemma that the audience faces. The speaker's main goal, then, is to help the audi-ence perceive its situation differently by initiating a moment of perception for the audience.[47]

Fable leans on that perception in lieu of—or alongside—straightforward "didactic explication."[48] As the title of an article by Gregory Carlson phrases it, "fables invite perception."[49] Its level of sensuous engagement aids fable's suggestive potency in the context of both oratorical performance and rhetorical education.

PARTNERS IN *ALOGOS*

But how is it that such a graphic genre as fable, used in the rough-and-tumble world of classical political oratory as a means of picturing pain and stirring fear, came to serve as the lead preparatory exercise for children? It's not as if the *progymnasmata* authors selected particularly anodyne examples. One clue is found in the word *pseudēs* in Theon's definition, which allows for the fiction that bestows eloquence on otherwise *aloga* animals. If children and animals were deemed partners in *aloga*, then speaking animals, perhaps paradoxically, provide more realizable models for children to hone their facility with words and arguments, while at the same time tapping their already lively imaginations.

The *progymnasmata* attributed to Hermogenes (second century CE) assigns the primary position to fable out of similar concerns for overcoming unruliness:

> Fable is regarded as the first exercise to be assigned to the young because it can bring their minds into harmony [*rhythmizein*] for the better. In this way they [i.e., teachers of grammar] think to form students while still tender [*hapalous*].[50]

The two key words in this passage—*rhythmizein* and *hapalous*—reveal ancient assumptions about the minds of children. To harmonize, *rhythmizein*, is of course the etymological ancestor of English rhythm, and it is frequently used with an educative valence.[51] The primary meaning, of course, has to do with timing and order—so here it can be read "ordering their minds for the better." The implication is that the minds (and even the souls) of children suffer from disorder or arrhythmia and need to be ordered, harmonized. This intimation coheres with a prevailing assumption among the ancients: the unruliness of human children—minds and bodies—aligns most closely with nonhuman animals, especially toward the beginning of their educational lives. The second key word, *hapalous*, a term of the flesh that sometimes refers specifically to young animals, supports such an interpretation.[52]

The shared place of animals and children on a wild-tame continuum moti-
vates a broad concern with education in general. But another crucial division
grafts onto the human child-beast relationship, pulling the educational focus
specifically toward rhetoric and complicating the easy separation between human and nonhuman animals: the possession of a facility with *logos*. And this is
where a strictly privative notion of *alogos* asserts itself most obviously. Put another way, the most notable way that animals and children converge is not in
their "softness," unruliness, or trainability, but in their perceived deficiencies
of *logos*, and here I mean for *logos* to contain its two most prominent ancient
valences: speech and reason.

In their very early phases, children too were deemed *aloga*, and as they
developed, they inhabited a somewhat liminal space with regard to *logos*, edg-
ing closer to a full adult human by means of a rhetorical education. The word
infant, as is widely known, derives from the Latin *infans*, one who cannot
speak.[53] An infant's wail was often described with verbs that also referred to
the bleating of sheep or goats and the bellowing of wild beasts.[54] Early in the
first book of *Institutes of Oratory*, where Quintilian treats the "elementary"
phase of education, he writes that "it would be a good idea, at this age, in order to develop the vocal organs and make the speech more distinct, to get the
child to rattle off, as fast as he can, words and verses designed to be difficult,
formed of strings of syllables which clash with one another, and are really
rocky, as it were: the Greeks call them *chalinoi*."[55] *Chalinoi* were literally bits
or curbs used on a horse.[56] Facility with words became a way to control bestial
unruliness, to move the child along the continuum from *alogos* to *logos*.

The relation between children and animals along the lines of *alogos* and
logos, wild and tame, together with the prominence of nonhuman animals in
fables, helps to account for fable's slide to the beginning of the rhetorical curriculum. What is missing, of course, from the ancient accounts is the perspective of children themselves on the animals. With a mixture of caution and
textual evidence, we can infer a kind of affinity. Ausonius, a fourth-century
Latin poet and rhetorician, sent the emperor Probus a book of fables to use
in educating his children, to which he appended an epigram expressing "his
wish that the fables, between fairy tales and lullabies, will accustom the addressee's son to laugh and learn simultaneously."[57] Quintilian, too, mentions
fable telling as a method for provoking laughter, and at the beginning of his
educational treatise he notes that Aesop's fables ought to "follow on directly
from their nurses' stories, *nutricularum*," intimating that fables may provide
similar nourishment.[58] Indeed, children may well have known the nonpriva-

tive version of *aloga* that I discussed in chapter 1. Such a view, I offer, persists in the positive associations with fable, the sweetness, the delight.

Synesius, a bishop of Ptolemais during the age when the *progymnas-mata* took hold, calls fables "a mere slight imitation of dreams" and notes that "Sophists have considered fables useful in teaching men to speak." He then goes on to make the connection: "Fable might be the starting-point: dream, the end; and by studying dreams a person would become, not only more eloquent, but actually wiser."[59] This Synesius connection, by linking fables to dreams, one of Aristotle's designated states of *phantasia* (sensation at a remove), acknowledges that learning potentially can happen in, with, and from *phantasia*. Recall from chapter 1 that in the *Metaphysics phantasia*—the world of impressions—is a mode of sensing, feeling, and thinking shared by all animals (along with *memoria*), so children possess it as well.[60] Fable's "picturing" quality taps this phantasic capacity by staging a meeting of creatures deemed fully capable of engaging in this sensory mode of participation.

PICTURING PAIN

So far I have considered uses of fable in deliberative oratory and rhetorical theory, theorized its workings through *phantasia*, specifically deliberative *phantasia*, and followed that version of fable into the *progymnasmata*, whose structure rests on a presumption of children and animals as partners in *aloga*.

Still, as I mentioned earlier, despite the *progymnasmata* authors' insistence on the tenderness of children, the manuals hardly blunt the violence of fable. Theon's discussion of fable references the earliest recorded fable, that of the hawk and the nightingale, from Hesiod's *Works and Days*. Here is Theon:

> When a fable is being told as a whole, it is also useful for the learner to become accustomed to make an elegant beginning in the middle of the story, as Hesiod does: "Thus said the hawk to the nightingale with speckled neck." From what is added, "he is a fool who tries to withstand the stronger," it is clear that a nightingale was quarreling with a hawk and then the hawk became annoyed and seized her and spoke these words.[61]

A simple adjective can anticipate and then magnify pain. Hesiod's version shows a nightingale with a "speckled neck" "gripped fast" in the "crooked" talons of a hawk.[62] The speckled neck detail, while not central to the fable's action, nevertheless serves at least two purposes. First, it conjures the nightingale, calling to mind one of the bird's distinguishing physical characteristics, and with it, its small size and even its pretty voice. Second, the phrase speck-led neck draws the eyes to the nightingale's neck, laying it bare, stressing the bird's vulnerability. Because the image of the nightingale would have been visually familiar, exhibiting such a variety of physical characteristics that sig-nify relational strengths and weakness, one or two words—tortoise, hare—can frame a predicament that would require a good deal of setup were the actors indistinct humans.

Other fables mentioned in the extant *progymnasmata* manuals that may be said to picture—or at least portend—pain include, from Theon, a camel that lost its ear and a drowned dog.[63] Pseudo-Hermogenes alludes to the nightin-gale detail once again as well as to a fable attributed to Archilochus that may have by this point evolved to depict a fox creating a circle of fire around a tree bearing a nest of eaglets whose mother was feeding them the fox's cubs.[64] Aphthonius the Sophist includes a fable in which cicadas nearly starve to death.[65]

The more dramatic and painful the situation of the fabulous animals, the easier it would have been to remember the narrative details. Chapter 5 will pursue this relation between *phantasia*, memory, fear, and pain into its me-dieval manifestations. For now it is worth noting that heightened sensation helps to achieve Theon's recommendation to make sure students' "minds have been filled with many fables," which prepares them to "imagine a fable suitable to the material at hand."[66] *Phantasia* of memory begets *phantasia* of invention. In the *progymnasmata* tradition, the beasts of fable become narra-tive martyrs for the causes of memory and of learning preparation, and their potent mix of pain and "sweetness" makes them the gateway to rhetorical education. The "seeds of all the art" were sown with narrative violence and suffering.

On one hand, this violence and suffering could and should be read as "anthropomorphic taming," to use Derrida's phrase.[67] Yet the treatment of fable in *progymnasmata* manuals does more than that. Fables begin with the plight of nonhuman animals and take seriously what the animals featured in the fable do as beings living in and moving through the world, which posits what the writers call credibility or plausibility.[68] The principle of plausibility is drawn out in the *progymnasmata* attributed to Hermogenes in what van Dijk calls his "profile of the [fable] genre."[69] That profile augments Theon's definition by building on what might be taken as the genre's central paradox: How can a false story picture truth? Put in terms of the plausibility principle, how can a talking fox be plausible? The *progymnasmata* writers wrestle with this paradox with different levels of intensity, but the answer comes down to this: as a false story that pictures the truth, the genre leans "truthward" not just through the clarity of its picture, but also by means of its usefulness and its persuasiveness. The Greek adjective here, *pithanon*, of course, generally means persuasive. The subsequent elaboration augments the *picturing truth* part of Theon's generic definition, and the discussion of fables' persuasiveness focuses on the animal characters:

> How would it become plausible? If we attribute appropriate things to the characters. For example, someone is arguing about beauty; let him be represented as a peacock. Cleverness needs to be attributed to someone; here, the fox is appropriate. For imitators of the actions of human beings, choose apes.[70]

The *pithanos* principle reins in the genre's fictitiousness in the service of something like "truth," and this is how the narrative blur of *phantasia* mingles the likelihood of animal actions based on lives and habits with the future-oriented blur of politics. Fables offer yet another way that nonhuman animals entered political lifeworlds of the ancients.

PICTURING DELIBERATION

If the fable genre enacts rhetorical vision (words conjuring images), then it also relies on the imagination—the faculty of *phantasia*—to conjure words for otherwise nonspeaking animals. Indeed, the manual attributed to Hermogenes frames the fable exercise this way:

> Sometimes fable needs to be expanded, sometimes to be compressed. How would this be done? If we sometimes recount the fable in a bare narrative, at other times invent speeches for the given characters.[71]

The author clarifies with a fascinating example that does not augment deliberative arguments so much as it stages a nonhuman deliberation:

> The apes gathered to deliberate about the need to found a city. Since it seemed best to do so, they were about to begin work. An old ape restrained them, saying that they will be more easily caught if hemmed in by walls.[72]

This compact overview of the fable is then expanded to illustrate the inventing of speeches:

The apes gathered to deliberate about building a city. One stepped forward and delivered a speech to the effect that they had need of a city: "For you see," he says, "how happy men are by living in a city. Each of them has his house, and by coming together to an assembly and a theater all collectively delight their minds with all sorts of sights and sounds," and continue in this way, dwelling on each point and saying that the decree was passed; then fashion a speech also for the old ape.[73]

This fable about simian orators, it should be noted, follows the same author's advice about using apes to imitate deeds of humans. Building cities, of course, is that particular animal's specialty. Several noteworthy features spring from this scenario. First, the students given such an assignment are asked to act as if they are apes acting as if they are men, redoubling a subjunctive cast. But the short expansion, in staying with apeness, marshals *topoi* about feeling and sensation: humans appear to be happy; they gather to take in sights and sounds.

John of Sardis incorporates this fabulous scenario into the *progymnasma* called *ēthopoeia*. *Ēthopoeia*, as John notes, is explicitly a way of expanding fable: "*ēthopoeia* occurs in almost all the exercises and is part of each, starting with fables."[74] Seeking to create models for expansion through *ēthopoeia*, John rounds out the deliberation by attributing these words to the dissenting ape:

> Living together in a city will be the cause of many evils for us; for we shall grow softer in some way. One's way of life and soft living naturally weaken the mind as well as the body. Then, lack of the necessities of life follows from those collected in a city, and from that famine results. Nor will we have means of safety; if men already lay hands on us when we are widely scattered, how will they not do so more easily when we are shut in a city? Worst of all as a group we shall be wholly wiped out, leaving no seed of our race."[75]

This dissenting view is fascinating for its adherence to the terms of the assignment. That the composer is speaking as an ape and not as a human is evident in the positing of humans as a threat to the species. John goes on to reflect on the work of *ēthopoeia* "creating a vivid impression of the subject" and also "creating pathos," both of which feed the picturing work of fable.

Such *ēthopoeia* involving animals may have been rare (with such limited extant resources it is difficult to tell), and if Aphthonius's distinctions are to be followed, the ape deliberation would actually count as *prosopopoeia*, the name for character making for which "everything is invented," including the character. By contrast, *ēthopoeia* in this scheme voices a specific human speaker, while *eidōlopoeia* speaks for the dead.[76] The different accounts of the distinctions between *ēthopoeia* and *prosopopoeia* can be confusing, though it is worth examining where Quintilian draws the line, because there the doubling of imagination in *prosopopoeia* intensifies *pathos*. Here is Quintilian: "In *prosopopoeia* we simulate the feelings [*adfectus*] of children, women, nations, and even voiceless things, and they are all entitled to their appropriate character."[77] The "voiceless things"—*mutarum rerum*—would include nonhuman animals.[78]

Marjorie Curry Woods and Manfred Kraus have both studied the fascinating tradition alluded to by Quintilian of practicing speaking for women, and both conclude that the practice persisted for schoolboys because of the need to practice displaying a wide range of feelings, which Kraus locates in the distinctive styles of remaining examples.[79] The dire picture presented by the ape imitated by John of Sardis fits in with that analysis even as it presents a composite picture—this time a future imagined by an imagined ape—nested *phantasiai*, fraught with fear. What is more, in John's ape's vision of the future, humans assume the same role as the wolves in Demosthenes's vision. The inhabiting of an ape's perspective as required by this instance of ethopoetic deliberation enables a picturing of the pain and suffering caused by humans. Such a perspective, though rare, is nevertheless enabled by fable's activation of *phantasia* and the need to practice vivifying otherwise uncertain futures.

Fable's domain is sensation and feeling; through deliberative *phantasia* it mixes invented pictures to sharpen the contours of an otherwise blurred future. As composite and kinetic means of picturing pain and imagining the future, fable's roles in oratory and rhetorical education—two otherwise distinct contexts—are surprisingly similar. They follow animal habits, imagine animal concerns, and depict animal suffering in a way that leaves a marked impression—remaining in memories, enchanting souls, envisioning futures. Fables, and especially beast fables, "containing seeds of all the art," begin to fill out the picture of nonhuman elements in rhetorical education. Following nonhuman animals further into the *progymnasmata* sequence, the task of the next chapter, shows the importance of rhetorical education for attitudes toward nonhuman animals in broader cultural formations, including those that would become crucial for scientific culture.

CHAPTER 4

Looking Beyond Belief: Paradoxical Encomia and Visual Inquiry

"The gnat, it is said, is like the elephant." So writes Michael Psellos, the eleventh-century (Byzantine) rhetor, scholar, and monk in one of four extant encomia—set speeches of praise—all written in honor of bugs.[1] Given their subject matter, the speeches may be further classified as "paradoxical encomia," traditionally defined as speeches praising matters otherwise deemed trivial or unexpected; the most famous extant prototype is Lucian's second-century encomium on the fly.[2] The encomia in this group extol the merits of a particular kind of bug: two are written for the flea, one each for the louse and the bedbug. The gnat comparison appears in the second encomium on the flea.[3] There Psellos goes on to compare the dance of the gnat to the elephant's battle dance, effectively (and deliberately, I think) enlarging the gnat, both in size and in his readers' estimation. In doing so, he exemplifies the guiding principle Cicero ascribes to Gorgias, the fifth-century Sophist, that oratory's "biggest distinction," its *maxime proprium*, is "to *magnify* a thing by praise."[4]

Psellos's gnat, temporarily rendered elephantine, expands by way of a visible material magnification. And when the gnat is shrunk back to typical size, the intensity of the elephant remains intact, such that the defining, praiseworthy feature becomes the gnat's compact power, its immense *dunamis*. For the remainder of the set piece, the elephant dwells in the gnat's nimble, whirring body, dancing about and sounding its trumpet. I will return to Psellos's bug encomia at the end of this chapter along with Lucian's "The Fly" as illustrations of a style of inquiry that persisted in the genre's long history, including their discussion in the *progymnasmata*, those durable exercises that often began with fable.[5]

In the *progymnasmata* manuals, encomium was a discrete exercise usually placed toward the middle of the sequence and practiced just before or after ekphrasis, vivid description.[6] Following the cumulative logic of the exercise sequence, ekphrasis and encomium feed on each other and work together to develop a style of inquiry that insists on *seeing things anew*, bringing them up close, engaging the senses with a disposition of amazement or wonder, the Greek word for which is *thauma*.[7] This inquisitive mode pushed composers to bracket or look beyond prevailing *doxa* or belief, the most literal meaning of paradox (*para* = beyond; *doxos* = belief). The strategies of description and praise that develop along these lines seek to consider nonhuman animals' form and power, their *dunamis*, in a way that frequently levels, and sometimes flips, persistent hierarchies among nonhuman animals. "Wonder," as historian Mary Beagon tantalizingly phrases it, "is a hungry passion."[8] When approached with a focus on nonhuman animals first, the *progymnasmata*, especially the exercises in the middle of the series, where sensation, language, and judgment converge (encomium, invective, comparison, ekphrasis), simultaneously feed on and nurture that passion and therefore may be seen as the bedrock of inquiry itself, including the kind of inquiry that would come to be called scientific. When eyes trained by these exercises turn on the natural world, the world of nonhuman animals in particular—on peacocks and crocodiles, flies, fleas, and lice—they need at times to squint, to carefully scrutinize the subjects for their marvelous qualities and describe them in a way that magnifies, measures, and compares them so that the audience can see them too.

The account offered in this chapter enriches and expands existing conceptions of rhetorical education, showing, for example, the embeddedness of natural history in Western rhetorical education, a matter I return to in chapter 6. Put simply, the kind of inquiry that engages natural history (and especially the sensible, sensuous forms and activities of nonhuman animals) depends on a pedagogy of wonder in the face of the as yet unknown but observable, and it ranks marvel above belief. Making such connections first requires a bit of unraveling, beginning with inquiry itself as taught through ancient exercises in ekphrasis. From there I move to the joining of paradox and encomium, attending first to the history of that joining and then to its hallmark strategies of amplification (magnification and comparison) before returning to Psellos and Lucian, where these strategies come alive, so to speak, by way of the tiniest living creatures.

EKPHRASIS AND THE VISUAL PEDAGOGY
OF THAUMATIC INQUIRY

My inquiry into inquiry, then, begins with Theon, whose treatment of ekphrasis marks a crucial entry point for animals into the art of describing from and for the senses.[9] That entry, however, has been somewhat obscured by translators' restriction of the Greek *prosōpa* (countenances, faces, characters, bodily presence) to humans.[10] Ruth Webb's study of ancient ekphrasis lingers on Aphthonius's "puzzling addition" in the fourth century "of plants and dumb animals" to the list of ekphrastic subjects.[11] But what Webb calls the "rather incongruous addition" of "interlopers" is very much in line with the models suggested in Theon's earlier manual, which includes ekphrases of three non-human animals native to Egypt: ibis, hippopotamus, and crocodile, as they appear in Herodotus's *Histories*.[12]

Coiled into Herodotus's descriptions of animals are methods and dispositions, styles of inquiry (*historia*) guided by wonder or amazement (*thauma*). The visual descriptions in Herodotus (especially of Egyptian culture and Egypt's flora and fauna) seek to know and to make vivid the unknown. Herodotus is, of course, most often touted as the father of history, yet *historia*, like many Greek terms, did not always have the specificity of its current cognate.[13] In fact, as scholars like to point out, *historia* was originally less concerned with the past per se than with inquiry, for the verb *historeīn* meant to inquire into or about a thing, to examine or observe, and even to give an account of what one has observed; *historia* generally named inquiry or systematic observation, or a written account of those inquiries.[14] Tellingly, then, from early on, inquiry itself (*historia*) was pressed into the same word as the narrative of that inquiry (*historia*): the methods of observing and showing the results of those observations were philologically bound together; the term at once marked a kind of knowing and a mode of telling. Recent work on the concept of *historia* confirms that the inquiry put forward by Herodotus was often marked by an accompanying attitude that in turn can be cast as a method of inquiry dependent on firsthand experience and visual witnessing.[15]

Here, in this distinctly Herodotean method of inquiry, grows wonder. The French historian François Hartog elucidates the role of wonder as a recurring *topos* in a tradition (epic) that preceded and informed Herodotus's approach.[16] In this tradition, *thauma* (*thōma* in Herodotus's Ionic dialect) names the extraordinary, the extreme, the strange or perplexing, and even just the surprising. Herodotus dwells on Egyptian fauna for precisely this reason, as he writes upon turning to matters of Egypt: "Concerning Egypt I will now speak at length, because nowhere are there so many marvelous things [*thōmasia*], nor in the whole world beside are there to be seen so many works of unspeakable greatness; therefore I shall say the more concerning Egypt."[17] As Stephen Greenblatt argues in the context of contact with the New World (a context he links with Herodotus), "The expression of wonder stands for all that cannot be understood, that can scarcely be believed. It calls attention to the problem of credibility and at the same time insists upon the undeniability, the exigency of the experience."[18] And in the Herodotean scheme, and later in the *progymnasmata*, wonder specifically maintains that "exigency of experience" through measuring, inspecting, drawing close.

What is more, *thauma*, wonder and amazement, frequently and often inevitably tips ekphrasis, or plain old description, into encomium, or praise.[19] Perhaps the best instance of this thaumatic pull of ekphrasis toward encomium is Herodotus's account of the crocodile, the last and longest ekphrasis mentioned in the *progymnasmata* manual attributed to Theon (and in fact the longest zoological ekphrasis in Herodotus). Here is the first part:

> I will now show what kind of creature is the crocodile. For the four winter months it eats nothing. It has four feet, and lives both on land and in the water, for it lays eggs and hatches them out on land, and it passes the greater part of the day on dry ground, and the night in the river, the water being warmer than the air and dew.[20]

This passage's opening sentence emphasizes the crocodile's nature, its *phusis*, placing this description and the other animal and plant ekphrases in the text firmly in the tradition of natural history of the kind that would later inspire the elder Pliny's thirty-seven-book *Natural History*, to which I will return in chapter 6.[21] From there, though, the description moves to the most distinctive, marvelous qualities of the reptile, most notably its size, its mouth movements, and its symbiotic relationship with the plover. It then slides smoothly into encomium:

> No mortal creature known to us grows from so small a beginning to such greatness; for its eggs are not much bigger than goose eggs, and the young crocodile is of a bigness answering thereto, but it grows to a length of seventeen cubits and more. It has eyes like pigs' eyes, and great teeth and tusks answering to the bigness of its body. It is the only animal that has no tongue. Nor does it move the lower jaw. It is the only creature that brings the upper jaw down upon the lower. It has also strong claws, and a scaly impenetrable

hide on its back. It is blind in the water, but very keen of sight in the air. Since it lives in the water, its mouth is all full within of leeches. All birds and beasts flee from it, except only the plover, with which it is at peace, because this bird does the crocodile a service; for whenever the crocodile comes ashore out of the water and then opens its mouth (and this it does for the most part to catch the west wind), the plover goes into its mouth and eats the leeches; the crocodile is pleased by this service and does the plover no harm.[22]

"Nature" (*phusis*) of course is both capacious and far from static, so it stands to reason that a description of an animal's "nature" would include physical characteristics and day-to-day habits, with a protracted account of the most curious habits—in this case the symbiotic relationship with the plover.[23] This passage also features a kind of quantitative *thauma*:[24] a length of "seventeen cubits and more," the ancient unit of measurement that referred generally to forearm length, would have been a wonder indeed, worthy of pause and of praise.

The way to achieve vividness is not to offer a comprehensive description but rather to focus on what is striking. As Theon sees it, the leading virtue of an ekphrasis is "clarity and the vividness [*enargeia*] which makes one almost see what is being spoken about."[25] And to achieve these virtues, Theon suggests that "one should avoid speaking at great length about useless things."[26] Instead, he implies, the focus ought to remain on the most compelling details, and the "qualities of the language should not be inappropriate to the nature of the subject."[27] And this is how Herodotus does it. His succinct description of the hippopotamus, instead of offering an inch-by-inch account of the Egyptian native, compares its features to animals more commonly known to Greeks in order to present a composite picture:

> For their outward form, they are four-footed, with cloven hoofs like oxen; their noses are blunt; they are maned like horses, with tusks showing, and have a horse's tail and a horse's neigh; their bigness is that of the biggest oxen. Their hide is so thick that when it is dried spearshafts are made of it.[28]

The composite itself constitutes a marvel inasmuch as hybrid animal bodies were deemed amazing and incongruous. The hippopotamus description reinforces Hartog's observation that "the eye of the traveler operates as a measure of *thoma* and the narrator makes his addressee 'see' the *thoma*, precisely by measuring its size."[29] Such a recounting brings the hippopotamus up close. To closely paraphrase Theon, one can almost see what is being spoken about.[30] Hence ekphrasis could be deemed a version of *phantasia*, in which the words do the seeing from a distance.[31]

To conclude this section and to complete the link between thaumatic impulse and an inquisitive way of looking, I want to dwell on a model ekphrasis to the peacock in which both are startlingly evident. The ekphrasis in question has been dated to the fourth century CE and attributed to Libanius, a teacher of the later *progymnasmata* author Aphthonius.[32] After a detailed description of the peacock's colors ("the gleaming gold color of its neck is combined with a glossy blue-back"),[33] the first-person description goes on:

> But since I also saw the movement of the bird, speech impels me to declare
> the paradoxical wonders [*paradoxa thaumata*] of its rapid movement as
> well; for having just now beaten its wings on both sides as if for flight, and
> having somehow forced them to form an arch over its head, it revealed itself
> as a most beautiful form of a statue and a shining temple, encouraging the
> viewer also to fall down and worship it, as one enslaved by the wonder of a
> shining statue.[34]

Speech, *logos*, moves the writer to declare the paradoxical wonders of this bird's movement, and he does so by narrating the effects those marvelous qualities—those *thaumata*—have on viewers, compelling them to fall down and worship *as one enslaved by wonder*.[35] Those who see the peacock in motion are overtaken, gripped by wonder that, as the use of the descriptor *paradoxa* suggests, exists beyond the edge of belief. It is no surprise that this particular ekphrasis ends with a meditation on how sight is preferable to hearing for "one who wishes to praise,"[36] for such would be the case with a peacock. This description shows how the firsthand witnessing belonging to inquiry (*historia*) opens itself up to wonder and shows the centrality of sensation to that process. In the face of nature, plodding description is thrown over by a regard for the marvelous and the wondrous. You have to see it to believe it.

The thaumatic stance toward nonhuman animals is heavily attested in all sorts of studies of animals and in various disciplines through the centuries, ranging from medieval romance to Victorian taxidermy.[37] *Thauma* and observational description remain tightly and noticeably entwined in the context of early modern scientific culture.[38] To brighten the line from Herodotus through the *progymnasmata* to these later versions of inquiry, I will first dwell briefly on the nonhuman animals in the encomium tradition.

ENCOMIUM AND PARADOX IN RHETORICAL THEORY

As is evident in Herodotus's description of the crocodile, and even more so in Libanius's of the peacock, the wonder-based inquiry encouraged by ekphrasis slides easily into encomium, the genre of praise that epideictic rhetoric frequently encompassed. The epideictic genre and encomia are well known for reinforcing established belief, or *doxa*.[39] In the strict oratorical sense, however, paradoxical encomia, encomia that run counter to established belief, have been around just about as long as the genre itself. The subgenre of encomium that most often hosted animals as subjects was of course the paradoxical encomium. The thaumatic method of ekphrasis complements the idea of paradox itself inasmuch as wonder and paradox both strain toward the unknown. The values reinforced by paradoxical encomium are novelty, surprise, and revelation—the very stuff of wonder. In addition to the literal meaning of the term (what is beyond or apart from belief or commonly held opinion), the term *paradoxos* was also used as a "title of distinction for accomplished athletes, musicians, and artists of all kinds."[40] The use of *paradoxos* to describe encomia recruits both sets of meanings: counterintuitive arguments, or arguments that stretch beyond established belief, have a zingy "wow" factor that distinguishes the word artists who invent them. The most famous example of an encomium composed in the paradoxical vein is Gorgias's *Encomium on Helen*. With *Helen*, Gorgias not only seeks to upend the commonly received narrative about how Helen ended up in Troy, he does so by laying out not one but four alternative explanations (she submitted to Paris by will of fate or the gods, or she was ravaged by force, or persuaded by words, or maddened by love), therefore upping the ante of distinction.[41] This famous encomium lays bare the primary meaning of paradox when attached to encomia: paradoxical encomia seek to praise the unpraisable.

The rhetorical force of paradox has been considered in a smattering of studies from several decades ago.[42] As Mark Moore puts it in one of these works, "[Paradox] defies the traditional basis of rhetorical action. It forces the reader and listener to consider something other than, or contrary to, commonly held beliefs, attitudes, and values; it forces an audience to contemplate a "new" knowledge and a different reality."[43] In the context of encomium, I would hazard, paradox formalizes the wonder of *thauma* on both the inventional and performance ends of a speech. Put another way, paradox is built on wonder, even as it amazes its audiences.

As I noted above, nonhuman animals were a favorite choice as encomiastic subjects, and encomia composed for them could be quickly evaluated as serious or not depending on the choice of animal (small, pesky ones often featured in the paradoxical variety). After noting that his discussion of topics for praising or blaming will equip his audience to "make both ourselves and any other person worthy of credence in regard to virtue,"[44] Aristotle quickly offers this aside:

> But since it often happens, both with and without earnestness, that not only a man or a god is praised but inanimate objects and any random one of the other animals, propositions on these subjects must be grasped in the same way.[45]

Here Aristotle, with perhaps a note of resignation, brings his advice in line with rhetorical custom: since humans praise both humans and nonhumans, his subsequent discussion will account for both.

The phrase "without earnestness" signifies the destabilizing force inanimate objects and nonhuman animals exert on the genre's gravity, and Aristotle dwells on this comic element in a discussion found in book 2.[46] Here Aristotle circles back to paradoxical encomia, this time using them to illustrate how homonyms can lead to verbal fallacies:

> Another [verbal fallacy] is by use of homonyms, as saying that a mouse [*mys*] is a worthy creature from which comes the most honored of all festivals; for the [celebration of the Eleusinian] *Mysteries* is the most honored of all. Or if someone delivered an encomium of the dog that included the Dog Star or [the god] Pan, because Pindar said [of Pan],
>
> > Oh blessed one, whom the Olympians call dog
> > Of the Great Goddess, taking every form.
>
> Or [if someone said that] because it is most dishonorable for there to be no "dog" thus clearly the dog is honored.[47]

The Greek is a bit tricky here, but the passage refers to a trend of comic punning. Aristotle's reasoning presumes that the mouse and the dog could hardly be honored, though the final reference leaves some room for that possibility, and Kennedy's note offers the possible traditions of dog as faithful attendant that Aristotle might be referring to.[48] These lines show that the difference between animal encomia crafted in jest and those composed in earnest was often keyed to the regard ancients already had for a particular species, and those estimations also at times loosely tracked with size, such that encomia to bumblebees and mice were deemed devoid of earnestness, while encomia to an ox or a horse were taken at face value.[49]

Where Aristotle saw the absence of earnestness, his contemporary Isocrates saw absurdity. In fact, in a passage that would become a touchstone for late antique writers, Isocrates sneers at the praising of things "trivial and base" in his own *Encomium on Helen*, singling out salt and bumblebees as existing examples to distinguish his choice of Helen as a subject of praise.[50] Even so, apart from Aristotle's generic mention of serious praise of animals, testimony of such speeches is spare. Burgess believes that the dearth of extant examples of paradoxical encomia owes to base associations, so that "this form of encomium is least likely to be preserved or even to be discussed in serious literature."[51] Paradoxical encomia appear to have suffered the same fate as fable in political oratory, as I discussed in the previous chapter. For further testimony about and extant models of animal encomia—both doxical and paradoxical— it is necessary to move into the Common Era, when they flourished and began to be preserved, taught, and imitated, beginning with the *progymnasmata* manuals.

PARADOXICAL PROGYMNASMATA

Despite the established tradition of paradox, the main *progymnasmata* manuals tend to presume earnest encomia to animals: those written to horses or oxen, animals deemed useful for humans and therefore worthy of praise. The model encomium to the ox, attributed to Libanius, places the ox above all animals (other than human) for its beauty and "the benefits it provides to men," thereby helpfully illustrating the kind of sincerity recommended in the manuals.[52] In a similar vein, an exemplary invective against deer, attributed to *progymnasmata* author Nicolaus in a collection of model exercises, reinforces existing *doxa* about timidity. The brief invective (*psogos*) mainly condemns deer's cowardice, especially in relation to their size, as with this sentence: "Given the magnitude possessed by their body, the big ones should certainly not be so seized with fear when pursued; others grow into the largest beasts of prey."[53] All four extant manual discussions of encomia—Theon's, Pseudo-Hermogenes's, Aphthonius's, and Nicolaus's—keep *doxa* at their center. Nicolaus perhaps hints at the reason for this doxical pull in his opening discussion of encomium, which acknowledges the genre's complexity and then notes, "Here it is necessary only to say as much as is appropriate for begin-ners."[54] The early manual writers appear to have deemed paradox beyond the reach of young students.

John of Sardis's ninth-century commentary on Aphthonius's *progymnas-mata* manual is the first to consider the paradoxical possibilities of encomium. They occur in Aphthonius's discussion of encomium versus *epainos*, where one (*epainos*) is directed at gods and is brief, while the other (encomium) is directed at mortals and tends to exhibit artistic skill. John, however, believes these two differences lead to a third. As he puts it, "*Epainos* is concerned with true things, encomion with the persuasive."[55] John's elaboration of this third distinction opens onto paradoxical encomia:

> Encomium imitates the praise of *epainos*, but it does not hold the honest assent from the encomiast. Doubtless whenever we praise pots or pebbles, as did Polycrates, or baldness or a fly, we are not absolutely commending in a state of wonder [*tethaumakotes epainoumen*] but are exercising ourselves in certain persuasive arguments.[56]

This passage is revealing as much for what it says about the purpose and method of the paradoxical as for its attribution of wonder to the encomiastic process. In other words, the paradoxical encomiasts are not necessarily prais-ing or epainizing (that is, putting forward incontrovertible truths), but instead are practicing thaumatic method by exploring all possible corners of praise. John's clarification calls attention to paradoxical encomium's value in the context of the *progymnasmata*: it exercises one's ability to praise.

The elaboration of Aphthonius's encomiastic subjects by John of Sardis is exceptional in this regard, owing to John's own historical context. John be-gins as the other *progymnasmata* writers begin (and Aristotle for that matter), by saying that the topics available for animal encomia are nearly the same as for human subjects, including the place they were born, as "a certain elephant in India or the crocodile in Egypt or the phoenix from Ethiopia, for the place swiftly establishes one's fatherland."[57] The next sentence is revealing for the way it directs vision and specifies those subjects deemed worthy of marvel (*thaumasomen*):

> One must see then what is remarkable about the places where certain ani-mals are born; hence one necessarily praises it if it is distinct, and the com-mon grew everywhere, but scrutiny of their place did not fail. For this in

itself we approve what is most common to all and we marvel at [*thauma-somen*] the nature of the animal.[58]

Here John reinforces the method of visual inspection I have been tracking by noting the reliable approach of examining a particular animal's place, its *chōra*. The word I have translated as scrutiny, *hē exetasis*, indicates close examination, a test, and more broadly undertaking an inquiry.[59] It therefore follows the visual instruction of Herodotean *historia* found in Theon's *progymnasmata*.[60] John's mention of the Egyptian crocodile also tacitly invokes Herodotus as well, highlighting once again the connection between ekphrasis and encomium.

"THE DISTINCTIVE BUSINESS OF PRAISE"

So far this chapter has followed two connected paths nonhuman animals took into the middle of the *progymnasmata*: the first, via Herodotean thaumatic inquiry of visual description (ekphrasis), and the second through encomium, as subjects of praise, doxical and paradoxical. These paths converge most noticeably in the persuasive technique of amplification (*auxēsis* in Greek; *amplificatio* in Latin). Aristotle notes amplification's importance for all branches of rhetoric in book 2, but in book 1 he tags epideictic rhetoric as its most obvious habitat: "In general, among the classes of things common to all the speeches, amplification is most at home in those that are epideictic."[61] Quintilian mentions amplification in the context of encomium, directly following this crucial line: "The distinctive business of praise is to amplify and adorn."[62] As Laurent Pernot observes in his examination of epideictic rhetoric, "Amplification does not mean 'development,' even less 'padding out.' It involves not lengthening the speech but increasing the size of the subject."[63] It bears repeating here that the paradoxical encomium—the subgenre I am focusing on—moves encomium from the "things generally agreed to" to a matter of contention, beyond *doxa*. But that move does not diminish the importance of amplification in such an effort, it amplifies it. A line from Quintilian's *Institutes of Oratory* indicates as much, when he singles out the impressiveness of amplifying: "Augmentation is the most potent when it lends grandeur even to comparative insignificance."[64] This promise of such potent amplification—amplification that strikes a chord of wonder—is very likely what drew figures like Lucian, Chrysostom, and Psellos, writers and teachers up for the challenge, to the paradoxical encomium.

One crucial technique of amplification in all encomia, but especially in paradoxical ones, is comparison, or *synkrisis*. It stands to reason: in order to praise the unpraisable, a promising strategy would be to compare the seemingly paradoxical subject with the doxical, to effectively coax outlandish praise into the realm of belief. Generally, comparison transfers value. As Quintilian frames it, using notably visual language, "One thing is magnified to augment another, and a transition is made by an inference to the thing which we wish to emphasize."[65] Such magnification is often achieved by a kind of comparative measuring, as explained by Aristotle, whose instruction on the matter of encomiastic amplification is simple: "And if you do not have material enough with the man himself, compare him with others."[66] The word for the act of comparing here, *antiparaballein*, suggests placing two comparates side by side, or measuring them against each other. Aristotle goes on to advise readers to compare (*sunkrinein*) the subject "with those held in high esteem," for "the subject is amplified and made honorable if he is better than [other] excellent ones."[67] In this instance, the subject of praise is what gets amplified: according to the comparison, it grows upward.[68]

The *progymnasmata* writers follow Aristotle's lead by taking care to consider the choice of measuring stick. The person or thing or (in these cases) animal one selects for comparison makes all the difference. Disparate quantitative size has an explicit place in Aphthonius's advice for comparison. For him comparison is "made by setting things side-by-side, bringing the greater together with what is compared to it."[69] The method he suggests—something like comparing "up"—results in a kind of betterment of the smaller/weaker comparate. In fact, such comparisons, according to Aphthonius, create forcefulness, a stylistic feature I discussed in chapter 2, by drawing out the marvelously strong, wondrous, forceful features of every topic. Such forcefulness is achieved "especially," he notes, when "comparing small things to bigger [*meizosi*] ones."[70] Aphthonius doesn't explain why comparing small things to bigger ones is a particular guarantor of *deinos*. Still, note the paired adjectives in his advice to "either set fine things beside good things or poor things beside poor things or good beside bad or small beside larger."[71] Of these paired adjectives, the smaller and larger are the only visible, empirically comparable features, while the others are value terms that, while still arguable, are less observable and therefore not *quite* as wondrous or marvelous. Given that comparison feeds directly into the encomium exercise, if taken to its logical extreme this reflection on the power of comparing across size, featured in what would become the most popular version of the *progymnasmata*, would end up with exactly the kind of paradoxical encomium that would seek out the tiniest of animals that, when compared with large hulking ones, as with Psellos's elephantized gnat, promise to maximize the force to the point of astonishment. Elephants, it turns out, can be the measure of small things.

THE INQUIRING EYES OF LUCIAN AND PSELLOS

From the threads of rhetorical theory, oratorical practice, and extant *progymnasmata* manuals, this chapter has spun an account of a rhetorical education grounded in wonder, methods of visual inquiry, and techniques of amplification that include description, magnification, and comparative measurement. Such a model of education encouraged students to push beyond existing beliefs, to seek new modes of praise and hence knowledge—even, tantalizingly, as my concluding nod to Robert Hooke will suggest, modes of looking that form the contours of scientific culture.

These aims and methods are startlingly evident in a handful of showpieces including Lucian's "The Fly" and Michael Psellos's tributes to bugs, encomia featuring the results of visual inquiry discussed so far. While this illustrative discussion could probably get by with just a focus on Lucian's famous composition, Psellos's bug set serves to show how the genre sustains and nourishes a drive to wonder and amplification through magnification and comparison more than a millennium after Lucian. In this way Psellos works as a Byzantine stepping-stone on the way to the Renaissance, when the paradoxical encomium would flourish mightily. Yet Psellos's encomia are more than that. The Psellos bug set is worth recovering for its preservation not just of a Lucianic heritage, but of classical ways of looking in the name and tradition of rhetorical education.[72]

The most noteworthy feature of Lucian's and Psellos's encomia is the sheer preponderance of comparison (*synkrisis*). In the first ten sentences of "The Fly," Lucian compares his subject with no fewer than ten other species. The first few sentences of the encomium use comparison to measure the fly's size: "The fly is not the smallest of winged creatures, at least in comparison with gnats and midges and things still tinier. On the contrary, she is as much larger than they as she is smaller than the bee."[73] After placing the fly on a spectrum of insect size, Lucian goes on to characterize the fly's unfeathered wings by contrasting them with those of birds, then likening them to those of grasshoppers, locusts, and bees, like whom the fly "has membranous wings, as much thinner than theirs as Indian cloths are more delicate and softer than Greek."[74] This relational comparison with Eastern fabrics carries a hint of exoticism that dates back to Herodotus, where it also feeds wonder.

Psellos's second encomium to the flea also begins with a complex relational comparison that proposes to follow the logical train of the previously discussed gnat-elephant commonplace to establish the flea's similarity to the panther: "The gnat, they say, is like the elephant. And in order that our speech may proceed according to method [*kath' hodon*], let us argue/prove that the flea is like the panther."[75] Taking the proverb as a springboard, Psellos sets forth the relational analogy: the flea is like the panther as the gnat is like the elephant. He immediately goes on to discuss nature's penchant for lessening the capability (*dunamis*) of big animals. Here he cites "the best of philosophers: for that which has grown in size loses its strength, just as that which is more capable of gathering into oneself is completed."[76] *Sustraphen* signals a powerful kind of compression; it is often used in the instance of a whirlwind, in reference to a compact body. This word has rhetorical meanings as well. When working with words, to "bring into a close form, compress" is to draw out the power and intensity of the pithy. So Psellos rehearses at the outset the logic behind the gnat-elephant relation, from which readers may deduce the flea-panther relation. Yet not only is the flea compared with the panther by way of the gnat-elephant relationship. The encomium that follows invokes sweet-smelling plants that appear in spring like the flea; it invokes as counterexamples wood worms, mites, and mosquitoes, which "arise partly out of mud, partly out of decay," whereas the flea can cleanly (and marvelously) "reproduce itself from itself."[77] Then in another passage where Psellos returns to the panther, the panther appears in a menagerie of other comparates. When describing the form of the flea, he writes:

> It's shaped like a pig but moves like a panther, and it sees like a lion without its shaggy glance; even more amazing, while nature forms its knitted brow, its leap, and everything for brutishness, all the flea's features crowded together harmonize in gentleness.[78]

This passage flips through two species (pig, panther) before dwelling for the remaining lines on the lion, whose form and movements are conjured by their fierce brutishness (*thēriōdian*), while the flea's constitution and movements are fashioned out of gentleness and rhythm, which for Psellos is cause for *thauma*.

Psellos's encomium to the bedbug compares it to the plover, thereby tacitly invoking Herodotus's ekphrasis of the crocodile: "Just as the Egyptian plover exults over the crocodile, getting the most pleasant rest and being sustained by leftovers, so this most pleasant animal lives together with us, binding on a certain part of our body. It makes food out of what has been seized and re-joices."[79] The subtle reference to Herodotus—or at least to a thaumatic quality of the symbiotic relationship between the crocodile and the plover—achieves a good deal here. The comparison performs ekphrasis, enlivening the flea-human relationship even as it figures the human body as a fierce crocodile from whom, as Herodotus notes, "all birds and beasts flee."[80]

While the plover passage in Psellos helps to brighten the fifteen-century line from his paradoxical encomia backward to Herodotean thaumatic ek-phrasis, other passages, though less obviously Herodotean, do still more to achieve the visual amplification this chapter has been concerned with. The descriptions here, in other words, function as discursive protomicroscopes. Here is his somatic description of the flea: "The head is suitably united with the remaining body, hence both raising and arching just as nature created the pig, and then it tapers to the bottom, and it might be said that the centermost spinal part holds up both ends of the body."[81] Here the flea-pig comparison ef-fectively zooms in to the neck area, enlarging it while panning midspine, where the flea's body arches upward. The effect of this description is an almost sus-pended magnification: the flea is held up as if by tweezers and enlarged as if by a microscope, but the suspension and magnification are achieved, marvel-ously, by words alone. And lest there be any doubt which of the comparates is superior, Psellos adds this line: "I compare this with the pig, not classing the flea with it, but further preferring it to the pig."[82]

Psellos's description of the bedbug works in a similar way, only it is cast in geometric language:

> Not even the shape of the animal can be faulted, for it is small and seems like a true circle, if you like, in equal shapes, even though the length does not quite stand with the width. It appears to be both, for it deceives the eye.[83]

The geometric comparisons here—the way the bedbug looks like but isn't really a true circle—confirm the measuring function of comparison, especially with the calculation of length in relation to width. This comparison is particu-larly intriguing, though, because it turns on deception. One of the bedbug's most amazing qualities is its near imperceptibility, and this deceptive shape plays into that thaumatic line of praise. After observing that this "marvelous [*thaumaston*] little animal"[84] "is not quite common by nature,"[85] Psellos uses this idea that they are not always "at hand" (*procheiron*) as a basis for compar-ing bedbugs to royalty, especially queens: "It does not even appear in public, but like the queens it is kept hidden from the crowd, and you will not readily get to behold this species."[86] Yet despite its assertion of queenly elusiveness, the encomium nevertheless offers an up-close glimpse of the bug in the geometric description above. Words step in where appearance and eyes fail.

Such suspended magnification through words is of course modeled on Lucian, whose methodical description of the fly's midsection closely resembles Psellos's description of the flea:

> As for its body, the head is very delicately attached to the neck and so is easily moved, not fixed like the head of a grasshopper. The eyes are prominent and have much the quality of horn. The breast is solid, and the legs grow right out of the waist, which is not at all pinched up as in wasps. As in them, the abdomen is armored and resembles a corselet in having flat zones and scales. She differs, however, from the wasp and the bee in that her weapon is not the hinder-part, but the mouth, or rather the proboscis; for, like the elephant, she has a trunk with which she forages, seizing things and holding them tenaciously, since it is like a tentacle at the end.[87]

The most striking part of this passage's comparisons is Lucian's use of insects (grasshoppers, bees, wasps) as countercomparates while offering the elephant as a direct comparate. The result is an account that distinguishes the fly from its more obvious counterparts through microinspection of the way its tiny parts fit together. The neck is not fixed but moves; the trunk seizes things and holds them fast. The gradual enlargement of the fly in this passage links to the colorful, glittery comparison to peacocks a few lines later when Lucian contemplates the texture of the insect's wings:

> Like grasshoppers, locusts and bees, she has membranous wings, as much thinner than theirs as Indian stuffs are more delicate and softer than Greek. Moreover they are bejeweled like peacocks, if [one] looks into [them] sharply when they spread and fly in the sun.[88]

The reference to exotic goods and their difference from Greek ones signals an ekphrastic, ethnographic style in this passage, as Lucian zooms in for an even closer view.[89] In both cases the passage's up-close description looks on behalf of the reader, upping the thaumatic ante. Both descriptive inquiries move through sight to sound, with Psellos noting how the bedbug "walks with noiseless foot, a testament to their gentle constitution."[90] Lucian's subject, though, does not fly like bats with a steady, oar-like movement of the wings, or like grasshoppers with a spring, or as wasps do, with a whizzing rush, but easily directs her course to any quarter of the air she will. She has also this characteristic, that her flight is not silent but musical: the sound is not shrill like that of gnats and midges, nor deep-toned like that of bees, nor fierce and threatening like that of wasps; it is much more melodious, just as flutes are sweeter than trumpet and cymbals.[91]

This passage continues the trend of distinguishing the fly from other insects, again the grasshoppers, wasps, gnats, midges, and bees. The move to musical instruments mirrors the earlier move to the elephant inasmuch as it attempts to clarify the (here) sonic distinction with another relational analogy: flies are to flutes as bees are to trumpets and cymbals—and here Lucian mixes in yet another sensation, that of honey-sweet taste (*melichroteroi*). Flutes are smooth and delightful whereas trumpets and cymbals clatter and jar. The method in both Lucian and Psellos seems to be, first, to distinguish small insects from others of their size and kind, to pluck their subject right out of a lineup of similar species. But then recognizing that this is not a sufficient warrant for praise, they must locate worthy comparates outside the assemblage of species (the elephant, a queen) or even in another realm entirely (a musical instrument, a geometric shape). With the flute comparison, amplification takes on the sonic meaning it later came to acquire.

The comparisons in the paradoxical encomia of Lucian and Psellos are complex and wide-ranging, and they activate sensation through words. Furthermore, these writers both heed Aphthonius's observation mentioned earlier that "every topic of syncrisis is quite forceful, but especially that comparing small things to greater ones," and they lean on the minuteness of their subjects to expand marvel.[92] They are fully aware of the same phenomenon reflected in *The City of God*, where Saint Augustine contends that "the smallest [of animals] are most admired, for we are more amazed at the work of tiny ants and bees than at the huge bodies of whales."[93] While Augustine's remark reveres divinity, the sentiment lingers "on the purely scientific side" as well, as Arthur Stanley Pease contends.[94] Augustine's sentiment of being struck by wonder nicely captures the *thauma* effect of these paradoxical encomia.

WONDERSTRUCK

Many of the comparisons in these paradoxical encomia work like Psellos's plover example in that they urge wonder or marvel. At times the marvel is self-evident, as with Psellos's own performative marveling over the spontaneous generation of lice from human skulls. Here is that passage:

> Rotting asses do not produce dung beetles, nor hippopotami wasps, nor bulls honeybees, nor foul water mosquitoes, [but] the louse (his novel tale) springs from the most noble animal, not when it is decayed, but while it breathes and is full of vitality. For it springs from the head of man.[95]

The emphatic prose here, along with the account of the louse's spontaneous generation from the human head—not unlike Athena's springing from Zeus's—are poised to generate marvel aplenty. Similar passages in which *thauma* is tacit but no less palpable appear throughout Lucian's "The Fly." In addition to the passages he culls from Homer, whose authority provides powerful testimony for Lucian's case, there is Lucian's own meditation on the fly's strength and the way the insect "wounds the skin of the ox and the horse as well as that of man."[96] He continues, describing how the fly "torments the elephant by entering his wrinkles and lancing him with her proboscis as far as its length allows."[97] Lucian also wishes to mention the greatest quality in the fly's nature: the way a fly corpse revives when sprinkled with ashes.[98]

Lucian's penultimate line mentioning *thauma* explicitly on the topic of large flies (horseflies, which the ancients called "soldier flies" or "dog flies"), is presented with the infinitive *thaumazein*, to mark out a quality of these large flies worthy of wonder:[99] that these particular kinds of flies are at once male and female, "like the child of Hermes and Aphrodite, who had two natures and double beauty."[100]

Each of Psellos's bug encomia includes grammatical forms of *thauma*. After describing the birth of the bedbug (the primary topos shared with encomia to humans), Psellos continues: "Once born, this marvelous [*thaumaston*] little animal does not change with the season (it is not that he is there now and then disappears), but he is a similar animal to humans in his life, and his birth can take place at any convenient time."[101] The encomium to the louse is infested with forms of *thauma*. Early on, Psellos compares the louse favorably with the flea, using the comparative adjective to say that its birth is more marvelous than that of the flea.[102] The theory of spontaneous generation, an enduring cause for wonder since at least Aristotle,[103] is enough to astound Psellos: "In this way the filtering and flowing steam might escape through the plate and generate the louse on the scalp in an incredible way."[104] This sentence, interestingly, deploys not a form of *thauma* but the adverb form of paradox, *paradoxōs*, indicating that spontaneous generation is incredible, that it lies beyond belief, while simultaneously asserting it as fact.

The louse encomium also explicitly challenges the belief that the bigger is better than the smaller, and it does so by comparing different animals to planetary bodies. The resulting passage attempts to harness and redirect wonder, and to that end it uses four forms of the word in five sentences, with the fifth sentence using the near synonym *agametha* (wonder, admire):

> We admire [*thaumazomen*] the rare more than the ordinary, and we are stunned more by the bigger than by the smaller.[105] Certainly there is nothing more remarkable [*thaumasiōteron*] and known as the sun. But when we saw the comet, we were more amazed [*apethaumasamen*]. And so in this way let us admire [*agametha*] swifts more than swallows, and the winged ant more than the elephant. Therefore the unusual birth is more marvelous [*thaumasiōteron*] than the ordinary one.[106]

This passage is itself marvelous for its celestial comparisons to earthbound animals. Psellos invokes the streaking, brilliant, short-lived comet—perhaps Psellos is referring to the appearance of Comet Halley in 1066, when Psellos would have been in his late forties—as rarer but smaller than the still remarkable but nevertheless regular and predictable sun. Yet the comet comparison, not unlike the gnat-elephant comparison at the beginning of *Oration* 27, serves as a much—*much*—bigger emblematic image, simultaneously magnifying and brightening the otherwise difficult-to-perceive louse. Psellos then moves to birds, advocating for the otherwise indistinctive swift over the swallow, beloved for foretelling spring, and from there to the tiny winged ant.[107] Psellos returns to the comet comparison later in the speech for a comparison that invokes the "vapors" the louse and the comet were thought to have in common:

> Indeed, just as offerings of the earth create falling stars and comets, those in our belly create a louse. In fact, according to a certain account our vapor may be gained from the earth, so the louse gains light from the comet. These amazing phenomena [*phainomena thaumasia*] occur in the celestial sphere, but nothing else emerges from our heads except this little creature.[108]

The ambition of the celestial comparison permeates the louse encomium, and much as ekphrases of comets must have stood in place of firsthand witnessing

because of their rarity, so Psellos's description of the louse relies on constructions that translate "it is said" (*phasi*): for example, "Even though the beast
originated in the skin, it is said [*phasi*] they are like sponges."[109]

Psellos's encomium of the louse effectively raises the genre's degree of difficulty by rendering visible this tiny parasite that Psellos says "remains invisible" "although the eyes see everything."[110] He underscores this difficulty
by emphasizing the paradoxical quality—the grand reversal of belief—that
his encomium has achieved when he addresses readers directly, instructing
them in this way: "Do not suppose I was hastily overturning things without
method, because I chose to study the unstudiable and I was willing to compare the incomparable."[111] Psellos's self-professed willingness to compare the
asynkrita, what cannot be brought together, places him squarely in the paradoxical genre; his insistence on praising the smaller as opposed to the bigger
situates him in the long sophistic tradition of making the weaker stronger.
Here he joins his predecessor Lucian, who illustrates this sophistic principle
perfectly with the lines mentioned earlier about the fly's dominion over oxen,
horses, and elephants. Indeed, both Lucian and Psellos marshal the sophistic
weaker/stronger tradition so effectively in the context of the animal world that
they end up challenging a belief far more enduring than the unpraisability of
insects. Their encomia, with their careful scrutiny of—and wonder at—the
origins and forms of these tiny buzzing creatures, trouble prevailing hierarchies of animal forms. The view that results attempts to see the world from
the perspective of insects. When the views of the bedbug, the flea, or the louse
are considered in this way, larger animals (humans especially) become home,
food, and birthplace.

At the close of the louse encomium, Psellos calls attention to this achieve-
ment, this reversal of *doxa*, when he asks his readers not to think that the
speech comes from ambition alone, for "the art demonstrates power even in
the most minuscule things."[112] He continues, "For I did not intend to write
an encomium to the louse (may I not be that insane!), but rather to be able to
show you how many things *logos* is capable of doing, and so that also by way
of looking at this example you can keep close also to the easier topics and
fasten yourself to imitation."[113] This passage, with its focus on the power of
logos, echoes parts of Gorgias's *Encomium to Helen*. But it goes further with a
commentary on learning. The word for fastening here, *prosartan*, indicates an
appendage or place of attachment. Psellos thus closes with a tacit but delightful analogy that presents his own encomium as the body onto which students
(the lice) are supposed to attach, to sustain their own art and strengthen their
rhetorical abilities.

LEVITY, LEARNING, AND SCIENTIFIC CULTURE

The delightful louse analogy embedded in Psellos's conclusion points to a feature of paradoxical encomia that I have yet to consider fully: the role of comic play, its educational and rhetorical features. Lucian's "The Fly" ends with this playful proverb: "Although still having much to say, I will stop the account, because I do not expect to be following the proverb 'to make an elephant out of a fly.'"[114] To make an elephant out of a fly is an ancient saying that apparently means about the same as making a mountain out of a molehill. The humor here is obvious, because the set piece twice invokes the elephant to amplify certain of the fly's qualities. In other words, Lucian has already done what he pretends to resist. The first time he makes a fly into an elephant by means of a physical comparison: "Like the elephant, [the fly] has a trunk with which it forages, seizing things and holding them tenaciously, since it is like a tentacle at the end."[115] The comparison of the fly's "trunk" to the elephant's achieves visual *auxēsis* through magnification. The second comparison to the elephant pits the fly against the elephant to the fly's advantage: "She even torments the elephant by entering his wrinkles and lancing him with her proboscis as far as its length allows."[116] The effect is similar to Psellos's comparison of the gnat to the elephant, which highlights the compactness of the gnat's strength. In both comparisons, Lucian and Psellos pull the view back a bit, shrinking the insect down to size. Lucian's passage still conjures an elephant, dancing around from the pain inflicted by this little creature, thereby magnifying the fly's *dunamis*. When it comes to the elephant, Lucian and Psellos have it both ways.

The effect of this comparison is what the twentieth-century rhetorical theorist Kenneth Burke would call "perspective by incongruity." As Burke sees it, such a move "appeals by exemplifying relationships between objects which our customary rational vocabulary has ignored."[117] At stake in the paradoxical encomium, its visual inquiry and thaumatic urging, is a stretching beyond the limits of existing "rational vocabulary." It encourages toying with language to see what (else) it can do.

The playfulness of Lucian's piece is one of the features that accounts for its enduring popularity. Yet while it is commonplace to refer to the paradoxical encomium as a jeu d'esprit,[118] this genre flourished, especially in later periods, as more than a trifle. Desiderius Erasmus himself, in the prefatory letter to his "Praise of Folly" (addressed to Thomas More), draws out one of the most compelling paradoxes of paradox: that levity has a serious side. After naming Lucian in a long line of amusing writers in whose footsteps he is following (including Homer and Virgil too), Erasmus has this to say about potential detractors:

> So let them make up stories about me if they wish, alleging that I have some-times played draughts for recreation, or ridden a hobby-horse if they would rather; for, considering that every way of living is permitted its appropriate recreation, it would be monstrously unfair to allow no diversion whatever to those who pursue literary studies, especially if nonsense leads to serious matters and absurd themes are treated in such a way that the reader whose senses are not wholly dulled gains somewhat more profit from these than from some men's severe and showy demonstrations. . . . For, as there is nothing more frivolous than to handle serious topics in a trifling manner, so also there is nothing more agreeable than to handle trifling matters in such a way that what you have done seems anything but trifling.[119]

What Erasmus underscores here is the promise of connectivity: humorous treatments of trifling subjects contain more potential for enlivening young minds than do "forbidding" subjects. In this way the paradoxical encomium can be seen to extend from fable, tapping into existing knowledge of and delight in nonhuman animals.

But Erasmus's last line hints at an even larger purpose, one that overlaps with the purpose of this chapter. Whether composed with a straight face or a crooked smile, paradoxical encomia draw on the skills of ekphrasis and comparison and thereby have the potential to provide serious exercise in amplification. Selecting small insects as subjects holds an additional promise of bearing down on amplification both in its traditional sense—generating topics to help elaborate a broader point—and in a more specific, focused sense, one that draws particularly on the ekphrastic skill of bringing before the eyes, which means producing an up-close inspection such that *logoi* (words) and the *logos* (the speech) both become tools of visual, and even scientific, magnification. In this way a key role of nonhumans in the *progymnasmata* is to stimulate the wonder that leads to careful scrutiny that can then lead to wonder, whether inspired by a burst of insight or by the idea of spontaneous generation. In short, as Erasmus intimates, amazement and amusement are complementary responses. The thaumatic urge inspired by heretofore underexamined and undervalued animals does both: wonder begets wonder, and mimesis follows not far behind.

Finally, this chapter has also been developing a subclaim about ways of looking cultivated by rhetorical encounters with nonhuman creatures. The presence of ekphrasis in Enlightenment science is indisputable. If Robert Hooke, the famous documenter of microscope use, worked to train its users how to see, as rhetoric scholar Jordynn Jack demonstrates,[120] he no doubt had a tradition to draw on—a tradition where words themselves did the enlarging, a tradition that cultivated the urge to examine carefully, what the classicist Arthur Stanley Pease includes on his list of serious impetuses of paradoxical encomia and describes as "a real scientific interest in the microscopic."[121] Perhaps it is no coincidence that Hooke's 1665 *Micrographia* featured depictions of the eyes of the fly[122] and a four-page foldout engraving of a magnified louse.[123] Like the paradoxical encomiasts, Hooke's descriptions favor minute animals, especially insects such as lice, gnats, flies, mites, and fleas. Likewise, the microscopic vision that results shows Hooke turning to larger species as comparates, so that the "two horns" of a magnified gnat "seem'd almost like the horns of an Oxe."[124] Of the "wandring mite" he writes:

> The head of this little Insect was shap'd somewhat like a Mite's, that is, it had a long snout, in the manner of a Hog's, with a knobbed ridge running along the middle of it, which was bestuck on either side with many small bristles, all pointing forward, and two very large pikes or horns, which rose from the top of the head, just over each eye, and pointed forward also.[125]

Even more compelling are Hooke's occasional thaumatic ekphrases that slide inexorably into encomia, such as the one to the bookworm, where Hooke gives himself over to wonder, professing that he "cannot chuse but remember and admire the excellent contrivance of Nature," or the one to the blue fly, which Hooke writes "is a very beautifull creature and has many things about it very notable." Hooke, we should recall, had read his Lucian.[126]

With this brief glance at Hooke I mean to suggest that the techniques of amplification developed by *progymnasmata*—description, measurement, magnification—played a discernible role in cultivating what Jack calls "a pedagogy of sight," "the explicit, didactic attempt to teach a new way of seeing to an audience."[127] Hooke, Jack contends, needed to "help his readers see microscopic objects as valid objects of study."[128] I am suggesting that to do so Hooke drew on a long and storied history of always straining past the known, stretching beyond *doxa* to find marvelous, praiseworthy qualities in tiny creatures. Visual inquiry and its urge toward the unknown, and therefore toward the more striking or marvelous, has its place in that history. The *progymnasmata*, that is, ought not to be confined to a narrow conception of rhetorical education. The urge to study and praise small animals, after all, was not spontaneously generated with the microscope but was most likely born of the same inclination toward the unseeable and the unknown manifest in the concepts and dispositions this chapter has laid out: *historia*, inquiry, thaumatic description, and laudation through magnification and comparative measurement. Much like Psellos's gentle louse on human bodies, this curious thaumatic mode of inquiry came to be appended to the *progymnasmata* and was nourished and sustained by them. These rhetorical exercises, and the habits of mind they cultivated, were long the lifeblood of inquiry itself.

CHAPTER 5

Nonhuman Animals and Medieval Memory Arts

To this point I have focused mainly on the texts and traditions used to instruct aspiring rhetors, whether in general approaches to rhetoric (as with Aristotle), advanced matters of style (as with Longinus and Demetrius), or preparatory schoolroom exercises, and I have shown how nonhuman animals kept sense perception at the fore of both composing and learning more generally. The lively capacities of *alogos*, the vivification at the center of zoostylistics, the energetic narratives enacted by fabulous animals, the sense of wonder inspired by the subjects of ekphrasis and paradoxical encomia all combine to form a vibrant, active, zoocentric side of instruction in rhetoric. Yet to leave the story at that would be to continue to treat these texts, especially the *progymnasmata*, the way they are too often treated, as a curriculum confined to a handful of manuals, a mere precursor to more elevated forms of learning. Instead, the *progymnasmata*, especially those sense-based components of learning presided over by nonhuman animals, wound their way into cultural practices and knowledge formations that ought to be considered—at the very least—an outgrowth of that curriculum.

To present such a case, this chapter follows nonhuman animals into medieval rhetoric, where memory arts would become their habitat. As Manfred Kraus and Marjorie Woods have established, and as I discussed in the context of Psellos's writings, the *progymnasmata* were still alive in certain regions during the time scholars call the medieval period (from the end of late antiquity through the fifteenth century).[1] These serial exercises lived, though, in more ways than the straightforwardly curricular: the capacities cultivated by the *progymnasmata*, especially those that came to life in the presence of animals, were complementary to—and complemented by—traditions that are usually given separate consideration. The case in point of this chapter is the astounding "memorial cultures" built and inhabited by medieval thinkers.[2]

As historian Raphael Samuel reminds us, memory served as the basis of both thought and learning in antiquity, and the same can be said of the medieval period—and then some.[3] Indeed, the enduring presumption that memory is indispensable to learning means that the idea of memory came embedded in the progymnasmatic program: the traditions of memory and of the *progymnasmata*, therefore, exceed complementarity and may be best viewed as both mutually enabling and deeply embedded within each other.

Writing in the thirteenth century, Albert the Great linked memory to the fable tradition—the entry point into the *progymnasmata*:

> What is marvelous [*mirabile*] is more moving than what is ordinary, and so when images of this metaphorical sort are made up out of marvels [*ex miris*] they affect the memory more than [do] those things that are particularly customary [*plus movent quam propria consueta*]. So indeed early philosophers translated their ideas in poetry, as the Philosopher says, because a fable, since it is composed out of marvels, is more affecting [*quia fabula, cum sit composita ex miris plus movet*].[4]

Here Albert presents a strong associative tie between memory and fable, expressly favoring memory images that are *composita ex miris*, composed out of marvelous or extraordinary things, the very same quality that positions non-human animals as ideal subjects of the paradoxical encomia discussed in the previous chapter. The association between memory and fable here hinges on the single most repeated lesson in medieval memory treatises: that memory is excited by the extraordinary. This observation, contained in nearly every medieval reflection on memory and derived from their two favorite ancient sources (Aristotle and [pseudo-]Cicero), automatically brings sensation to the fore of both the faculty and the art of memory. Albert's close engagement with the ancient treatises on memory shows him locating memory in the soul's seat of sensation rather than in the rational part.[5] But this location does not prevent a wonder-guided memory from forming the very basis of rational investigation. Indeed, according to Mary Carruthers, memorial cultures locate in memory "the matter with which human intellect most directly works."[6]

In fact, tied to Albert's foundational assumption about the importance of sensation to memory is the presumption of the sensational considered above: the commonplace idea that extraordinariness aids retention and that in this realm too both wonder and retention are crucial for learning and inquiry. When Albert expounds on the implications of the affecting wonder doctrine, he offers Aristotle's still famous observation from the *Metaphysics* that wonder is the basis of philosophy itself, on both individual and historical levels.[7] Here is Albert:

> From this it appears that "from wondering [*ex admirari*] about befores and afters then and now is the beginning of philosophical thinking" because what is marvelous [*mirum*] by its vigorous motion [*vehementi motu*] produces questioning [*facit quaerere*] and thence gives rise to investigation and recollection.[8]

The processes of memory and of inquiry are barely distinguishable, though Albert, landing on the vigorous motion of *mirum*, the wonderful, nevertheless attempts to clarify matters. In doing so he places the memory arts on either side of inquiry—as both prior to and resulting from reflective consideration. Albert thus has it both ways, and he plays a visible role in linking memory to invention and creativity, a relation drawn out compellingly by Carruthers in *Craft of Thought*.[9]

Furthermore, passages like Albert's tell us even more about the particular size and frequently zoopoetic shape of medieval innovations when it came to memory. Importantly, the Latin *vehementi* (vigorous, powerful, mighty) that modifies the question-inducing motion (*motu*) in Albert's reflections was usually reserved for living beings. Albert's conclusions about memory and thought therefore hint at how nonhuman animals occupied medieval memorial edifices. In fact, in the context of memory arts, animal memory images were deliberately conjured for their stickiness: their kinetic vigor and their ability by turns to puzzle, frighten, amuse, and amaze were thought to help fix words and things in the memory. This paradox of arresting and captivating movement will serve as a focal point in this chapter. Quintilian's foray into memory turns on the paradox of memory, without which all "the effort" described in the *Institute*'s first ten books would be void (*inanis*), "unless all the other parts are retained, as it were, by this animating principle."[10] The idea of retention through animation conveyed here by the words *spiritu continentur* offers a suitable frame for this chapter's discussion of nonhuman animals in medieval memory arts.[11]

Medieval memory artists took seriously the principle of adhesion through amazement I described above, and they braided it together with Aristotle's writings on memory, specifically, I'll suggest, his theory of the perceptive (visual) faculty *phantasia* as it pertains to memory. In brief, the uniquely medieval entwinement of Herennial (technical) memorial tradition with an Aristotelian (philosophical) approach to memory results in performance-enhanced *phantasia*. This jacked-up *phantasia* is the best way to make sense of this chapter's guiding animal image: an otherwise confounding appearance of a ram in medieval commentaries on two central memory texts, Aristotle's *De memoria* and the *Rhetorica ad Herennium*. The ram itself, bearing super-sized testicles, best illustrates the compensatory *phantasia* central to medieval theories of memory.

Before following this marvelous ram and his extraordinary testicles through the otherwise staid and pious world of medieval commentaries, to help readers fully appreciate what animals appear to have enabled for the development of memory arts, I will say a word or two about the Ciceronian and Aristotelian strands of medieval memorial culture, providing a context for the distinct ancient traditions that fed medieval mnemotechnics. It's difficult, after all, to separate the theories of mind, and even meaning, from the practical, technical approaches to memory aids, especially in the context of rhetorical learning and performance. For the purposes of this book, animals inform and inhabit both the practical mnemotechnic approach to memory and the philosophical approach, and in the context of medieval memory arts, the two combine to form a potent version of *phantasia*, of which the ram is a remarkable illustration—though, as I'll show at the chapter's end, not the only one.

ARISTOTLE'S *DE MEMORIA*

The account of memory given by Aristotle in *De memoria et reminiscentia* (*On Memory and Recollection*) emphasizes images, association, corporeality, and *pathos* such that the processes of memory involve conjuring corporeal, affective images that stimulate memory (also corporeal), often construed as an "affection." Early on in *De memoria* Aristotle links memory to *phantasia*, which I discussed in earlier chapters as an inner capacity for sight, and he does so through thought: "Memory, even of the objects of thought, implies a mental picture, *phantasmatos*."[12] This observation, which follows from his famous claim that images are central to thought itself,[13] leads Aristotle to point out what he believes is obvious (*phaneron*): that memory and *phantasia* belong to the same part of the soul.[14] As I discussed in chapter 1, in Aristotle's schema, memory is one of the blurry-eyed situations that draws on the faculty of *phantasia*. Others include seeing at a distance, gazing at a reflection in water or burnished bronze, as well as dreams and delusions. The common feature of these instances of *phantasia* is "a kind of fuzziness":[15] where one faculty (vision) blurs, another (*phantasia*) steps in to clarify. Aristotle, recall, refers to *phantasia* in the *Rhetoric* as "a kind of weak sensation."[16] The inherent weakness of *phantasia* is its indirectness: it works at a remove. And while the weakness of memory as *phantasia* is not mentioned explicitly in the leading Aristotelian texts consulted during the medieval period, it is most certainly implied in *De anima* and *De memoria*, where the philosopher wrangles with *phantasia*'s tendency to err.

That slip of memory comes installed in Aristotle's very definition of memory: "Memory, then," he asserts in book 1 of *De memoria*, "is neither sensation nor judgment, but is a state or affection of one of these, when time has elapsed."[17] The time lapse between impression and recollection, a constitutive feature of memory, is also its primary weakening force: in the context of recollection, the passage of time can blunt the *phantasmata*, the images of *phantasia*, themselves. This blunting, I contend, or the inherent strain-inducing weakness of memorial *phantasia*, creates a need for compensation. And the idea that memory systems stand as an instance of *phantasia*, where the *phantasmata* are devised for the very purpose of future retrieval, introduces both the need and the possibility for a kind of compensatory *phantasia*.[18]

A passage in *De anima* makes explicit the link to mnemonic systems in the context of characterizing *phantasia* as "a *pathos* that lies in our power whenever we choose (for it is possible to bring before the eyes [*pro ommatōn gar esti poiēsasthai*], like those who make [*tithemenoi*] and form images [*eidōlopoioūntes*] in their memories)."[19] Here *eidōlopoioūntes* designates the act of creating an image especially in the mind, in the context of *phantasia*.[20] The word at the beginning of this definition, *pathos*, is best understood, as Richard Sorabji notes, as "anything one undergoes." Furthermore, "the *pathē* of the soul are accompanied by pleasure or pain" and lead to change, *kinēsis*.[21] Thus anger and a memory image can each comfortably assume the label of a *pathos*: both incite change.

In contrast to mirror images or straining to identify someone approaching from a distance, which rely on *phantasia* to "fill in" what can't be directly perceived, memory images can be created and therefore may be devised with an eye toward recall. *Phantasia*, already an affection, can be infused and thereby reinforced with *pathos* in the emotional sense more familiar to students of Aristotle's rhetoric. In this way, *pathos* joins with and reinforces *pathos*, resulting in a heightened, more potent *phantasma*, an image that is seared onto the soul (to use Aristotle's sense of the process). The potency of a *phantasia* as *pathos*, therefore, increases when memory images are themselves designed to be highly affective, even disturbing: "In *phantasia*," Aristotle notes in *De anima*, a few lines after mentioning *phantasia* in the context of memory, "we are like spectators looking at something dreadful or encouraging in a picture."[22] This line might inspire contemporary readers to think of memory images as a work of art displayed in a museum, and the critical distance allowed by memory is pretty much the point: the distance created by memory's weakness also allows for pleasure, even delight, through disturbing images. Such a sentiment drives Aristotle's famous discussion of the spectacle in the *Poetics* about the pleasure of contemplating images that would otherwise be painful to witness.[23] Though Aristotle doesn't say it explicitly in the *Poetics*, this idea of pleasurably contemplating images of things we could not bear to look at directly is underwritten by the idea of *thauma* or wonder. What he does suggest, however, when he specifies "vile beasts or corpses" is that nonhuman animals are exemplary in the context of pleasure enabled by contemplating terrifying, *pathos*-ridden things from a distance. The double bond of *pathos* in the context of *phantasia* is therefore crucial for memory systems.

When discussing recollection (*anamnēsis*), the more learning-friendly version of memory, Aristotle uses the language of associative *kinēsis*, effectively drawing out the transformative dimension of *pathos*: "Acts of recollection occur when one *kinēsis* naturally [*pephuken*] succeeds another."[24] Then he follows this observation with a nod to habit [*ethisthēnai*]: "But it happens that some impulses [*kinoumenous*] become habitual to us more readily from a single experience than others do from many; and so we remember some things that we have seen once better than others that we have seen many times."[25] This observation—that an image viewed once can be more memorable than an image seen time and again—reappears in the *Rhetorica ad Herennium* and receives a good deal of attention from medieval scholars of memory as well. Those one-time affecting images are seared onto the soul precisely because they stand out: they are striking; they *astound*.

In the Aristotelian tradition, then, recollective memory, as a version of *phantasia*, tends toward weakness and is aided by a chain of (kinetic) associated images.[26] Whether those chains are devised deliberately or simply occur matters less than the association itself. As Carruthers and Ziolkowski present it, "Aristotle taught also that *every memory is composed of two aspects*: 'a likeness' or 'image,' which is visual in nature (*simulacrum*), and an emotional resonance or coloring (*intentio*), which serves to 'hook' a particular memory into one (or perhaps more) of a person's existing networks of experience. *Memory works by association*."[27] Aristotle's formulation in *De memoria* is as follows: "It is only at the moment when the state or affection has been induced that there is memory."[28] Aristotle cares more about the fact of the induction of *pathos* or *hexis* than he does about forming that induction into a step-by-step program. A need for such a program, for techniques of recollection, would be fulfilled by the author of the *Rhetorica ad Herennium*, whom the medievals referred to lovingly, if mistakenly, as Tully.

RHETORICA AD HERENNIUM

Accounts of the memory arts put forth in the *Rhetorica ad Herennium* pro-liferate now as they did during the medieval period.[29] At base, the *Rhetorica ad Herennium* was a—if not *the*—central resource for medieval thinkers and writers, and its special value was drawn from the advice on memory offered in book 3.[30] According to Francis Yates, "The mediaeval artificial memory rested . . . entirely on the memory section of *Ad Herennium*."[31] That section of the *Rhetorica ad Herennium*, then, is crucial to the work of this chapter.

There, in a passage designed to guide the creation of memory images, im-ages meant not to just bring something before the eyes but to fix it in the mind, the anonymous author offers nature itself (*ipsa natura*), as a guide:

> When we see in everyday life things that are petty, ordinary, and banal, we generally fail to remember them, because the mind is not being *stirred* [*commovetur*, set in violent motion, disturbed] by anything *novel* [*nova*] or *marvelous* [*amirabili*]. But if we see or hear something exceptionally base [*egregie turpe*], dishonourable, extraordinary [*inusitatum*], great, un-believable [*incredible*], or laughable, that we are likely to remember a long time. Accordingly, things immediate to our eye or ear we commonly forget; incidents of our childhood we often remember best. Nor could this be so for any other reason than that ordinary things easily *slip* from the memory while the *striking* and *novel stay* longer in mind.[32]

A sunrise, the sun's movement through the day, and the sunset, he reasons, are *nemo admiratur, a wonder to no one* (wondered at by no one), because they are *vulgari* or common. Solar eclipses, on the other hand, are *mirantur* (wondrous).[33] Nature, continues the writer, is not stirred (*non exsuscitari*) by the ordinary but rather is *commoveri* by the novel or striking, *novitate et in-signi*: the new and unfamiliar. *Exsuscitari* is often used to refer to the stirring (by some external element) of a sleeping person and so translates variously "to stir up, rouse up, awaken, set in motion."[34] When linked to descriptors from earlier in the passage, the disturbing, the wondrous, or the marvelous all become means of awakening. The suggestion, when it comes to memory, is that people's minds are in something like sleep mode and then go from rest to motion: they are *stirred* by wonder. The second verb, *commoveri*, stirs things up even more: the marvelous or striking image simply causes a commotion. Such vigorous movements, as Carruthers has pointed out, form the theoretical basis of memory arts in the medieval period. The requisite commotion, the need for energetic stirring, also helps account for the preponderance of animals in memory treatises.

In fact, the *Rhetorica ad Herennium* specifically posits animals as exemplary images at the very beginning of its discussion of memory arts, when the author divides the components of artificial memory—backgrounds and images. Here the author offers architectural examples for backgrounds ("a house, an intercolumnar space, a recess, an arch or the like")[35] and nonhuman animals for images: "An image," he writes, "is, as it were, a figure, mark, or portrait of the object we wish to remember; for example, if we wish to recall a horse, a lion, or an eagle, we must place its image in a definite background."[36] The *loci* of this passage are by now quite familiar to scholars of memory and of rhetoric. The author here names a deliberate emplotment, a spatial placing of the memory objects, figured in this passage as images. The word translated here as images, *imagines*, tilts toward similitudes, likenesses, copies. They are visualized similitudes, pictures in thought, along the lines of Aristotelian *phantasiai*. That the author illustrates the very idea of *imagines* with a trio of nonhuman animals—a horse, a lion, an eagle—signals a persistent handiness of animal variety of the kind I discuss in chapters 2 and 3.

Yet once the Herennial discussion is under way, the images become far more outlandish than the straightforward instances of fabular, zoopoetic species recall might allow. Noteworthy too in the contrast between *loci* and *imagines* is the relative fixity of backgrounds compared with the lively images. Arches, once built, tend to remain still, whereas animals can be fixed only temporarily, through depiction. And even depictions tend to present an animal in motion, as with Homer's writhing snake. As Carruthers puts it, "Mnemonic images are called 'agent images' in rhetoric, for they both are 'in action' and 'act on' other things."[37] This idea of agent images, Latin *imagines agentes*, derives directly from the long-heeded Herennial advice:

We ought, then, to set up images of a kind that can adhere longest in the memory. And we shall do so if we establish likenesses as striking as possible; if we set up images that are not many or vague, but doing something [*si non multas nec vagas, sed aliquid agentes imagines*]; if we assign to them exceptional beauty or singular ugliness; if we dress some of them with crowns or purple cloaks, for example, so that the likeness may be more distinct to us; or if we somehow disfigure them, as by introducing one stained with blood or soiled with mud or smeared with red paint, so that its form is more striking, or by assigning certain comic effects to our images, for that too, will ensure our remembering them more readily.[38]

Once again, the author favors the notion of a striking and active image. But here the methods of astounding are themselves vivified by staining and smearing to incite something like horror or at least surprise.

The paradox inherent in this advice—that one fixes through dramatic motion, that order is somehow preserved through *commotion*—preserves and perpetuates the double pathos of *phantasia* put forward by Aristotle: the most adhesive images, that is, are not just set in motion, but set in vigorous motion. In other words, to stir things up these images need to not merely move, but to *disturb*. And animals, because of their variety, their lively energy, the way they can be caught in motion, and the wonder and marvel they elicit, frequently show up in this context. Animals, that is, exude what Carruthers calls "mnemonic *usefulness*."[39]

An animal body—or part of an animal body—features curiously in the *Rhetorica ad Herennium*'s illustrative and well-known memory image. The image, directed to a hypothetical prosecutor trying to retain the details of the "many witnesses and accessories" to an act of murder by poison is as bizarre as it is enduring in medieval accounts of memory, so I want to dwell on it here before tracking it into those accounts.

> We shall picture the man in question as lying ill in bed. . . . And we shall place the defendant at the bedside, holding in his right hand a cup, and in his left tablets, and on the fourth finger a ram's testicles. In this way we can record the man who was poisoned, the inheritance, and the witnesses.[40]

Caplan's textual note reads as follows: "*Testiculi* suggests *testes* (witnesses). Of the scrotum of the ram purses were made; thus the money used for bribing the witnesses may perhaps also be suggested."[41]

It's all well and good to know what the ram's testicles indicate, and the explicit mnemonic link to witnessing provides a tantalizing connection to the painful witnessing work assumed by animal characters in fables (discussed in chapter 3). Still, the very fact that ram testicles are chosen as a memory aid in the first place might be worth further consideration, especially with an eye to how *testiculi animalum* were taken up in medieval memory texts. The *Rhetorica ad Herennium*'s blithe advice to visualize a pair of ram's testicles on the end of the defendant's fourth finger has a curious afterlife in medieval memory texts, even as it captures the attention of contemporary theorists.[42] Yet it is rather odd, especially given the link I am drawing here between agentful images and nonhuman animals, that these parts are cleaved from the animal body. Perhaps recognizing this oddity yet acknowledging the shock value of using testicles as mnemonic devices, medieval commentators and memory theorists breathed new life into the testicle images, reattaching them to the animal bodies, enlarging them, even in one unforgettable instance (for that is the point), giving them a swift kick. The medieval interpretive comments on and allusions to this passage, that is, provide a stark contrast to the neat, almost incidental Herennial organ, envisioned on a human finger like a thimble. In the rest of this chapter, I will follow the images of animal testicles through medieval commentaries and memory texts, beginning with those of the ram in the litigation tableau, considering the strength that animals accumulated in the context of memory images and portraying as vividly as possible the resulting interwoven Aristotelian-Herennial theory of compensatory *phantasia* in medieval memory arts.

TESTICULI ANIMALUM

It is probably not surprising that contemporary medieval scholars, like the commentators they study, have tended to dwell on the testicular imagery. John O. Ward, Mary Carruthers and Jan Ziolkowski, and Jody Enders have therefore already delineated the manuscript lineage my argument is based on.[43] The earliest known and perhaps most curious medieval elaboration on the *Rhetorica ad Herennium*'s image of ram testicles is found in an eleventh-century commentary titled *Etsi cum Tullius*, which has been authoritatively attributed to William of Champeaux, a philosopher who taught both at Notre Dame and at the monastery of Saint Victor.[44] In the *Rhetorica ad Herennium*, the ram testicles are mentioned with a casualness that belies their oddity, yet William mentions them repeatedly in his commentary on this passage, offering a number of possible meanings while effectively redrawing the original image to amplify and animate it, making it more memorable. William even concludes his discussion of the Herennial image tableau by mentioning the testicle-witness association one last time at the very end of his commentary on the *Rhetorica ad Herennium*'s summative reminder of why this image-locus method facilitates memory, *poterimus per hoc facile meminisse*. The method, that is, works "if we use the arrangement of the objects—the order—and the characterization of the images, that is, if we keep in mind both the place where the image is located and what thing it is the image of, just as the testicles are [an image] of the witnesses."[45] With this final mention of the testicles as an example of what an image can evoke, William leaves his readers with what would become the most memorable element in the tableau. But even more interesting than William's end-game fixation on the testicle imagery are the interpretive liberties he takes a few lines earlier:

> We will depict the culprit before him holding a cup of poison in his right hand, in his left hand tablets, and through this we will signify that that man killed him with poison for the sake of his inheritance. He adds also, in order that the witnesses may be evoked, that he was holding ram testicles with that finger which is called "medical," symbolizing through them the witnesses to the potion and to the poison (because it is contrived using the ram's testicles, which are poisonous); or he said "of a ram" symbolizing what the defender will do against witnesses harassing and upsetting the accused himself with their horns.[46]

With this passage, William expounds on the significance of the ram testicles, reading into them valences that are based first in the word (*testes* = witnesses or testicles) and then in testicular imagery itself. The etymological reading, that is, is followed by an alternative reading that gives body to the ram testicles by associating them with the horns. The horns themselves in this passage (*ipsum reum cornibus*) are described as upsetting the accused. The word for "upsetting" here, *inquietantes*, is often rendered "disquieting" (the verb Carruthers uses in her translation of this line), and it more commonly means "disturbing."[47] William's expansion on the *Rhetorica ad Herennium* passage therefore takes seriously the advice given earlier in the Roman text that the most memorable images are novel, large, or unseemly. Indeed, William's commentary on those lines singles out *res mirabiles et magnas*, things amazing and great/large, as well as *turpe*, unsightly or repulsive, as particularly memorable.[48]

William continues that emphasis by mentioning all possible disturbing dimensions of a ram's testicles. His account effectively rebodies the ram itself, committing a retro-reversal of the modern phrase "grow a pair," which is to say that in William's commentary the pair of testicles grows a body, one complete with—and complemented by—a pair of threatening horns. William's interpretation of the ram testicle imagery is remarkable, then, not just for the liberties it takes, but for its proliferation of imaginative associations.

Not that he was fabricating these associations. All the possible ideas William associates with testicles in general (e.g., the word's kinship with witness), and with ram testicles in particular (e.g., their poisonous properties, their intimidating horns), can be documented. Pliny's *Natural History*, as an example, singles out the "wildness" of a ram (an uncut sheep), which he says can be "restrained by boring a hole in the horn close to the ear.[49] Perhaps the unsavoriness Galen attributes to the testes of rams, bulls, and the like later became associated with poison.[50] The Bodleian bestiary, which likely post-dated William but nevertheless drew on long-standing cultural associations found in the enduring bestiary genre, has this to say: "Rams are like Apostles because these animals have very powerful foreheads and always overthrow whatever they strike."[51] The point here, then, is that William appears to have contemplated fairly deeply the meaning and force of the testicular imagery.

From there the newly bodied wild ram takes on a life of its own in subsequent commentaries,[52] even charging into Albert the Great's thirteenth-century commentary on Aristotle's *De memoria*, where Albert invokes the *Rhetorica ad Herennium*'s tableau to develop Aristotle's point about memory's chain of associations. Notably, Albert invokes the memory scene in a discussion of the potential impairments of "mental image making" caused by inadvertent associations formed with incidental images. To minimize the risk of damaged *phantasia* (*corruptus laedit phantasiam*), Albert recommends a retreat from busy, well-lit public places to private, dimly lit places.[53] And this is the spot in the commentary where Albert sees fit to invoke and vivify the ram from the Tullian memory image:

> This is why Tully, in the art of memory that he sets forth in his second *Rhetoric*, prescribes that when forming images we seek out dark places containing little light. Because recollection seeks out many images and not one, he prescribes that we take what we want to retain and recollect, that we figure it in many images, and that we assemble the images. For example, if we wish to recall the person who opposes us in a court case, we should imagine some ram in the dark with great horns and great testicles coming against us; for the horns prompt us to recall our opponent and the testicles prompt us to recall the arrangement of those testifying.[54]

In the passage leading up to this reference, Albert uses the word *phantasia* three times, beginning with the idea of the corrupt or impaired faculty. The strenuous emphasis Albert places on the limitations of *phantasia*'s image-making capacity bespeaks the scholar's intimate familiarity with Aristotle's lengthy discussions of *phantasia* elsewhere, especially in *De anima*, the basis of another Albertian commentary, where Aristotle presents *phantasia* as a weak form of perception.

What we have in the *De memoria* commentary, then, is an intricate weaving together of perceptual memory theories found in Aristotle and the *Rhetorica ad Herennium*. The resulting account emphasizes the advice found in the *Rhetorica ad Herennium* as well as Aristotle's theoretical account of *phantasia*. Albert, notably, refuses to settle for pointing out the weakness of memorial *phantasia* and instead turns to the image itself to preemptively compensate for that weakness. The resulting memory image takes seriously the *imagines agentes* principle. The testicles have been cropped from the original tableau, enlarged, bodied, and set in motion: the ram is coming against us (*contra nos venientem*). Francis Yates, writing in the mid-twentieth century, presents this Albertian passage with the equivalent of a scholarly gasp. Noting that it "gives one rather a fright," Yates even half seriously suggests that the image is more like a hallucination resulting from too much nighttime memory work on Albert's part than a serious technique.[55] But I am suggesting otherwise. The vividness of the image is owed instead to Albert's extreme faithfulness to Aristotle's version of *phantasia*, and a resulting urge to bring "Tully" into the service of that tradition. The image is not a product of Albert's own dim recollection of the *Rhetorica ad Herennium* but rather is a deliberate and creative emendation that results from an innovative and intertextual reading of memory images.

In fact, the next mention of Tully in Albert's commentary on *De memoria* also references the nature as memory guide passage. Once again, key to that passage is its distinction between "ordinary things," which "easily slip from the memory while the striking and novel stay longer in mind."[56] The observation resonates—perhaps even originates—with Aristotle, who notes in book 2 of *De memoria* that "we remember some things that we have seen once better than others that we have seen many times."[57] According to Albert, the comparative strength of one-time viewing over habitual viewing is owing to a "twofold circumstance":[58] age and, more important for the present discussion, what he calls "the dispositional circumstance [*dispositio rei*] of that which disturbs the soul."[59] This circumstance, continues Albert, is rife with disturbing motion—he uses the descriptor *vehemens* twice in close succession (*destructio scilicet vehemens, et abominatio vehemens*), for such "profound disturbances enter into the soul and remain there a long time."[60] Albert's commentary then invokes the *Rhetorica ad Herennium* for the second time: "For these reasons, as Tully teaches, 'we remember for a longer time some things we see only once than others that we have seen and come to know many times.'"[61] Albert concludes matter-of-factly, "Therefore when we recollect, we are first stirred [*movemur*] then according to some one of the previous old motions impressed upon us [*aliquem priorum et antiquorum motuum nobis impressorum*]."[62] The words *movemur* and *motum* in this passage present a cluster of possible meanings, marking an intensity of motion—a disturbance, an affection, a stirring. Such words serve as the focal point for the rest of the meaty paragraph, offering an important explanation for why Albert's ram has a body and why it is coming at his readers.

The other noteworthy feature of the full-bodied ram image and Albert's deliberate choice to darken the background (a choice that, as Ward notes, contravenes the advice in *Rhetorica ad Herennium* that backgrounds be neither too bright nor too dim) is the removal of *loci*. Put simply, the image itself replaces the *locus*—the ram's body becomes the background, setting it in motion. The section in *De bono* where Albert reflects on the advice about memory that Cicero gives at the end of book 3 shows Albert questioning the role of the *loci* or backgrounds and suggesting that his beloved author didn't offer a full picture of how to fashion them:

> Further it seems that he [Tully] has taught incompletely [*imperfecte tradidit*] the rules for the backgrounds in which the images of things to be remembered are deposited, because many other things are useful as places for remembering besides those he defined.[63]

Albert finds in "Tully himself" (*ipse Tullius*) permission to innovate: "'If we are not content with our ready-made supply of backgrounds, we may create a region for ourselves and obtain a most serviceable distribution of appropriate backgrounds.'" His conclusion succinctly settles the matter: *Ergo multitudo confundet memoriam*, a "multitude" of images "will confound the memory." From there he proceeds to cite the Herennial placement of the sick man in bed to exemplify how Tully "teaches us to refer to images" (*ipse enim docet imagines referre*).[64] His objection to the crowd of images in this tableau persists, though. When it comes to creating images, Albert inclines to the rare, spare, and unique, and he finds much in the *Rhetorica ad Herennium* to bolster his case. After quoting a host of passages, all of which have been considered in this chapter, Albert concludes:

From all these quotations it appears that for the artificial memory disci-
plined study is required in images and contents and words and much else
besides, so that our images may be rare and conspicuous, and thus it seems
that these may not be predetermined images which we employ for remembering all sorts of things, as we employ letters for signifying every sort of
thing in writing.[65]

The upshot of Albert's meditation on the nature of memory images is this: images are not codes to be learned and reused. They are idiosyncratic creations
and must be devised anew with an eye to the memorable; they must anticipate
and compensate for *phantasia*'s lapses and weakness. This reflection, therefore, helps show why Albert's ram image in his commentary on Aristotle dif-
fers so radically from the one put forward in the *Rhetorica ad Herennium*. He
redraws the image to make it his own and one for his age.

The ram that, as Carruthers puts it, "runs amok" in Albert's commentary[66]
therefore exemplifies compensatory *phantasia*, the innovative theoretical
emendation that medieval commentators made to the text based on a revision-
ary account of what is in that text. Albert is no aberration. In addition to his
predecessor William of Champeaux, whom he is thought to follow, Albert's
student Saint Thomas Aquinas channels the ram's effects (if not the ram itself) in his detailed discussions of Aristotelian *phantasia*, which notes the
importance of binding abstract ideas to particular images and also points out
the memorial work of vigor and wonder.[67] What's more, Albert's full-bodied,
large-testicled charging ram can be found in Thierry of Chartres, Alanus, and
Guarino.[68] His is a variation on a theme, but a deliberate, amplified, theoreti-
cally informed variation, built on a composite of Aristotelian and "Tullian"
approaches to memory.

MARVELOUS TURPITUDE

A remarkable exemplum of Albert's distinctly medieval compensatory *phantasia* may also be found in Thomas Bradwardine's fourteenth-century treatise "On Acquiring a Trained Memory." On the topic of images, Bradwardine
notes that "there are four considerations: size, nature, order, and number."[69]
"Their size," he continues, "should be moderate. . . . But their nature [*qualitas*] should be wondrous and intense [*mirabilis et intensa*] because such
things are impressed in memory more deeply [*in memoria imprimuntur
profundius*] and are better retained."[70] This passage links memory work to

the ekphrastic wonder explored in the previous chapter, hinting at the embeddedness of progymnasmatic principles in memorial culture. Bradwardine elaborates the tandem qualities of *mirabilis et intensa*, offering specific techniques for maximizing the impressiveness of an image, thereby compensating for any phantasic weakness. If it is all right for the size of an image to be moderate (*media*), everything about the quality ought to eschew moderation. Bradwardine puts this requirement in very particular terms:

> Such things are for the most part not moderate but extreme, as something greatly beautiful or ugly [*turpe*], joyous or sad, worthy of respect or derision, a thing of great dignity or vileness, or maybe a person who has been injured with an enormous open wound flowing with a remarkable river of blood, or in some other way made ugly [*deturpatum*], having strange clothing and every bizarre embellishment, the color also very brilliant and intense, such as intense, fiery red, and the whole color strongly altering its appearance. The whole image should have some other quality such as movement [*motionem*], that thus it may be commended to memory more effectively than through tranquility or repose.[71]

This passage, replete with words for the hideous or base, indicated by the number of words derived from *turpe*, the unseemly, or even foul, focuses on intensities and the extremes, *extrema*, as opposed to the mediums: things are secured in memory through an intensification of their most sensible features. Their *qualitas vero sit mirabilis et intensa*: their true condition, their *nature*, as Carruthers's translation renders *qualitas*, must not only be *mirabilis*, that is, wondrous, marvelous, extraordinary, amazing, *strange*. It must also be *intensa*, which translates as intense but also denotes a bend, an exaggerated distension. This distension shows up in Bradwardine's examples, particularly in the distorted, contorted animal bodies featured in his exemplary memory image for the signs of the Zodiac. Here is the lengthy passage:

> Suppose that someone must memorize the twelve signs of the Zodiac, that is the ram, the bull, etc. So he might, if he wished to, make for himself in the front of the very first location a very white ram standing up and rearing on his hind feet, with golden horns. And he might put a very red bull to the right of the ram, kicking the ram with his rear feet; standing erect, the ram with his right foot might kick the bull in his large and super-swollen testicles [*magnos et ultra modum inflatos*], causing a copious effusion of

blood. And by means of the testicles [*et per testiculos*] one will recall that it is a bull, not a castrated ox or a cow.[72]

With this gory, astonishing image, there is certainly no chance that one seeking to memorize the signs of the zodiac will mistake the bull for a cow. The image of Taurus and his *testiculos magnos* stands in marked contrast to the detached ram testicles in *Rhetorica ad Herennium*. Whereas in the *Herennium* they are perched, like thimbles, on the fourth finger,[73] their associations perhaps dwelling in the postmortem uses of ram testicles,[74] Bradwardine, in the tradition of his more recent predecessors, finds the testicles much more impressive if they are equipped with nerves, engorged with blood, and swiftly kicked. Their "superswollen" state (*ultra modum inflatos*) is eye-popping enough to work as a mnemonic, but the blood drawn by the ram's hoof helps plant the image, sealing the memory by way of an empathetic wince. It probably goes without saying that Bradwardine's invoked audience is largely male.

The bull testicles in his zodiacal example exhibit on a number of levels the grotesque intensity Bradwardine suggests. First there is their distended quality marked by the cluster of words (*super, magnos, inflatos*). But the other mode of intensity is their fiery redness (*rubissimum*), which not only draws the eyes to that particular body part but effectively widens those eyes. The composite figure also adds the additional characteristic prescribed by Bradwardine's discussion of *qualitas*: *motionem*. The testicles are receiving a kick from the ram.

Note that the next figure in the zodiacal chain is human, a woman whose body is ripped open and is being attacked by the animals around her:

> In a similar manner, a woman may be placed before the bull as though laboring in birth, and in her uterus as if ripped open from her breast may be figured coming forth two most beautiful twins, playing with a horrible, intensely red crab, which holds captive the hand of one of the little ones and thus compels him to weeping and such outward signs, the remaining child wondering yet nonetheless touching the crab in a childish way.[75]

Alternatively, Bradwardine casually suggests, the bull can be the one to "miraculously" give birth "so that the principle of economy of material may be observed." Another human, a virgin, appears on the other side of Aries, after a "dreadful lion," "who with open mouth and rearing on its legs" attacks her, ripping her clothing. In her right hand she might hold scales, while "on her left may be placed a scorpion horribly stinging her so that her whole arm is swollen."[76]

This suggested part of Bradwardine's shocking tableau continues an age-old narrative of violence against mythical women. In this case the women's figures offset the motion of the animals. For starters, the first one is clearly dispensable, replaceable by the more miraculous birthing bull, but even more notably, the women stand in sharp contrast to the animals.[77] Or rather they *lie* in sharp contrast, suffering the active stings of the scorpion, the lion's violent assault. The only active movement attributed to these figures is childbirth (though that is undercut with an "as though" and appears to name her position more than a vigorous activity), and that of the virgin who "could strive to balance the scorpion in the aforementioned scales."[78] The virgin's striving is in the service of maintaining the chain of images.

The Gemini babies are intriguing here because they divide the labor of suffering and of marveling, with one ensnared by the crab's pincers and the other wondering, *admirante*, touching the crab "in a childish way."[79] The second twin, that is, models the kind of contemplative, sensory response the entire memory image ought to inspire. The chain of images therefore continues:

> Then in the front of the second location might be placed an archer with suitable equipment, holding an astounding bow fully extended, in which might be an even more astounding arrow, and he could strive to shoot arrows at a goat standing erect slightly farther back in the same location, remarkably hairy and shaggy, having a weird-looking horn and a golden, luxuriant beard. And he might hold in his right foot a most remarkable jug full of water, in his left foot unusual fishes, onto which he pours crystal-clear water from the water vessel.[80]

The second locus adds in the *imagines agentes* of a male archer, striving to shoot a goat. But it is the goat's position that I want to note here. Apart from his "remarkable" (*mirabiliter*) hairiness and shagginess and his "weird-looking horn" (one gets the sense that Bradwardine is growing weary of the image invigoration), the goat is both image and locus. All the beasts in this image—the ram, the bull, the lion, and the goat—are positioned on their hind legs, a stance that allows a number of things. First, the upright stance increases the motion and allows a curved verticality that helps keep the circle of images going, offering a spatial, connective advantage. In the case of the bull, the stance allows a full view of the distended testicles, which are explicitly the point of attention in part because they distinguish the animal as a bull and in part (or mostly, I'd suggest) because they are *turpe*, repulsive.

In addition to the erect animal bodies, at once in motion but also splayed open, with the ram "standing up and rearing on his hind feet"—there is nothing more surprising than a wild beast rearing (like the ram) or leaping (like the lion). Standing on the hind hooves also frees the front hooves to be imagined carrying something, as with a goat Bradwardine presents just after the zodiac discussion, in the same stance and holding "in his right foot a most remarkable jug full of water, in his left foot unusual fishes, onto which he pours crystal-clear water from the water vessel."[81] The stance simultaneously allows for memorable action (the erect ram is still able to plant a kick in the bull's groin), and it also enlarges the body so that it becomes a field itself, able to contain images. The bull's stance, similarly, exposes the genitals, making them at the same time visible (hence memorable) and vulnerable to attack by the adjacent ram. In the cases of both the ram and the bull, that is, the upright stance splays—*displays*—the animal body in a way that enables the *imagines agentes* to serve simultaneously as image and as locus, a field in which to display images. The key Herennial divisions of *loci* and *imagines* converge neatly into one; animal bodies are carved up, not unlike a pig on a spit or a sheep spread over an altar, yet are still very much alive and, well, kicking.[82]

It is worth noting again how this segment of memorial culture may have been fed by the imaginative, descriptive skills cultivated by the *progymnasmata*: Bradwardine's circle of zodiacal images is highly ekphrastic and features the comparative measurement central to *thauma* embedded in that tradition. While these images of lively betesticled wild animals are a long way from the abstracted testicles in the *Rhetorica ad Herennium*, they still developed on that text's logic, which favors the "marvelous" (*admiribali*), the "exceptionally base" (*egregie turpe*), and the "extraordinary" (*inusitatum*) over the everyday (*cotidianas*) and the banal (*usitatas*).[83] From this logic, combined with Aristotle's account of *phantasia*'s limits, springs a medieval model of memory image making built on the idea of compensatory *phantasia* in which wild animals, bucking and charging, feature with some prominence.

The very qualities that commended animals to early rhetorical theory and style theorists—their variety, their striking movements and features, their beauty and their ugliness (recall Demetrius's reflections on cacophonous sounds discussed in chapter 2), their woundability, their potential for incongruity—were exactly the qualities that lent them mnemonic usefulness. And so Albert's expressed preference for fable as the mode of memory making, the preference with which this chapter began, indicates the mutual imbrication of the *progymnasmata* and memory traditions. Medieval memorial traditions stand as a crucial outgrowth of the fabular, ekphrastic, zoopoetic skill of the *progymnasmata*.

The bestiary, a medieval genre modeled after the ancient *Physiologus*, combining elements of fable and natural history, likely figures into this textual lineage. In *The Book of Memory*, Carruthers argues that bestiaries taught "mental imaging, the systematic forming of 'pictures' that would stick in the memory and could be used . . . to mark information."[84] Relatedly, the thirteenth-century teacher and philologist John of Garland offers as one of his two primary aids for memory "the *voces animantium* of diverse animals."[85] According to Carruthers, "the *voces animantium* is a list of the habits and physical features thought to characterize the animals and birds; it was disseminated both as a simple listing and, in an expanded semi-narrative form, as the Bestiary."[86] Carruthers amasses compelling evidence that bestiaries were used as memory books.[87]

Even so, chronicling the moving of animals deep into the recesses of medieval minds risks leaving behind real animals and the blood they spill. It bears mentioning, then, what the wild growth of memory arts during this period owes to the extraordinary labor and animal sacrifice that went into producing material for manuscripts and for transcribing the manuscripts themselves.[88] Animal urine was used in rubrication, the application of bold, reddish ink to highlight important material or organize indexes and also to deepen memory. Indeed, the smearing and staining suggested by the beloved "Tully" was itself an early form of *phantasic* rubrication. Nonhuman animals, in short, quite literally saturate medieval memorial cultures, melding Aristotelian theory with processual Herennial advice and aiding development of memory arts featuring a robust theory of compensatory *phantasia*.

CHAPTER 6

Accumulatio, Natural History, and Erasmus's *Copia*

Nature is not silent but speaks to us everywhere and teaches the observant man many things if she finds him attentive and receptive.

ERASMUS, "The Godly Feast," 1522[1]

No discipline is so remote from rhetoric that you cannot use it to enrich your collection.

ERASMUS, *De copia*, 1512[2]

Consider the advice offered by the famous humanist Desiderius Erasmus in his 1512 treatise *De duplici copia verborum ac rerum*, "On Two-fold Copia of Words and of Things," which I will hereafter call *De copia*:

> There are also appropriate characteristics to be observed in fables, and this no one will be able to manage unless he has observed and studied the natures of living creatures, and knows that the elephant is quick to learn and reverent, the dolphin an enemy of the crocodile and a friend of man, that the eagle builds its nest on heights, that the beetle has a habit of pushing along balls of dung in which it mates and reproduces, and disappears during the season when eagles are incubating, that the lark lays its eggs in harvest-fields, that the hedgehog likes ranging about and is an enemy to snakes. All this, and less well-known facts too, may be easily discovered in Aristotle, Pliny, and Aelian.[3]

These two sentences, one long, one short, seemingly a curious mash of fable and natural history, appear in Erasmus's treatment of how to describe (of all things) people. Compressed into this passage are a number of assumptions about the overlapping worlds of human and nonhuman animals, about the relation between habits and character, about cross-species friendliness and animosity, about past authorities on such matters and the significance of those authorities for Erasmus's present, about the importance of combining first-hand observation with intensive study, and about the dependence of fable on such "things" or facts of nature.

To simply document the astonishing variety of ways that Erasmus engages the shared worlds of animals (human and nonhuman) would result in a breathless and paratactic compendium of passages not unlike some of Erasmus's own publications.[4] At times Erasmus uses animals in ways that could be described as deeply anthropocentric, presuming and exploiting a hierarchy of humans over other animals in, for example, his reflection on children's civility in which he sternly observes that using the tongue to lick something sweet off a dish "is for cats, not for people," and making a trumpet noise with the nose "is for horn-blowers and elephants."[5] Yet that very anthropocentrism feeds a kind of ethical stance toward animals, one that leads Erasmus to inveigh against hunting and war on the same page and for the same reason: their disregard for the living.[6] Erasmus's famous satire "Praise of Folly" contains a dizzying array of references to animals and animal lives; his *Adages*, a meditative compilation of proverbs, refers to nearly every animal imaginable (mainly because it collects every proverb Erasmus was able to coax out of the near and distant past); his *Parallels* offers direct comparisons of animal dispositions within and across species, and his colloquies, which range from matters more obviously linked to nonhuman animals (hunting) to less obviously connected ones (sympathy and religion), attend to the natural world and feature any number of dogs, rabbits, wolves, sheep, and even, in "Sympathy," a monkey and a weasel (to which I will return later in this chapter).[7] His "Declamation on the Subject of Early Liberal Education for Children" invokes, in various places, bears, elephants, oxen, monkeys, and puppies.[8] Perhaps most intriguing, the interlocutors in the enduringly popular and highly imaginative "The Right Way to Speak Latin and Greek: A Dialogue," are a bear and a lion; the bear advises the lion on the sort of training in the classical languages she ought to seek for her newborn cub.[9]

Given the impossibility of charting all these animal-constituted writings in a single chapter, I have chosen to place Erasmus's treatise on abundance, *De copia*, at the center of this one. There are good reasons for this focus beyond *De copia*'s enduring renown and its centrality to rhetorical education in the West.[10] As a comprehensive manual for creating abundance (the best translation of the Latin word *copia*),[11] *De copia* offers the most lucid articulation of Erasmus's signature method such that compressed into the treatise are commitments and tendencies visible throughout his body of work. It therefore works as something of a hub for this chapter's discussion of how nonhuman animals animate Erasmus's approach to abundance.

That approach can be most concisely characterized as collecting and storing for future use bits of information about the world, including—but by no means only—appealing turns of phrase. As such, the method, which aimed at cultivating what Thomas Sloane calls "resourcefulness"—and I would stress the audible *fullness* in this word—drew on and helped shape the prevailing early modern habit of accumulation.[12] Close examination of Erasmus's cumulative approach reveals an abiding fondness for natural history, specifically (though by no means exclusively) for the writings of the Roman scholar and statesman Pliny the Elder, the first-century CE author of the thirty-seven-book *Natural History*. Erasmus himself contributed to translations of Aristotle, Lucian, and Pliny, but Pliny received special mention in several instances discussed below.[13] *De copia* is itself studded with references to Pliny, to nonhuman animals, and to natural history. As such, the treatise offers a starting point for detailing the specific ways that natural history and rhetoric, as arts of inquiry, supported and sustained each other during the late fifteenth and early sixteenth centuries.

By developing and building as a central concept *"accumulatio"* (accumulation) and showing how the *accumulatio* of observations from natural history entwined with the art of rhetoric in the work of Erasmus, this chapter sheds new light on Erasmus's method of *copia* and on Renaissance rhetoric more generally. What emerges from this investigation is a stronger sense of rhetoric's embeddedness within and centrality to early modern culture and natural history; and that sense, yet again, depends in part on the sensory effects of accumulation: this time the overwhelming and sometimes stifling density of a crowd, the dazzling spectacle of a seeming infinite variety of words and of things. A weighty materiality, a piling up of things, drives Erasmus's method of *copia*. This materiality, made manifest through a broad method of *accumulatio*, comes readily into view when we examine Erasmus's engagements with nonhuman animals. And further inspection of those engagements turns up a pedagogical stance that holds up certain nonhuman animals as purveyors of feeling, as models of ethical relations and of rhetorical invention. Animals, for Erasmus, do not merely fill one's own storehouse; they call forth deep meditations on feeling, on concord and discord, and on productivity itself. Nonhuman animals continue, that is, to hold up—even encourage the generation of—*logos* by living, moving, sensing, and feeling. After considering *accumulatio* in rhetoric and early modern culture, I consider specifically Erasmus's advice to study, to observe, and to imitate the habits and inclinations of certain living creatures. I conclude by elaborating the model of memory that results from these activities, what might usefully be called "collected memory," a memory enabled and sustained by nonhuman animal movements, sensations, and feeling, studied, observed, and imitated.

ACCUMULATIO

It is well attested if not a commonplace among Renaissance historians that the early modern period was an age of accumulation, a time when Europeans adhered to what historian of science Paula Findlen calls a "principle of plenitude."[14] That principle, and the practices of *accumulatio* it motivated, resulted in the growth during the fifteenth, sixteenth, and seventeenth centuries of zoological gardens as well as the emergence of curiosity cabinets, museums, and grottos, all of which frequently featured animals, whether painted, stuffed, or breathing and roaming in cages or pits.[15] The widespread collecting habit, encouraged by expanding trade and exploration and also by the development of print technology, fed a seemingly insatiable quest for knowledge. This period's growth of inquiries into nature—known most commonly as natural history—has been documented most notably by Paula Findlen and Brian Ogilvie as constitutive of the conditions of and quest for abundance in cities across Europe.[16] Ann Blair's work fills out—and helps account for—the breadth and sweep of accumulation by examining "the preoccupation with accumulating and managing information among the learned in the Renaissance," and in doing so it lands on a kind of information obsession, or what she calls "info-lust."[17] Erasmus's rhetoric nestles between the preoccupations with accumulating information and with accumulating stuff (though, as I will discuss later in the chapter, information was considered stuff as well).[18] *Accumulatio*, the Latin term for accumulation, for Erasmus was the road to rhetorical profusion. As such, *De copia* teaches strategies for accumulating and organizing the things—*res*—accumulated.

The narrowest meaning of *accumulatio* names a particular rhetorical figure in which an orator strings together similar phrases to emphasize a point.[19] For Quintilian, the approach took the form of a figure he describes as "congeries of words and sentences identical in meaning."[20] In subtle contrast, the *Rhetorica ad Herennium*, the text that exerted so much influence during the medieval period, labels this approach *frequentatio*, a crowding together. Embedded in the rhetorical figure of *accumulatio* is the word's broader meaning, the act of heaping or piling, as in *accumulatio*'s general definition: "a heaping up."[21] Pliny the Elder uses a form of the word in his *Natural History*, in a discussion of tree cultivation, to indicate heaping up earth around the roots of plants.[22] This act of heaping up soil provides a rich analogy for what I suspect *accumulatio* was doing both in Erasmus's approach to language and in the early modern culture of collecting more generally: *accumulatio* was a strategy for preserving and nurturing life and—by extension—knowledge through and about life. It was a heaping up of stuff for a larger purpose, a growth, be it sheer display of wealth, a better understanding of the world, the establishment of social networks, or in Erasmus's case for the sake of future eloquence.[23] As a mode of living and as a mode of writing, *accumulatio* presumes the importance of matter and what matter can do, whether in a motley heap or in an organized collection (the latter was the prevailing preference at the time). And the final reason Pliny's soil heap matters is that it shows the heaping of material things (*res*) in the interest of growth, expansion, protection, and transformation.

And so it is important to leave *accumulatio* as open to Pliny's heap of dirt as to Quintilian's congeries of words. At stake in the relation between the two is the very relation that guided Erasmus's approach to *copia*, that between *res* and *verba*, things and words. The material density of the heaping-up strategy, which bears some similarity to the Greek *hyperochē* and to magnitude discussed in chapter 2, creates an equally sensuous material effect that the visual alone does not fully capture: there can be a breathtaking quality to the sheer density of things, and that quality is pronounced when the accumulated things are varied, as with ever-popular menageries, and as with Erasmus's braggadocio display of nearly two hundred ways to express pleasure over a letter from a friend.[24]

The act of accumulation, then, figures prominently into Erasmus's approach to rhetoric. As Jeanne Fahnestock puts it, "Erasmus transformed amplification through accumulation into a great vortex pulling in all the other elements of rhetorical theory."[25] Here accumulation is the means to amplification, a rhetorical practice considered in depth in chapter 4. But amplification through accumulation is qualitatively—and, importantly, quantitatively—distinct from the amplification through magnification or enlargement necessitated by the minuscule insects discussed in that chapter (recall the up-close inspections of Lucian's fly and Psellos's louse). Put simply, while amplification through magnification expands the size of one thing, amplification through accumulation expands by accruing many things. If *copia* is the faculty Erasmus seeks to develop, then *accumulatio* is behind nearly every technique he offers for developing it, ranging from practice-oriented techniques where a pile of prose is generated as a way to exercise one's *copia* muscles, to the accumulation of words and things, the very stuff of *copia*.[26]

The accumulation of animals as things (*res*) and the accumulation of facts (also *res*) about animals were mutually informing modes of *accumulatio* best considered not just side by side, but together, as interlinked. *Accumulatio* takes slightly different forms in relation to *verborum* (words) than it does to *rerum* (things), the two parts of Erasmus's famous treatise on *copia*. Erasmus's quick sketch in *De copia* of what abundance of things entails leads with three approaches, "the collecting [*congenerindis*], stretching [*dilatandis*], and amplifying or increasing [*amplificandis*] by means of arguments, examples, comparisons, similarities, dissimilarities, contrasts, and other like procedures."[27] This description may fruitfully be placed next to his discussion of exercises in expression, which falls on the side of words. Put simply, the accumulation of stuff to say, and the stretching and enlarging of that stuff leads to the accumulation in the saying. *Accumulatio* in the context of Erasmian *copia* is, at base, generative.

Before moving to specific ways that animals and natural history help constitute Erasmian methods of accumulation, I want to linger briefly on Erasmus's description of practice necessary for developing *copia*, because that description suitably sets up the sensed feature that *copia* brings forth: density, weight, mass. And, as it happens, the description invokes an ancient legend involving a growing animal:

> Here it will be best to copy the expertise of the famous Milo of Croton and develop our powers gradually, first of all rendering it twice, then three times, and eventually treating it over and over again, so as to attain such facility in the end that we can vary it in two or three hundred ways with no trouble at all.[28]

Central to Erasmus's reference to the legendary wrestler and his exemplary incremental approach to strength training is, of course, the calf Milo carried uphill every day, from its birth until it was a full-grown bull. Milo's calf becoming bull is crucial to the logic of *accumulatio* and its relation to nonhuman animals. In this famous and easily conjured tale, what matters is the ever-increasing weight of the animal. As the animal accumulates body mass in the smallest of increments, so too do Milo's "powers" increase incrementally through the daily exercise of lifting and carrying the growing animal.[29] The bull's comparate here is the impressive—because countable—pile of sentences that can be churned out with increasing ease by a student training in

Erasmus's method. The image of Milo's growing calf is particularly useful because it offers a material—which is to say visible, felt, and therefore imaginable—instantiation of increasing mass. And so the word image does not fully capture what is going on with the Milo detail: when Erasmus invokes Milo traveling uphill under the mass of the bull, he also imports a feeling of density, of sheer weight, and therefore the laborious feat, of abundance.

After encouraging daily practice with incrementally increasing challenge, Erasmus moves to another approach, this one more directly cumulative, which involves mining words and phrases from the works of highly regarded authors:

> We must keep our eyes open to observe every figure of speech that they use, store it in our memory once observed, imitate it once remembered, and by constant employment develop an expertise by which we may call upon it instantly.[30]

This three-step plan—observe, store, and imitate—has *accumulatio* at its core, especially as it designates memory as the storage place, a point I will return to later. For now it is important to note that collection, or *accumulatio*, is not just the end point, but a necessary precursor to the faculty *copia*. The sensuous force of this approach to *copia* is more evident in another passage in which Erasmus advocates *copia* as a desirable way to approach language. There he assumes a wondering disposition toward the vibrancy of nature similar to the one I discuss in chapter 4. Shortly after introducing variety by way of Quintilian, Erasmus has this to say:

> Variety is so powerful in every sphere that there is absolutely nothing, however brilliant, which is not dimmed if not commended by variety. Nature above all delights in variety; in all this huge concourse of things, she has left nothing anywhere unpainted by her wonderful technique of variety. Just as the eyes fasten themselves on some new spectacle, so the mind is always looking round for some fresh object of interest. If it is offered a monotonous succession of similarities, it very soon wearies and turns its attention elsewhere, and so everything gained by the speech is lost all at once.[31]

A rich passage itself, this four-sentence excerpt introduces a number of ideas folded into Erasmus's notion of *copia*. First, it identifies variety as a—if not *the*—leading advantage for "studying the subject of *copia*," the title of the section in which the passage appears. And it does so with a host of vibrant references to sensation as audience access points, to gaining and holding their attention. Erasmus begins with the light metaphor (brilliant/dimmed) to illuminate variety's *vim*, that familiar word indicating strength, force, power, and energy. He also sutures sensation to attention by focusing on the eyes, *oculi*, and their tendency to be detained, *detinentur*, here translated as fasten, by *adspectu rerum magis*, a magical aspect of things. Erasmus's reference to painting also links sensation to variety. Just as important as the stress on sensation in this passage is the twofold role Erasmus ascribes to nature (*natura*): it is both the source of and the model for variety. The observation that "nature above all delights in variety" (*gaudet ipsa natura vel imprimis varietate*), assigns nature prime place in variety, and the painting analogy mentioned above describes the ingenuity (*artificio*) or technique of nature.

In the midst of all these commendations of variety, an anxiety underwrites Erasmus's mini-encomium of nature as the "leader in variety, and that anxiety is detectable in the phrase Knott translates "in all this huge concourse of things" (*in tam immense rerum turba*). The Latin, I think, exceeds this translation, though the collection of words "all," "huge," and "concourse" gesture to variety's tendency to overwhelm. *Turba*, in particular, a word that cropped up repeatedly in relation to the disturbing images of animals in medieval memory tableaux in chapter 5, in this context might find a more suitable translation in the chaos of many, or *the crowd*. By this account, abundance is achieved through the sheer number of things, *rerum*, discernible by means of their variety, their differentiation from each other. In Erasmus's account, variety satisfies the roving spirit (the word here is *animus*); the eyes need variety, as do the ears. So much is intimated by the question posed in the line just preceding this passage: "Who has got ears patient enough to put up even for a short time with a speech totally monotonous?"[32] The *turba*—in this case the crowded density—of variety becomes a leading feature of *copia*. When it comes to words, the undifferentiated lot of them is cause for concern, as when Quintilian, Erasmus's source here, warns against "the assembly of a disorderly crowd of words" (*turban tantum modo congregat*). *Congregat*, incidentally, usually indicates a flock of birds swarming. These fleeting bird-words, Quintilian implies, must be sorted, cataloged, and stored in a deliberate way. Amplifying Quintilian's point, Erasmus recommends maintaining order this way:

> One should collect a vast supply of words like this from all sides out of good authors, provide oneself with varied equipment, and, as Quintilian remarks, heap up riches so that we find we have a wealth of words to hand whenever we require it. It will not be sufficient to prepare a copious appa-

ratus or an abundant store of words unless you have them not only at the ready but in full view, so that they present themselves to the eyes even if you are not looking for them. But here we must take special care not to do what some do and use the first thing that presents itself out of the heap in any context without exercising any choice at all.[33]

Again, variety is the focus here, this time achieved through the act of collecting (*contrahenda*). This passage, which appears under the heading "Variety of Expression," urges a continuous awareness of what has been collected, and a sensuous one at that. The discussion redirects the distinctly Aristotelian notion of bringing before the eyes, which Aristotle generally treated as an audience-directed phenomenon in domains of play writing and speech writing. But when Erasmus urges keeping the "abundant store of words" spread before the eyes (*ostendant oculis*), he is talking about the eyes of a rhetor who will, at a future point, return to the store. Erasmus vivifies *accumulatio* by means of the incrementally increasing weight of Milo's calf and with an encomium to nature's variety. Underlying those treatments of growth and variety is an ability to measure what accumulates, and in order to measure something there needs to be a thing (or things) to measure. The measuring inheres in the incremental numbering and differentiation of the ways the same sentiment is presented—first two, then three, and then two hundred and three hundred: the strings of words become countable things.

A brief word on things, then. In the Latin vocabulary, the tiny word *res* pulls a lot of freight. Primarily, it translates as thing, as in a material object, substance, or possession, sometimes with added stress, for example, "an actual thing," emphasizing the thingness of the thing. In legal spheres, it can mean a case or lawsuit; in military ones, a battle or campaign; and in political spheres, as is commonly known, *res* lingers in "republic" (*res publica*), affairs of the state or (more literally) public stuff.[34] It can also, in point of fact, mean plainly "fact," which leads to another set of meanings that bends things on themselves: things about things, whether known or said (*res* is both singular and plural). This doubling and recombination of things pressed into the notion of thing as fact leads an annoyed Brian Vickers to attribute to scholars a "crass misunderstanding" that confuses *res* as "things of the speech" and *res* as "three-dimensional objects."[35] Jeanne Fahnestock tries to clarify Erasmus's division of his treatise on *copia* into *copia verborum* and *copia rerum*—abundance of words and abundance of things—in this way: "This confusing distinction between *matter* and *words* simply means that the prompts for expanding offered in Book II [*copia rerum*] are not formal to begin with, as they are in Book I [*copia verborum*], where they are directed by figures of speech."³⁶ Yet it is also the case that ambiguity persists in the term's latitude. When, for example, Quintilian observes that things are more durable or stronger (*firmior*) than words, it is unclear from the context of his example whether he is talking about the subject matter or facts or the actual things—in this case purple quilts—Cicero refers to in the example under discussion.³⁷ And the difference may well be negligible. For his part, Erasmus helpfully describes his method for *de rerum copia* by means of an analogy to nothing other than a three-dimensional object, a piece of merchandise:

> The first method of enriching what one has to say on any subject is to take something that can be expressed in brief and general terms, and expand it and separate it into its constituent parts. This is just like displaying some object for sale first of all through netting or inside a wrapping, and then unwrapping it and opening it out and displaying it fully to the eyes.³⁸

This passage proves Vickers's and Fahnestock's point about confusion over *res* even as it points to the materiality of *res* as subject matter, or even of words. For without a thinglike conception of *res*, how else would one inspect (or even count) what accumulates?

There is a strong correlation, overlap even, between the broad cultural tendency to accumulate *res* as things and the rhetorical gravitation toward accumulating *res* as known things, or even words as things. In fact, in his elaboration of the "twofold" condition of *copia* (*duplicem esse copiam*), Erasmus admits that "these two aspects"—by which he means *copia* of words and *copia* of things—"are so interconnected in reality that one cannot easily separate one from the other, and that they interact so closely that any distinction between them belongs to theory rather than practice."³⁹ The Latin word for interconnected here is *conjunctae*, which means connected, joined, harmonious, or even married. The richness of *copia*, for Erasmus, comes down to both, together, indicated as well by the word *duplici*—twofold—in the treatise's extended title. Erasmus elaborates the importance of such balance in the opening lines of his treatise "On the Method of Study": "In principle, knowledge as a whole appears to be of two kinds, of things and of words."⁴⁰ After pithily giving temporal precedence to knowledge of language but preference to knowledge of things (*verborum prior, rerum potior*), Erasmus goes on to discuss how they are indispensable to each other: "A person who is not skilled in the force of language is, of necessity, short-sighted, deluded, and unbalanced in his judgment of things as well."⁴¹ As with *copia*, knowledge of words and knowledge of things (including things about things) are conjoined and interdependent.

In their productive movement back and forth on a sliding scale of "thing-ness," Erasmus's *De copia* and the theories therein further embed his work in the European culture of accumulation. Concentrating on nonhuman animals helps to focus the point: the increasingly popular menageries, zoos, and cu-riosity cabinets provided inspiration and material for Erasmus's accumula-tions. But whereas in the broader culture of collecting distinction came with the number, volume, variety, and rarity of things possessed—a collection with a lion or an African parrot would draw more attention than a collection of, say, hounds—with collecting words and things for the purposes of *copia*, distinc-tion came with what one was able to do with the collection.[42] In other words, how one was able to mobilize the accumulation (the *rerum* and *verborum* gathered) in the service of eloquent prose made all the difference for show-casing the accumulated stuff. It is one thing to develop, Milo-like, a faculty of word generation, or to be aware of the stunning variety presented by things of nature, but it is another thing altogether to know how and when to call on those resources. Even though Erasmus cautions that accumulation is not all there is to this enterprise, in *De copia* he mainly focuses on building reserves of things to say and ways to say them. The way Erasmus moves from teaching to accumulate to teaching to work from the accumulated may be more clearly seen by concentrating on three distinct but complementary approaches to nonhuman animals. Those approaches—to study, to observe, and to imitate—begin with Pliny's *Natural History*, which served as both resource and arche-type for Erasmus's *accumulatio*.

STUDY (PLINY)

With the culture of accumulation as a backdrop, especially accumulation of things of nature, I want to return to Erasmus's suggestions for amassing things *about* animals—to study, to observe, and to imitate—beginning with the ex-hortation to study. Erasmus's short colloquy on *copia*, of which *De copia* is a significant expansion, contains the plain assertion that "comparisons of things [*rerum similitudines*] are taken from natural science [*Physica*]; you must memorize the qualities of a great many of them."[43] I will return to the link between accumulation and memory in this chapter's conclusion. What, or really whom, to study is a pressing question, and Erasmus had at hand a variety of ancient sources about *rerum natura*, including Oppian, the Greek author of fishing treatises, as well as the *Opera omnia* of Aristotle, for the 1531 edition of which Erasmus composed a preface.[44] But his leading source for things about the nature of things (and things about nature) can be found in the thirty-seven-volume work of Pliny the Elder, *Naturalis historia*, which translates literally as inquiry into nature or natural history.

Erasmus's "On the Method of Study" ranks Pliny first among resources for teachers, just after an exhortation to "range through the entire spectrum of writers so that he reads in particular all the best, but does not fail to sample any author, no matter how pedestrian."[45] A few lines later, though, Erasmus allows for extreme busyness and lack of resources: "If someone suffers from lack of time or books, Pliny alone will furnish an immense amount of information, Macrobius and Athanaeus much, and Gellius a variety of things."[46] Here Pliny tops the list of authors recommended by Erasmus; the *Natural History* on its own, though not ideal, is nevertheless deemed sufficient. Pliny effectively offers a shortcut to comprehensiveness.

Pliny himself was a great accumulator, and he presents his work as such, figuring the *Natural History* as a storehouse rather than a book and noting that he has therein assembled, by his own accounting, twenty thousand "things worthy of attention" (*rerum dignarum cura*).[47] As Ann Blair notes, "Humanists and early modern pedagogues embraced Pliny as the consummate model of abundant reading and note-taking."[48] And the early moderns weren't the only ones to value Pliny; his *Natural History* held pride of place both in the manuscript tradition and in the early history of printing. According to E. W. Gudger, about two hundred manuscripts from antiquity and the medieval period are extant.[49] The *Natural History* was the first natural history to be read in print and was printed early and often.[50]

Pliny's appeal during the early modern period no doubt inhered in his status as the most prodigious of the ancients on the matter of nature. The entwined cultures of display and of erudition, as Paula Findlen notes, shaped natural history as a mode of inquiry, and the flexibility and neutrality resulting from its status "as a universal discipline, prior to political, social and moral order" helped solidify its import.[51] Also not to be underestimated in the early modern culture of accumulation is the sheer heft of Pliny's work. Aude Doody's description of the *Natural History* as "a monumental account of the nature of things, always threatening to flatten the reader under the weight of its knowledge" hints at the material force of his work, especially as it was taken up—hoisted would not be the wrong word—by humanist scholars such as Erasmus.[52] According to Findlen, who details the tilt toward Pliny (and away from Aristotle) among the Italian naturalists of the sixteenth century, the naturalists preferred Pliny because he "allowed them to revel in the particularity and infinity of the world."[53] That paradoxical but defining feature of Pliny's work—the balance of bold expansiveness with painstakingly minute detail—plays out on every page of the *Natural History* and cumulatively, on all the pages together, as well.

The combination of particularity and seemingly endless reach held strong appeal for Erasmus, whose preface to a 1525 edition of the *Natural History* claims that the work "presents all knowledge with remarkable conciseness."[54] He adds, "Pliny's subject is the world."[55] He then poses a question with a flourish of incredulity, laying bare the thread of empire running through the culture of accumulation: "Could you imagine anything more absurd than to rule the world and not know what it is?"[56] Erasmus embellishes Pliny's own characterization when he asserts that the *Natural History* "is not simply a work, but a treasure house, a veritable encyclopaedia of all that is worth knowing."[57] This statement follows an elaborate and perhaps hyperbolic encomiastic comparison of Pliny to city builders:

> Real distinction belongs to those who, by building bridges, harbours, baths, and aqueducts, have created works which combine grandeur with utility. But if you were to select from all such things the one which stands out above all others, could anything compare with this work which Pliny left us as the living and breathing monument of his genius?[58]

To say that Erasmus thought highly of "this marvelous gift" would be an understatement. Erasmus's incorporation of Pliny's *rerum natura* laid an infrastructure for cross-disciplinary exchange between scientific knowledge and rhetoric.[59]

The approach Pliny takes to animals may be characterized as description mixed with narrative. Each of Pliny's descriptive treatments of an animal species, as Roger French notes in his book-length study of ancient natural history, generally contains the following components:

> (i) the principal characteristics of the plant or animal, given to it by providence for man's use, physical, medical and moral; (ii) sympathies and antipathies that it has for other living things as an expression of the innate powers, its nature-of-the-thing; (iii) its history in relation to man and the arts: how they became known and how they participated in the growth of the human arts; (iv) craft-knowledge and (v) portents associated with it.[60]

A peculiar tension inheres in the relation between the first of Pliny's descriptions and the remaining four. Pliny believed, on one hand, that plants and other animals besides humans exist for human use and, on the other hand, that study of the "nature of the thing" reveals observable relations among animals other than humans, relations that often do not involve humans at all. The elephant shows extreme gentleness toward weaker animals: "If it gets among a flock of sheep it will remove with its trunk those that come in its way, so as not unwittingly to crush one."[61] Lions detest the pranks of monkeys, and camels dislike horses.[62] The urge to document interspecies relations is sometimes frustrated by Pliny's tendency to treat one species at a time. Toward the end of book 10, for example, Pliny pauses to dwell on observable relations that persist "besides the various facts that we have stated about each species in their places"; "for animals have certain kinds of warfare and of friendships, and the feelings [*adfectus*] that result from them."[63] He then catalogs instances of birds' snatching other birds' eggs and food, disrupting each other's habitats, and generally quarreling, followed by a shorter reflection on "friendships" that "occur between peacocks and pigeons, turtle-doves and parrots, blackbirds and turtle doves, the crow and the little heron in a joint enmity against the fox," and so on.[64] Indeed, despite the species-by-species organization of the work, it is this effort to illustrate "sympathies and antipathies" across species, or what Pliny calls "concordant and discordant things that exist in nature," that Pliny himself marks as the unifying principle in the "whole of this work."[65]

Pliny's own unifying principle—the observable concord and discord between and among animals that coexist—appears to have seeped into Erasmus's work.[66] The lines of sympathy and enmity on view in cross-species interactions made those interactions particularly suitable for Erasmus's effort, capturing his imagination as they did and providing endless bases for comparison to human life and to rhetorical activity. Erasmus's devotion, his aspiration to become the Pliny of language, manifests itself in at least three ways: in his explicit instructions to study Pliny; in countless attributed and unattributed references to material Erasmus himself gleaned from the *Natural History*; and, perhaps less obvious though no less important, in his embrace of a model of rhetoric based on concord and discord.[67]

Erasmus thoroughly and effectively embedded natural history into his method of *copia*. That embeddedness helped to establish rhetorical education as fertile ground for what Findlen calls "the formation of a *scientific culture*," which she describes as "the broadening of the activities that we subsume under the category of science into new arenas: the court, the academy,

the pharmacy, the piazza, the marketplace, the museum."[68] Rather than further subsuming rhetorical education under "the academy," I offer that Erasmus's widespread training in and methods for rhetorical production, situated
so early in the lives of students across Europe, aided the very broadening into
the areas Findlen names. *De copia*, after all, was the leading early modern
rhetoric textbook; between 1512 and 1580, 168 editions were published.[69] As
Lisa Jardine details, Erasmus was very savvy when it came to publishing and
self-promotion; he was himself a hub in the publishing industry.[70] In his preface, Erasmus heaps praise on the labor of restoring the work of Pliny: "The
restoration of even a single passage will win for a man an honorable place
among the learned, for such is the splendor of Pliny's name and such the at-
traction and usefulness of his work."[71] Erasmus appears to have hitched his
aspirations to the success of the *Natural History*.

But mainly Pliny provided a treasure house model filled with a wealth of
material. In *De copia*, Pliny's treatments of animals feature most prominently
in Erasmus's discussion of comparison, and they also show up in his advice
for description, especially the Aristotelian technique of *enargeia*, vividness,
Erasmus's fifth method of enrichment, which consists "mainly in the description of things, times, places, persons."[72] Under the category "description of
things" falls just about everything that is not a time, a place, or a person. Here
Erasmus advises selectivity when the matter is serious, but when "the whole
business has no purpose but pleasure, as is usually the case with poetry, and
with display pieces which are handled precisely for the purposes of exercising and demonstrating one's ingenuity, one may indulge rather more freely
in graphic descriptions of this sort."[73] With this observation about pleasure,
developing one's "ingenuity," and also displaying it, Erasmus is now squarely
in the territory of ekphrasis and encomium considered in chapter 4. What
follows is a seemingly exhaustive list of the things vividly described by the
likes of Homer, Virgil, and Ovid, ranging from snowstorms to seditions to
processions to incantations to hunts. The catalog then turns to "descriptions
of living creatures":

> Like the electric ray and the porcupine in Claudian; the phoenix both in
> Claudian and Lactantius; the parrot in Ovid's *Amores* and in Statius; ser-
> pents in Lucan 9; all kinds of fish in Oppian; in Pliny the physical appear-
> ance, nature, and habits of countless living creatures, together with their
> natural enemies and allies, and in particular his description of the gnat; in
> Virgil the depiction of the horse and the ox and the wonderful portrayal of
> the bee . . .[74]

This discussion of describing living creatures bears close resemblance to the treatments of ekphrasis in the *progymnasmata*, especially Theon's manual, which pointed to ekphrases of specific animals in ancient writings.[75] Whereas Theon directs aspiring rhetors to Herodotus's descriptions of animals native to Egypt (the ibis, the hippopotamus, the crocodile), Erasmus includes a whole range of writers, genres of writing, and species from far-flung places. And whereas Erasmus singles out writers' names alongside their notable descriptions of particular animals (e.g., Claudian's electric ray and porcupine, Ovid's parrot, and Lucan's serpent), his treatment of Pliny stands out in this passage for his association not with accounts of particular types or species of animal, but (again) with detailed descriptions of "countless living creatures" (*innumerabilium animantium*). Erasmus recommends Pliny in a singular way yet again, this time for his expansiveness, as a resource for a seemingly infinite number of specific things to say.

Pliny's concentration on the concord and discord of the natural world itself amplifies a core principle of Erasmian humanism, the doctrine of *via diversa*, literally "different way," an approach that heeds the world's complexity and meets it by alternative paths rather than ever the same one. Thomas Sloane places *via diversa* at the center of his reading of Erasmus's rhetoric. Rhetoric is, after all, as Sloane puts it somewhat paradoxically, "anchored in contingency," and therefore needs approaches that keep open multiple avenues to knowledge/thought/small-*t* truth.[76] By following and expounding on the lives and habits of Pliny's animals, Erasmus arrives, again and again, at the twin ideas of contingency and responsiveness.

That animals act as sensuous guides for ways of living and responding becomes most apparent when Pliny appears in Erasmus's own collections, his *Parallels* and his *Adages*, exemplary compilations that effectively did the work of accumulation for readers, works he refers to in *De copia* as serving this very purpose.[77] His collection of adages expanded with each edition, growing more than fivefold from about 800 proverbs with commentary in the 1500 edition to a count of 4,251 at the time of his death.[78] Its change in title—from *Adagiorum collecteana*, "Collection of Adages" (1500), to *Adagiorum chileades*, "Thousands of Adages" (1508)—reflected an immense labor of accumulation. The proverbs amassed there frequently center on animals, a fact that has caused consternation in at least one of Erasmus's twentieth-century editors.[79]

A few extended examples of animal proverbs and parallels from these compendiums will help show how Pliny guided Erasmus's attitude toward specific nonhuman animals and pulled him different ways, *via diversa*. The adage "with ears lowered" is, according to Erasmus, "taken from work-animals who show how they feel by the movement of their ears, just as humans do with their brows and eyes."[80] The reflection combines results of his study of Pliny with other sources and implies observation:

> For, as Pliny says in book eleven, only to humans did nature give ears that do not move. The ears of work-animals and almost all quadrupeds prick up when they are listening, are languid when they are tired, twitch when they are frightened, and almost completely prick up when they are angry; they droop when the animals are sick. This is why Flaccus writes, "I droop my ears like an ill-tempered ass / When it takes up too heavy a load on its back." In fact, even today those whose hopes are disappointed are said "to lower their ears" and "to have droopy ears."[81]

Erasmus's amplification of this adage follows his own recommended method of drawing on a range of sources (study) even as it shows him comparing humans and other animals, drawing out the logic of applicability that constitutes proverbs. In the context of the *Natural History* the immovable ear detail first moves into a cross-species reflection on radically different ear morphology exhibited by stags, mice, seals, and dolphins. From there Pliny reflects on the correspondence between particular movements of beasts' ears and beasts' feelings, the catalog of which Erasmus reproduces in order.[82] These observations about the ears of quadrupeds—be they pricked or twitching, languishing or drooping—were very likely to cohere with observations of both Pliny's and Erasmus's readers. The reference to Horace's *Satire* reinforces the commonplace observations.

Erasmus's mention of Pliny's observation about humans' immovable ears follows an explicit comparison: "just as humans do with their brows and eyes."[83] In other words, humans are presented as making up for a deficit— the lack of movable ears—with other movable features. Even today, when speaking of humans, we use a version of "pricked up one's ears" to indicate captivated attention that is more likely to be visible through a tilted head, a furrowed brow, a forward lean. The point here seems to settle on readable countenances across species. And of course that *lowered* ears—*demissis auriculis*—are the ones that become proverbial must be acknowledged.

Erasmus also discusses at some length the Greek adage "adopt the outlook of the polyp."[84] The Greek word *polupodos* means simply "many footed," so the word could apply to the octopus as well as to the simpler coral-dwelling relatives of anemones still known as polyps, the ones that bend and sway. Erasmus's elaboration, especially his citation of Theognis, suggests he means an octopus. The lesson Erasmus gleans at first from this adage is "suit our-selves to every contingency in life, acting the part of Proteus, and changing ourselves into any form as the situation demands."[85] The age-old lesson of changing hues relates directly to Erasmus's instructions in *De copia*'s discus-sion of variety and attention, "to turn one idea into more shapes than Proteus himself is supposed to have turned into."[86] As Peter Mack notes in his consid-eration of this adage, though, Erasmus quickly equivocates, denouncing any reading of the adage that would lead to "a disgusting type of flattery . . . or an improper changeability in behavior."[87] The lesson, then, is to be attentive to the situation, easygoing and versatile, but not sycophantic.

Erasmus's penchant for comparison, for finding lessons for life and for rhe-torical practice in the material and observable lives of animals, evident in the adages, becomes the main event in his *Parabolae*. Mack describes this work as "a notebook of Erasmus's reading before the quotations have been transferred to a commonplace book."[88] Indeed, Erasmus's 1514 dedicatory letter to Pieter Gillis acknowledges as much:

> Of late, as I reread Aristotle, Pliny, and Plutarch for the enrichment of my
> *Adagiorum chiliades*, and cleared Annaeus Seneca of the corruptions by
> which he was not so much disfigured as done away with altogether, I noted
> down by the way these passages, to make an offering for you which I knew
> would not be unwelcome.[89]

From each of the authors mentioned, Erasmus draws comparisons from a va-riety of domains—nautical, religious, fiduciary, literary, culinary, medical—but animal lives feature in all the sources and appear with the most frequency. So from Plutarch Erasmus gleans a grumbling comparison of overly dependent students to nestlings' harassment of parent birds; several references to horses and bits, including this gem: "The horse is turned by the bit, the ship by the rudder; and men are steered by words"; a comparison of kitchen flies to op-portune friends, and of the octopus to friendship.[90] From Seneca, Erasmus records parallels between the phoenix and men of distinction (both rare); be-tween a purebred horse and a great talent who won't be burdened with public office; and this fascinatingly direct comparison of animals to passions: "No animal, tame or wild, is obedient to reason, for it has none; and the passions are like that."[91]

This last parallel deserves attention, for it encapsulates with rare directness enduring presumptions about animals and feeling that this book has brought to the fore. Erasmus draws these lines from Seneca's "Moral Letters to Lucilius." This particular comparison between animals and passions is more elaborate in Seneca, where tigers and lions illustrate the connection:

> Just as no animal, whether wild or tamed and gentle, obeys reason, since nature made it deaf to advice; so the passions do not follow or listen; however slight they are. Tigers and lions never put off their fierceness; they sometimes moderate it, and then, when you least expect it [*minime expectaveris*], their softened fierceness is roused to savageness.[92]

These fierce cats, here working as animal embodiments of *adfectus* or intense feelings, passions, nearly leap off Seneca's page just after the phrase "when you least expect it" or, to stress the looking built in to the verb *ex-specto*, when you aren't quite looking out. The comparates (animals and passions) collapse into one leaping, roaring image at this point: tigers and lions are not merely like the passions; they display, become, and incite them, with ferocious, unpredictable, and nerve-jangling intensity. The shift to the second person here (when you least expect it), that is, plays on humans' and other animals' fear of the lion's spring. Erasmus's version tames the comparison somewhat, herding the lions and tigers into a more oblique "some animals" of another comparison.[93] These animals, according to Seneca, are not equipped to hear reason. They don't speak its language. They are *alogos*, and look at what they do in the absence of *logos*. Or better, *look out*.

According to Erasmus, the final section of the *Parallels*, containing comparisons drawn from Aristotle, Pliny, and Theophrastus, are the ones that required expansion.[94] As translator R. A. B. Mynors notes, the "great bulk of the material" in this section is gleaned from Pliny's *Natural History*, which accounts for this part of the book's also containing the greatest density of parallels drawn from the lives, habits, and bodily states of nonhuman animals.[95] And so Erasmus likens the elk's thick skin to certain men's imperviousness to words; a crocodile's friendliness with the plover that cleans its teeth parallels a tyrant's self-interested kindness; an overly affectionate monkey that smothers its young to death with hugs is likened to child-spoiling parents.[96] From Pliny too, Erasmus draws a parallel between the beaver's purported tendency to castrate itself when being pursued by hunters for its genitals and the wise man's sacrifice of his possessions, surely also his downfall.[97]

Pliny's account of animal lives, therefore, is not merely an encyclopedia but is also a record of cultural observations about cross-species relations, a document of nature's astonishing variety. Erasmus follows his lead, attending to that relationality, to the observable concord and discord, the principle of *via diversa. Via diversa* informs Erasmus's rhetoric, and in general his approach to all things. The cross-species relationality stands out especially when Erasmus appears to be following his own advice to complement study with first-hand observation.

OBSERVE (THE MONKEY)

Which brings me to a little monkey. Toward the end of his lengthy discussion of description, Erasmus lingers over the importance of observation to description: "To give a satisfactory account of all these things not only requires skill and imagination, but it is very helpful to have seen with your own eyes what you wish to depict."[98] Erasmus's friendship with Thomas More in fact gave him the opportunity to observe cross-species interactions in More's own collection of animals. Evidence of that observation appears in Erasmus's correspondence, and he weaves what may have been the results of the observation into his colloquy on friendship.

In a self-described "portrait" of More that Erasmus included in a 1519 letter to the German humanist Ulrich von Hutten, Erasmus describes his friend's love for collecting animals:

> He takes a particular pleasure in contemplating the shapes, character, and behavior of different living creatures. Thus there is hardly any kind of bird of which he does not keep one in his household, and the same with any animal that as a rule is rarely seen, such as monkey, fox, ferret, weasel, and the like. Besides these, if he sees anything outlandish or otherwise remarkable, he buys it greedily, and has his house stocked with such things from all sources, so that everywhere you may see something to attract the eyes of the visitor; and when he sees other people pleased, his own pleasure begins anew.[99]

This description of More's fondness for observing animals is fascinating for a number of reasons, the first being the very existence of More's menagerie. Second, the passage underscores the work of collections during this period. No longer restricted to monarchs and conquerors, diverse collections of remarkable creatures and objects were amassed, in England anyway, by the middle class.[100] The passage works by bringing eyes before the eyes in the form of a guest's drifting and delighted attention and therefore coaxes from More's household the same point found in *De copia*'s discussion of nature's brilliant variety and its ability to meet the needs of wandering eyes and ears, easily bored. But then there are the specific kinds of animals: the monkey, the fox, the weasel. A monkey in fact appears in another famous portrait of More's household, this one originally completed by the painter Hans Holbein the Younger. The painting depicts one little monkey—More's favorite—scrambling up the skirt of More's second wife, Alice.[101] It is probably not a reach to surmise that Erasmus himself shared More's pleasure in observing the animals and was therefore a frequent source of More's own pleasure.

That the historical painter Frank Cadogan Cowper included a monkey in his 1910 work titled *Erasmus and Thomas More Visit the Children of King Henry VII at Greenwich, 1499* suggests that the monkey came to be associated with More's own character, thanks in large part to Erasmus's epistolary portrait. And one of More's monkeys makes a cameo appearance in a colloquy Erasmus published at the end of the summer of 1531, a summer he spent hosting scholars from Kraków who themselves were immersed in Pliny's *Natural History*.[102] Here the monkey and its "associates"—namely a weasel and a rabbit—return Erasmus to a point so often underscored by animal interactions as documented in this book: that all animals are partners in feeling, and in the context of conflicting animal interests, the feeling of sensation stretches to apparent feelings and actions of harmony and rivalry.

The colloquy, titled "Amicitia," which may be translated as friendship or even sympathy, is a dialogue rooted in Pliny's assertion at the end of the *Natural History* that his whole work documents the "sympathies and antipathies" of nature (the title of Erasmus's colloquy repeats the Latin word used by Pliny). The interlocutors in "Amicitia," who bear the names of two young scholars Erasmus hosted that summer, Ephorinus and John (Boner), trade story after story, derived from both study and observation, of animals' dispositions toward each other. There are assertions of "mutual enmity between foxes and kites," merlins and foxes, both presented as understandable; whereas interspecies rivalry between swans and eagles, ravens and orioles, crows and owls, and eagles and wrens perplexes the colloquy's characters.[103] Ephorinus and John also exchange stories obliquely attributed to grooms and cowherds of an ox's preference for a particular ox, a horse's for a particular horse.[104] Ephorinus, as the older of the two, is the epitome of *copia* and therefore has the most to say, until John, worried that he will contribute nothing to the discussion, relates what he once observed with his "own eyes at the house of the distinguished Englishman, Thomas More." The anecdote John proceeds to offer begins with "a large monkey" kept by More, "which at the time, as it happened, was allowed to run loose in order to recover from a wound." As John continues, his description turns into an interspecies drama:

At the end of the garden was a rabbit hutch, and a weasel had designs on the rabbits. The monkey would watch this from a distance, quietly and idly, as long as he saw the rabbits were in no danger. But after the weasel had pried the pen loose from the wall and there was now danger that the rabbits, exposed to attack from the rear, would fall prey to the enemy, the monkey dashed up and by climbing on a board pulled the pen back to its former position so skillfully that a man could not have done it better—plain evidence of the fondness monkeys have for rabbits. The rabbits themselves didn't understand their danger but kissed their enemy through the fence. The monkey came to the rescue of innocence imperiled.[105]

The three creatures in John's vignette illustrate the intricate workings of discord and concord even as they reaffirm prevailing assumptions about animals' dispositions and characters. Indeed, Ephorinus responds to the tale in this way: "Monkeys delight in all young animals and love to fondle and embrace them," an observation gleaned from Pliny.[106] In this way the colloquy weaves together insights about animal and plant life gleaned from study and from observation, exactly the advice Erasmus gives in *De copia* for generating things to say. The monkey-weasel-rabbit anecdote nicely captures the intensity of feeling especially on the part of the observers and listeners, even as it names and violates the presumed hierarchy of animal life, for in this case, the monkey was able to use its dexterity to reposition the rabbit pen with more skill than even a human.

In the context of the colloquy, the anecdote leads Ephorinus first to wonder if the monkey was properly rewarded (he was, with a scrap of bread) and then to return to Pliny's sentiment at the end of *Natural History*, and the unifying principle of the colloquy: the world teems with concordant and discordant relations. That allusion to Pliny's own unifying principle harks back to the idea of human and nonhuman animals as partners in feeling, discussed in this book's introduction, this time linking it to the raison d'être of rhetoric itself: differently aligned interests, discordant inclinations. And while the line between amusing stories and ethical insight is nearly imperceptible in Erasmus, this anecdote exploits that imperceptibility, tacitly suggesting that humans might learn from monkeys. Such an idea is brought out at the colloquy's conclusion when John complains that he does not "yet see the point of all this talk." Ephorinus lays out part of the lesson this way: a person "should avoid the company of those characters he finds incompatible with his own and associate with those to whom he is drawn by natural sympathy."[107] This sentiment connects to the adage listed first as a "favorable omen" in Erasmus's *Adagia*, "friends hold all things in common" (*amicorum communia omnia*). There, as in the colloquy, he elaborates the adage with reference to Christian virtue and social harmony.[108] That such insight can be conveyed through the conflicting interests and wiles of monkeys and weasels means that Erasmus plumbs the depths of his own study and his observations—of Pliny's storehouse and More's menagerie, both model collections.[109]

IMITATE (BEES)

Study and observation alone, of course, do not make a good orator, and Erasmus knows this well. Indeed, study and observation feed and draw from the broader culture of accumulation, which, as Susan Stewart argues in her consideration of collecting, "replaces production with consumption."[110] Yet the aim of Erasmus's *copia* diverges from the culture of accumulation at this very point: the point of rhetorical accumulation is production. The collection of things—insights, ideas—gleaned from observation and from study needs to be accessible for later use. Indeed, in several places in *De copia* Erasmus worries about the "undigested multitude of things" that might result from his method of accumulation.[111] For a suitable model of accumulation that does not end with the mere fact of accumulation, Erasmus turns to bees, following a long line of writers in advising his readers to imitate them.

The place where bees enter Erasmus's picture is crucial for his overall point about the act of accumulating. Late in *De copia* he advises students on how to organize their material in a navigable way:

> Prepare for yourself a sufficient number of headings, and arrange them as you please, subdivide them into appropriate sections, and under each section add your commonplaces and maxims; and then whatever you come across in any author, particularly if it is rather striking [*insignias*], you will be able to note down immediately in the proper place, be it an anecdote or a fable or an illustrative example or a strange incident or a maxim or a witty remark or a remark notable for some other quality or a proverb or a metaphor or a simile.[112]

These lines of course—instructions for how to keep a commonplace book—are themselves historical gems.[113] But equally interesting for historians of rhetoric is the subsequent expansion of these instructions, because Erasmus explicitly urges disciplinary variety, the source of this chapter's second epigraph: "No discipline is so remote from rhetoric that you cannot use it to enrich your collection."[114] After a trek through mathematics and numbers, seemingly the furthest from rhetoric ("Mathematics seems utterly remote, yet it will provide you with comparisons),"[115] Erasmus settles in again with *"physica"* (natural science) and lists useful similes and examples, hewing closely to Pliny without naming him.[116] With the handy Latin *itaque*, a common adverbial transition suitable for comparisons, and one that carries everything forward in the name of method—*and so, in this way*—Erasmus winds up his discussion of how and what to aggregate from such a range of disciplines with an elaborate and well-known comparison to the cumulative work of bees:

> In this way a studious one will flit like a diligent little bee through all the gardens of authors, will light on every blossom collecting a little nectar from all parts, and carry it back to its hive. Since there is such an abundance [*fecunditas*] of this material [*rerum*] that all will not be able to be enjoyed, [the student] will choose the most extraordinary and fit it into the structure of his own work.[117]

With this advice to act as bees toward other writings, Erasmus invokes a long tradition of bee comparisons.[118] Earlier in the treatise he mentions Virgil's famous reflection on bees. Pliny all but bows to the bees, assigning them "chief place" among the insects and devoting the largest proportion of book 11 to details about their lives and labors.[119] Perhaps the most intriguing feature of Erasmus's passage, though, is the way bees model both comprehensiveness and finitude—the bee visits "all the gardens" and collects from "all the parts" but a little nectar, only the most extraordinary, *praecipua*, a word that signals peculiarity or distinction. The repetition of forms of the adjective *omnis* (all) in this passage gestures to expansiveness and even infinity, while the selectivity of the distinct offers a necessary limit. Bees effectively keep Erasmus tied to Pliny's particular yet infinite world.

Indeed, Erasmus's *Parallels* extracts an impressive thirteen comparisons from Pliny's discussion of bees, and in his preface to the 1525 edition of the *Natural History*, Erasmus makes special note of a passage of Pliny's on bees that he worked to restore.[120] The insight in *De copia* about drawing from multiple disciplines—all the gardens—inheres in this lengthy reflection on material drawn from Pliny:[121]

> Bees do not collect everything indiscriminately from every source, but bee-glue from one place, pitch-wax from another, from another propolis, from another bee-bread or offspring or honey. In the same way one should not

expect to find everything in the same author, but select from each the most useful thing he has. From poets and orators one gets splendor of language, from logicians skill in arguments, from philosophers a knowledge of nature, from theologians the principles of the good life.[122]

Here Erasmus coaxes readers to note what kinds of things one might extract from what kinds of authors, augmenting his point in *De copia* about the usefulness—the specific usefulness—of a variety of disciplinary perspectives. Again, particularity resides with seeming infinity, guiding and promoting the principle of *via diversa*.

Bees may be found in several of Erasmus's works. For instance, in his dialogue on Latin style, titled *Ciceronianus*, the character Bulephorus follows a description of Cicero's broad reading and careful selection with "examples offered us by nature."[123] His first example expounds on bees:

Bees don't collect the material for making honey from just one bush, do they? No, they flit in their wonderful busy way round every type of flower, herb, and bush, often going far afield for the stuff to store in their hive. And what they bring is not honey to begin with. They turn it into a liquid in their mouths and inner parts, and then reproduce it, transmuted into their own substance; in it one recognizes not the taste or smell of any flower or shrub the bee has sipped, but a creation of the bee itself, compounded from all the contributory elements.[124]

This passage emphasizes the idea of the compound—the having been compounded (*temperatum*)—a transformation so radical that the smells and tastes of the mingled substances are no longer discernible.

Comprehensiveness, selectivity, transformation, particularity sipped from infinity.[125] These are the bee principles Erasmus deems worthy of imitation. After all, as the pithy adage Erasmus attributes indirectly to Sappho formulates it, *neque mel, neque apes*: no bees, no honey.[126]

COLLECTED MEMORY

Without bees, too, Erasmus might be left without a way to animate the process of accumulation and might find himself with a collection of flat and useless objects, what Terence Cave, in a reading of Quintilian on memory and *copia*, calls "a store of inert goods."[127] The movement of the bee and the transformability of the nectar both matter a good deal for Erasmus's method. And that transformability helps drive home the point of this book: in the context of rhetoric and language, nonhuman animals keep things moving and changing. They keep sensation at the fore. When it comes to memory, that all-important faculty for the art of rhetoric, a "store of inert goods" will not get you far, but a storehouse buzzing and oozing with varied substances resulting from lively activity might do the trick.

Mary Carruthers's wide-ranging study of medieval memory contains a fascinating meditation on the significance of bees (and birds as well) for conceptions of memory.[128] The contents of medieval memory "were imagined as alive (animals and birds) or as materials to be used richly in the commerce of creative thought (coins, jewels, food)."[129] Erasmus's model of memory falls very much in this tradition, harking back to the ancients, as it did for the medievals. Erasmus's cumulative method of study yields a *thesaurus* or storehouse (a word he uses repeatedly, as do Quintilian and Cicero), a collected memory. But his talk of storing things accumulated in topical "nests" or pigeonholes (the Latin word is a form of *nidus*)[130] and his repetition of ancient advice to imitate bees make learning and storing a matter of keeping for later use.

Pliny devotes considerable attention to honey making, describing how bees must collect nectar from flowers and leaves and carry it in their stomachs. The substance that will become honey, then,

> having been sipped from foliage and pastures and having been collected into the stomachs of bees—for they throw it up out of their mouths, and in addition being tainted by the juice of flowers, and soaked in the corruptions of the belly, and so often transformed, nevertheless it brings with it the great pleasure of its heavenly nature.[131]

The process as Pliny presents it may be tainted (*corruptus*), but the pleasure (*voluptatem*) of honey of course derives from its sweetness, and its invention must also tinge the words themselves with that quality.[132] And so the bees entail not only buzzing and flitting but also, with time, sweetness; and used in the context of *copia*, they keep alive the enduring Homeric notion of honeyed words.[133] Indeed, Erasmus's short colloquy on copiousness includes this paragraph under the heading "comparison by simile": "'Your letter was more delectable than all ambrosia or nectar.' 'Your letter was sweeter to me than any honey.' 'Your kind epistle far surpassed all carob and Attic honey and sugar, nectar, and ambrosia of the gods,'" which then concludes with this principle: "Whatever is enhanced by sweetness can be utilized here."[134]

Of course bees and honey were by no means Pliny's only concern, and Erasmus advises his compilers to "memorize the quality of a great many" of the subjects of natural science. Animals, or things about animals, collected through study and observation in the context of rhetorical education, draw on, replicate, and arguably feed the broader trend of accumulation and of accumulating animals, but only to a point, and that point is inventional and also, as it turns out, ethical.

While it may be tempting and not wholly incorrect to conclude that such replication implicates rhetorical education in exploitation and cruelty toward animals, the close observation of animals seems to have had (for the time at least) mixed implications for human dispositions toward other species. Erasmus, like his friend Thomas More, believed hunting to be wasteful, foolish, and unnatural.[135] In a particularly sharp critique of "the cruelty of man," Erasmus inveighs against the "tyranny of the stomach" that leads people to eat the ox "who had supported the ungrateful family for so long with his hard labor."[136] Erasmus is by no means the first to worry about the customs supporting such cruelty, and he raises this point as part of his amplification of the adage "war is sweet to one who has not tried it."[137] Life—in all its variegated, harmonious, and discordant forms—mattered to Erasmus and fed his outlook.

And so study, observation, and imitation yield a variety of relations with nonhuman animals, some of them contradictory. They are at once figured as brutes, beneath humans, and as marvels of nature. Bees and Milo's growing calf inspire awe, and both in their own ways heed a principle of *accumulatio*. *Accumulatio* in the context of rhetorical abundance therefore results in collected memory, but that memory, thanks in part to the work of nonhuman animals—studied, observed, and imitated—is far from inert and teems with the active and interactive material of nature, in all its rich and sensuous variety. Variety, after all, brings energy to every sphere, including all the disciplines Erasmus believes rhetoric should draw from. This includes the hue-changing cuttlefish and the nimble, dexterous monkey as much as the flitting bee, transforming its collected substances into abundant sweetness.[138] In these ways and for these reasons Erasmus kept animals alive in his method of *copia*, feeding the sensuous side of rhetoric and drawing out contradictory—even incommensurable—modes of relation. Decades ago, Walter Ong placed Erasmus in a group of historical figures who took a "rhetorical approach to life."[139] And nonhuman animals, especially as manifest in natural history, brought life to Erasmus's theory of rhetoric.

At the Feet of Rhetorica

Consider the sketch shown in figure 1, a reproduction of one of sixteen en-graved "symbolic images" (*icones symboles*) of the liberal arts—this one depicts rhetoric—that organized the holdings by subject matter at a Milanese library in the early part of the seventeenth century.[1] Other emblems of Rhetorica re-ceive—and received—more attention than this one, despite its fascinating ex-plication in a speech (or sermon) delivered in 1626 by Christophoro Giarda, a Barnabite priest and teacher of rhetoric.[2] A mere glance at the emblem Giarda describes (which I will refer to as Giarda's Rhetorica) will suggest its par-ticular allure for this study. Rhetorica holds in her right hand a snake-wound scepter known as the caduceus; her left makes the gesture of an orator.[3] Her ornate robes epitomize the flowering of the stylistic component of rhetoric.[4] Throughout this book, though, my analysis has resided for the most part in the accompaniments shown in the lower third of the image, tucked into the folds of Rhetorica's skirt: on her left a three-headed beast, and on her right a blazing cauldron and golden spurs. I will begin, as I have thus far, with the beast(s) at the other end of the golden chains descending from Rhetorica's mouth, the links between language and nonhuman animals perhaps nowhere more visible. On Giarda's reading, the three chains signify high, middle, and low style, and they evoke the image—well known at the time—of Gallic Her-cules, "his tongue pierced with fine chains" that link to the ears of his follow-ers, an image made available to early moderns by Erasmus's 1512 translation of "Gallic Hercules" by Lucian of Samosata and emblematized by Andrea Alciato in 1531.[5]

RHETORICA

FIGURE 1. *Rhetorica*, Christoforo Giarda, *Bibliothecae Alexandrinae Icones Symbolicae*, 1628. By permission of the Folger Shakespeare Library.

But the nature and identity of the beasts themselves have puzzled the handful of rhetoric scholars who have considered Giarda's Rhetorica in any sustained way. Heinrich Plett calls them "the three-headed hell-hound Cerberus," but that interpretation is, I think, undermined by the appearance of three distinct species.[6] Raymond B. Waddington, in a remarkable encyclopedia entry on rhetoric's iconography, opts for a more opaque and incongruous reading of the "rather jolly, three-headed monster," a revival of an image of rhetoric as a chimera depicted by the early emblematist Achille Bocchi.[7] But Bocchi's writhing lion-goat-serpent monster, a fascinating image on its own, bears little resemblance to this one.[8] Famous art historian Ernst Gombrich does not even hazard a guess. He describes the chains, the fiery pot, and the entwined serpents that form Rhetorica's caduceus but oddly makes no mention of the three-headed beast.[9] Giarda himself offers little help in this regard; the Latin motto that accompanies the first edition uses a rather generic epithet "*domitrix ferarum*," tamer of animals, to characterize Rhetorica's relation to the beasts; that phrase was excised for the second edition.[10] Giarda's lecture mentions, almost in passing, that the chimeric animal bears witness to Rhetorica's victory.[11] The nature of Rhetorica's three-headed beast deserves further scrutiny. Using visual antecedents from the then relatively new tradition of emblem books, I will offer an alternative account of the image. That interpretation allows me to reflect on the importance of rhetoric to a fuller picture of animal-human relations, and "full" here ought to be taken in two ways: comprehensiveness and material, sensible density—an account of rhetoric that brims with its many moving, lively, active, entangled elements. Giarda's Rhetorica therefore allows me to revisit arguments I have been making throughout this book for a livelier conception of rhetoric's past, even as the nature of the beast presents a mystery worth trying to solve.

EMBLEMATIC ANTECEDENTS

Two important visual clues about the beast in Giarda's Rhetorica appear in Cesare Ripa's *Iconologia*, the most consulted Renaissance compendium of ancient Egyptian, Greek, and Roman allegorical figures. First published in 1593 without images, the *Iconologia* of 1603 was augmented by woodcut illustrations, and the book subsequently became a resource for painters, sculptors, woodcut makers, and engravers such as the artist who created the sixteen liberal arts for the library at Giarda's school.[12]

The first visual clue appears in the illustration of Ripa's *Persuasione* (1613), seen in figure 2. As described by Ripa, the figure of Persuasion is shown here

PERSVASIONE.

FIGURE 2. *Persuasione* (Cesare Ripa, *Iconologia*, 1613). Getty Research Institute, Los Angeles (2822-310).

bound with a golden cord, the end of which restrains another three-headed beast.

Whereas Giarda does not identify the beast heads in his Rhetorica, Ripa's description dwells on the tricephalic animal, a cat, a dog, and a monkey. According to Ripa's accompanying description, each animal face adds to a dispositional composite:

> The three-faced animal shows the need for three things, each of which must be had to result in persuasion. The first must be benevolence, as shown on the face of the dog who fawns for her interest. It also must be teachable in order to persuade, as shown by the monkey, who of all the other animals

seems to understand the concepts of men; and still he must maneuver with care, as shown by the cat, who is diligent in its actions, and attentive. She is holding the rope of said animal with both hands, because if persuasion does not have these harbingers, she does not exist, or moves weakly.[13]

As Helen F. North points out, the three dispositional qualities embodied by the dog, cat, and monkey—benevolence, teachability, and attentiveness—align with the "the familiar aims of the Exordium of a speech, going back at least to the rhetorician Theodectes in the fourth century B.C."[14] Ripa's three bestial heads therefore keep with the findings of this book, embodying as they do attitude and feeling, rhetoric's less than rational qualities. Ripa's parting observation about the indispensability of these qualities refers directly to the rope she grips with both hands—they are important, and without them persuasion, the third of three central movements of rhetoric (to teach, to delight, to move), grinds to a halt. The attitudinal force of Ripa's chimera is fascinating in itself, and the image also invokes a variety of sensations. The golden cord, not unlike the golden chains as style in the image discussed by Giarda, signify, according to Ripa, "the sweetness of eloquent speech, which binds us to others."[15] A number of components exhibited by Ripa's Persuasion and Giarda's Rhetorica support my theory that the artist consulted Ripa: the golden cord and chains, the beast with three heads and their placid dispositions. Yet for all that the beast of Giarda's Rhetorica does not quite resemble the cat-dog-monkey trio. The heads themselves must convey a different set of associations.

A second important clue appears in the illustration, new to the 1613 edition of Ripa's *Iconologia*, of the figure Consiglio (fig. 3). As the description, also newly expanded for the edition, explains, Consiglio holds in his right hand a book that serves as an owl's perch; he stands on a dolphin and a bear and wears around his neck a long chain bearing a large rounded heart.[16] And there, perched like a falcon on Consiglio's left hand, are three disembodied heads that bear a striking resemblance to the beasts of Giarda's Rhetorica.

Ripa's description characterizes them as a wolf, a lion, and a dog. He presents the tree animal heads as the past, present, and future, and on the same page he links them to prudence.[17] The chimeric component of Giarda's Rhetorica, on my reading, fuses the animal heads held by Ripa's Consiglio with the beast restrained by his Persuasion.[18] Such fusions were not at all uncommon, and this particular fusion acknowledges how rhetoric exceeds persuasion.

Ripa's own source for the temporal associations with the wolf-lion-dog trio, the *Saturnalia* of the fifth-century Roman writer Macrobius, was treasured during the early modern period, and its first book, where the relevant

FIGURE 3. *Consiglio* (Cesare Ripa, *Iconologia*, 1613). Getty Research Institute, Los Angeles (2822-310).

description appears, primarily concerns the Roman calendar and documents the variety of ways of worshiping the sun.[19] The specific passage Ripa cites is Macrobius's description of Sarapis, the sun god at Alexandria:

> The city bordering on Egypt, which boasts of Alexander of Macedon as its founder, worships Sarapis and Isis with an almost crazed veneration. Yet the city gives evidence that it is really offering up that worship to the sun under Sarapis' name, when it sets a basket atop his head or joins to his image the statue of a three-headed creature: its middle head—the largest—has the appearance of a lion; on the right the head of a dog rears up, tame and fawning, and the left part of the neck ends in the head of a rapacious wolf. A serpent with its coils binds these figures together, while its head returns

to the god's right hand, which keeps the monster at bay. The lion's head, then, points to the present time, poised for action, powerful and urgent, between the past and the future, while the wolf's head signifies time past, because the memory of bygone events is snatched up and carried off; similarly, the image of the fawning dog represents future events, which hope— uncertain though it is—presents to us with winning aspect.[20]

Macrobius's striking association of the wolf with the past, the lion with the present, and the dog with the future derives its reading from qualities distinct to each species. Note how vividly Macrobius presents each head: the "powerful and urgent" lion, "poised for action"; the snatching and transporting wolf; the "fawning" dog. Such dispositional tendencies are the reason nonhuman animals show up so frequently in the emblem tradition and—as I argued in chapters 2 and 4—in its partner art of stylistic depiction. The dog, pure futurity, may hold still in the depiction, but the depiction entails the dog's bounding, paradoxically encapsulating its movement. And the lion, too, works paradoxically by mediating what by definition is not mediated—immediacy, the now. The wolf is particularly noteworthy here because his violent and hungry snatching vivifies the act of forgetting, making it paradoxically memorable. For such was the work of descriptions like Macrobius's: to seal open the phantasic eyes of memory in much the same way as Albert the Great's charging ram discussed in chapter 5.[21]

To my eyes, trained in rhetoric, the association of this complex figure with time and with prudence stands out as the most suggestive evidence that the heads of the beast depicted in Giarda's Rhetorica are wolf, lion, and dog.[22] Rhetoric scholars know that the link between rhetoric and prudence is crucial, in Robert Hariman's phrasing, for a "full realization of rhetoric as a reflective practice that contributes to the common good."[23] Victoria Kahn, reflecting on early humanism, follows two assumptions about prudence from the quattrocento humanists to at least Erasmus: "First, the prudence or practical reason that is deliberation about action in a social and political context is also at work in the artist's production of a work of art. Prudence is, in this sense, the precondition of artistic decorum, just as it is of ethical decorum."[24] The upshot of Kahn's observation—and her book more generally—is that art, prudence, and rhetoric were coiled as tightly together as the serpent wrapped around the wolf-lion-dog trio in Cartari's icon of Sarapis.[25]

The beast's three heads also evoke Aristotle, for whose theories of rhetoric prudence was paramount.[26] Aristotle's *Rhetoric* had been translated into the Italian vernacular in the sixteenth century (and into Latin even earlier), thereby increasing the likelihood that the creator of the Rhetorica emblem for the library at Milan would have been familiar with that text; indeed, Ripa cites the first book of Aristotle's *Rhetoric*.[27] Also familiar, then, were the three genera of Aristotelian rhetoric: judicial, the genre concerned with past actions in a forensic sense; epideictic, that of the present; and deliberative, which, doglike, looks toward an as yet unknown future.[28] Giarda's Rhetorica compresses into the tricephalic beast a notion of temporality, its movement, and the pressing simultaneity of past, present, and future, a simultaneity that disrupts even Aristotle's attempt at tidy distinctions.

CONSTITUTIVE BEASTS, RHETORIC'S FEELING

Together with its Ripan forebears, Giarda's icon therefore renders visible, there at the feet of Rhetorica, the argument I have been making in this book about the constitutive role of nonhuman animals. The constitutive point is glaringly and wonderfully made by Persuasion's two-handed grip on the leash and by Ripa's description, the concluding line of which notes that without this cord she either does not exist or moves but weakly.[29] As such, the cord and Giarda's chains restrain and control, of course, but they also connect and coordinate the fantastical human and beast figures, making them move together, the three-headed beast an animate and animating, sensed and sensing force.

A similarly animate point is conveyed in the case of Giarda's Rhetorica by the object that appears in apposition to the wolf-lion-dog beast: the blazing pot—and the passions its burning evokes—instantly transforming what it comes in contact with. Giarda mentions the pot in a few places. The pot's fire is the likely reference in the phrase *terroris fulmen*, included in the motto appended to the image in the second edition of Giarda's lectures, which translates "fire of terror"; *fulmen* often denotes a flash, as in lightning, and so it depicts the sudden transformation of state that happens when one becomes engulfed in, say, anger or fear, or strong sensation; indeed, Aristotle's explanation of the senses in *De anima* begins by likening them to fire in that they can exist only in relation to external bodies, in what he calls potentiality.[30] Giarda explains the fiery pot with more detail: "If he is to be effective, the orator must first burn himself. For this reason, a blazing pot has been placed discreetly beside her."[31] The fiery pot therefore conjures the theory most pointedly formulated by Quintilian that all attempts at passion (*adfectus omnes*) will "inevitably languish, unless they are kindled into flame by voice, face, and bearings of virtually the whole body."[32]

Given the connections this book has followed, the otherwise odd elements of Giarda's engraved subject are perhaps not as surprising as they might have been. *Phantasia*, the sensuous capacity that reinforces, replaces, and depends on direct sensation, has figured prominently into my account of nonhuman animals in the history of rhetoric, and *phantasia*'s imaginative and pedagogical prospects may be located in the emblem tradition as well. Emblems of course prompted encomiastic expositions, as in the case of Giarda, and as with fable, the animals featured there keep things moving.

Indeed, in many ways Ripa's Persuasion and Giarda's Rhetorica, as part of the emblem tradition, bundle together a number of the areas this book documents as those where nonhuman animals became crucial for rhetoric. By several accounts, the emblem tradition carried on that of the otherwise fading memory arts discussed in chapter 5, and, of course, it famously served a pedagogical function as well.[33] It was, after all, the job of emblems to encourage a kind of instantaneous bringing before the eyes of the kind Aristotle discussed at length in the *Rhetoric*. Gombrich, too, points out relations among emblems, feeling, and sensation: "In Giarda the ultimate function of the visual symbol is to kindle love through vision. In Ripa we are nearer the established view of the didactic image as a substitute for and supplement of the written word."[34] Fables as allegories are embedded in the very definition of emblem; early modern emblem books were both the visual equivalents of and counterparts to fable and to Erasmian *copia*.[35] If emblems gather together all these places where nonhuman animals appear in the context of rhetoric—the sensuous feelings persistent in *alogos* first theorized by Aristotle, zoostylistics, fables, ekphrastic and encomiastic description, memory arts, *copia*—then bestial emblematic accompaniments to rhetoric and persuasion intensify the effect of that felt presence. It is no wonder a single-headed beast would not suffice for Ripa's Persuasion or for the Rhetorica of Giarda's artist.

EMBLEMS, ANIMAL STUDIES, TRANSDISCIPLINARY RHETORIC

Despite its prominence and durability, and despite the frequent iconographic appearance of nonhuman animals, the emblem tradition remains largely separate from animal studies. This exclusion is likely because, like fable, emblems are judged to be open-and-shut cases of cooptation, of the use of animals in service of a seemingly fusty and outdated notion of symbols, far removed from animal lives.[36] Yet to ignore that tradition altogether is to miss a major part of the felt presence, the lived movement, the spirit and the energy with which nonhuman animals historically enlivened and helped materialize the less than rational features of communication, deliberation, persuasion, and eloquence—language in all its transactional, rhetorical manifestations. In other words, there is more to the story than the one-way absorption told by anthropocentrism.

As the chapters of this book demonstrate, nonhuman animals bring energy to language in its broadest, fullest conception—verbal and bodily, rational and sensuous—and to the teaching and theorizing of its artful use. In that context in particular, attention to nonhuman animals draws out a powerful and decidedly sensuous history of rhetoric, one that refuses an account of rhetoric as a collection of disembodied, cerebral concepts and demands a reconsideration of concepts themselves as the material, enacted, lived, bodily, sensuous, and sense-activating things they are. In documenting that relation, this account of nonhuman animals in the history of rhetoric stands as a reminder that what seems merely metaphorical or even decorative usually harks back to a persistent, transactional, material relation. Indeed, as Nietzsche formulates it, the transference of metaphor begins with sense perception, an observation that potentially deactivates the adjective "mere" when it comes to metaphor.[37] The particular relations between language, rhetoric, and different kinds of animals documented in this book shape and are shaped by imaginative, sensuous activity, activity not always beginning or ending with human animals, but arising in what might be called cross-species partnerships.

I chose to end this book by inspecting the nonhuman animals in these astonishing early modern emblems less to decipher a hieroglyphic code than to follow their *phantasic* suggestiveness, their ability to enliven the imagination.[38] That following joins the other followings in this book to make explicit the constitutive capacity of nonhuman animals in relation to matters of rhetoric. Despite attempts to cleave animals from language once and for all, animals repeatedly found their way back in, and importantly so. Aristotle's famous denial of language to animals, as chapter 1 suggests, also had an underexplored attributive and binding force, as it makes all living animals partners in sensation. Dwelling with that insight as a possibility rather than dismissing it as an error of denial helps to more productively read animal relations back through rhetoric's key texts and traditions. Such an examination does not always follow the script of contemporary animal studies, in part because scholarship that capitulates so fully to that script struggles to add much to what begin to seem like preset conclusions about hierarchies.

And so, while I have engaged the spirit of animals studies by beginning foremost with the bees, the bedbugs, the crocodiles, the birds, and the dogs that, along with other animals, turn up in premodern and early modern rhetorical theory and rhetorical education, I do not always arrive at the same conclusions. Rather than finding everywhere a firm hierarchy of human over nonhuman, I have tried throughout this book to take seriously what animals besides human ones have long brought to the art of rhetoric. Yet despite the fact that the texts and teachings I have considered have humans at their center, the art of rhetoric is not just an open-and-shut case of nonhuman animals serving human ones in a field. Indeed, nonhuman animals were partnered with human ones in the context of feeling, and certain strains of and moments in rhetorical theory showcase that partnership. Reexamining the seemingly most human art from the point of view of transactional, cross-species partnership helps account for the way animals frequently turn up in traditions of style, endured as teachers of deliberation and sensuous language, lingering in—or charging through—medieval memory arts, enlivening the matter of early modern *copia*, and persisting in emblems of eloquence. And that accounting is enabled by suspending a conclusion of one-way cooptation as well as a presumption of deliberateness. In other words, in all likelihood human actants of Western rhetoric's past did not deliberately work to include nonhuman animals in rhetoric's texts and traditions. It may be that they had no choice. This book considers nonhumans too, in all their lively energy, and what Pliny characterizes as concordant and discordant relations with each other, as actors in rhetorical theory. Nonhumans drew in their human counterparts, inviting wonder and amazement, and that world mixing became a potent and underconsidered feature of language itself, its learning, its use.

My brief concluding trek into early modern bestial-rhetorical emblemata by no means exhausts the subject, but it does reinforce visually my claims about the persistent presence of nonhuman animals in rhetorical theory and rhetorical education. Giarda's and Ripa's ekphrastic, encomiastic subjects also return to arguments I have been making throughout the book about the interpretive and historical costs of omitting rhetoric and rhetorical theory from studies of animals in the critical humanities, and about the importance of remaining open to transdisciplinarity, refusing strict periodizing in a way that ties together, in this instance, areas of study that were more blended and fluid in the premodern and early modern West. Such a disciplinary confluence is difficult to see from the standpoint of the inexorably divided disciplines of the twenty-first century, yet it is crucial to remember it for the sake of interpretive rigor.[39] Rhetoric may not be deemed central to the liberal arts (or what US institutions call the humanities) these days, but it was then, and in profound and durable ways that this book has documented, ways that others working in allied traditions (literature, philosophy) have heretofore only barely considered.

My own choice in this book, then, has been to tack loosely with key teaching texts, specifically those in the Aristotelian and school manual (*progymnasmata*) vein. This choice stems from what I see as the need to acknowledge the importance of these traditions to studies of poetics, of philosophy, and of scientific culture. That the *progymnasmata* are malleable and are still today adapted to education in a variety of contexts, including religious ones, only increases the stress I have placed on their cultural and educational significance. Sensation-wise, my findings often highlight and perhaps replicate, which is to say follow, a historical preference for the visual, but not without acknowledging the omnipresence and simultaneity of other senses, especially the sonic and the haptic, though there is surely work to be done on notions of taste and smell. After all, in the theories and traditions this book has examined, *phantasia*, rhetoric's primary mode of activating sensation, whether through the deliberative imagining of painful futures or the conjuring of memories, both facilitates and is facilitated by all faculties of sensation, especially those that join to register pleasure and pain. Such findings are only a small part of the story of rhetoric and sensation, but they are integral to this one, which began with, and has at every turn been constituted by, nonhuman animals.

NOTES

INTRODUCTION

1. Aristotle, *Rhetoric*, 2.3.1380a.24–26 (my translation).

2. Homer, *The Odyssey* 14.33–35; trans. Robert Fagles, 302. Cunning: *kerdosunē*.

3. Aristotle, *The "Art" of Rhetoric*, trans. John Henry Freese, 186n*a*; Aristotle, *Rhetoric: A Theory of Civic Discourse*, trans. George A. Kennedy, 122n19.

4. Liliane Bodson, "Motivations for Pet-Keeping," 27–41. For a discussion of animals in archaic life, see John Heath, *The Talking Greeks*, 1–6: "Animals were never merely mirrors of ideology but living, breathing, odorous, and unwitting partners in a struggle for survival" (4). For a brief but wide-ranging discussion of dogs in the context of ancient pet keeping, see Michael MacKinnon, "Pets," 270–74. There are also literary and dramatic pre-texts for this instance. See the taxonomy of nonverbal canine communication developed by R. M. Harriott, "The Argive Elders, the Discerning Shepherd and the Fawning Dog: Misleading Communication in the *Agamemnon*," 14. See also James M. Redfield's lengthy and illuminating discussion of dogs in Homer in *Nature and Culture in the "Iliad*," 193–203. Two additional relevant works are Saara Lilja, *Dogs in Ancient Greek Poetry*, and Gilbert P. Rose, "Odysseus' Barking Heart."

5. Mark Payne, *The Animal Part*, 8; George A. Kennedy, "A Hoot in the Dark"; see also Debra Hawhee, "Looking into Aristotle's Eyes."

6. Kennedy, "Hoot"; Alex C. Parrish, *Adaptive Rhetoric*. See especially Parrish's discussion of ants and dogs, 43–44. Diane Davis is at work on a book that draws out implications that biological animal research holds for rhetoric and rhetorical theory. See also Davis, "Creaturely Rhetorics." For an account of Kenneth Burke's ruminations on animal communication, see Debra Hawhee, "Kenneth Burke's Jungle Book."

7. Jacques Derrida, *The Animal That Therefore I Am*.

8. For a lucid discussion of the terminology of "animal studies" versus "animality studies," see Marianne DeKoven, "Why Animals Now?" 368n3. I don't wish to elide the philosophical

distinctions between the two terms, but from this point I will use "animal studies" to refer to current work in these emerging fields in the critical humanities.

9. Many works in animal studies productively bring together philosophy and literature. See, for example, Karl Steel, *How to Make a Human*; Payne, *Animal Part*; Erica Fudge, *Perceiving Animals*. Gordon Lindsay Campbell, editor of the remarkable *Oxford Handbook of Animals in Classical Thought and Life*, notes in his introduction to the volume that his "main interest" had been "in literary and philosophical animals in the ancient world," but that in response to encouragement from the anonymous readers and Oxford University Press editors, he "broadened out the book to include the realities of animals in the ancient world," xv.

10. The best work here has remarkable revelatory power, demonstrating, for example, culturally embedded notions of violence in the case of Steel's work in *How to Make a Human* on medieval logics of dominion, or a "cosmic citizenship" by focusing on animals in Shakespearean drama as Laurie Shannon does in *The Accommodated Animal*.

11. Susan Crane, *Animal Encounters*, 4.

12. Crane, *Animal Encounters*, 3, brings "literary approaches to genre, language, gender, and culture with perspectives from evolutionary biology, taxonomy, language acquisition, ethology, and environmental studies." DeKoven makes important connections between feminist theory and posthuman studies of animals and animality ("Why Animals Now?," 366–67). Shannon's *Accommodated Animal* works magisterially at the border of literature and law.

13. Of course there were various points of flourishing, but the exercises do not seem to have disappeared entirely at any one point. See Donald Lemen Clark, "The Rise and Fall of Progymnasmata in Sixteenth and Seventeenth Century Grammar Schools."

14. Chapters 3 and 4 focus on the *progymnasmata*, on which the scholarship in rhetorical studies is vast. Donald Lemen Clark and George Kennedy both offer useful introductions; see Clark, "Rise and Fall," and Kennedy, ed. and trans., "Introduction," in *Progymnasmata: Greek Textbooks of Prose Composition and Rhetoric*, ix–xvi. For the *progymnasmata* in the early modern period, see Francis Johnson, "Two Renaissance Textbooks of Rhetoric: Aphthonius' 'Progymnasmata' and Rainolde's 'A Booke Called the Foundacion of Rhetorike'"; Thomas Baldwin, *William Shakspere's Small Latine and Lesse Greeke*, vol. 2; and Manfred Kraus, "Aphthonius and the Progymnasmata in Rhetorical Theory and Practice." See also the discussion by Christy Desmet, "Progymnasmata, Then and Now," 188–90. A case in point of the costs of ignoring rhetoric's texts and traditions may be found in a recent book-length consideration of literary character by Bruce Boehrer, whose exclusive reliance on a poetic tradition misses a major source for the act of characterization: the *progymnasma ethopoeia*, often referred to as characterization, which emerges directly from skills built in the fable exercises, frequently using nonhuman animals, as I discuss in chapter 3 (Boehrer, *Animal Characters*). For a broader work on Shakespeare and early modern education, see Lynn Enterline, *Shakespeare's Schoolroom*.

15. John Muckelbauer, "Domesticating Animal Theory," 98.

16. Davis, "Creaturely Rhetorics," 91. Parrish's *Adaptive Rhetoric* springs from a healthy resistance to the field's habit of recoiling from arguments based in biology. Parrish's mission, on my reading, is in step with feminist biologist Elizabeth A. Wilson, *Psychosomatic: Feminism and the Neurological Body,* and also of course Donna Haraway, e.g., "In the Beginning Was the Word: The Genesis of Biological Theory," and more recently, Haraway, *The Companion Species Manifesto*. Like Davis, Parrish works to challenge such foundational presumptions.

17. One of the most compelling portrayals of this violent relationship is by Steel, *How to Make a Human*.

18. Derrida, *Animal*, 29.

19. See Jagna Brudzińska, "Aisthesis"; Terry Eagleton, *The Ideology of the Aesthetic*; Charles H. Kahn, "Sensation and Consciousness in Aristotle's Psychology," 3; and Stephen Halliwell, *The Aesthetics of Mimesis*. "Aesthetics as a term and in its root meanings points us to the sensuous experience of art," writes James I. Porter in the opening page of his *Origins of Aesthetic Thought in Ancient Greece*, 1. He continues, "Driving aesthetics back to the level of sensation, but without halting there, has the virtue of putting the act of attending back in touch with matter and materiality, the senses, and experience" (4-5).

20. Greek writers in Byzantium dwelled on *aisthēsis* as sensation. See Stratis Papaioannou, "The Aesthetics of History: From Theophanes to Eustathios."

21. Richard Sorabji, "Body and Soul in Aristotle," 66.

22. Aristotle, *Posterior Analytics* 2.19.99b.34-36, trans. Tredennick and E. S. Forster.

23. Brian Massumi's account of this distinction, via Deleuze, is perhaps the most often cited by rhetorical scholars (*Parables for the Virtual*, 27-28). See also Eric Shouse, "Feeling, Emotion, Affect." I also have to wonder if absorbing emotion into such a cognitive category is desirable or even accurate.

24. David Konstan, *The Emotions of the Ancient Greeks*, x.

25. Daniel Heller-Roazen, *The Inner Touch*, 21.

26. Ann Cvetkovich, *Depression: A Public Feeling*, 4. To be clear, I believe the terminological reach Cvetkovich exploits also obtains in the ancients' use of the terms.

27. Henry George Liddell, Robert Scott, and Sir Henry Stuart Jones, *Greek-English Lexicon*, s.v. "πάθος." For discussions of *pathē* as feelings, see Eugene Victor Walter, *Placeways: A Theory of Human Environment*, 123-24; Aristotle, *Nicomachean Ethics*, trans. and ed. Terence Irwin, 256n. John M. Cooper writes, "In studying these chapters [from book 2 of the *Rhetoric*] it is important to bear in mind that Aristotle means to discuss throughout states of *feeling*—passions or emotion, conditions in which one's mind or consciousness is affected, moved, or stirred up" ("An Aristotelian Theory of the Emotions," 242).

28. For historical reflections on rhetoric and touch, see Shannon Walters, *Rhetorical Touch*.

29. Konstan, *Emotions*, 33-34. For a counterargument about pleasure and pain as not strictly sensation in Aristotle, see Kahn, "Sensation and Consciousness," 23-24, 66-67nn.

30. Davide Panagia, *The Political Life of Sensation*, 27.

31. Massumi, *Parables*, 97.

32. Massumi, *Parables*, 25.

33. Jenny Rice, too, favors feeling in her ecological study of public discourse on matters of development (*Distant Publics*, 48-55). In *Ambient Rhetoric*, Thomas Rickert attends to affective dimensions of attunement, which can't ignore matters of sensation. Brian Ott incorporates sensation when theorizing affect in rhetoric, especially in the context of cinema ("The Visceral Politics of *V for Vendetta*). Ott and Diane Marie Keeling describe affects as "extradiscursive 'moments of intensity'" in "Cinema and Choric Connection: *Lost in Translation* as Sensual Experience," 381n34. For a brief discussion of feelings and affect in the discipline of speech communication, see Joshua Gunn and Jenny Edbauer Rice, "About Face/Stuttering Discipline," 215-19. See also Debra Hawhee, "Rhetoric's Sensorium." Joshua Gunn's work on

sensorium and on sound studies usefully lays out the stakes of sensation for rhetorical studies; see in particular "Speech Is Dead; Long Live Speech."

34. Heller-Roazen, *Inner Touch*, 55.

35. Debra Hawhee and Christa Olson, "Pan-Historiography: The Challenges of Writing History across Time and Space."

36. Cicero and Quintilian's frequent use—and Seneca the Elder's work with the phrase "colors of rhetoric"—is a case in point, as well as a starting point for inspecting the ways the Romans thought rhetoric engaged the senses. See Mark Bradley, *Colour and Meaning in Ancient Rome*, 111–27.

37. Derrida, *Animal*, 416.

38. This observation appears at the beginning of Quintilian's treatment of delivery, in which he notes that voice and gesture appeal to the eye and the ear respectively, "the two senses by which all emotion penetrates to the mind" (Quintilian, *The Orator's Education*, 11.3.14, trans. Donald A. Russell, 91).

39. Aristotle, *Rhetoric* 3.11.4.1412a.10, translation mine. For a wonderful book-length study of Homer in Aristotle, see Marilee Mifsud, *Rhetoric and the Gift*.

40. Stuart Clark, *Vanities of the Eye*; Janice Neri, *The Insect and the Image*.

41. Mary Carruthers, *The Book of Memory: A Study of Memory in Medieval Culture*; Frances A. Yates, *The Art of Memory*.

CHAPTER ONE

1. Aristotle, *De anima* 2.2.413b.3–5, trans. W. S. Hett.

2. Aristotle, *Nicomachean Ethics* 2.9.1109b.23-24: En tē aisthēsei hē krisis. See Aristotle, *Nicomachean Ethics*, 2nd ed., trans. and ed. Terence Irwin, 201.

3. "We begin, as is often the case with these debates, with Aristotle" (Erica Fudge, *Brutal Reasoning*, 15); "Since Aristotle, man (as used in most texts) has been defined as the 'rational animal,' distinguished from other animals by his (and, more recently, her) ability to think and to reason" (Kari Weil, *Thinking Animals: Why Animal Studies Now?*, xv); Laurie Shannon uses more nuance than is typical: "Consistent with his glossing of man as the 'political animal' (and less consistent with his voluminous accounts of actual animals, Aristotle begins the long, Western philosophical characterization of nonhumans as *un*-political animals" (*Accommodated Animal*, 54); Cary Wolfe credits Derrida with the observation that Aristotle "inaugurates an entire philosophical tradition of thinking the difference between human and non-human animals in terms of the human's ability to properly 'respond' to its world rather than merely 'react' to it—a capacity made possible (so the story goes) by language" ("Flesh and Finitude," 9). Perhaps it is ironic, since Derrida has set so many people on this path, that Derrida himself, at the very end of *The Beast and the Sovereign*, 348–49, locates biopolitical and zoopolitical possibilities in the very *Politics* passage where scholars locate the division full stop.

4. Heath, *Talking Greeks*, 7. See also Heller-Roazen, who writes that Aristotle offered *zōon logon echon* in distinction from the pre-Socratic philosophers who "accepted no such partition between man and the other beasts" (*Inner Touch*, 91).

5. Note that the exact phrase does not occur in Aristotle but is a foreshortened version of

anthrōpos . . . monon gar echei logon (*Politics* 7.12.1332b.5–6). Heidegger may have been the first to shorten this phrase. See Martin Heidegger, *Plato's "Sophist,"* 12; see also Stuart Elden, "Reading Logos as Speech: Heidegger, Aristotle and Rhetorical Politics." Its counterpart, *aloga zōa*, very common in the *progymnasmata* and discussed more thoroughly in chapters 3 and 4, also implicitly refers to Aristotle's formulation.

6. Heath, *Talking Greeks*, 5, for example, is extremely focused on *logos* and the "rejection" of nonhuman animals from the world of *logos*. This focus is of course not incorrect, but it does skim over the perceptual abilities on which *logos*—the conveying of those perceptions—depends. Jessica Moss's account of *logos* is useful for drawing out these implications ("Right Reason in Plato and Aristotle"). The commonplace reading stops with *logos* but does not acknowledge the perception it entails. So Eve Browning Cole puts it this way: "Humans alone possess the crucial faculty of significant speech (*logos*), in which they make judgments concerning what is better and worse" ("Theophrastus and Aristotle on Animal Intelligence," 46). And R. G. Mulgan: "Man has *logos* which allows him to indicate the advantageous and disadvantageous and the right and the wrong" ("Aristotle's Doctrine That Man Is a Political Animal," 444). Note that these readings are by no means incorrect; they simply stress the conveying work of *logos* over—and to the exclusion of—the perceptive work it depends on.

7. Derrida, *Animal*, 35.

8. Moss is helpful on this score; see especially *Aristotle on the Apparent Good*, 8–9, 20–21.

9. Richard Sorabji, *Animal Minds and Human Morals*, 7. See also his related piece, "Esprits d'animaux," 355.

10. Aristotle, *Politics* 1.2.1253a.7–18, translation slightly modified from Lord, 4. As an aside, while the "nature has come this far" line might strike contemporary ears as somehow evolutionary, it is important to note that this is a spatial/spectral remark rather than a remark about change across time. In *History of Animals* Aristotle makes incremental allowances across the ancient spectrum of life, observing that "nature moves from the non-living to animals little by little" (7.1.588b4–5). This translation appears in G. E. R. Lloyd's discussion of "fuzzy natures" in *Aristotelian Explorations*, 74.

11. Greek: logon de monon anthrōpos echei tōn zōōn.

12. Aristotle, *Politics* 1.2.1253a.8–9, trans. Lord, 4.

13. Interestingly, though, *mallon* is the comparative and not the superlative (*malista*), so humans are more political than other animals rather than *the most political* of animals. The distinction may be minute, but the comparative force is nevertheless intriguing. Mulgan considers and rejects another reading of *mallon* as "rather than" ("Aristotle's Doctrine," 443–45).

14. Aristotle, *History of Animals* 1.1.488a.8–9, trans. Peck, 19. Indeed, John Cooper holds that the passage cannot be read correctly without reference to *History of Animals*: "What we learn from the *Historia Animalium* theory and its extension in *Politics* 1.2.1253a7–18 is that active participation in a city's life is that single function (*ergon*) which all the human beings belonging to that city perform together, and in the performance of which their character as political animals consists" ("Political Animals and Civic Friendship," 69). David J. Depew's indispensable extended reading of *History of Animals* anticipates Cooper's conclusions ("Humans and Other Political Animals in Aristotle's *History of Animals*"). For a ranging analysis that considers Aristotle's presumptions about human nature vis-à-vis political life, see Carnes

Lord, "Aristotle's Anthropology." See also Mulgan, "Aristotle's Doctrine." For a consideration of the interanimation of political and economic perspectives on animals, see Richard Bodéüs, "L'animal politique et l'animal économique."

15. So Mulgan: "In addition to voice (φωνή) which allows the expression of pleasure and pain and which is found in other animals man has λόγος which allows him to indicate the advantageous and disadvantageous and the right and the wrong" ("Aristotle's Doctrine," 444). And Bernard Yack: "But logos gives to human beings the capacity to calculate and communicate advantage and harm—the ability to indicate the consequences that may follow from any given action, as well as to communicate pain and pleasure" (*The Problems of a Political Animal*, 65). See also David J. Depew, "Humans and Other Political Animals," 157, and Wolfgang Kullmann, "Der Mensch als politisches Lebewesen bei Aristoteles." Cooper writes: "They [humans] also have language, which is necessary in order for them to communicate these conceptions to one another" ("Political Animals," 68).

16. As Malcolm Heath puts it: "The richness of Aristotle's concept of perception is rooted in his zoological perspective" ("Cognition in Aristotle's Poetics," 52).

17. Residing in this discussion is of course the idea of the articulate versus the inarticulate voice, which Aristotle alludes to in several places in his corpus: e.g., *Rhetoric* 3.2.1405.13–15; *History of Animals* 1.1.488a.32–33; the most lengthy consideration occurs in *De anima* 2.8.419a–421a8. For more on *phōnē-logos*, see Joshua Gunn, "Speech Is Dead," and Joshua Gunn and Mirko M. Hall, "Stick It in Your Ear: The Psychodynamics of iPod Enjoyment." For a brief discussion of "the basic criterion of articulacy" as manifest in the early modern period, see R. W. Serjeantson, "The Passions and Animal Language, 1540–1700," 428. For a meditation on voice in relation to political life, see Adriana Cavarero, *For More Than One Voice: Toward a Philosophy of Vocal Expression*, especially part 1, "How Logos Lost Its Voice." See also James I. Porter, "Rhetoric, Aesthetics, and the Voice."

18. Aristotle, *Nicomachean Ethics* 9.9.1170b.10–15, translation modified from *Nicomachean Ethics: A New Translation*, trans. Robert C. Bartlett and Susan D. Collins, 205.

19. Here I am interpreting ἐν τῷ (ἐν τῷ συζῆν καὶ κοινωνεῖν λόγων καὶ διανοίας), at 9.9.1170b.12–13 with purposive force.

20. I would simply point out that for humans, too, eating sometimes forestalls the sharing of words and thoughts.

21. This reading fits with Moss's recent and very striking argument that *logos* in ethical texts of Plato and Aristotle ought to be read as *account* ("Right Reason"). Moss's reading holds implications for all theorists and historians of rhetoric working with ancient texts, inasmuch as it calls into question the standard line of *logos* meaning reason or speech.

22. See Debra Hawhee, *Moving Bodies*, 141–44. For a foundational discussion of individuation and rhetoric, see Maurice Charland, "Constitutive Rhetoric: The Case of the Peuple Québécois."

23. Jill Frank, *A Democracy of Distinction: Aristotle and the Work of Politics*, 160.

24. Sorabji, *Animal Minds*, 58; Moss, *Aristotle on the Apparent Good*, 40–43.

25. Aristotle, *History of Animals* 1.1.488b.24–26, trans. Peck, 19.

26. Aristotle, *Nicomachean Ethics* 2.9.1109b.9, trans. Irwin, 201. Irwin's commentary calls attention to the way the "in" here indicates dependence.

27. For more on touch as the crucial animal sense, see Rebecca Steiner Goldner, "Touch and Flesh in Aristotle's *De Anima*," 435–46; S. H. Rosen, "Thought and Touch: A Note on Aristotle's *De Anima*"; and Richard A. Lee and Christopher P. Long, "Nous and Logos in Aristotle," 366.

28. I opted to call this second kind of *aisthēsis* deliberative because the perceptions themselves provide the material for deliberation in Aristotle's scheme.

29. Aristotle, *Rhetoric* 1.11.1370a.28–29, trans. Kennedy, 88. Greek: phantasia estin aisthēsis tis asthēnes.

30. Aristotle, *De anima* 3.3.427b.15–25, translation modified from Hett, 157.

31. Aristotle, *De anima* 3.3.428a.5–6, trans. Hett, 159.

32. Aristotle, *De anima* 3.3.428a.15–16, translation modified from Hett, 159.

33. Moss, *Aristotle on the Apparent Good*, 4.

34. Aristotle, *De anima* 3.3.429a.5–9, translation modified from Hett, 163.

35. The idea of portability here overlaps with Michele Kennerly's assessment of *phantasia* as a mode of transport ("Getting Carried Away: How Rhetorical Transport Gets Judgment Going").

36. See Aristotle, *De anima* 3.7.431b.7–8.

37. As Heller-Roazen puts it: "Aristotle lays bare a principle that remains merely implicit elsewhere in his account of the soul, although it profoundly determines the entire doctrine of *aisthēsis*. This is the principle that all sensation occurs in time, and more precisely, at one time in particular—namely, 'now'" (*Inner Touch*, 52). See also *De memoria* ("On Memory and Recollection"), where Aristotle describes memory as "a state induced by a mental image [*phantasmatos*]" and notes that it "pertains to the primary sense-faculty, *aisthētikou*" (*De memoria* 451a.15–18, trans. Hett, 299).

38. Aristotle, *De anima* 3.11.434a5–10.

39. Hawhee, "Looking into Aristotle's Eyes," 148. For more detailed discussions of deliberative *phantasia*, see Moss, *Aristotle on the Apparent Good*, 144–52; Martha Craven Nussbaum, "The Role of *Phantasia* in Aristotle's Explanation of Action"; Harry Wolfson, "The Internal Senses in Latin, Arabic, and Hebrew Philosophic Texts."

40. Aristotle, *Generation of Animals* 1.23.731a.33–34, translation modified from Peck. Greek: ē d' aisthēsis gnōsis tis.

41. Aristotle, *De anima* 3.9.432a.15–18, trans. Hett, 181.

42. Aristotle, *Metaphysics* 1.1.980a27–69, trans. Tredennick, 3.

43. Aristotle, *Nicomachean Ethics* 6.7.1141a.27–29, trans. Rackham, 343.

44. Aristotle, *Parts of Animals* 2.2.648a.3–11, trans. Peck, 119, 121. Perhaps even more remarkable is the passage at 2.4.650b22–27: "An animal which has the thinner and clearer sort of fluid in it has also a more mobile faculty of sensation [*eukinētoteran tēn aisthēsin*]" (139).

45. Aristotle, *Nicomachean Ethics* 3.8.1116b.24–26, trans. Rackham, 167.

46. Aristotle, *Nicomachean Ethics* 3.8.1117a.5, trans. Rackham, 169.

47. *Paraplēsion d' exousi ti*. Aristotle, *Nicomachean Ethics* 3.8.1117a.11, translation mine.

48. *Allōn zōōn* is in the genitive case, which can, among other things, indicate possession or comparison.

49. Aristotle, *Rhetoric* 1.9.1366a.28–31, trans. Kennedy, 75–76.

50. Greek: ton auton tropon.

51. For an account of the dogs as performing bodily syllogisms, see Debra Hawhee, "Toward a Bestial Rhetoric," 85.

52. Aristotle, *Rhetoric* 1.11.1369b.33–35. The translation is from Dorothea Frede, "Mixed Feelings in Aristotle's *Rhetoric*," 267. See also Eugene Garver's treatment of emotions and deliberative rationality (*Aristotle's* Rhetoric: *An Art of Character*).

53. For more on pain as disturbance of equilibrium, and on the Platonic roots of this medical approach, see Frede, "Mixed Feelings," 258–85.

54. Aristotle, *Rhetoric* 1.11.1370a.16–17, trans. Kennedy, 88. Greek: kai ou an hē epithumia enē, hapan hēdu. See also 1.11.1369a1–4 and Frede, "Mixed Feelings," 266.

55. Konstan treats pleasure and pain as types of sensation; cf. *Emotions*, 34. Cooper is probably the most accurate on this question of whether pleasure is a sensation when he answers, basically, "sometimes": "Aristotle's words for pleasure [cover] . . . everything from some bodily sensations to mental attitudes and responses ranging from simple liking or being pleased or glad about something to elation and vivid enjoyment" ("Rhetoric, Dialectic, and the Passion," 190). Stephen Leighton does not treat pleasure and pain as sensation per se but favors them as alterations (see my discussion below) ("Aristotle and the Emotions," 206–37). Martha Nussbaum views pain and pleasure as cognitive categories (though it is not clear to me how she arrives at this interpretation from the passages she cites) (*Upheavals of Thought*, 63–64).

56. Aristotle, *Rhetoric* 1.11.1370a.27–28, trans. Kennedy, 88. This passage no doubt informs George Kennedy's reflections on the "convocations of crows" on his university campus, as I will discuss in chapter 2 ("Hoot," 5); see also Debra Hawhee, "Toward a Bestial Rhetoric."

57. Aristotle, *Rhetoric* 1.11.1371b.12–17, trans. Kennedy, 91.

58. The "homophily principle" names "the principle that a contact between similar people occurs at a higher rate than among dissimilar people" (Miller McPherson, Lynn Smith-Lovin, and James M. Cook, "Birds of a Feather: Homophily in Social Networks," 416).

59. Glossing the jackdaw proverb (koloios para koloion or koloios poti koloion) with the birds of a feather proverb has become common; see George A. Kennedy, trans., *On Rhetoric: A Theory of Civic Discourse*, 91n211. See also Liddell, Scott, and Jones, *Greek-English Lexicon*, s.v. "κολοιός," 973. At *Eudemian Ethics* 7.5.1239b.19–21, Aristotle makes a similar though more general observation: "For this reason the voices and habits and company of kin are most pleasant to each other, *even among other animals*." Translation from Eve Browning Cole, "Theophrastus and Aristotle on Animal Intelligence," 48. Emphasis in Browning Cole's translation.

60. Aristotle, *Nichomachean Ethics* 8.1.1155a.34. Plato also cites "the old proverb" in *Phaedrus* 240c.

61. For consideration of the senses and sensible objects, see the treatise of Aristotle's bearing that name, as well as *De anima*, where Aristotle observes that "if the soul is moved, the most plausible view is that it is moved by the sensible objects" (1.3.406b.10–11, trans. Hett, 35). See also the discussion of these concepts in Thomas Kjeller Johansen, *The Powers of Aristotle's Soul*, 137–45.

62. Aristotle, *Rhetoric* 1.11.1371a.16, trans. Kennedy, 90.

63. Aristotle, *Rhetoric* 2.6.1384a.21–22, trans. Kennedy, 134.

64. Aristotle, *Rhetoric* 2.6.1384a.33–35, trans. Kennedy, 134.

65. Aristotle, *Rhetoric* 2.6.1384b.23–24, trans. Kennedy, 135.

66. I choose not to stress the diminutive forms here, following the suggestion by Herbert Weir Smyth that *thērion* especially "is diminutive in form, but not in meaning." *A Greek Grammar for Colleges*, 235. Worrying over the diminutives only gets Kennedy into murky interpretations, such as his gloss in the 1990 version of his translation, discussed below (George A. Kennedy, trans., *On Rhetoric: A Theory of Civic Discourse*, 147n61).

67. Kennedy, *On Rhetoric*, 135n50.

68. Kennedy, *On Rhetoric*, 147n61.

69. Greek: ta toiauta allon tropon huparchein. Aristotle, *Nicomachean Ethics* 6.13.1144b. 8–9, trans. Rackham, 369.

70. Aristotle, *Nicomachean Ethics* 6.13.1144b.9–10, translation modified from Irwin, 98.

71. Moss, "Right Reason," 190. I also find the conception of *nous* as a kind of "intuitive insight" to be extremely helpful here. See Lee and Long, "Nous and Logos in Aristotle," 348.

72. Aristotle, *Nicomachean Ethics* 6.13.1144b.10–12, trans. Irwin, 98.

73. This passage, of course, raises questions about disability. Part of the point about the need to share perceptions, though, presumes differences across sense-based *aisthēsis*. The case of disabled bodies relying on a different gathering of senses makes the point about varieties of sense perception. Indeed, disability studies is indispensable to a contemporary ethical account of sensation. See Bill Arning, "Prosthetics," 194–98, and Jay T. Dolmage, *Disability Rhetoric: Critical Perspectives on Disability*. See also Hawhee, "Rhetoric's Sensorium."

74. In chapter 3 on fables I offer a more in-depth treatment of this association.

75. Aristotle, *Rhetoric* 2.4.1382a.10–11, translation mine.

76. Homer, *Iliad* 16.259–265, trans. Lombardo, 312.

77. And also the elegance of Lombardo's translation.

78. Thomas K. Johansen points out that "functions like *phantasia*, pleasure, pain and desire" are secondary features of the soul "which definitionally depend on the primary features" ("Parts in Aristotle's Definition of Soul: *De Anima* Books I and II," 51). In this case the primary feature is perception, *aisthēsis*. Johansen's account is compelling and seems to me correct, and the place of *pathē* also invites consideration for my purposes.

79. Moss's explanation of why she uses the term cognition to discuss some of these nonrational processes pinpoints the difficulty I have with the term: "'Cognition,' writes Moss, "may sound exclusively intellectual to some ears, but I use it, along with the more idiomatic 'finding,' for lack of a better general term." She also explains, crucially, that "there is nothing specially rational or intellectual about cognition," noting that an animal with a strictly haptic sense "counts as a cognizer" (*Aristotle on the Apparent Good*, 3). I do continue to worry about the work the term has come to do and opt instead for a kind of "discernment" (a word Moss uses as well).

80. Kahn, "Sensation and Consciousness," 4–5; also quoted in Heller-Roazen, *Inner Touch*, 24–25. The most comprehensive account of Aristotle's *De anima* as a delineation of faculty psychology ("powers of the soul") is offered by Johansen, *Powers of Aristotle's Soul*.

81. Aristotle, *De anima* 2.2.413b.2, trans. Hett, 75. Greek: to de zōon di atēn aisthēsin prōtos.

82. Aristotle, *De anima* 2.2.413b.23–25, trans. Hett, 77. Aristotle repeats this at 2.2.414b. 4–5: "That which has sensation knows pleasure and pain, the pleasant and the painful, and that which knows these has also desire; for desire is an appetite for what is pleasant," trans. Hett, 81.

83. Aristotle, *De anima* 2.2.414b.2–7, trans. Hett, 81.

84. Konstan, *Emotions*, 34; E. M. Cope, *An Introduction to Aristotle's Rhetoric*, 238.

85. Aristotle, *De anima* 2.5.416b.33–34. I favor this translation offered in Heller-Roazen, *Inner Touch*, 25.

86. Aristotle, *De anima* 2.5.416b.34–35, my translation. The Greek is dokei gar alloiōsis tis einai. See also 2.4.415b.23–25.

87. The *pathē* turn up very early in *De anima* too, though, as in this passage at 1.1.403a.17–19, trans. Hett, 15: "Probably all the affections of the soul [*tēs psuchēs pathē*] are associated with the body—anger, gentleness, fear, pity, courage, and joy, as well as loving and hating; for when they appear the body is also affected [*paschei*]. There is good evidence for this. Sometimes no irritation or fear is expressed, though the provocations are strong and obvious." For a book-length consideration of the promise of *alloiōsis* for rhetoric, see Jane S. Sutton and Marilee Mifsud, *A Revolution in Tropes: Alloiostrophic Rhetoric*. This book was published after I wrote this chapter, confirming my own developing suspicion of the term's promise for rhetorical theory, and happily fulfilling that promise.

88. Aristotle, *Movement of Animals* 7.701b.17–23, trans. Forster, 465; emphasis mine.

89. Liddell, Scott, and Jones, *Greek-English Lexicon*, s.v. "βάλλω," 304–5.

90. *Oxford English Dictionary Online*, s.v. "Metabolism," accessed November 12, 2014, http://www.oed.com.ezaccess.libraries.psu.edu.

91. Aristotle, *De anima* 3.3.429a.1–2.

92. Amélie Oksenberg Rorty formulates the *pathē* as follows: "*Pathē* have double-entry bookkeeping: they are identified by a conjunction of physical and psychological changes that themselves generate further changes" (Rorty, "Structuring Rhetoric," 15).

93. For a fascinating discussion of the role of emotion in Aristotle's moral philosophy and an account compatible with the one given here, see Sherman, *Making a Necessity of Virtue*, 248–62.

94. Aristotle, *Rhetoric* 2.1.1377b.6, trans. Kennedy, 112. Greek: Epei d' heneka kriseōs estin hē rhētorikē.

95. Hawhee, "Looking into Aristotle's Eyes," 150.

96. Aristotle, *Rhetoric* 2.1.1378a.19–21, translation modified from Kennedy, 113. While Kennedy's translation notes that the *pathē* are "accompanied by," I have opted for a stronger, less corollary conception of *epetai*, for in addition to attend or accompany, it can also mean follow or trace, or even heed or obey. The move from mere accompaniment to a following gives the felt experience even more of a clear and central role in shaping judgment. Also, as discussed already, *krisis*, judgment, is not limited to humans. See Juha Sihvola, "Emotional Animals: Do Aristotelian Emotions Require Beliefs?," 142.

97. Aristotle, *Rhetoric* 2.1.1377b.30–32. See Kennedy's translation, 112. Note too that Aristotle does not mention physical differences. I am sensitive to the implications of his omission, as is Dolmage, *Disability*.

98. Leighton, "Aristotle and the Emotions," 207.

99. What's more, pleasure and pain are not mere accessories to his definition of *pathē* but are integral to it. This is "stronger than simple concurrence" (Leighton, "Aristotle and the Emotions," 219).

100. Aristotle, *Rhetoric* 2.2.1378a.30–32, trans. Kennedy, 116.

101. I am not the first to point out that scholars may be leaping to cognition a bit prematurely when it comes to Aristotle's emotion. As Sherman writes, "There is a temptation to regard the discernment of the particulars as primarily the function of cognitive rather than affective capacities. . . . But on a more comprehensive Aristotelian account, discernment of the particulars is not regarded as a purely cognitive function" (*Making a Necessity of Virtue*, 248).

102. Moss's reading of *logos* as "account," while restricted to ethical treatises, may well apply in rhetoric, at least in certain places where the subject is not obviously speech or "a speech" ("Right Reason").

103. The astonishing wolves, from Homer, *Iliad* 16.155–63, are considered more fully in chapter 2.

104. The commonplace translation of this word as simile in the discussion of metaphor, while fair enough because of similitude, nevertheless risks oversimplifying the discussion in book 3, chapter 4 to what is likely the most commonly retained distinction learned in American high school English classes, that between metaphor and simile. The point of this passage, however, is not to distinguish the two, but to show how metaphor relies on a fundamental—and visible—likeness.

105. Aristotle, *Rhetoric* 3.4.1406b.20–24, trans. Kennedy (though I have removed his parentheses in the interest of clarity), 205.

106. Aristotle, *Rhetoric* 3.4.1406b.27–29, 32–34, trans. Kennedy, 205.

107. Aristotle, *Rhetoric* 3.4.1407a.2–4, 8–10, trans. Kennedy, 206.

108. Aristotle, *Rhetoric* 3.4.1406b.30, trans. Kennedy, 205.

109. Aristotle, *Rhetoric* 3.4.1406b.36–1407a, trans. Kennedy, 205.

110. Steven H. Lonsdale, *Creatures of Speech*, 10.

111. Lonsdale, *Creatures of Speech*, 7.

112. Lonsdale, *Creatures of Speech*, 10.

113. Aristotle, *Rhetoric* 3.11.1411b, trans. Kennedy, 222.

114. Kennedy, *On Rhetoric*, 222n116.

115. Liddell, Scott, and Jones, *Greek-English Lexicon*, s.v. "ἄφετος, -ον," 288.

116. Isocrates, "To Philip," trans. George Norlin, 127. For a discussion of Macedonia, see George Norlin, "Introduction," xlii.

117. Liddell, Scott, and Jones, *Greek-English Lexicon*, s.v. "ἐνέργεια," 565. See also Kennedy, *On Rhetoric*, 222n117.

118. See Chung-Hwan Chen, "Different Meanings of the Term *Energeia* in the Philosophy of Aristotle," 57–58.

119. Aristotle, *De anima* 2.5.417a.12–14, trans. Hett, 97.

120. Aristotle, *De anima* 2.4.415b.9–10, translation mine.

121. Aristotle, *De anima* 2.4.415b.26, translation modified from Hett, 89.

122. Aristotle, *Rhetoric* 3.11.1412a.10, trans. Kennedy, 223.

123. For example, at the beginning of chapter 2 of the *Rhetoric*, book 3, Aristotle notes, "To deviate [from prevailing usage] makes language seem more elevated . . . as a result, one should make the language unfamiliar, for people are admirers of what is far off, and what is marvelous is sweet," 3.2.1404b.8–12, trans. Kennedy, 198.

124. Aristotle, *Rhetoric* 3.3.1406b.15–16, trans. Kennedy, 204.

125. Robert E. Bell, *Women of Classical Mythology: A Biographical Dictionary*, 365. See also Homer, *Odyssey* 19.585–90.

126. Aristotle, *Rhetoric* 3.3.1406b.15–19, trans. Kennedy, 204.

127. Aristotle, *Rhetoric* 3.7.1408b.20, trans. Kennedy, 211.

CHAPTER TWO

1. Homer, *Iliad* 3.151-55, trans. Murray and Wyatt, 139, 141.

2. Homer, *Iliad* 3.144, trans. Murray and Wyatt, 139.

3. Homer, *Iliad* 3.155, trans. Murray and Wyatt, 141.

4. Wyatt's gloss on the "lily-like" epithet is even more pointed: "the adjective 'lily-like' applied to the voice seems a striking instance of the transference of an epithet from one field of sense perception to another." Homer, *Iliad*, trans. Murray and Wyatt, 141n2.

5. Steve Reece, "Homer's Winged and Wingless Words: ΠΤΕΡΟΕΙΣ/ΑΠΤΕΡΟΣ," 261.

6. Paolo Vivante, "On Homer's Winged Words," 1–12; Richard P. Martin, *The Language of Heroes*, 45. See also W. E. Gladstone, "The Reply of Achilles to the Envoys of Agamemnon," 844.

7. Martin, *Language of Heroes*, 35.

8. Vivante, "On Homer's Winged Words," 6.

9. Vivante, "On Homer's Winged Words," 8–9.

10. Martin, *Language of Heroes*, 36.

11. Martin, *Language of Heroes*, 36–37.

12. Gladstone, "Reply of Achilles," 844.

13. Walter J. Ong, "World as View and World as Event," 638.

14. The dates, of course, are called into question along with authorship. One school of thought posits that *On the Sublime* is actually Dionysius's promised text on style; see Malcolm Heath, "Longinus on Sublimity." For an argument that translates into an earlier (first-century BCE or CE) date for *On the Sublime*, see Casper C. de Jonge, "Dionysius and Longinus on the Sublime: Rhetoric and Religious Language," 273–74n5. Longinus probably ought to be rendered "Longinus," given the likelihood that this text was not written by him; see Jeffrey Walker, *Rhetoric and Poetics in Antiquity*, 118–20. I prefer to avoid the distraction of quotation marks and will therefore note the tenuousness of authorship here. On the controversy around Demetrius's identity, see Doreen C. Innes, "Introduction," in *Poetics*, 23:312–24.

15. Kathy Eden, *The Renaissance Rediscovery of Intimacy*, 1–2.

16. Cicero, *De oratore* 3.59.223, translation modified from Rackham. For a consideration of this line in the context of bodily rhetoric, see Debra Hawhee, *Bodily Arts*, 222.

17. See the note on dating above. Dionysius of Halicarnassus is the only one of these three authors whose dates and identity are relatively certain (he wrote during the Augustan period in Rome at the turn of the era).

18. Rosi Braidotti, "Animals, Anomalies, and Inorganic Others," 528.

19. G. E. R. Lloyd, *Science, Folklore, and Ideology: Studies in the Life Sciences in Ancient Greece*, 53.

20. Donald Lateiner, "Nonverbal Communication in the Histories of Herodotus," 86.

21. George A. Kennedy, "A Hoot in the Dark," 5, 14, and 13.

22. Kennedy's gloss on the term *energeia* in book 3 notes that "the English cognate is *energy*." While Kennedy chooses to translate the term actualization, he notes that "vivification" is another possibility, and I opt for that here because of its foregrounding of life/liveliness (Kennedy, *On Rhetoric*, 222n117).

23. Quintilian, *Orator's Education* 6.2.29; see Simon Goldhill's translation of this passage, "What Is Ekphrasis For?," 4.

24. Goldhill, "What Is Ekphrasis For?," 4.

25. Longinus, *On the Sublime* 15.1–2, trans. W. Hamilton Fyfe and Donald A. Russell, 216n1. Per the translators, the adjectival form of pathos (*pathētikon*) was added by Kayser, an early editor.

26. The full phrase translated here as inspired by strong emotion is hup' enthouasiasmou kai pathous. *Enargeia* relates to, but ought not be confused with, *energeia*. Kennedy, *On Rhetoric*, 222n117, notes that the confusion is common. This is likely because of the slim difference between the terms (an epsilon for an alpha)—*energeia, enargeia*—and also the fact that *energeia* shows up in Aristotle's discussion of "bringing before the eyes," which directly relates to vividness, *enargeia*.

27. Kennerly draws out this transportative quality of *phantasia* in "Getting Carried Away," 270–76.

28. Longinus, *On the Sublime* 10.3, translation modified slightly from Fyfe and Russell, 201.

29. Longinus, *On the Sublime* 15.2, translation mine.

30. Longinus, *On the Sublime* 15.2, translation modified from Fyfe and Russell, 217.

31. Longinus, *On the Sublime* 15.2, translation modified from Fyfe and Russell, 217.

32. Longinus, *On the Sublime* 15.3, translation mine; Greek: hekasta epi tōn megethōn.

33. Longinus, *On the Sublime* 15.3, translation mine; cf. Homer, *Iliad* 20.170.

34. Homer, *Iliad* 20.167, trans. Murray and Wyatt, 379.

35. Longinus, *On the Sublime* 15.3, trans. Fyfe and Russell, 217.

36. Longinus, *On the Sublime* 15.4, translation mine.

37. Longinus, *On the Sublime* 15.4, translation mine.

38. Longinus, *On the Sublime* 15.5, translation mine.

39. Ned O'Gorman, "Longinus's Sublime Rhetoric, or How Rhetoric Came into Its Own," 73.

40. Longinus, *On the Sublime* 15.9, translation modified from Fyfe and Russell, 223.

41. Longinus, *On the Sublime* 15.11, translation modified from Fyfe and Russell, 225.

42. Demetrius, *On Style* 217, trans. Innes and Roberts, 479.

43. Hawhee, "Looking into Aristotle's Eyes," 143.

44. Aristotle, *Rhetoric* 3.2.1405b, trans. Kennedy, 201.

45. Aristotle, *Rhetoric* 3.2.1405b, translation mine.

46. Demetrius, *On Style* 255, trans. Innes and Roberts, 497.

47. Demetrius, *On Style* 49, trans. Innes and Roberts, 381.

48. Demetrius, *On Style* 49, trans. Innes and Roberts, 381.

49. Quintilian, *Orator's Education* 8.6.31, trans. Russell, 443.

50. Giambattista Vico, *The Art of Rhetoric*, 151. See also Jeanne Fahnestock, *Rhetorical Style*, 51.

51. See Jeffrey Walker, "Dionysius of Halicarnassus," 139; Stephen Usher, trans., introduction to *Dionysius of Halicarnassus: Critical Essays*, 3–4.

52. As Usher puts it, Demetrius's *On Style*, Dionysius's *On Composition*, and Longinus's *On the Sublime* "are more or less complementary to one another." "Introduction," *Dionysius of Halicarnassus: Critical Essays*, 3.

53. In opting to render the title of Dionysius's treatise as "On Composition" (Peri syntheseōs onomatōn), I am explicitly rejecting the common translation of "On Literary Composition." In doing so I follow Casper de Jonge, who rightly notes that "the adjective 'literary' carries connotations that do not entirely fit Dionysius' introduction to his work." *Between Grammar and Rhetoric*, 42. An even more literal translation of the title, as de Jonge points out, would be "the putting together of words," 41.

54. Dionysius, "On Literary Composition" 15, trans. Usher, 111.

55. Dionysius, "On Literary Composition" 16, trans. Usher, 113.

56. Aristotle, *Rhetoric* 3.2.1405b.6, trans. Freese, 353.

57. Dionysius, "On Literary Composition" 15, trans. Usher, 111.

58. Dionysius, "On Literary Composition" 15, trans. Usher, 111n2.

59. Homer, *Iliad* 12.207, trans. Murray and Wyatt, 571.

60. Henry George Liddell, Robert Scott, and Sir Henry Stuart Jones, *Greek-English Lexicon*, s.v. "κλάζω," 955; see also John Heath's comparison of Homeric animal cries with animal cries in Aeschylus, *The Talking Greeks* 222–23.

61. Dionysius, "On Literary Composition" 16, translation modified from Usher, 115. It should be noted, of course, that different languages put forward distinctive onomatopoeia, a phenomenon that points to the cultural habit inhering in the notion of *phusis*, or the importance of ears trained in particular ways, resulting in mimetic variation. Thanks to Davida Charney for the exchange at ISHR 2015 that helped me see the need for this qualification.

62. Dionysius, *Lysias* 11; this passage is translated in Jeffrey Walker, *The Genuine Teachers of This Art*, 225.

63. Dionysius, *Lysias* 16, translation mine.

64. Dionysius, "On Literary Composition" 16, trans. Usher, 113.

65. See de Jonge, *Between Grammar and Rhetoric*, 75.

66. Walker, *Genuine Teachers of This Art*, 224–26.

67. Aristotle, *Rhetoric* 3.1.1404a.8, trans. Kennedy, 196.

68. De Jonge, *Between Grammar and Rhetoric*, 75.

69. Aristotle, *Rhetoric* 3.1.1404a.8, trans. Kennedy, 196. I discussed this passage in chapter 1 and will discuss it further below.

70. Demetrius, *On Style* 94–95, translation slightly modified from Innes and Roberts, 409.

71. Homer, *Odyssey* 9.391–94, trans. Murray and Dimock, 345.

72. Homer, *Iliad* 16.155–63, trans. Murray and Wyatt, 175.

73. Demetrius, *On Style* 220, trans. Innes and Roberts, 479.

74. Aristotle, *Rhetoric* 3.1.1404a.8, trans. Kennedy, 196.

75. For a consideration of speech gesture in the context of twentieth-century theories of language evolution, see Hawhee, *Moving Bodies*, 106–24.

76. Longinus, *On the Sublime* 15.1, trans. Fyfe and Russell, 215.

77. Liddell, Scott, and Jones, *Greek-English Lexicon*, s.v. "ὄγκος," 1197.

78. Euripides, "Ion" 15, trans. Kovacs, 323.

79. Roberts, 393nb, thinks it is quoted from memory and not exact.

80. Demetrius, *On Style* 66, trans. Innes and Roberts, 393.

81. Demetrius, *On Style* 66, trans. Innes and Roberts, 393.

82. Demetrius, *On Style* 66, trans. Innes and Roberts, 393.

83. Aristotle, *Poetics* 7.1450b.23–25, trans. Stephen Halliwell, 55.

84. Aristotle, *Poetics* 7.1450b.33–1451a.5, trans. Halliwell, 55-7.

85. Thomas B. Farrell, "Sizing Things Up: Colloquial Reflection as Practical Wisdom." See also his related article (but note that this posthumously published essay contains an erroneous spelling: *megathos* instead of *megethos* for magnitude) ("The Weight of Rhetoric: Studies in Cultural Delirium").

86. Farrell, "Sizing Things Up," 6. Short but substantive discussions of *megethos* appear in Ned O'Gorman, "Longinus's Sublime Rhetoric," 77, and Hawhee, "Looking into Aristotle's Eyes," 149.

87. Farrell, "Sizing Things Up," 6.

88. Farrell, "Sizing Things Up," 6.

89. Farrell, "Sizing Things Up," 7.

90. Farrell, "Sizing Things Up," 7.

91. Aristotle, *Poetics* 7.1450b.33–34, trans. Halliwell, 55.

92. Farrell, "Sizing Things Up," 7.

93. Aristotle, *Poetics* 7.1451a.9–15, trans. Halliwell, 57.

94. Aristotle, *Poetics* 4.1448b.9–12, trans. Halliwell, 37, 39.

95. For a fascinating art-based discussion of human actors in animal costumes in the archaic period, see Mary Louise Hart, "Choral Dance in Archaic Athens," 19–28.

96. Longinus, *On the Sublime* 9.5, translation modified from Fyfe and Russell, 187.

97. Longinus, *On the Sublime* 9.5, trans. Fyfe and Russell, 187.

98. Longinus, *On the Sublime* 9.5, trans. Fyfe and Russell, 187.

99. Longinus, *On the Sublime* 35.2–3, trans. Fyfe and Russell, 277.

100. Demetrius, *On Style* 75, trans. Innes and Roberts, 399.

101. Demetrius, *On Style* 76, translation modified from Innes and Roberts, 399.

102. Demetrius, *On Style* 127, trans. Innes and Roberts, 429.

103. Demetrius, *On Style* 133, trans. Innes and Roberts, 431.

104. Demetrius, *On Style* 133; translation modified from Innes and Roberts, 433.

105. Homer, *Odyssey* 19.518–19, trans. Murray and Dimock, 273.

106. Gregory Nagy, *Poetry as Performance: Homer and Beyond*, 7.

107. Homer, *Odyssey* 19.524, trans. Murray and Dimock, 273.

108. Nagy, *Poetry as Performance*, 8–16. For a reading of the nightingale image's complexity, see Emily Katz Anhalt, "A Matter of Perspective: Penelope and the Nightingale in *Odyssey* 19.512–534."

109. Demetrius, *On Style* 142, trans. Innes and Roberts, 437, 439.

110. Demetrius, *On Style* 145, trans. Innes and Roberts, 439.

111. Demetrius, *On Style* 145, trans. Innes and Roberts, 439.

188 *Notes to Pages 60–67*

112. Demetrius, *On Style* 145, trans. Innes and Roberts, 439nd; cf. Aristotle, *History of Animals* 7.597b24, trans. Balme, 137.

113. Aristotle, *History of Animals* 7.597b.24–26, trans. Balme, 137. Inasmuch as the owl was thought to imitate human actions, the anthropomorphism in this passage perhaps isn't as straightforward as Demetrius suggests—positing *mimēsis* seems qualitatively different from ascribing human qualities to nonhumans. But that might be beside the point of charm.

114. Demetrius, *On Style* 157, trans. Innes and Roberts, 447; cf. Aristotle, *History of Animals* 8.619a16, trans. Balme, 299.

115. See Ben Edwin Perry, "Demetrius of Phalerum and the Aesopic Fables," and Gert-Jan van Dijk, *Ainoi, Logoi, Mythoi: Fables in Archaic, Classical, and Hellenistic Greek*, xiv.

116. Demetrius, *On Style* 158, trans. Innes and Roberts, 447.

117. Demetrius, *On Style* 159, trans. Innes and Roberts, 447.

118. Demetrius, *On Style* 160, trans. Innes and Roberts, 449.

119. Demetrius, *On Style* 161, trans. Innes and Roberts, 449.

120. Demetrius, *On Style* 304, trans. Innes and Roberts, 525.

121. Demetrius, *On Style* 304, trans. Innes and Roberts, 525.

122. Demetrius, *On Style* 296, translation modified from Innes and Roberts, 519.

123. Demetrius, *On Style* 296, trans. Innes and Roberts, 519.

124. Liddell, Scott, and Jones, *Greek-English Lexicon*, s.v. "πλάσσω," 1412.

125. For a discussion of dogs in antiquity, see R. H. A. Merlen, *De Canibus: Dog and Hound in Antiquity*, 25–65. See also Timothy Howe, "Domestication and Breeding of Livestock: Horses, Mules, Asses, Cattle, Sheep, Goats, and Swine."

126. Demetrius, *On* Style 296–98, trans. Innes and Roberts, 519, 521.

127. Quotation drawn from C. C. W. Taylor, "Aristippus," 49.

128. Homer, *Odyssey* 17.290–304.

129. At *Iliad* 21.79, Lycaon reminds Achilles that he once brought him the price of one hundred oxen, whereas Eurycleia, the daughter of Ops, cost Laertes a mere twenty oxen (*Odyssey* 1.431). For a discussion of how such animals became sacred during the classical and Hellenistic periods, see Signe Isager, "Sacred Animals in Classical and Hellenistic Greece," 15–20.

130. Demetrius, *On Style* 298, translation modified from Innes and Roberts, 521.

131. Dionysius of Halicarnassus, "Demosthenes" 54, trans. Usher, 443.

132. Longinus, *On the* Sublime 43.3, trans. Fyfe and Russell, 297.

133. Longinus, *On the* Sublime 43.3, trans. Fyfe and Russell, 297.

134. Longinus, *On the* Sublime 43.3–4, trans. Fyfe and Russell, 297.

135. Demetrius, *On Style* 89, 274, trans. Innes and Roberts, 407, 507.

136. Demetrius, *On Style* 89, trans. Innes and Roberts, 407.

137. Demetrius, *On Style* 89, trans. Innes and Roberts, 407.

138. Demetrius, *On Style* 274, trans. Innes and Roberts, 507.

139. Demetrius, *On Style* 274, trans. Innes and Roberts, 507.

140. Demetrius, *On Style* 9, trans. Innes and Roberts, 353.

141. Michael Osborn, "Rhetorical Depiction," 76.

142. Osborn, "Rhetorical Depiction," 80.

143. Osborn, "Rhetorical Depiction," 87.

144. Demetrius, *On Style* 259, trans. Innes and Roberts, 499.

145. Demetrius, *On Style* 260, trans. Innes and Roberts, 499, 501.

146. Demetrius, *On Style* 261, trans. Innes and Roberts, 501.

147. Demetrius, *On Style* 261, trans. Innes and Roberts, 501.

148. Demetrius, *On Style* 8, trans. modified from Innes and Roberts, 353.

149. Longinus, *On the Sublime* 20.2, trans. Fyfe and Russell, 237.

150. Longinus, *On the Sublime* 20.3, trans. Fyfe and Russell, 237.

151. Longinus, *On the Sublime* 21.1–2, trans. Fyfe and Russell, 239.

152. Liddell, Scott, and Jones, *Greek-English Lexicon*, s.v. "κέντρον," 939.

153. Pseudo-Lucian, "In Praise of Demosthenes" 20, trans. M. D. Macleod, 261.

154. Eupolis, "Demoi" 102, in *Eupolis: Poet of Old Comedy*, trans. Ian C. Storey, 14.

155. Babrius, "Fables" 2.14–16, trans. Perry, 141.

156. See Perry's note in his Loeb translation of Babrius for an in-depth explanation of the associations with iambic verse, which at the time was linked with the bitter, stinging mood of satire (*Babrius and Phaedrus*, trans. and ed. Ben E. Perry, 4na).

CHAPTER THREE

1. Plutarch, "Demosthenes" 23.3; see also Thomas Martin's discussion of Alexander's conquests in *Ancient Greece from Prehistoric to Hellenistic Times*, 192–93.

2. As with many Plutarch-reported details, this one (the telling of the fable) is contested as historical fact. My concern is as much with the report of his responding with fable, though. Since Demosthenes alludes to the fable only through bare plot, I have offered here the closest Aesopian fable, amended to include the surrender detail as indicated by Plutarch; "Demosthenes" 23.4, trans. Perrin, 57. As Aristotle indicates, fables have flexible forms, especially in the context of oratory. See Ben Edwin Perry, "Appendix: An Analytical Survey of Greek and Latin Fables in the Aesopic Tradition," 450; Aesop, *Aesop's Fables*, trans. Laura Gibbs, 20. For a consideration of veracity and a lengthy discussion of this fable and its alleged context, see Gert-Jan van Dijk, *Ainoi, Logoi, Mythoi: Fables in Archaic, Classical, and Hellenistic Greek*, 292–96. See also (and especially) Leslie Kurke's fascinating discussion of fables in oratory, *Aesopic Conversations: Popular Tradition, Cultural Dialogue, and the Invention of Greek Prose*, 156–58. See also the authoritative text, Aesop, *Aesopica*, ed. Ben Edwin Perry. For an excellent overview of sources on ancient fable, see Jeremy B. Lefkowitz, "Aesop and Animal Fable," 6–7.

3. Van Dijk, *Ainoi, Logoi, Mythoi*, 293.

4. The evidence for the logic of comparison shows up repeatedly in rhetorical treatments of fable. See, for example, van Dijk's *Ainoi, Logoi, Mythoi*, excerpts G48 and G49 (60), from C. Chirius Fortunatianus and Iulius Victor, respectively, both of which count fable *loci circa rem a simili*, which is to say arguments made by drawing a comparison. Aristotle's treatment of fable as example places it next to comparison. See discussion below.

5. Liddell, Scott, and Jones, *Greek-English Lexicon*, 9th ed., s.v. "μονόλυκος" (singularly fierce wolf).

6. Plutarch, "Demosthenes," 23.5. For more on Demades and Athenian political life, see Christian Habicht, *Athens from Alexander to Antony*, 17–22.

7. "Fable 63: Demades the Orator," in *Aesopica*, ed. Ben Edwin Perry, 345–46, translation mine.

8. Derrida, *Animal*, 37.

9. "I take my cue," writes (spoke) Derrida, "from the title of our program. Indeed, that title obliges us to cross the animal with autobiography." Derrida, *Animal*, 37. On the Cerisy conference that occasioned the seminar/lecture from which Derrida's bracing and formative work was drawn, see Mary-Louise Mallet, foreword to Derrida, *Animal*, ix.

10. Crane, *Animal Encounters*, 42–48.

11. Lefkowitz, "Aesop and Animal Fable," 1.

12. John of Sardis, "Selections from the Commentary on the *Progymnasmata* of Aphthonius Attributed to John of Sardis," 181.

13. I do not wish to diminish the political dimensions of epideictic rhetoric, for more on which see Kathleen S. Lamp, *A City of Marble*.

14. Nicolaus the Sophist, "The Preliminary Exercises of Nicolaus the Sophist," in *Progymnasmata*, trans. George Kennedy, 135n18; John of Sardis, "*Progymnasmata* of Aphthonius," 185. For a history of the psychagogic tradition, see John Jasso, "Psychagogia: A Study in the Platonic Tradition of Rhetoric from Antiquity to the Middle Ages."

15. Aristotle, *De anima* 3.11.434a5–10.

16. Debra Hawhee, "Looking into Aristotle's Eyes," 148. For more detailed discussions of deliberative *phantasia*, see Jessica Moss, *Aristotle on the Apparent Good*, 144–52; Martha Craven Nussbaum, "The Role of *Phantasia*"; and Wolfson, "Internal Senses."

17. Ned O'Gorman, "Aristotle's *Phantasia* in the *Rhetoric*: *Lexis*, Appearance, and the Epideictic Function of Discourse," 22 (citing *De anima* 434a).

18. Aristotle, *De anima* 3.7.431b.3–6, translation modified from Sachs, 148.

19. Aristotle, *De anima* 3.3.427b.15–25, trans. Hett, 157.

20. Aristotle, *Poetics* 4.1448b.9–12, trans. Halliwell, 34.

21. The effect I am describing here is something like the faded layering of a palimpsest, as I suggest in an analysis of Demosthenes's "Epitaphios"; see Hawhee, "Looking into Aristotle's Eyes," 156–57. Michael Halloran first suggested the palimpsest analogy to me, and I remain grateful for his suggestion.

22. Aristotle, *Rhetoric* 2.20.5, 1393b, trans. Kennedy, 162–63.

23. The phrase here is *talla dialechtheis*, which Kennedy (162) renders as saying other things at some length, and which Freese (275) translates more simply as after many arguments.

24. Aristotle, *Rhetoric* 2.20.6.1393b, trans. Kennedy, 163.

25. Aristotle, *Rhetoric* 2.20.7.1394a.

26. Aristotle, *Rhetoric* 2.20.7–8.1394a, trans. Kennedy, 163.

27. "Dunētai to homoion horan." Aristotle, *Rhetoric* 2.20.7.1394a.

28. Aristotle, *Rhetoric* 1.2.1355b.1–2. See Kennedy's translation, 37.

29. Aristotle, *Rhetoric* 3.11.1412a, trans. Kennedy, 223.

30. Van Dijk, *Ainoi, Logoi, Mythoi*, 72; Arti Mehta, "How Do Fables Teach? Reading the World of the Fable in Greek, Latin and Sanskrit Narratives," 145–46.

31. Aristotle, *Rhetoric* 2.5.1382a.1, translation modified from Kennedy, 128.

32. Aristotle, *Rhetoric* 2.21.1394a.9, trans. Kennedy, 164. For the lively account of enthy-

meme that informs my own here, see Jeffrey Walker, "The Body of Persuasion: A Theory of the Enthymeme."

33. Aristotle, *Rhetoric* 2.20.1394a.9, trans. Kennedy, 164.

34. The corresponding phrases here are "ho de martus pantachou pithanos" and "heis chrēsimos."

35. Aristotle, *Rhetoric* 1.15.1375b, trans. Kennedy, 106.

36. As such, this reading of the witness passages in Aristotle further corroborates Leslie Kurke's book-length case for fables as part of a tradition of *sophia*; see Kurke, *Aesopic Conversations*.

37. Pseudo-Hermogenes, *Progymnasmata* 1; "The Preliminary Exercises Attributed to Hermogenes," in Kennedy, *Progymnasmata*, 75; Aphthonius, "The Preliminary Exercises of Aphthonius the Sophist," in Kennedy, *Progymnasmata*, 96; see also van Dijk, *Ainoi, Logoi, Mythoi*, 58, 62.

38. Nicolaus, "Preliminary Exercises," 135.

39. Nicolaus, "Preliminary Exercises," 135.

40. I will have more to say about sweetness in the context of the enduring image of the honeybee in chapter 6. For a bracing examination of sweetness in medieval rhetoric, see Mary Carruthers, "Sweetness." The Greek word used by Nicolaus is the genitive case of *hēdutēs*.

41. Aristotle, *De anima* 3.7.431b.9–10, trans. Hett, 179.

42. "Logos pseudēs eikonizōn alētheian." Liddell, Scott, and Jones, *Greek-English Lexicon*, s.v. "εἰκονίδιον," 484, citing Aphthonius's version, translate the phrase's last two words as giving a semblance of truth, while van Dijk (5) makes a convincing case for nudging *alētheian* to "reality." Kennedy, *Progymnasmata* 23, translates the line as a fictitious story giving an image of the truth, thereby stressing the *eikon-* root of *eikonizōn*. I prefer Perry's translation for its preservation of the image word with "picturing," xx.

43. Ben Edwin Perry, introduction to *Babrius and Phaedrus*, xx.

44. Aphthonius (in *Progymnasmata*, trans. Kennedy, 96) and Nicolaus the Sophist (in *Progymnasmata*, trans. Kennedy, 193) both repeat it, as does John of Sardis (in *Progymnasmata*, trans. Kennedy, 177) in his commentary on Aphthonius. Only Hermogenes does not.

45. Aelius Theon, "The Exercises of Aelius Theon," in *Progymnasmata* 4.72, trans. Kennedy, 23.

46. Aelius Theon, "Exercises," 6.

47. Mehta, "How Do Fables Teach?," 13–14.

48. Mehta, "How Do Fables Teach?," 157.

49. Gregory I. Carlson, "Fables Invite Perception."

50. Pseudo-Hermogenes, "Preliminary Exercises," 74.

51. Liddell, Scott, and Jones, *Greek-English Lexicon*, 9th ed., s.v. "ῥυθμίζω."

52. Liddell, Scott, and Jones *Greek-English Lexicon*, 9th ed., s.v. "ἁπαλός." For example: "And as a lion easily crushes the little ones of a swift hind, when he has seized them with his mighty teeth, and has come to their lair, and takes from them their tender life [*hapalon*], and the mother, though she happens to be very near, cannot protect them, for on herself too comes dread trembling, and swiftly she darts through the thick brush and the wood, sweating in her haste before the mighty beast's attack" (*Iliad* 11.114–15, trans. Murray and Wyatt, 501).

53. The Greek counterpart might be *nēpios*, as both John Heath and Richard Janko suggest; see Heath, *The Talking Greeks*, 94–95; Janko, *The Iliad: A Commentary*, 83–84, 266.

54. Liddell, Scott, and Jones, *Greek-English Lexicon*, 9th ed., s.v. "βληχάζω" and "βρυχάομαι." See also Mark Golden, *Children and Childhood in Classical Athens*, 9.

55. Quintilian, *Orator's Education* 1.1.37, trans. Donald A. Russell, 83.

56. Quintilian, *Orator's Education* 1.1.37, trans. Russell, 82n19.

57. Ausonius, "Epigrammata 9," 68; see also van Dijk, *Ainoi, Logoi, Mythoi*, 61.

58. Quintilian, *Instituties of Oratory* 6.3.44 ("Laughter"), 1.9.2 ("Nurse's Stories").

59. Synesius, "On Dreams" 13, trans. William Saunders Crawford, 482.

60. Aristotle, *Metaphysics* 1.1.980a27–69.

61. Aelius Theon, "Exercises," 25; Hesiod, *Works and Days* 202.

62. Hesiod, *Works and Days* 202, translation mine.

63. Aelius Theon, "Exercises," 25 (camel), 26 (dog). These fables correspond to Perry, *Aesopica*, 117 and 133.

64. Pseudo-Hermogenes, "Preliminary Exercises," 74.

65. Aphthonius, "Preliminary Exercises," 96.

66. Aelius Theon, "Exercises," 26.

67. Derrida, *Animal*, 37.

68. The Greek is *pithanon*; the author of the Hermogenic text narrates these qualities as a "sketch" provided by "the ancients," his predecessors who "think it right for [fable] to be fictitious, but in all cases to be useful for some aspect of life. In addition, they want it to be plausible [*pithanon*]." Pseudo-Hermogenes, "Preliminary Exercises," 74.

69. Van Dijk, *Ainoi, Logoi, Mythoi*, 57.

70. Pseudo-Hermogenes, "Preliminary Exercises," trans. Kennedy, 74.

71. Pseudo-Hermogenes, "Preliminary Exercises," trans. Kennedy, 74.

72. Pseudo-Hermogenes, "Preliminary Exercises," trans. Kennedy, 74–75.

73. Pseudo-Hermogenes, "Preliminary Exercises," trans. Kennedy, 75.

74. John of Sardis, "*Progymnasmata* of Aphthonius," trans. Kennedy, 213.

75. John of Sardis, "*Progymnasmata* of Aphthonius," trans. Kennedy, 213.

76. Aphthonius, "Preliminary Exercises," trans. Kennedy, 115.

77. Quintilian, *Orator's Education* 11.1.41, translation modified from Russell, 31.

78. Disagreement on these various terms for speaking for other beings was widespread. For additional sources, see Malcolm Heath, "Theon and the History of the *Progymnasmata*," 154. Theon refers to the large category as *prosopopoeia*, and his treatment notably closes by marking the exercise as "most receptive of character and emotion" or feeling, ēthōn kai pathōn; see Aelius Theon, "Exercises," 47.

79. And so Kraus: "In every case, we notice a highly emotional language characterized by short, even elliptic sentences, by questions and exclamations, by frequent use of anaphora and repetition." "Rehearsing the Other Sex: Impersonation of Women in Ancient Classroom Ethopoeia," 460–61; Marjorie Curry Woods, "Weeping for Dido: Epilogue on a Premodern Rhetorical Exercise in the Postmodern Classroom."

CHAPTER FOUR

1. These encomia are included in Littlewood's edition of Psellos's minor orations, Michael Psellos, *"Lusus ingenii,"* in *Oratoria minora*, ed. Antony Robert Littlewood, 94–115. Translations are mine, though I gratefully acknowledge the insights of Manfred Kraus, Vessela Valiavitcharska, and Jeffrey Walker, whose readerly responses helped me make a few stubborn passages more accurate and readable.

2. See, for example, Henry Knight Miller, "The Paradoxical Encomium with Special Reference to Its Vogue in England, 1600–1800," 145.

3. Psellos, *"Lusus ingenii"* 27, ed. Littlewood, 98.

4. Cicero, *Brutus* 12.47, translation mine. Latin: quod iudicaret hoc oratoris esse maxime proprium, em augere posse laudando.

5. For a consideration of a broader tradition of insects in ancient literature, see Rory Egan's treatment in "Insects," 183–84, which, in addition to Lucian's "The Fly," mentions the mock epic titled *Culex* (mosquito), attributed to Virgil, as well as Virgil's *Georgics*, book 4, which rather famously praises the world of bees.

6. Only Theon ordered ekphrasis before encomium; the manuals attributed to Hermogenes, Aphthonius, and Nicolaus all place it after. George A. Kennedy provides a helpful chart of the treatises' order of treatment in his introduction to *Progymnasmata*, xiii.

7. The lexical manifestations of *thauma* are themselves a marvel in their sheer number. The most common occurrences are (of course) the verb and adjective forms, *thaumazō* and *thaumastos* or *thaumasios*. Magnification is preinstalled in the related verb *thaumastoō*, whose passive form is still "marvel" but in active constructions is translated as magnify. Liddell, Scott, and Jones, *Greek-English Lexicon*, 9th ed., s.vv. "θαῦμα," "θαυμάζω," "θαυμάσιος," and "θαυμασμός/θαυμαστός."

8. Beagon's focus is on classical antiquity, but her case is built on the writings of Pliny the Elder, who figures prominently in chapter 6 of this book. See her "Wondrous Animals in Classical Antiquity," 415.

9. For some time scholars tentatively assumed that "Theon" referred to Aelius Theon, the Alexandrian Sophist of the first century CE. Malcolm Heath, in "Theon and the History of the *Progymnasmata*," has recently made a strong case that the manual was written by a different, much later, separately verified rhetorician called Theon.

10. Here are the opening lines of Theon's ekphrasis exercise as translated by Kennedy: "Ecphrasis [*ekphrasis*] is descriptive language, bringing what is portrayed clearly before the sight. There is ecphrasis of persons [*prosōpa*] and events and places and periods of time" (45); on *prosōpon*, see Liddell, Scott, and Jones, *Greek-English Lexicon*, 9th ed., s.v. "πρόσωπον." Ruth Webb, *Ekphrasis, Imagination, and Persuasion in Ancient Rhetorical Theory and Practice*, 62–67, mentions the Herodotus examples in parentheses but does not overtly try to square their presence with her bewilderment about Aphthonius's addition of animals. That Aphthonius felt the need to add nonhuman animals as a separate item is in itself interesting, and Webb's discussion of the relation to encomiastic subjects, and especially the table she includes, are fruitful in this regard; animals are far from Webb's chief concern. G. E. R. Lloyd, *Science*, 31–32, notes tension in Aristotle's *History of Animals* around the term *prosōpon*. Even when used to

refer specifically to a human (as in Homer), *prosōpon* usually invokes that person's *bodily* form. Herodotus uses *prosōpon* to indicate the hooked beak of the ibis (*prosōpon de es ta malista epigrupon*) in the passage cited by Theon, suggesting that Theon too was drawing on the face-countenance-front meaning rather than the human-person meaning. Elsewhere in Greek writings, the attested uses of *prosōpon* for nonhumans are many: Xenophon refers to the cheerful countenances of hounds ("On Hunting," 4.2 "*tōn prosōpōn phaidrai*"), and Aristotle uses the term in *History of Animals* to refer to a mare's face (8.66.631a5) and to the foreheads of deer (6.29.579a2).

11. Webb, *Ekphrasis*, 79.

12. Aelius Theon, *Exercises*, 45; for these snippets, see also Webb, *Ekphrasis*, 79.

13. Of course it often does. Good entry points to the scholarship on *historia* include Gianna Pomata and Nancy G. Siraisi, "Introduction" to *Historia: Empiricism and Erudition in Early Modern Europe*; Christian Meier, "Historical Answers to Historical Questions: The Origins of History in Ancient Greece"; and Roger French, *Ancient Natural History*.

14. Liddell, Scott, and Jones, *Greek-English Lexicon*, 9th ed., s.v. "ἱστορία."

15. Rosalind Thomas sketches the "prevalent and popular image of Herodotus" as "that of the curious traveller, ready to listen to whatever he is told, anxious like the modern anthropologist to record traditions as they were told to him; tolerant and open-minded" (*Herodotus in Context*, 213). She further draws out the explicitly rhetorical force of Herodotus's mode of *apodeixis*, its use as demonstration or display, and links it, tantalizingly, to medical observations in the Hippocratic tradition, where it is used almost interchangeably with its cognate *epideiknumi*. Several converging contexts—philosophical demonstration, medical demonstration, demonstration as argumentation—help Thomas argue that *apodeiknumi* often contains "the sense of 'show decisively'" (222), and that it carries a reverence for the visible (221–25).

16. Hartog reads the word as it is used in Hesiod as "not only 'a marvel' but also 'a miracle as an object of stupefaction'" (*The Mirror of Herodotus*, 231–32).

17. Herodotus, *Histories* 2.35, trans. Godley, 315, 317.

18. Stephen Greenblatt, *Marvelous Possessions*, 20. Greenblatt's context of colonization is certainly relevant here as well.

19. Webb, in *Ekphrasis*, 79, presuming an earlier Theon, argues that *ekphrasis* becomes more encomiastic with later *progymnasmata* writers. This engagement with Herodotus may well complicate Webb's presumption.

20. Herodotus, *Histories* 2.68.1, trans. Godley, 355.

21. See Valeria Viatcheslavova Sergueenkova, "Natural History in Herodotus' *Histories*," 32.

22. Herodotus, *Histories* 2.68, trans. Godley, 355, 357. I have altered Godley's translation of the Greek *troxilos* to read plover because it returns later in this chapter in lines by Michael Psellos. The species, according to Godly, is the Egyptian plover, *Hoplopterus armatus*. See also Liddell, Scott, and Jones, s.v. τροχίλος.

23. For a recent book-length consideration of *phusis*, see Gerard Naddaf, *The Greek Concept of Nature*. For *phusis* in relation to a network of terms and linked to rhetoric, see Megan Foley, "*Peitho* and *Bia*: The Force of Language," 83.

24. For a discussion of *thauma* produced through measuring the size of something, see Hartog, *Mirror*, 236.

25. Aelius Theon, "Exercises" 119, translation by Webb, *Ekphrasis*, 198.

26. Aelius Theon, "Exercises" 119, translation by Webb, *Ekphrasis*, 198.

27. Aelius Theon, "Exercises" 119, translation by Webb, *Ekphrasis*, 198.

28. Herodotus, *Histories* 2.71, trans. Godley, 359.

29. Hartog, *Mirror*, 236.

30. Aelius Theon, "Exercises" 47.

31. As Froma I. Zeitlin observes of *ekphrasis*, "First and foremost are the qualities of *enargeia* (vividness), *sapheneia* (clarity), and *phantasia* (mental image), which, taken together, aim to turn listeners (or readers) into viewers and to evoke an emotional response through an appeal to the immediacy of an imagined presence" ("Figure: Ekphrasis," 17).

32. As Craig Gibson points out in an introduction to his translation of Libanius, this attribution is contested; see "Introduction" to *Libanius's "Progymnasmata": Model Exercises in Greek Prose Composition and Rhetoric*, trans. Craig A. Gibson, xiv; see also Richard Foerster and Karl Münscher, "Libanios."

33. Libanius, *Progymnasmata* 24.6; *Libanius's "Progymnasmata,"* trans. Gibson, 487.

34. Libanius, *Progymnasmata* 24.7, trans. Gibson, 487.

35. Greek: dedoulōmenon tō thaumatī.

36. Libanius, *Progymnasmata* 24.9, trans. Gibson, 487.

37. On medieval romance, see Lorraine Daston and Katharine Park, *Wonders and the Order of Nature, 1150–1750*, 88–110. For Victorian taxidermy see Rachel Poliquin, *The Breathless Zoo: Taxidermy and the Cultures of Longing*, 11–42.

38. I am following Paula Findlen's use of "scientific culture" in *Possessing Nature*, 9, in order to avoid the pitfalls of naming a set of practices as "science" per se, which risks anachronistically narrowing the scope.

39. For discussions of epideictic's role in reinforcing traditional values, see Chaïm Perelman and Lucie Olbrechts-Tyteca, *The New Rhetoric: A Treatise on Argumentation*, 47–51; Jeffrey Walker, *Rhetoric and Poetics in Antiquity*, 7–8; Ned O'Gorman, "Aristotle's *Phantasia*," 30; Laurent Pernot, *Epideictic Rhetoric*, 27–28, 78–86; and Theodore C. Burgess, *Epideictic Literature*.

40. Liddell, Scott, and Jones, *Greek-English Lexicon*, 9th ed., s.v. "παράδοξος."

41. For a discussion of the rhetorical work of possibility in this speech, see John Poulakos, *Sophistical Rhetoric in Classical Greece*, 68–71.

42. Michael J. Hyde, "Paradox: The Evolution of a Figure in Rhetoric"; Mark Paul Moore, "Rhetoric and Paradox: Seeking Knowledge from the 'Container and Thing Contained'"; and A. E. Malloch, "The Techniques and Function of the Renaissance Paradox." Brian Vickers discusses paradox in the Renaissance, "*King Lear* and Renaissance Paradoxes," and Rosalie L. Colie's *Paradoxia Epidemica* takes on medieval and Renaissance thought. Frances Yates raises issues with Colie's account in "Paradox and Paradise."

43. Moore, "Rhetoric and Paradox," 14.

44. Aristotle, *Rhetoric* 1.9.2.1366a, trans. Kennedy, 76.

45. Aristotle, *Rhetoric* 1.9.2.1366a, translation modified from Kennedy, 76.

46. The phrase is *chōris spoudēs* (separately from or without earnestness), which Kennedy translates as in jest and Freese translates as not serious ("seriously or not"), 91.

47. Aristotle, *Rhetoric* 2.24.1401a, trans. Kennedy, 185.

48. Kennedy, *On Rhetoric*, 185n191.

49. Amusement and laughter attach to the practice of encomizing animals—especially tiny, seemingly insignificant ones—in the context of Attic comedy, especially that of Aristophanes. Burgess in *Epideictic Literature* (157) attributes to the Athenians "a native keenness in detecting the ridiculous" and notes their "great fondness for representing it" on his way to arguing that the paradoxical encomium is inspired by comedy's entrance into prose. Indeed, comedy can hardly be ignored as an important context for the growth of paradoxical encomia, a point I will return to later. The comedies of Aristophanes did much to cultivate a fondness for play.

50. Isocrates's contemporary, the Sophist Polycrates, is the likely target here, for encomia on these topics are attributed to him. Plato, *Symposium* (177B) refers to an encomium on salt by an unknown writer. Jeffrey Walker, *The Genuine Teachers of This Art*, 103–4, discusses Isocrates's resistance to paradoxical themes.

51. Burgess, *Epideictic Literature*, 157.

52. Libanius, *Progymnasmata* 6, trans. Gibson, 259.

53. "Blame of Deer" (*Psogos elaphou*) 8.28–29 (my translation). It is included in a group of sample *progymnasmata* attributed to Nicolaus, as collected in *Rhetores Graeci*, ed. Christianus Walz, 350–51.

54. Nicolaus, *Progymnasmata* 47, trans. Kennedy, "Preliminary Exercises," 154.

55. John of Sardis, *Commentarium in Aphthonii Progymnasmata*: "true things" (*alēthōn*); "the persuasive" (*tou pithanou*); translation mine based on Rabe's Latin edition of John of Sardis, *Commentarium in Aphthonii progymnasmata* 123.1.

56. John of Sardis, *Aphthonii progymnasmata* 123.1, translation mine based on Rabe edition.

57. John of Sardis, *Aphthonii progymnasmata* 125.3–5, translation mine based on Rabe edition.

58. John of Sardis, *Aphthonii progymnasmata* 125.5–9, translation mine based on Rabe edition.

59. Liddell, Scott, and Jones, *Greek-English Lexicon*, 9th ed., s.v. "ἐξετάζω."

60. *Histeon* comes from *oīda*; inf., *eīdein*, to see; *histeon de*—one must see.

61. Aristotle, *Rhetoric* 1.9.39.1368a; for a discussion of amplification in book 2, see 2.19.4.1391b.

62. Quintilian, *Orator's Education* 3.7.6, my translation. Latin: sed proprium laudis est res amplificare et ornare.

63. Pernot, *Epideictic Rhetoric*, 87.

64. Quintilian, *Orator's Education* 8.4.3, translation mine.

65. Quintilian, *Orator's Education* 8.4.16, trans. Russell, 399. Latin: ut aliud crescat, aliud augetur, inde ad id quod extolli volumus ratione transitur.

66. Aristotle, *Rhetoric* 1.9.38.1368a, trans. Kennedy, 82.

67. Aristotle, *Rhetoric* 1.9.38.1368a, translation modified from Kennedy, 82. See Liddell, Scott, and Jones, *Greek-English Lexicon*, 9th ed., s.v. "ἀντιπαραβάλλειν."

68. The subsequent discussion in this passage serves to further suture comparison and praise together with amplification: "Amplification [*auxēsis*], with good reason, falls among forms of praise, for it aims to show prominence, and prominence reveals beauty. Thus, even if there is no comparison with those held in high esteem, it is necessary to compare [the person

praised] with others [*tous allous*], since superiority [even over them] reveals excellence" (Aristotle, *Rhetoric* 1.9.1368a.39, translation modified from Kennedy, 82).

By this point in the discussion, comparison is deemed so integral to the amplification-praise pair that Aristotle can move swiftly from a mention of superiority or prominence (*hyperochē*) to the act of comparison itself. The *progymnasmata* tradition follows Aristotle's lead in binding together comparison and encomium. Even though they are two separate exercises, *synkrisis* is explicitly folded into the *progymnasmata* encomium by several of the manual writers, just as encomium is mentioned in several of the treatments of *synkrisis*. Pseudo-Hermogenes's discussion of *synkrisis* notes the use of encomiastic topics. His discussion (see Kennedy, *Progymnasmata*, 84) emphasizes the enormous flexibility of the tool. The same can be said about Theon's discussion of *synkrisis* (Kennedy, *Progymnasmata*, 53–54). The manual attributed to Hermogenes puts it this way: "The best source of argument in encomia is derived from comparisons, which you will utilize as the occasion suggests" (*Progymnasmata* 17, trans. Kennedy, 82).

69. Aphthonius, "Preliminary Exercises," trans. Kennedy, 113.

70. Aphthonius, "Preliminary Exercises," trans. Kennedy, 113. Here the word *deinos*, especially with the intensifier *kathapax*, suggests the activation of something like *thauma*, wonderment.

71. Aphthonius, "Preliminary Exercises," trans. Kennedy, 113–14.

72. Their situation, of course, is also very different: although composed in the second century, Lucian's "The Fly" delighted audiences far and wide, especially during the Renaissance, when the speech was frequently reproduced and imitated. The most notable translators of Lucian into Latin are Desiderius Erasmus and Thomas More, and though Lucian's work saw a revival during the early modern period, Byzantine scholars (among them Psellos), by keeping Lucian very much in play, helped make that revival possible. In contrast to Lucian's tribute to the fly, though, Psellos's bug set has remained relatively obscure apart from the Greek text edited by Littlewood and a German translation by Margarethe Billerbeck and Christian Zubler; see Michael Psellus, "*Lusus ingenii*," in *Oratoria minora*, ed. Antony Robert Littlewood, 94–115; "Michael Psellos, Enkomien: Text und Übersetzung," in *Das Lob der Fliege von Lukian bis L. B. Alberti: Gattungsgeschichte, Texte, Übersetzungen und Kommentar*, ed. Magarethe Billerbeck and Christian Zubler, 118–32. It is a little odd that so few of the scholars who have worked on Psellos's paradoxical encomia recognize that he was explicitly writing in the vein of Lucian. See, for example, Jorge Marcos de la Fuente, "El insecto como tema retórico y poético." For more on Psellos's background, particularly as it relates to the study and history of rhetoric, see Jeffrey Walker, "Michael Psellos on Rhetoric: A Translation and Commentary on Psellos' Synopsis of Hermogenes"; Herbert Hunger, *Die hochsprachliche profane Literatur der Byzantiner*, 131–32.

73. Lucian, "The Fly" 1, trans. A. M. Harmon, 83.

74. Lucian, "Fly" 1, trans. Harmon, 83.

75. Psellos, "*Lusus ingenii*" 27.1–2, ed. Littlewood, 98, translation mine.

76. Psellos, "*Lusus ingenii*" 27.10–11, ed. Littlewood, 98: "gathering into oneself" (*eis heauto sustraphen*), translation mine.

77. Psellos, "*Lusus ingenii*" 27.18–19, 20–21, ed. Littlewood, 98. Here Psellos relies on the theory of spontaneous generation put forth in book 3 of Aristotle's *Generation of Animals*. The scholarship on Aristotle's theory of spontaneous generation is vast. See Henry Harris, *Things Come to Life: Spontaneous Generation Revisited*; Allan Gotthelf, "Teleology and Spon-

taneous Generation in Aristotle: A Discussion"; D. M. Balme, "Development of Biology in Aristotle and Theophrastus: Theory of Spontaneous Generation"; James Lennox, "Teleology, Chance, and Aristotle's Theory of Spontaneous Generation"; and for an early overview and intervention that gives mention to nineteenth-century theories, see Eugene S. McCartney, "Spontaneous Generation and Kindred Notions in Antiquity." For a thoroughgoing account of the theory's uptake in Darwin's time, see James E. Strick, *Sparks of Life: Darwinism and the Victorian Debates over Spontaneous Generation*.

78. Psellos, *"Lusus ingenii"* 27.95–99, ed. Littlewood, 101, translation mine.

79. Psellos, *"Lusus ingenii"* 29.59–63, ed. Littlewood, 10, translation mine.

80. Herodotus, *Histories* 2.68, trans. A. D. Godley, 357.

81. Psellos, *"Lusus ingenii"* 27.88–93, ed. Littlewood, 100–101, translation mine.

82. Psellos, *"Lusus ingenii"* 27.93–94, ed. Littlewood, 101, translation mine.

83. Psellos, *"Lusus ingenii"* 29.68–71, ed. Littlewood, 109–10, translation mine.

84. Psellos, *"Lusus ingenii"* 29.48, ed. Littlewood, 109, translation mine.

85. Psellos, *"Lusus ingenii"* 29.52–53, ed. Littlewood, 109, translation mine.

86. Psellos, *"Lusus ingenii"* 29.53–54, ed. Littlewood, 109, translation mine.

87. Lucian, "Fly" 2, translation modified from Harmon, 85.

88. Lucian, "Fly" 2, translation modified from Harmon, 83.

89. The *kai mēn* that introduces this sentence (here translated as moreover) often marks something deserving special attention, and the optative's conditional, *blepoi*, "if [one] looks," gently urges readers to look with a tantalizing glimpse of what they will see if they do, much as Psellos's bedbug description notes that not just anyone gets to see the queen, though it's obvious that people would elbow their way to the front of a crowd were such a glimpse possible.

90. Psellos, *"Lusus ingenii"* 29.55–56, ed. Littlewood, 109, translation mine.

91. Lucian, "Fly" 2, trans. Harmon, 83, 85.

92. Aphthonius, "Preliminary Exercises," trans. Kennedy, 114.

93. Augustine, *The City of God against the Pagans* 22.24, trans. William M. Green, 335.

94. Pease, "Things without Honor," 32.

95. Psellos, *"Lusus ingenii"* 28.30–35, ed. Littlewood, 103.

96. Lucian, "Fly" 6.1–3, trans. Harmon, 89.

97. Lucian, "Fly" 6.3–4, trans. Harmon, 89.

98. Lucian, "Fly" 7.4–7, trans. Harmon, 89, 91.

99. *"Thaumazein axion."* Lucian, "Fly" 12.6; see Harmon's translation, 93.

100. Lucian, "Fly" 12.7–8, translation mine.

101. Psellos, *"Lusus Ingenii,"* 29.48–50, ed. Littlewood, 109, translation mine.

102. *"Thaumasiōteron."* Psellos, *"Lusus ingenii"* 28.13, ed. Littlewood, 102, translation mine.

103. For a discussion of spontaneous generation focused on Aristotle and acknowledging the role of *thauma*, see Lloyd, *Aristotelian Explorations*, 104–25.

104. Psellos, *"Lusus ingenii"* 28.41–44, ed. Littlewood, 103–4, translation mine.

105. *Ekplēttometha*, expel or drive out, here translated as stunned, carries secondary meaning having to do with sensation, amazement, sudden shock, or "any sudden, overpowering passion." Liddell, Scott, and Jones, *Greek-English Lexicon*, 9th ed., s.v. "ἐκπλήσσω."

106. Psellos, *"Lusus ingenii"* 28.16–20, ed. Littlewood, 102–3, translation mine.

107. See John Pollard, *Birds in Greek Life and Myth*, 31–32.

108. Psellos, "*Lusus ingenii*" 28.54–57, ed. Littlewood, 104, translation mine.

109. Psellos, "*Lusus ingenii*" 28.98, ed. Littlewood, 105, translation mine.

110. Psellos, "*Lusus ingenii*" 28.114, ed. Littlewood, 106, translation mine.

111. Psellos, "*Lusus ingenii*" 28.73–76, ed. Littlewood, 105, translation mine.

112. Psellos, "*Lusus ingenii*" 28.119–20, ed. Littlewood, 106, translation mine.

113. Psellos, "*Lusus ingenii*" 28.121–24, ed. Littlewood, 106, translation mine, though I am especially grateful to Manfred Kraus for his assistance with this stubborn passage.

114. Lucian, "Fly" 12, translation mine.

115. Lucian, "Fly" 3, trans. Harmon, 85.

116. Lucian, "Fly" 6, trans. Harmon, 89.

117. Kenneth Burke, *Permanence and Change*, 90.

118. Theodore C. Burgess asserts that the *paradoxon encomion* "is a mere display of ingenuity, a *jeu de langage*." *Epideictic Literature*, 157.

119. Desiderius Erasmus to Thomas More, [Paris?], 9 June [1511], in *The Correspondence of Erasmus 2: Letters 142–297 (1501–1514)*, *Collected Works of Erasmus*, 2:163–64.

120. Jordynn Jack, "A Pedagogy of Sight: Microscopic Vision in Robert Hooke's *Micrographia*."

121. Pease, "Things without Honor," 33. For a wonderful and thorough account of the precursors—ancient, medieval, and early modern—to seventeenth-century science, see Catherine Wilson, *The Invisible World: Early Modern Philosophy and the Invention of the Microscope*. Wilson uses the term protoscience, but mainly to refer to the seventeenth century (see especially 56 for her reasons).

122. Robert Hooke, *Micrographia, or Some Physiological Descriptions of Minute Bodies Made by Magnifying Glasses*, 196.

123. Jack, "Pedagogy of Sight," 192.

124. Hooke, *Micrographia*, 185.

125. Hooke, *Micrographia*, 206.

126. Hooke, *Micrographia*, 210 (bookworm), 182 (blue fly). Hooke cites Lucian in *Micrographia*'s discussion of the magnified edge of a razor (5). Thanks to Jeanne Fahnestock for sending me in this direction.

127. Jack, "Pedagogy of Sight," 193.

128. Jack, "Pedagogy of Sight," 193.

CHAPTER FIVE

1. Manfred Kraus, "Grammatical and Rhetorical Exercises," and Marjorie Curry Woods, "Weeping for Dido." Periodization, of course is not without its critics. See Jennifer Summit and David Wallace, "Rethinking Periodization."

2. The term memorial cultures is Mary Carruthers's (*The Book of Memory*, 240; *The Craft of Thought*, 144).

3. Raphael Samuel, *Theatres of Memory*, vii.

4. Albertus Magnus, *De bono*, translation modified from "Appendix B: Albertus Magnus: *De Bono*, tractatus 4, quaestio 2, 'De partibus prudentiae,'" trans. Mary Carruthers in *Book of Memory*, 359.

5. "Memoria est pars sensibilis animae et non rationalis per se [memory is part of the sensory soul and not of the rational *per se*]." Albertus Magnus, *Opera omnia*, ed. H. C. Kühle, B. Geyer Feckes, and W. Kübel, vol. 28, quaestio 2: *De partibus prudentiae*, 245.

6. Carruthers, *Craft of Thought*, 144.

7. Aristotle, *Metaphysics* 1.2.982b.12–14, trans. Tredennick, 13: "Dia gar to thaumatzein hoi anthrōpoi kai nun kai to prōton ērxanto philosophein [It is through wonder that men now begin and originally began to philosophize]."

8. Translation modified from Albertus Magnus, *De bono*, trans. Carruthers in *Book of Memory*, 359.

9. Carruthers, *Craft of Thought*, 10–16.

10. Quintilian, *Orator's Education* 11.2.1, trans. Donald A. Russell, 59.

11. I am following Russell's translation/interpretation (59) of *spiritus*'s ablative (*spiritu*) as an ablative of instrument ("by this animating principle").

12. Aristotle, *De memoria* 1.450a.13–14, trans. Hett, 293.

13. "It is impossible even to think without a mental picture" (*De memoria* 1.449b.32). This statement repeats and explicitly invokes the following *De anima* passage: "The soul never thinks without a mental image" (3.7.431a.17–18, trans. Hett, 177). See my discussion of these notions in chapter 1.

14. Aristotle, *De memoria* 1.450a.23.

15. See also Hawhee, "Looking into Aristotle's Eyes," 143.

16. Aristotle, *Rhetoric* 1.11.1370a.28–29, trans. Kennedy, 88.

17. Aristotle, *De memoria* 1.449b.24, trans. Hett, 291.

18. Another instance of *phantasmata* being devised might be rhetorical language itself (see Hawhee, "Looking into Aristotle's Eyes," 139–65, for an argument in that direction).

19. Aristotle, *De anima* 3.3.427b.18–22, translation modified from Hett, 157.

20. Liddell, Scott, and Jones, *Greek-English Lexicon*, 9th ed., s.v. "εἰδωλοποίησις," 484.

21. Richard Sorabji, *Aristotle on Memory*, 69.

22. Aristotle, *De anima* 3.3.427b.26–27, trans. Hett, 157.

23. The sentiment continues, "We enjoy contemplating the most precise images of things whose actual sight is painful to us, such as the forms of the most vile beasts and of corpses" (Aristotle, *Poetics* 4.1448b.9–13, trans. Halliwell, 37–38).

24. Aristotle, *De memoria* 2.451b.12–13, trans. Hett, 301.

25. Aristotle, *De memoria* 2.451b.17–18, trans. Hett, 301.

26. Aristotle, *De memoria* 2.451b.25–27, trans. Hett, 303: "Generally speaking, it is when other impulses, such as we have mentioned, have first been aroused that the particular impulse follows."

27. Mary Carruthers and Jan Ziolkowski, introduction to *The Medieval Craft of Memory*, 8 (emphasis in original).

28. Aristotle, *De memoria* 2.451a.23–24, trans. Hett, 299.

29. In addition to all of Mary Carruthers's books cited in this chapter, key texts are Yates, *Art of Memory*; Lina Bolzoni, *The Gallery of Memory*; Philippe Codognet, "The Logic of Memory and the Memory of Logic"; Douwe Draaisma, *Metaphors of Memory*; Jody Enders, *Rhetoric, Memory, Violence*; Grover Zinn, "Hugh of Saint Victor and the Art of Memory"; and Gillian R. Evans, "Two Aspects of *Memoria* in Eleventh and Twelfth Century Writings."

30. For more on the influence of *Rhetorica ad Herennium* as half of a pair of texts attributed to Cicero, see John O. Ward, "The Medieval and Early Renaissance Study of Cicero's *De Inventione* and the *Rhetorica ad Herennium*."

31. Yates, *Art of Memory*, 55.

32. [Cicero], *Rhetorica ad Herennium* 3.22.35, trans. Caplan, 219, with emphasis and key Latin terms added.

33. Indicative passive plural verb; literally, "wondered at."

34. Charleton T. Lewis and Charles Short, *A Latin Dictionary*, s.v. "exsuscito," 706.

35. [Cicero], *Rhetorica ad Herennium* 3.16.29, trans. Caplan, 209.

36. [Cicero], *Rhetorica ad Herennium* 3.16.29–30, trans. Caplan, 209.

37. Carruthers, *Craft of Thought*, 16.

38. [Cicero], *Rhetorica ad Herennium* 3.22.37, trans. Caplan, 221.

39. Carruthers, *Book of Memory*, 177.

40. [Cicero], *Rhetorica ad Herennium* 3.20.33, trans. Caplan, 215.

41. [Cicero], *Rhetorica ad Herennium*, trans. Caplan, 214–15nb.

42. The commentary tradition will occupy this chapter. For a good example of the image's work in contemporary theory, see the chapter titled "*Medico Testiculi Arietini:* On the Ring Finger a Ram's Testicles" in Tom Tyler's *Cifarae: A Bestiary in Five Fingers*, 109–62.

43. The relevant work here is Mary Carruthers, "Rhetorical *Memoria* in Commentary and Practice," 224–25; Carruthers's survey of the imagery gave rise to this chapter's preliminary hunch. See also Jody Enders, *Rhetoric, Memory, Violence*, 83–87. Special thanks to John O. Ward, who generously shared with me his transcriptions of the Champeaux manuscript, the most important manuscript for my analysis of the Aristotelian and Herennial lines.

44. For the authorship and date of this manuscript, see Karin M. Fredborg, "The Commentaries on Cicero's *De Inventione* and *Rhetorica ad Herennium* by William of Champeaux," whose case for William of Champeaux appears to have received broad acceptance by medieval scholars. See also Constant J. Mews, "*Logica* in the Service of Philosophy: William of Champeaux and His Influence."

45. Latin: Si utemur dispositione formarum, id est ordine, et notatione imaginum, id est si bene retinebimus et quo loco posita sit imago et que res sit imago cuius rei, sicut testiculi testium (William of Champeaux, *Etsi cum Tullius*, ed. John O. Ward, 73). Special thanks to Dr. Ryan McConnell for consulting with me on this translation.

46. "Reum tenentem poculum potionum in dextera, in sinistra tabulas, et per hoc significabimus istum interfecisse illum ueneno pro hereditate. Addit et ad designandos testes illum tenentem cum illo digito qui medicus uocatur testiculos arietinos, significans per eos testes potionis et ueneni quod designatur per testiculos arietis qui uenenosi sunt, vel dixit arietinos significat quod deffensor aget contra testes arietantes et ipsum reum cornibus suis inquietantes" (William of Champeaux, *Etsi cum Tullius*, ed. Ward, 73).

47. Carruthers works with these lines in "Rhetorical *Memoria*," 224–25.

48. "Meminisse nisi res mirabiles et magnas, sicut stellam que apparuit tempore anglici regis. Si iterum uidemus res *usitatas* non solemus meminisse nisi nouas; sed si uidemus aliquid multum *turpe* aut multum honestum inter homines tamen inauditum et cetera" (William of Champeaux, *Etsi cum Tullius*, ed. Ward, 75).

49. Pliny, *Natural History* 8.72, trans. Rackham, 131, 133.

50. Galen, *On the Properties of Foodstuffs* {*De alimentorum facultatibus*} 3.5–6 ("On Testes"), trans. Owen Powell, 121: "Those of younger animals are better, but the testes of bulls, male goats and rams are distasteful, difficult to concoct and unwholesome. . . . But they remove the testicles of goats and sheep for both reasons [eating and usefulness]. The testicles of all the above animals are difficult to concoct and unwholesome, but nourishing when well concocted. Their defects and virtues parallel what was said about flesh. For just as the flesh of sheep is superior in all respects, so too are their testes, to the same extent."

51. Richard Barber, ed., *Bestiary: MS Bodley 764*, 80.

52. Carruthers, *Book of Memory*, 178, notes that "this aggressive ram with large testicles . . . had become the standard academic gloss on this passage by the time Albertus wrote," and in "Rhetorical *Memoria*" (224) she pieces together a compelling lineage for the altered image, beginning with William of Champeaux, through Thierry of Chartres, Alanus, and Guarino.

53. Albertus Magnus, "Commentary on Aristotle, *On Memory and Recollection*," trans. Ziolkowski, in *The Medieval Craft of Memory*, ed. Carruthers and Ziolkowski, 138; see Carruthers, *Craft of Thought*, 260, for a discussion of "the lower-light, 'obscure' aesthetic familiar to Albertus," which Carruthers designates "Gothic gloom."

54. Albertus Magnus, "Commentary on Aristotle," trans. Ziolkowski, 138.

55. Yates, *Art of Memory*, 68–69.

56. [Cicero], *Rhetorica ad Herennium* 3.22.35, trans. Caplan, 219. See also Albertus Magnus, *De bono*, trans. Carruthers in *Book of Memory*, 353.

57. Aristotle, *De memoria* 2.451b.19–21, trans. Hett, 301.

58. Albertus Magnus, "Commentary on Aristotle," trans. Ziolkowski, 141.

59. Albertus Magnus, *Opera omnia* 9:111, translation mine.

60. Albertus Magnus, "Commentary on Aristotle," 14, translation modified from Ziolkowski, 142.

61. Albertus Magnus, "Commentary on Aristotle," trans. Ziolkowski, 142.

62. Albertus Magnus, "Commentary on Aristotle," trans. Ziolkowski, 142; Latin text added from Albertus Magnus, *Opera omnia*, ed. Borgnet, 9:102.

63. Albertus Magnus, *De bono*, trans. Carruthers in *Book of Memory*, 350; Latin text in Albertus Magnus, *Opera omnia*, ed. Kühle et al., 247.

64. Albertus Magnus, *De bono*, trans. Carruthers in *Book of Memory*, 351, translation modified.

65. Albertus Magnus, *De bono*, trans. Carruthers in *Book of Memory*, 353.

66. Carruthers, *Book of Memory*, 178.

67. Thomas Aquinas, "Commentary on Aristotle, *On Memory and Recollection*," trans. John Burchill in *The Medieval Craft of Memory*, 153–88. See in particular lesson 2 (161–65), which discusses *phantasia* and phantasms in depth. For the point about vigor and wonder, see 166.332: "Yet it happens that things which one receives in boyhood are firmly held in the memory because of the vigor of its movement, just as it happens that things about which we wonder are imprinted more in the memory. We wonder, especially, however, at the new and unusual: hence a greater wondering about things, as if they were unusual, affects the young who are going about in the world for the first time."

68. Carruthers discusses the relevant passage in these successors in "Rhetorical *Memoria*," 224.

69. Thomas Bradwardine, "On Acquiring a Trained Memory," trans. Mary Carruthers in *The Medieval Craft of Memory*, 208.

70. Bradwardine, "Trained Memory," trans. Carruthers, 208.

71. Bradwardine, "Trained Memory," trans. Carruthers, 208; Latin text edited by Carruthers in Bradwardine, "De memoria artificiale adquirenda," 36, lines 49–59.

72. Bradwardine, "Trained Memory," trans. Carruthers, 209–10; Latin text edited by Carruthers in Bradwardine, "De memoria artificiale adquirenda," 37, lines 92–99.

73. Caplan's gloss on this passage helpfully elaborates on the symbolism here: "According to Macrobius, *Sat.* 7.13.7–8 (ed. Kaster), the anatomists spoke of a nerve which extends from the heart to the fourth finger of the left hand (the *digitus medicinalis*), where it interlaces into the other nerves of that finger; the finger was therefore ringed, as with a crown. [Cicero], *Rhetorica ad Herennium*, trans. Caplan, 214–15nb.

74. [Cicero], *Rhetorica ad Herennium*, ed. Caplan, 215nb, notes the ancient use of animal testicles as money sacks.

75. Bradwardine, "Trained Memory," trans. Carruthers, 210; Latin text edited by Carruthers in Bradwardine, "De memoria artificiale adquirenda," 37, lines 100–104.

76. Bradwardine, "Trained Memory," trans. Carruthers, 210.

77. For an alternative reading emphasizing the witnessing function of Bradwardine's zodiacal women, see Enders, *Rhetoric, Memory, Violence*, 86–88.

78. Bradwardine, "Trained Memory," trans. Carruthers, 210.

79. Bradwardine, "Trained Memory," trans. Carruthers, 210; Latin text edited by Carruthers in Bradwardine, "De memoria artificiale adquirenda," 37, lines 103–5.

80. Bradwardine, "Trained Memory," trans. Carruthers, 210–11; Latin text edited by Carruthers in Bradwardine, "De memoria artificiale adquirenda," 37, lines 112–18.

81. Bradwardine, "Trained Memory," trans. Carruthers, 210.

82. Although the subject matter is beyond the scope of this chapter, it bears mentioning that the memory images of the gospels Mark, Luke, and John that derive from a popular and widely imitated anonymous fifteenth-century blockbook and are reprinted by Carruthers and Ziolkowski feature an eagle, a lion, and an ox, respectively, all on hind legs, bodies splayed in this manner, with symbols of the narratives to be memorized from gospel chapters; see "A Method for Recollecting the Gospels," in *The Medieval Craft of Memory*, ed. Mary Carruthers and Jan Ziolkowski, 255–93.

83. [Cicero], *Rhetorica ad Herennium* 3.22.35, trans. modified from Caplan, 219.

84. Carruthers, *Book of Memory*, 160.

85. Carruthers, *Book of Memory*, 158. In addition to Carruthers's discussion on 158–59, for even broader historical context see also Lillian B. Lawler, "Zoologically Speaking," 671–82.

86. Carruthers, *Book of Memory*, 159.

87. See especially her discussion of Philippe de Thaon's bestiary, which instructs readers, "Hold in memory. This is important" (160).

88. See, for example, Bruce Holsinger, "Of Pigs and Parchment: Medieval Studies and the Coming of the Animal," and Jay David Bolter and Richard Grusin, *Remediation: Understanding New Media*, 35–36.

CHAPTER SIX

1. Desiderius Erasmus, "The Godly Feast," trans. Craig R. Thompson, *Collected Works of Erasmus*, 39:175.

2. Desiderius Erasmus, "*Copia*: Foundations of the Abundant Style" (De duplici copia verborum ac rerum commentarii duo), trans. Betty I. Knott, *Collected Works of Erasmus*, 24:638.

3. Erasmus, *De copia*, trans. Knott, *CWE*, 24:585.

4. Here I am thinking of his *Adages* and *Parallels*, compilations of (respectively) proverbial and comparative material, which I will discuss later in the chapter.

5. Desiderius Erasmus, "On Good Manners for Boys" (De civilitate morum puerilium), trans. Brian McGregor, *Collected Works of Erasmus*, 25:284, 275.

6. The comparison may be found in a number of places in Erasmus's work, but it is at its highest pitch in a long elaboration on the adage "war is sweet for those who have not tried it," especially in a reflection on the "tyranny of the stomach," which Erasmus claims "reached the point that no animal was ever safe from the cruelty of man" (*Adages IIIiv1 to IVii100*, trans. Denis L. Drysdall, vol. 35 of *Collected Works of Erasmus*, 409. See also the critique of hunting in "Praise of Folly" (Stultitiae laus), trans. Betty Radice, *Collected Works of Erasmus*, 27:112–13; see also his colloquy on hunting, "Hunting (Venatio)," in *Colloquies 1*, trans. and ed. Craig R. Thompson, 109–12, vol. 39 of *Collected Works of Erasmus*.

7. Erasmus, "Hunting," trans. Thompson, *CWE*, 39:109–12; Desiderius Erasmus, "Sympathy" (Amicitia), trans. Craig R. Thompson, 1033–55, vol. 39 of *Collected Works of Erasmus*.

8. Desiderius Erasmus, "A Declamation on the Subject of Early Liberal Education for Children" (De pueris statim ac liberaliter instituendis declamation), trans. Beert C. Verstraete, *Collected Works of Erasmus*, 26:297–346.

9. Desiderius Erasmus, "The Right Way of Speaking Latin and Greek: A Dialogue" (De recta latini graecique sermonis pronuntiatione dialogus), trans. Maurice Pope, *Collected Works of Erasmus*, 26:368–475. Brian W. Ogilvie discusses humanist philology of the late fifteenth century compared with natural history (*The Science of Describing*, 6). In Erasmus, we see an odd combination of the two. In a headnote to the Dialogue, translator Maurice Pope points out that "The Right Way of Speaking" was "one of the foundation charters of the classical education . . . in European schools from the sixteenth to the twentieth century" (348).

10. Jeanne Fahnestock notes that with *De copia* "Erasmus produced the greatest single work" on copiousness (*Rhetorical Style*, 391). Similarly, Peter Mack's remarkable chapter on Erasmus notes that *De copia* "defined and established the centrality of amplification for the next eighty years" (*Renaissance Rhetoric*, 76); Mack also discusses Erasmus's influence in the sixteenth century (*A History of Renaissance Rhetoric, 1380–1620*, 76–103). See also Heinrich F. Plett, *Rhetoric and Renaissance Culture*, 23–24; Thomas O. Sloane, "Schoolbooks and Rhetoric: Erasmus's *Copia*."

11. As George Kennedy notes, *copia* translates in this instance simply as abundance (*Classical Rhetoric and Its Christian and Secular Tradition from Ancient to Modern Times*, 206). It is tempting, to be sure, to make *copia* into an adjective, as so many scholars do, yielding translations such as "abundant style," or to add a prepositional phrase linking the abundance to language, "abundance in [or of] language." Doing so, however, risks deemphasizing the comprehensive approach to abundance that Erasmus in fact developed. Thomas Sloane makes

a similar point in relation to the Toronto edition's title *Foundations of Abundant Style* (*On the Contrary*, 60).

12. Sloane, *On the Contrary*, 56–79. See also Sloane, "Schoolbooks and Rhetoric," 113–29.

13. For an account of Erasmus and the publishing world, see Lisa Jardine, *Worldly Goods*, 155–56. Jardine gives Pliny and Erasmus prominent places in her account of the economy of early printing: Pliny as a commodity and Erasmus as a well-connected figure in the world of print production.

14. Paula Findlen, *Possessing Nature*, 64. See also an early intervention by Lisa Jardine, who marvels at "how reluctant we are to include acquisitiveness among the defining characteristics of the age which formed our aesthetic heritage" (*Worldly Goods*, 12).

15. Zoo histories offer details about such circumstances. See, for instance, Vernon N. Kisling Jr., "Ancient Collections and Menageries," and Eric Baratay and Elisabeth Hardouin-Fugier, *Zoo: A History of Zoological Gardens in the West*, 29–34. For a wonderful and wide-ranging theoretical history of taxidermy, see Poliquin, *Breathless Zoo*, and Barbara M. Benedict, *Curiosity*.

16. For this point, in addition to Findlen's book cited above, see Paula Findlen, "Inventing Nature: Commerce, Art, and Science in the Early Modern Cabinet of Curiosities," 301.

17. Ann M. Blair, *Too Much to Know*, 11.

18. I refer to Erasmus's "rhetoric" deliberately, despite Thomas Conley's insistence that Erasmus did not write about rhetoric (*Rhetoric in the European Tradition*, 120). For a discussion of why Conley's passing assertion is misleading because it is based on a "curiously foreshortened" and therefore a short-shrifted account of Erasmus, see Sloane, *On the Contrary*, 71–72.

19. Arthur Quinn and Lyon Rathbun, "Accumulatio," 1.

20. "Congeries quoque verborum ac sententiarum idem significantium." Quintilian, *Orator's Education* 8.4.26–27, translation mine.

21. Charleton T. Lewis and Charles Short, *A Latin Dictionary*, s.v. "accumulatio."

22. "In very warm localities growers heap (*adcumulant*) earth over the roots in summer and cover them up, to prevent the heat of the sun from parching them." Pliny, *Natural History* 17.31.140, trans. Rackham, 99.

23. Paula Findlen takes up the idea of "collecting as [Europeans'] key to understanding their world" (*Possessing Nature*, 3). Susan M. Pearce treats the social basis of collecting (*On Collecting*, 4).

24. Erasmus, *De copia*, trans. Knott, *CWE*, 24:348–54. These variations are followed by two hundred variations of "Always, as long as I live, I shall remember you" (354–65). See Fahnestock, *Rhetorical Style*, 395.

25. Fahnestock, *Rhetorical Style*, 395.

26. For the language of *copia* as a "faculty," see *De copia*: "It remains for me now to give some brief advice on the exercises by which this faculty [*facultas*] may be developed" (trans. Knott, *CWE*, 24:303).

27. Erasmus, *De copia*, translation modified from Knott, *CWE*, 24:301.

28. Erasmus, *De copia*, trans. Knott, *CWE*, 24:303.

29. Quintilian's choice of the sentence "Milo carried a grown bull which he had been used to carry as a calf" as a model sentence for declension work implies the approach elaborated here by Erasmus (see Quintilian, *Orator's Education* 1.9.5).

30. Erasmus, *De copia*, trans. Knott, *CWE*, 24:303.

31. Erasmus, *De copia*, trans. Knott, *CWE*, 24:302.

32. Erasmus, *De copia*, trans. Knott, *CWE*, 24:302.

33. Erasmus, *De copia*, trans. Knott, *CWE*, 24:307.

34. Lewis and Short, *Latin Dictionary*, s.v. "res"; *OED Online*, s.v. "res publica," last modified December 2014; *OED Online*, s.v. "republic," last modified December 2014.

35. Brian Vickers, "'Words and Things'-or 'Words, Concepts, and Things'?, 302.

36. Fahnestock, *Rhetorical Style*, 397.

37. Quintilian, *Orator's Education* 8.4.25–26.

38. Erasmus, *De copia*, trans. modified from Knott, *CWE*, 24:572.

39. Erasmus, *De copia*, trans. Knott, *CWE*, 24:301.

40. Desiderius Erasmus, "On the Method of Study" (De ratione studii ac legendi interpretandique auctores), trans. Brian McGregor, *Collected Works of Erasmus*, 24:666.

41. Erasmus, "On the Method of Study," trans. McGregor, *CWE*, 24:666.

42. Baratay and Hardouin-Fugier, *Zoo*, 29; Vernon N. Kisling Jr., "Preface," in *Zoo and Aquarium History*; Findlen, "Inventing Nature," 300. On rarity in the context of book collections, see Jardine, *Worldly Goods*, 192.

43. Desiderius Erasmus, "A Short Rule for Copiousness" (Brevis de copia praeceptio), in *Colloquies 1*, trans. and ed. Craig R. Thompson, vol. 39 of *Collected Works of Erasmus*, 169.

44. See Desiderius Erasmus to John More, Freiburg, 27 February, 1531 (Letter 2432, preface to *Aristotelis opera*, Basle, J. Bebel), in *Opus epistolarum Des. Erasmi Roterodami*, vol. 9, *1530–1532*, ed. P. S. Allen, H. M. Allen, and H. W. Garrod, 133–40.

45. Erasmus, "On the Method of Study," 667.

46. Erasmus, "On the Method of Study," 667.

47. Pliny, preface to *Naturalis historia*, 0.17, translation mine. As Gian Biagio Conte notes, though, the sum total of index items for all the books of the work is 34,000, and "the discrepancy between the two sums has not yet been adequately explained" (*Genres and Readers: Lucretius, Love Elegy, Pliny's Encyclopedia*, trans. Glen W. Most, 67, 163n2). The figuring of his work as a storehouse is an inference following from the assertion that "as Domitus Piso says, it is not books but store-houses that are needed, *thesaurus oportet esse, non libros*. Pliny, "Preface," *Natural History*, trans. H. Rackham, vol. 1, 0.17. On Pliny's intellectual and philosophical heritage, see Mary Beagon, *Roman Nature: The Thought of Pliny the Elder*, 26–54.

48. Ann M. Blair, *Too Much to Know*, 18.

49. E. W. Gudger, "Pliny's *Historia Naturalis*: The Most Popular Natural History Ever Published," 270–71.

50. According to Charles Nauert Jr., the first print edition of Pliny's multibook tome was published in 1469 at Venice by the printer Johannes de Spira. During the fifteenth century, there were a total of fifteen incunable Latin editions and three incunable Italian editions. During the sixteenth century, scores of editions, in Latin and vernaculars, were published ("Humanists, Scientists, and Pliny," 76).

51. Paula Findlen, "Courting Nature," 3.

52. Aude Doody, *Pliny's Encyclopedia*, 1.

53. Findlen, *Possessing Nature*, 62.

54. Desiderius Erasmus to Stanislaus Thurzo, Basel, Letter 1544, 8 February 1525, in The *Correspondence of Erasmus: Letters 1535-1657*, ed. Charles Nauert Jr. and Alexander Dalzell, vol. 11 of *Collected Works of Erasmus*, 29. The edition was published by Froben at Basel and edited by Erasmus; see the headnote (26) to the letter.

55. Erasmus to Thurzo, Basel, Letter 1544, 8 February 1525, *CWE*, 11:29.

56. Erasmus to Thurzo, Basel, Letter 1544, 8 February 1525, *CWE*, 11:29.

57. Erasmus to Thurzo, Basel, Letter 1544, 8 February 1525, *CWE*, 11:27.

58. Erasmus to Thurzo, Basel, Letter 1544, 8 February 1525, *CWE*, 11:27.

59. For evidence that this infrastructure facilitated cross-disciplinary exchange beyond Erasmus's own writing, see the careful and illuminating study of Renaissance *progymnasmata* and the 1569 edition of Pliny's *Natural History* by classical scholar María Violeta Pérez Custodio, "Plinio el Viejo y los *progymnasmata*: La edición complutense de la *Naturalis historia* de 1569," 973–96.

60. Roger French, *Ancient Natural History*, 248.

61. Pliny, *Natural History* 8.7.23, trans. Rackham, 19.

62. Pliny, *Natural History* 8.18, 8.26.

63. Pliny, *Natural History* 10.95, trans. Rackham, 423.

64. Pliny, *Natural History* 10.96, trans. Rackham, 425.

65. Pliny, *Natural History* 37.15, trans. modified from Eichholz, 209.

66. Indeed, in an observation that may reveal his motivation for publishing editions of *Natural History*, Erasmus notes, "This single work has made, and continues to make, many a man's reputation. For however obscure a man may have been, once he puts his hand to Pliny's text, people take notice." Erasmus to Thurzo, Basel, Letter 1544, 8 February 1525, *CWE*, 11:27.

67. This model of rhetoric is drawn most explicitly from Erasmus by Sloane, *On the Contrary*.

68. Findlen, *Possessing Nature*, 9. The Italian naturalism Findlen studied might be situated fruitfully in the context of rhetorical education. See also Edward H. R. Tatham, "Erasmus in Italy."

69. Mack, *Renaissance Rhetoric*, 76.

70. Lisa Jardine, "Inventing Rudolph Agricola."

71. Erasmus to Thurzo, Basel, Letter 1544, 8 February 1525, *CWE*, 11:29–30.

72. Erasmus, *De copia*, trans. Knott, *CWE*, 24:577.

73. Erasmus, *De copia*, trans. Knott, *CWE*, 24:580.

74. Erasmus, *De copia*, trans. modified from Knott, *CWE*, 24:581.

75. This treatment of description is probably an instance of the breaking apart of the *progymnasmata* in the service of amplification as described by Manfred Kraus, "Aphthonius and the *Progymnasmata*," 62.

76. Sloane, *On the Contrary*, especially 8–11.

77. "Quite a number of [striking metaphors] can be collected from proverbs. . . . These I myself have labored to collect." Erasmus, *De copia*, trans. Knott, *CWE*, 24:335.

78. Margaret Mann Phillips, *The "Adages" of Erasmus: A Study with Translations*, 3.

79. "The animal stories show the *Adages* at its most frivolous and least modern. They form a kind of Bestiary, entirely from classical sources, usually Plutarch, Aesop or Pliny" (Phillips, *"Adages" of Erasmus*, 18).

80. Desiderius Erasmus, "With ears lowered" (Demissis auriculis), in *Adages IViii1 to Vii51*, ed. John Grant and Betty I. Knott vol. 36 of *Collected Works of Erasmus*, 278.

81. Erasmus, "With ears lowered," *CWE*, 36:278–79.

82. Pliny, *Natural History* 11.50.136–37, trans. Rackham, 517, 519. Pliny's discussion also, interestingly, veers into gender- and culture-based assertions about the amount of money women spend on pearl earrings and the custom among men in the East of sporting gold on their ears.

83. Erasmus, "With ears lowered," in *CWE*, 36:278.

84. Desiderius Erasmus, "Adopt the outlook of the polyp" (Polypi mentem obtine), *Adages Ii1 to Iv100*, trans. Margaret Mann Phillips, ed. R. A. B. Mynors, vol. 31 of *Collected Works of Erasmus*, 133–36. See Jeffrey Walker's wonderful discussion of "Theognis's Octopus" (Theognis is the archaic poet to whom Erasmus attributes the proverb), "Theognis' Octopus: On Poetry as Rhetorical Transaction," in *Rhetoric and Poetics in Antiquity*, 139–53. For a discussion of the octopus as the Greek instantiation of cunning intelligence, see Marcel Detienne and Jean-Pierre Vernant, *Cunning Intelligence in Greek Culture and Society*, 34; Hawhee, *Bodily Arts*, 55–57; Franziska Schnoor, "Octopuses, Foxes and Hares: Animals in Early Modern Latin and German Proverbs," 2:536–37.

85. Erasmus, "Adopt the outlook of the polyp," *CWE*, 31:133–34.

86. Erasmus, *De copia*, trans. Knott, *CWE*, 24:302; see also Adage IIii75, "As many shapes as Proteus" (Proteo mutabilior), in Desiderius Erasmus, *Adages III1 to IIvi100*, trans. R. A. B. Mynors, vol. 33 of *Collected Works of Erasmus*, 113–15.

87. Erasmus, "Adopt the outlook of the polyp," *CWE*, 31:134. Peter Mack discusses this adage at length in "Rhetoric, Ethics, and Reading in the Renaissance," *Renaissance Studies* 19, no. 1 (2005): 10–12.

88. Mack, *Renaissance Rhetoric*, 89.

89. Desiderius Erasmus, *Parallels* (Parabolae sive similia), trans. R. A. B Mynors, in *Literary and Educational Writings 1*, ed. Craig R. Thompson, vol. 23 of *Collected Works of Erasmus*, 130.

90. Erasmus, *Parallels*, trans. Mynors, *CWE*, 23:180 (birds), 183 (this reference to a horse follows another reference to bit use), 191 (flies), 193 (octopus).

91. Erasmus, *Parallels*, trans. Mynors, *CWE*, 23:201 (phoenix), 217 (horse), 214 (animals and passions).

92. Seneca, *Epistle* 85.8, "On Some Vain Syllogisms," in *The Epistles of Seneca*, vol. 2, *Epistles 66–92*, translation modified from Richard M. Gummere, 291.

93. "Some animals even when tame revert without warning to their native ferocity; you can tame a vice but must never trust it" (Erasmus, *Parallels*, trans. Mynors, *CWE*, 23:214.

94. "In anything under the heading 'From Aristotle and Pliny' the application of the image is my own invention" (Erasmus, *Parallels*, trans. Mynors, *CWE*, 23:134).

95. Erasmus, *Parallels*, ed. Mynors, *CWE*, 23:219n1.

96. Erasmus, *Parallels*, trans. Mynors, *CWE*, 23:240 (elk), 250 (crocodile), 252–53 (monkey).

97. Erasmus, *Parallels*, trans. Mynors, *CWE*, 23:222. This capacity of beavers had been long documented in medieval bestiaries and Plutarch. For a catalog of bestiary references to the self-castrating beaver, see Debra Hassig, "Sex in the Bestiaries," 89.

98. Erasmus, *De copia*, trans. Knott, *CWE*, 24:582.

99. Desiderius Erasmus to Ulrich von Hutten, Antwerp, Letter 999, 23 July 1519, in *Cor-*

respondence of Erasmus, ed. P. B. Bietenholz and R. A. B. Mynors, vol. 7 of *Collected Works of Erasmus*, 19.

100. Keith Thomas, *Man and the Natural World*, 110. See also Bruce Boehrer, "Introduction: The Animal Renaissance," 18–22.

101. Because the original (1523) painting was destroyed in a 1698 fire, these details are gathered from Holbein's preparatory drawing as well as later copies. See Stanley Morison, *The Likeness of Thomas More*, 18–21.

102. On that summer, see the extensive headnote to the Toronto translation of "Sympathy": Erasmus, "Sympathy," *CWE*, 40:1035. See also Halina Kowalska, "Anselmus Ephorinus of Freideberg, c. 1505-December 1566," 436–37; "Jan Boner of Cracow, 1516–12 September 1562," 166–67.

103. Erasmus, "Sympathy," *CWE*, 40:1042.

104. Erasmus, "Sympathy," *CWE*, 40:1045.

105. Erasmus, "Sympathy," *CWE*, 40:1043.

106. Erasmus, "Sympathy," *CWE*, 40:1043; Pliny, *Natural History* 8.80.

107. Erasmus, "Sympathy," *CWE*, 40:1046.

108. Erasmus, "Between Friends All Is Common" (Amicorum communia omnia), in *Adages I i1 to I v100*, trans. Phillips, *CWE*, 31:29.

109. For a deeper inspection of how Erasmus attempts to reconcile the adage "friends hold all things in common" with "the violence of a world characterized by difference rather than similarity," see Timothy Hampton, "'Turkish Dogs': Rabeleis, Erasmus, and the Rhetoric of Alterity," 61.

110. Susan Stewart, *On Longing*, 156. Barbara Benedict is equally (and understandably) suspicious of the culture of collecting, reading curiosity cabinets, for example, as an exercise in power, as a removal of objects from circulation (*Curiosity: A Cultural History of Early Modern Inquiry*, 10). My point from here is that Erasmian collecting worked differently, in an economy of production and recirculation.

111. Latin: indigesta rerum turba. Erasmus, *De copia*, translation mine.

112. Erasmus, *De copia*, trans. Knott, *CWE*, 24:638.

113. See Ann Moss, *Printed Commonplace-Books and the Structuring of Renaissance Thought*, 106–11.

114. Erasmus, *De copia*, trans. Knott, *CWE*, 24:638.

115. Erasmus, *De copia*, trans. Knott, *CWE*, 24:638.

116. For example, a point about elephants' mating practices is taken from Pliny's *Natural History* (8.13), as is an observation about dolphins accompanying their young until they are "quite grown up" (*grandior*) (9.21).

117. Erasmus, *De copia*, trans. modified from Knott, *CWE*, 24:639.

118. For a wonderful treatment of the bee as "textual harvester" in subsequent centuries, see Krista Kennedy, "The Daw and the Honeybee: Situating Metaphors for Originality and Authorial Labor in the 1728 Chambers' *Cyclopaedia*." And for a helpful sorting-through of the "tangled skein" of bee lore, see B. G. Whitfield, "Virgil and the Bees: A Study in Ancient Apicultural Lore," 100, and more recently Archibald Allen, "Virgil's Acquisitive Bees." For bees during the Renaissance in particular, see Jonathan Woolfson, "The Renaissance of Bees."

119. Pliny, *Natural History* 11.4–23.

120. Erasmus, *Parallels*, trans. Mynors, *CWE*, 23:259–61. For the bee detail, see Erasmus to Thurzo, Basel, Letter 1544, 8 February 1525, *CWE*, 11:30.

121. Pliny, *Natural History* 11.16.

122. Erasmus, *Parallels*, trans. Mynors, *CWE*, 23:260.

123. Desiderius Erasmus, "The Ciceronian: A Dialogue on the Ideal Latin Style" (Dialogus Ciceronianus), in *Literary and Educational Writings 6*, trans. Betty I. Knott, ed. A. H. T Levi, vol. 28 of *Collected Works of Erasmus*, 402. The explicit logic in this satire is this: "If the example of your idol does not convince you, let us look at the examples offered us by nature."

124. Erasmus, *Ciceronian*, trans. Knott, *CWE*, 28:402.

125. Peter Stallybrass, in his meditation on invention, charts bee work and the work of writing comparatively using a visual table ("Against Thinking," 1582).

126. Greek: mēte meli mēte melissas. Desiderius Erasmus, "No bees, no honey" (Neque mel, neque apes), in *Adages Ivi1 to IX100*, trans. R. A. B. Mynors, vol. 32 of *Collected Works of Erasmus*, 44.

127. Terence Cave, *The Cornucopian Text: Problems of Writing in the French Renaissance*, 7.

128. Carruthers, *Book of Memory*, 38–46.

129. Carruthers, *Book of Memory*, 38.

130. Erasmus, *De copia*, trans. Knott, *CWE*, 24:638. For a discussion of *nidus* as pigeonhole, see Carruthers, *Book of Memory*, 42.

131. Pliny, *Natural History* 11.12.

132. For a characteristically brilliant history of "sweetness" in premodern rhetoric, see Mary Carruthers, "Sweetness," 999–1013.

133. Charles Segal mentions Homer's use of "honeyed words" in "Kleos and Its Ironies in the *Odyssey*," 35 and 40.

134. Erasmus, "Short Rule for Copiousness," *CWE*, 39:168.

135. See in particular Erasmus, "Praise of Folly," trans. Radice, *CWE*, 27:112–13; Thomas More, *Utopia*, 64: "Taking such relish in the sight of death reveals, in the Utopians' opinion, a cruel disposition, or else one that has become so through the constant practice of such brutal pleasures."

136. Erasmus, "War is a treat," in *Adages IIIiv1 to IVii100*, trans. Denis Drysdall, ed. John Grant, vol. 35 of *Collected Works of Erasmus*, 409.

137. Erasmus, "War is a treat," trans. Drysdall, *CWE*, 35:399–440.

138. Erasmus, "On the Method of Study," *CWE*, 24:677 (cuttlefish).

139. Walter J. Ong, *Ramus, Method, and the Decay of Dialogue*, 291.

CONCLUSION

1. The library, at the behest of a Milanese diplomat and emblematist named Carlo Bossi, was attached to the Barnabite Institute of San Alessandro in Milan, and the priest Christophoro Giarda deemed it a successor to the famous—and famously destroyed—library at Alexandria; Giarda refers to the library several times and in his title of a collection of lectures, "Ad candidum lectorem," in *Bibliothecae Alexandrinae icones symbolicae*, n.p., on the images at the

Alexandrine Library. E. H. Gombrich speculates that Bossi, an emblematist himself, may have drawn up the plan for the set of engravings ("*Icones Symbolicae*: The Visual Image in Neo-Platonic Thought").

2. To my knowledge, none of Giarda's sermons have been translated into English. Heinrich Plett includes snippets of translation in *Rhetoric and Renaissance Culture*, 508–11, as does Gombrich in *Symbolic Images: Studies in the Art of the Renaissance*; see also Gombrich, "*Icones Symbolicae*," 188–92. Giarda's speech on Rhetorica is the lengthiest lecture in the lot (the printed version runs fourteen pages, four pages longer than the next longest, "Sacred Scripture," which runs ten). Such elaborate attention is not surprising given Giarda's position as a teacher of rhetoric. Perhaps the most familiar image of Rhetorica is the one featured in a fifteenth-century collection misleadingly called "Tarot Cards of Mantegna." See Raymond B. Waddington, "Iconography," 368. Waddington discusses the Giarda treatment at length; see below. Plett calls the tarot image "one of the most prominent icons of Rhetorica" (*Rhetoric and Renaissance Culture*, 507). Speaking from the present moment, that much is surely true: the image of the helmeted and arms-bearing figure has been adopted as the insignia of the journal *Rhetorica* and graces the cover of the collection on women and rhetoric edited by Andrea Lunsford, *Reclaiming Rhetorica*. For a more in-depth consideration of the Mantegna image, see Carly S. Woods and Michele Kennerly, "Moving Rhetorica."

3. For a discussion of the caduceus, see Simon Hornblower and Antony Spawforth, eds., *Oxford Classical Dictionary*, s.v. "Hermes," 690–91. In his sixteenth-century poem *The Faerie Queene* (2.12.41.6), Edmund Spenser describes the caduceus as "the rod of *Mercury*," "Th' infernall feends with it he can asswage." The mid-sixteenth-century painting *Allegory of Rhetoric* by Perin del Vaga (Pietro Bonaccors) features a caduceus ("An Allegory of Rhetoric Holding a Caduceus," *Wikigallery*, accessed May 5, 2015, http://www.wikigallery.org/wiki/painting_284875/Perino-del-Vaga-%28Pietro-Bonaccors%29/An-allegory-of-Rhetoric-holding-a-caduceus), as does Gilles Rousselet's print *La Retorique* from the series *The Liberal Arts* (*Les arts liberaux*), *La Retorique* (*Rhetoric: a Young Woman Standing in a Decorated Interior with a Caduceus in Her Right Hand and a Closed Fan in Her Left Hand*), 1633–35, engraving, $11^{15}/_{16}$ in. $\times$ $8\frac{3}{8}$ in., The Metropolitan Museum of Art, New York, accessed May 5, 2015, http://www.metmuseum.org/collection/the-collection-online/search/399271. For a sturdy and spirited survey of serpents as symbols, including a chapter-length treatment of the caduceus, see M. Oldfield Howey, *The Encircled Serpent*, 71–78.

4. Numerous accounts point to this flourishing. For one concise statement about early modern style that undergirds the rest of the remarkable book of which it is a part, see Fahnestock, *Rhetorical Style*, 8.

5. The quotation in the description is from Andrea Alciato: Alciati, *A Book of Emblems*, 208. See also Erasmus, "Preafatio, sev Hercules Gallicus," in *Opera omnia: Recognita et adnotatione critica instructa notisque illustrata*, 591–93; Andrea Alciato, "Eloquentia fortitudine praestantior," *Emblematum liber* (Augsburg: Heinrich Steiner, 1531); viewable at "Alciato at Glasgow," Glasgow University Emblem Website, http://www.emblems.arts.gla.ac.uk/alciato/facsimile.php?id=SM18_E6r.

6. Plett, *Rhetoric and Renaissance Culture*, 509.

7. Waddington, "Iconography," 373.

8. Achille Bocchi, *Symbolicarum quaestionum de universo genere* 5.137. I should mention, though, that following Giarda's main motto is an image of a chimeric character with horns and scales, lying in repose and bearing a tantalizing resemblance to Bocchi's figure; see Giarda, *Icones symbolicae*, 73.

9. Gombrich, "*Icones Symbolicae*," 192.

10. Plett, *Rhetoric and Renaissance Culture*, 508–9.

11. "Chymerae victoria testatur." Giarda, *Icones symbolicae*, 87.

12. A helpful overview of the *Iconologia*'s publication history is offered by Edward A. Maser, "Introduction," in *Cesare Ripa: Baroque and Rococo Pictorial Imagery*, vii–xxi. Voicing what appears to be a common assumption among scholars of Renaissance art, art historian Elizabeth McGrath observes that "*Iconologia* was clearly and explicitly aimed from the start at artists, and certainly on them had its greatest influence" ("Personifying Ideals," 364). For a compelling instance of adaptation of Ripa, also by an Italian artist, see Lothar Freund, "'Good Counsel': An Adaptation from Ripa," 81–82.

13. Ripa, *Iconologia* (1613), part 2, 145, translation mine.

14. Helen North, "Emblems of Eloquence," 429.

15. Ripa, *Iconologia* (1613), part 2, 143–44.

16. The bear embodies anger and the dolphin haste, both of which, according to the depiction, must be stemmed if wise counsel is to be achieved and upheld. See Freund, "'Good Counsel,'" 81.

17. Ripa, *Iconologia* (1613), part 1, 130. Erwin Panofsky helpfully historicizes the wolf-lion-dog image in his quest to make better sense of the *Allegory of Prudence*, a work by the famous Italian painter Titian, completed between 1565 and 1570. Panofsky's visual-historical account of Titian's wolf-lion-dog configuration lays the groundwork for my interpretation of the beasts in the Rhetorica image in question as part of that same tradition. See Panofsky, *Meaning in the Visual Arts*.

18. An audience member at a January 2016 lecture I delivered at the University of Pittsburgh wondered whether the animal I am identifying as a lion in Giarda's image is in fact a lion, given the seeming absence of a mane. It is difficult to tell, since the animal is depicted in profile, but the mane appears to be drawn on the lower part of the animal's head and upper chest, not unlike the corresponding animal in Ripa's Consiglio.

19. For a thorough consideration of the textual tradition of the Saturnalia, with a strong focus on the medieval manuscript tradition, see Robert A. Kaster, *Studies on the Text of Macrobius' "Saturnalia."*

20. Macrobius, *Saturnalia* 1.20.13–15, trans. and ed. Robert A. Kaster, 1:274–75.

21. Macrobius is the explicit source of the image of Sarapis (or "Sol") as depicted in two other mid-sixteenth-century image books: Vincenzo Cartari's *Imagini delli Dei de gl'Antichi* (*Images of the Ancient Gods*), and Giovanni Pierio Valeriano Bolzani's *Hieroglyphica*, both first published in 1556. Geographically, the association with Sarapis reinforces the wolf-lion-dog interpretation of the *signum triceps* in Giarda's *Rhetorica*: Sarapis's main sanctuary was in Alexandria, and the Serapeum was among the cultural monuments for which Alexandria was best known. Others included the gymnasium, the museum, and, of course, its library, the apparent namesake of the one at Giarda's school. See Dominic W. Rathbone, "Alexandria (1)," 60; Richard Gordon, "Serapis," 1317–18; Giarda, *Icones symbolicae*, 2–3.

22. Valeriano Bolzani, *Hieroglyphica*, mentions the dog-lion-wolf heads in his description of *prudentia* (160), and he also mentions prudence in his description of *eloquentia* (157).

23. Hariman, "Theory without Modernity," 3–4. See also Eugene Garver's book on Aristotle's *Rhetoric*, presented as a "history of prudence," *Aristotle's "Rhetoric": An Art of Character*, 5–6, 232–48; Lois S. Self, "Rhetoric and Phronesis: The Aristotelian Ideal," 134–35; and Janet Atwill's brilliant (and, for me, formative) discussion of Aristotle's notion of practical art, which features prominently (*Rhetoric Reclaimed*, 162–89).

24. Victoria Kahn, *Rhetoric, Prudence, and Skepticism in the Renaissance*, 39.

25. Vincenzo Cartari, "Imagine di Serapi Dio," in *Imagini delli Dei de gl'Antichi*, 56.

26. See Eugene Garver, *Aristotle's "Politics,"* 101.

27. According to Plett, "Aristotle's *Rhetoric* was translated into Latin by Georgius Trapezuntius (Paris, 1475?; Lyons, 1541). Italian translations of Aristotle's *Rhetoric* and *Poetics* were produced by Bernardo Segni in 1549" (*Rhetoric and Renaissance Culture*, 17); see also Ripa, *Iconologia* (1613), 127.

28. Aristotle, *Rhetoric* 1.3.4.1358b.

29. "Tiene la corda di detto animale con ambi le mani, perché se la persuasion non ha questi messaggieri, o non si genera, o debolmente camina" (Ripa, *Iconologia*, 145).

30. *De anima* 2.5.417a.5–8.

31. "Sed, ut hoc efficiat, ardeat orator primum necesse est. Quamobrem sapienter olla feruens apposite est" (Giarda, *Icones symbolicae*, 90).

32. Quintilian, *Orator's Education*, 11.3.2–3, trans. Russell, 87. For more on Quintilian during later periods, see John O. Ward, "Quintilian and the Rhetorical Revolution of the Middle Ages"; for the Italian Renaissance in particular, see Virginia Cox, "Rhetoric and Humanism in Quattrocento Venice."

33. See in particular Plett's thorough and suggestive account of *Memoria Poetica* in *Rhetoric and Renaissance Culture* (226–49) and Francis Yates's *The Art of Memory* (135–62); Peter M. Daly, *The Emblem in Early Modern Europe: Contributions to the Theory of the Emblem*; Douglas Radcliff-Umstead, "Giulio Camillo's Emblems of Memory"; Bolzoni, *The Gallery of Memory*, 3–22; Grover A. Zinn, "Hugh of Saint Victor and the Art of Memory," 231. Peter Daly admits that emblem scholars "have paid too little attention to the rhetorical dimension of emblem pictures" (*Emblem in Early Modern Europe*, 155). For an early consideration of emblems and learning, see Robert J. Clements, "Emblem Books and the Revival of Learning."

34. Gombrich, *"Icones Symbolicae,"* 184.

35. Central to the embedding of fable in emblems is the bestiary tradition, which flourished in the medieval period. For more on the bestiary, see in particular Beryl Rowland, "The Art of Memory and the Bestiary"; Florence McCulloch, *Mediaeval Latin and French Bestiaries*; and Richard Barber, ed. *Bestiary: MS Bodley 764*.

36. And even though they continue to be published, studies of animal emblems remain distinct from current animal studies conversations. For a case in point, see Simona Cohen, *Animals as Disguised Symbols in Renaissance Art*.

37. Friedrich Nietzsche, "On Truth and Lying in the Extra-moral Sense," 246–57.

38. I will admit to being drawn into the question of the animals' identity out of dissatisfaction with existing accounts.

39. I don't wish to claim anything close to cross-disciplinary comprehensiveness. For

example, save for a few mentions of Saint Augustine and passing references to the religious affiliation of men such as Psellos, Erasmus, and Giarda, religion has not featured all that prominently in my analysis. Such an omission is mainly because I chose to focus on the more secular strand of thought beginning with Aristotle and moving into school manuals (*progymnasmata*). The religion-animals-rhetoric connection presents one of many opportunities for further research that I hope other scholars soon pursue. An excellent starting point for such an effort would be Laura Hobgood-Oster, *Holy Dogs and Asses: Animals in the Christian Tradition*.

BIBLIOGRAPHY OF PRIMARY SOURCES

This bibliography includes translations and ancient-language editions of sources I consulted for this book. Loeb editions cited here were consulted for Greek and Latin; I cite those translations in the endnotes.

Aesop. *Aesopica: A Series of Texts relating to Aesop or Ascribed to Him or Closely Connected with the Literary Tradition That Bears His Name*. Edited by Ben Edwin Perry. Urbana: University of Illinois Press, 1952.

———. *Aesop's Fables*. Translated by Laura Gibbs. Oxford: Oxford University Press, 2002.

Albertus Magnus. "Commentary on Aristotle, *On Memory and Recollection*." In *The Medieval Craft of Memory: An Anthology of Texts and Pictures*, edited by Mary Carruthers and Jan Ziolkowski, translated by Jan Ziolkowski, 118–52. Philadelphia: University of Pennsylvania Press, 2002.

———. *De bono*, tractatus 4, quaestio 2 'De partibus prudentiae.'" In *The Book of Memory: A Study of Memory in Medieval Culture*, translated by Mary Carruthers, 345–60. Cambridge: Cambridge University Press, 2008.

———. *Opera omnia*. Vol. 9, *Liber de memoria and reminiscentia, parvara naturalia*. Edited by Auguste Borgnet. Paris: Vivès, 1890.

———. *Opera omnia*. Vol. 28, *De bono*. Edited by H. Kühle, C. Feckes, B. Geyer, and W. Kübel. Münster: Aschendorff, 1951.

Alciati, Andrea. *A Book of Emblems: The "Emblematum Liber" in Latin and English*. Edited and translated by John F. Moffitt. Jefferson, NC: McFarland, 2004.

Aphthonius. "The Preliminary Exercises of Apthonius the Sophist." In *Progymnasmata: Greek Textbooks of Prose Composition and Rhetoric*, 89–127. Translated by George A. Kennedy. Atlanta: Biblical Society of America, 2003.

Aquinas, Thomas. "Commentary on Aristotle, *On Memory and Recollection*." In *The Medieval Craft of Memory: An Anthology of Texts and Pictures*, edited by Mary Carruthers and Jan Ziolkowski, translated by John Burchill, 153–88. Philadelphia: University of Pennsylvania Press, 2002.

Aristotle. *Ars rhetorica*. Edited by W. D. Ross. Oxford Classical Texts. Oxford: Oxford University Press, 1991.

———. *The "Art of Rhetoric."* Translated by John Henry Freese. Loeb Classical Library 193. Cambridge, MA: Harvard University Press, 1991.

———. *De anima*. Translated by W. S. Hett. In *Aristotle in Twenty-Three Volumes*, vol. 8. Loeb Classical Library 288. Cambridge, MA: Harvard University Press, 1975.

———. *De memoria et reminiscentia* [*On Memory and Recollection*]. Translated by W. S. Hett. In *Aristotle in Twenty-Three Volumes*, 8:287–313. Loeb Classical Library 288. Cambridge, MA: Harvard University Press, 1975.

———. "Eudemian Ethics." In *Athenian Constitution, Eudemian Ethics, Virtues and Vices*, translated by H. Rackham. In *Aristotle in Twenty-Three Volumes*, 20:198–475. Loeb Classical Library 285. 1935. Reprint, Cambridge, MA: Harvard University Press, 1996.

———. *Generation of Animals*. Translated by A. L. Peck. In *Aristotle in Twenty-Three Volumes*, vol. 13. Loeb Classical Library 366. Cambridge, MA: Harvard University Press, 1942.

———. *History of Animals, Books 1-3*. Translated by A. L. Peck. Loeb Classical Library 477. 1965. Reprint, Cambridge, MA: Harvard University Press, 2001.

———. *History of Animals, Books 7-10*. Translated by D. M. Balm. Loeb Classical Library 439. Cambridge, MA: Harvard University Press, 1991.

———. *Metaphysics, Books 1-9*. Translated by Hugh Tredennick. Loeb Classical Library 271. Cambridge, MA: Harvard University Press, 1989.

———. "Movement of Animals." In *Parts of Animals*, translated by E. S. Forster. In *Aristotle in Twenty-Three Volumes*, 12:440–79. Loeb Classical Library 323. Cambridge, MA: Harvard University Press, 2006.

———. *The Nicomachean Ethics*. Translated by H. Rackham. In *Aristotle in Twenty-Three Volumes*, vol. 19. Loeb Classical Library 73. Cambridge, MA: Harvard University Press, 1990.

———. *Nicomachean Ethics*. Translated and edited by Terence Irwin. 2nd ed. Indianapolis, IN: Hackett, 1999.

———. *Nicomachean Ethics: A New Translation*. Translated by Robert C. Bartlett and Susan D. Collins. Chicago: University of Chicago Press, 2011.

———. *On Rhetoric: A Theory of Civic Discourse*. Translated by George A. Kennedy. 2nd ed. New York: Oxford University Press, 2007.

———. "On Sense and Sensible Objects." Translated by W. S. Hett. In *Aristotle in Twenty-Three Volumes*, 8:214–83. Loeb Classical Library 288. Cambridge, MA: Harvard University Press, 1975.

———. *Parts of Animals*. Translated by A. L. Peck. In *Aristotle in Twenty-Three Volumes*, vol. 12. Loeb Classical Library 323. Cambridge, MA: Harvard University Press, 2006.

———. "Poetics." Translated by Stephen Halliwell. In *Aristotle in Twenty-Three Volumes*, 23:28–141. Loeb Classical Library 199. Cambridge, MA: Harvard University Press, 1995.

———. *Politics*. Translated by H. Rackham. In *Aristotle in Twenty-Three Volumes*, vol. 21. Loeb Classical Library 264. 1932. Reprint, Cambridge, MA: Harvard University Press, 1998.

———. *Politics*. Translated by Carnes Lord. 2nd ed. Chicago: University of Chicago Press, 2013.

———. "Posterior Analytics." In *Posterior Analytics* and *Topica*, translated by Hugh Tredennick and E. S. Foster. In *Aristotle in Twenty-Three Volumes*, 2:24–261. Loeb Classical Library 391. Cambridge, MA: Harvard University Press, 1960.

Augustine, *The City of God against the Pagans, Books 21-22*. Translated by William M. Green. Loeb Classical Library. 1972. Reprint, Cambridge, MA: Harvard University Press, 2003.

Ausonius. *The Works of Ausonius*. Edited by R. P. H. Green. Oxford: Clarendon Press, 1991.

Babrius. "Fables." In *Babrius and Phaedrus*, trans and ed. Ben E. Perry, 1–249. Loeb Classical Library 436. Cambridge, MA: Harvard University Press, 1965.

Barber, Richard, ed. *Bestiary: MS Bodley 764*. Woodbridge: Boydell Press, 1999.

Bocchi, Achille. *Symbolicarum quaestionum de universo genere*. Reproduction of 1574 edition (Bologna). New York: Garland, 1979.

Bolzani, Giovanni Pierio Valeriano. *Hieroglyphica*. Lyon: Pauli Frellon, 1610.

Bradwardine, Thomas. "De memoria artificiale adquirenda." Edited by Mary Carruthers. *Journal of Medieval Latin* 2 (1995): 25–43.

———. "On Acquiring a Trained Memory." In *The Medieval Craft of Memory: An Anthology of Texts and Pictures*, edited by Mary Carruthers and Jan Ziolkowski, translated by Mary Carruthers, 204–14. Philadelphia: University of Pennsylvania Press, 2002.

Cartari, Vincenzo. *Imagini delli Dei de gl'Antichi*. Venice: Euangelista Deuchino, 1625.

Cicero. "Brutus." In *Cicero V*, translated by G. L. Hendrickson, 5:18–293. Loeb Classical Library 342. Cambridge, MA: Harvard University Press, 1988.

[Cicero]. *Rhetorica ad Herennium*. Translated by Harry Caplan. Loeb Classical Library 403. Cambridge, MA: Harvard University Press, 1954.

———. *De oratore*. Translated by H. Rackham. Loeb Classical Library 348 and 349. Cambridge, MA: Harvard University Press, 1992.

Demetrius. "On Style." Translated by Doreen C. Innes and W. Rhys Roberts. In *Aristotle in Twenty-Three Volumes*, 23:344–525. Loeb Classical Library 199. Cambridge, MA: Harvard University Press, 1995.

Dionysius of Halicarnassus. "Demosthenes." In *Critical Essays*, translated by Stephen Usher, 1:232–455. Loeb Classical Library 465. Cambridge, MA: Harvard University Press, 1974.

———. "Lysias." In *Critical Essays*, translated by Stephen Usher, 1:4–99. Loeb Classical Library 465. Cambridge, MA: Harvard University Press, 1974.

———. "On Literary Composition." In *Critical Essays*, translated by Stephen Usher, 2:14–243. Loeb Classical Library 466. Cambridge, MA: Harvard University Press, 1985.

Erasmus, Desiderius. *Adages Ii1 to Iv100*. Translated by Margaret Mann Phillips, edited by R. A. B. Mynors, 29–470. Vol. 31 of *Collected Works of Erasmus*. Toronto: University of Toronto Press, 1982.

———. *Adages Ivi1 to IX100*. Translated by R. A. B. Mynors, 3–281. Vol. 32 of *Collected Works of Erasmus*. Toronto: University of Toronto Press, 1989.

———. *Adages IIi1 to IIvi100*. Translated and edited by R. A. B. Mynors. Vol. 33 of *Collected Works of Erasmus*. Toronto: University of Toronto Press, 1991.

———. *Adages IIIiv1 to IVii100*. Translated by Denis Drysdall, edited by John N. Grant, 3–551. Vol. 35 of *Collected Works of Erasmus*. Toronto: University of Toronto Press, 2005.

———. *Adages IViii1 to Vii51*. Translated by John N. Grant and Betty I. Knott, 3–630. Vol. 36 of *Collected Works of Erasmus*. Toronto: University of Toronto Press, 2006.

——. "The Ciceronian: A Dialogue on the Ideal Latin Style" (Dialogus Ciceronianus). In *Literary and Educational Writings 6*, translated by Betty I. Knott, edited A. H. T. Levi, 323-48. Vol. 28 of *Collected Works of Erasmus*. Toronto: University of Toronto Press, 1986.

——. *Copia: Foundations of the Abundant Style* (De duplici copia verborum ac rerum commentarii duo). In *Literary and Educational Writings 2*, translated by Betty I. Knott, edited by Craig R. Thompson, 296-659. Vol. 24 of *Collected Works of Erasmus*. Toronto: University of Toronto Press, 1974.

——. "A Declamation on the Subject of Early Liberal Education for Children" (De pueris statim ac liberaliter instituendis declamation). Translated by Beert C. Verstraete, 297-346. Vol. 26 of *Collected Works of Erasmus*. Toronto: University of Toronto Press, 1974.

——. *Desiderii Erasmi Roterodami opera omnia*. Vol. 1. Leiden: Patri Vandera, 1703.

——. Desiderius Erasmus to John More, Freiburg, 27 February 1531. [Letter 2432. Preface to *Aristotelis opera*, Basel: J. Bebel]. In *Opus Epistolarum Des. Erasmi Roterodami*, vol. 9, *1530-1532*, edited by P. S. Allen, H. M. Allen, and H. W. Garrod, 133-40. Oxford: Oxford University Press, 1938.

——. Desiderius Erasmus to Thomas More [Paris?], 9 June [1531]. [Letter 222.] In *Correspondence: Letters 142-197*, translated by R. A. B. Mynors and D. F. S. Thomson, 161-64. Vol. 2 of *Collected Works of Erasmus*, Toronto: University of Toronto Press, 1975.

——. "The Godly Feast." Translated by Craig R. Thompson, 171-243. Vol. 39 of *Collected Works of Erasmus*. Toronto: University of Toronto Press, 1997.

——. "Hunting" [Venatio]. In *Colloquies*, translated and edited by Craig R. Thompson, 109-12. Vol. 39 of *Collected Works of Erasmus*. Toronto: University of Toronto Press, 1997.

——. "Letter to Ulrich von Hutten, Antwerp, Letter 999, 23 July 1519." In *Correspondence of Erasmus*, translated by P. B. Bietenholz and R. A. B. Mynors, 15-25. Vol. 7 of *Collected Works of Erasmus*. Toronto: University of Toronto Press, 1987.

——. "Letter to Stanislaus Thurzo, Basel, Letter 1544, 8 February 1525. In *Correspondence of Erasmus*, ed. Charles Nauert Jr. and Alexander Dalzell, 26-31. Vol. 11 of *Collected Works of Erasmus*. Toronto: University of Toronto Press, 1994.

——. "On Good Manners for Boys" (De civilitate morum puerilium). Translated by Brian McGregor. *Collected Works of Erasmus*, 25:273-89. Toronto: University of Toronto Press, 1985.

——. "On the Method of Study." (De ratione studii ac legendi interpretandique auctores). Translated by Brian McGregor. *Collected Works of Erasmus*, 24:666-702. Toronto: University of Toronto Press, 1974.

——. *Parallels* [Parabolae sive similia]. In *Literary and Educational Writings 1*, Translated by R. A. B. Mynors and edited by Craig R. Thompson. Vol. 23 of *Collected Works of Erasmus*. Toronto: University of Toronto Press, 1978.

——. "Praise of Folly" [Stultitiae laus]. Translated by Betty Radice. *Collected Works of Erasmus*, 27:86-153. Toronto: University of Toronto Press, 1986.

——. "Preafatio, sev Hercules Gallicus." In *Opera omnia: Recognita et adnotatione critica instructa notisque illustrata*, edited by Christopher Robinson, 1:591-93. Amsterdam: North-Holland, 1969.

———. "The Right Way of Speaking Latin and Greek: A Dialogue" (De recta latini graecique sermonis pronuntiatione dialogus). Translated by Maurice Pope. *Collected Works of Erasmus*, 26:368–475. Toronto: University of Toronto Press, 1985.

———. "A Short Rule for Copiousness" (Brevis de *copia praeceptio*). In *Colloquies 1*, translated and edited by Craig R. Thompson. *Collected Works of Erasmus*, 39:164–70. Toronto: University of Toronto Press, 1997.

———. "Sympathy" (Amicitia). *Colloquies 1*, translated and edited by Craig R. Thompson. *Collected Works of Erasmus*, 39:1033–55. Toronto: University of Toronto Press, 1997.

Eupolis. "Demoi." In *Eupolis: Poet of Old Comedy*, translated by Ian C. Storey, 12–16. Oxford: Oxford University Press, 2003.

Euripides. "Ion." In *Euripides*, translated by David Kovacs, 4:322–515. Loeb Classical Library 10. Cambridge, MA: Cambridge University Press, 1999.

Galen. *On the Properties of Foodstuffs* (De alimentorum facultatibus). Translated by Owen Powell. Cambridge: Cambridge University Press, 2003.

Giarda, Christophoro. *Bibliothecae Alexandrinae icones symbolicae*. Milan: I. B. Bidellinin, 1628. Reprint, New York: Garland, 1979.

Hermogenes. *Opera*. Edited by Hugo Rabe. Stuttgart: Teubner, 1969.

Hermogenes [Pseudo-Hermogenes]. "The *Preliminary Exercises* Attributed to Hermogenes." In *Progymnasmata: Greek Textbooks of Prose Composition and Rhetoric*, translated by George Kennedy, 73–88. Atlanta: Society of Biblical Literature, 2003.

Herodotus. *Histories (The Persian Wars)*. Translated by A. D. Godley. 2 vols. Loeb Classical Library 117, 118. Cambridge, MA: Harvard University Press, 1999.

Hesiod. "Works and Days." In *Theogony, Works and Days, Testimonia*, edited and translated by Glenn W. Most, 86–153. Loeb Classical Library 57. Cambridge, MA: Harvard University Press, 2006.

Homer. *Iliad*. Translated by Stanley Lombardo. Indianapolis, IN: Hackett, 1997.

———. *Iliad*. Translated by A. T. Murray and William F. Wyatt. 2 vols. Loeb Classical Library 170, 171. Cambridge, MA: Harvard University Press, 1999.

———. *Odyssey*. Translated by A. T. Murray and George E. Dimock. 2 vols. Loeb Classical Library 104, 105. Cambridge, MA: Harvard University Press, 1995.

———. *The Odyssey*. Translated by Robert Fagles. New York: Penguin Books, 1996.

Hooke, Robert. *Micrographia, or Some Physiological Descriptions of Minute Bodies Made by Magnifying Glasses*. London: J. Martyn and J. Allestry, 1665.

Isocrates. "To Philip." In *Isocrates I*, translated by George Norlin, 1:246–339. Loeb Classical Library 209. Cambridge, MA: Harvard University Press, 1928.

John of Sardis [Ioannis Sardiani]. *Commentarium in Aphthonii progymnasmata*. Edited by Hugo Rabe. Leipzig: Teubner, 1928.

———. "Selections from the Commentary on the *Progymnasmata* of Aphthonius Attributed to John of Sardis, Including Fragments of the Treatise on *Progymnasmata* by Sopatros." In *Progymnasmata: Greek Textbooks of Prose Composition and Rhetoric*, translated by George Kennedy, 173–228. Atlanta: Society of Biblical Literature, 2003.

Libanius. *"Progymnasmata": Model Exercises in Greek Prose Composition and Rhetoric*. Translated by Craig A. Gibson. Atlanta: Society of Biblical Literature, 2008.

Longinus. "On the Sublime." Translated by W. Hamilton Fyfe and Donald Russell. In *Aris-

totle in Twenty-Three Volumes, 23:160–307. Loeb Classical Library 199. Cambridge, MA: Harvard University Press, 1995.

Lucian. "The Fly." Translated by A. M. Harmon. In *Lucian*, 1:82–95. Loeb Classical Library 14. Cambridge, MA: Harvard University Press, 2006.

Lucian [Pseudo-Lucian]. "In Praise of Demosthenes." Translated by M. D. Macleod. In *Lucian*, 8:237–302. Loeb Classical Library 432. Cambridge, MA: Harvard University Press, 1967.

Macrobius. *Saturnalia*. Translated and edited by Robert A. Kaster, vol. 1, bks. 1–2. Loeb Classical Library 510, Cambridge, MA: Harvard University Press, 2011.

"A Method for Recollecting the Gospels." In *The Medieval Craft of Memory: An Anthology of Texts and Pictures*, translated by Mary Carruthers and Jan Ziolkowski, 255–93. Philadelphia: University of Pennsylvania Press, 2002.

More, Thomas. *Utopia*. Edited by George M. Logan. Translated by George M. Logan and Robert M. Adams. 3rd ed. New York: W. W. Norton, 2011.

Nicolaus. *Nicolai progymnasmata*. Edited by Iosephus Felten. Leipzig: Teubner, 1913.

Nicolaus the Sophist. "Nikolaou Sophistou progymnasmata." In *Rhetores graeci*, edited by Leonhard von Spengel, 3:449–98. Leipzig: Teubner, 1856.

———. "Progymnasmata." In *Rhetores graeci*, edited by Christianus Walz, 1:266–420. Osnabrück: Otto Zeller, 1968.

———. "The Preliminary Exercises of Nicolaus the Sophist." In *Progymnasmata: Greek Textbooks of Prose Composition and Rhetoric*, translated by George Kennedy, 128–72. Atlanta: Society of Biblical Literature, 2003.

Plato, "Phaedrus." In *Plato I: Euthryphro, Apology, Crito, Phaedo, Phaedrus*, translated by Harold North Fowler, 412–579. Loeb Classical Library 36. 1914. Reprint, Cambridge, MA: Harvard University Press, 1990.

———. "Symposium." In *Plato III: Lysis, Symposium, Gorgias*, translated by W. R. M. Lamb, 80–245. Loeb Classical Library 166. 1925. Reprint, Cambridge, MA: Harvard University Press, 1991.

Pliny. *Natural History*. Vol. 3, bks. 8–11. Translated by H. Rackham. Loeb Classical Library 353. Cambridge, MA: Harvard University Press, 1940.

———. *Natural History*. Vol. 5, bks. 17–19. Translated by H. Rackham. Loeb Classical Library 371. Cambridge, MA: Harvard University Press, 1950.

———. *Natural History*, vol. 10, bks. 36–37. Translated by D. E. Eichholz. Loeb Classical Library 419. Cambridge, MA: Harvard University Press, 1962.

Plutarch. "Demosthenes." In *Lives*, translated by Bernadotte Perrin, 1–79. Loeb Classical Library 99. Cambridge, MA: Harvard University Press, 2004.

Psellos [Psellus], Michael. "Enkomien: Text und Übersetzung." In *Das Lob der Fliege von Lukian bis L. B. Alberti: Gattungsgeschichte Texte, Übersetzunge und Kommentar*, edited by Margarethe Billerbeck and Christian Zubler, 118–32. Bern: Peter Lang, 2000.

———. "Lusus ingenii." In *Oratoria minora*, edited by Antony Robert Littlewood, 94–115. Leipzig: Teubner, 1985.

Quintilian. *The Orator's Education*, vol. 1, bks. 1–2. Translated by Donald A. Russell. Loeb Classical Library 124. Cambridge, MA: Harvard University Press, 2001.

————. *The Orator's Education*, vol. 3, bks. 6–8. Translated by Donald A. Russell. Loeb Classical Library 126. Cambridge, MA: Harvard University Press, 2001.

————. *The Orator's Education*, vol. 5, bks. 11 and 12. Translated by Donald A. Russell. Loeb Classical Library 494. Cambridge, MA: Harvard University Press, 2001.

Ripa, Cesare. *Iconologia di Cesare Ripa Perugino*. Siena: Florimi, 1613.

Seneca. *The Epistles of Seneca*, vol. 2, epistles 66–92. Translated by Richard M. Gummere. Loeb Classical Library 76. Cambridge, MA: Harvard University Press, 1920.

Spenser, Edmund. *The Faerie Queene*. Edited by A. C. Hamilton. 2nd ed. New York: Routledge, 2013.

Synesius. "On Dreams." In *Synesius the Hellene*, translated by William Saunders Crawford. London: Rivingtons, 1901.

Theon, Aelius. "The Exercises of Aelius Theon." In *Progymnasmata: Greek Textbooks of Prose Composition and Rhetoric*, translated by George A. Kennedy, 1–72. Atlanta: Biblical Society of America, 2003.

van Dijk, Gert-Jan. *Ainoi, Logoi, Mythoi: Fables in Archaic, Classical, and Hellenistic Greek*. Leiden: Brill, 1997.

Vico, Giambattista. *The Art of Rhetoric* (Institutiones oratoriae, 1711–1741). Translated by Giorgio A. Pinton and Arthur W. Shippee. Value Inquiry 37. Amsterdam: Rodopi, 1996.

Webb, Ruth. "Appendix A: Translations." In *Ekphrasis, Imagination, and Persuasion in Ancient Rhetorical Theory and Practice*, 197–211. Surrey: Ashgate, 2009.

William of Champeaux. "Etsi cum Tullius." Edited by John O. Ward. Unpublished manuscript, 2014.

Xenophon. "On Hunting." In *Scripta minora*, translated by E. C. Marchant and G. W. Bowersock, 366–457. Cambridge, MA: Harvard University Press, 1968.

Ackroyd, Peter. *The Life of Thomas More*. New York: Doubleday, 1998.

Allen, Archibald. "Virgil's Acquisitive Bees." *Classical Quarterly* 60, no. 1 (2010): 258–61.

Andrews, Edna, and Yishai Tobin. *Toward a Calculus of Meaning: Studies in Markedness, Distinctive Features and Deixis*. Philadelphia: John Benjamins. 1996.

Angelidi, Christine. *A History of Byzantine Literature (850–1000)*. Athens: National Hellenic Research Foundation Institute for Byzantine Research, 2006.

Anhalt, Emily Katz. "A Matter of Perspective: Penelope and the Nightingale in *Odyssey* 19.512–534." *Classical Journal* 97, no. 2 (December 2001): 145–59.

Arnhart, Larry. "Aristotle, Chimpanzees and Other Political Animals." *Social Science Information* 29, no. 3 (1990): 477–557.

Arning, Bill. "Prosthetics." In *Sensorium: Embodied Experience, Technology, and Contemporary Art*, edited by Caroline A. Jones, 194–98. Cambridge, MA: MIT Press, 2006.

Ashworth, William B. "Emblematic Natural History of the Renaissance." In *Cultures of Natural History*, edited by Nicholas Jardine, Emma Spary, and James A. Secord, 17–37. Cambridge: Cambridge University Press, 1996.

Atwill, Janet M. *Rhetoric Reclaimed: Aristotle and the Liberal Arts Tradition*. Ithaca, NY: Cornell University Press, 1998.

Baldwin, B. "Lucian as Social Satirist." *Classical Quarterly* 11, no. 2 (1961): 199–208.

Baldwin, Thomas. *William Shakspere's Small Latine and Lesse Greeke*. Vol. 2. Urbana: University of Illinois Press, 1944.

Balme, D. M. "Development of Biology in Aristotle and Theophrastus: Theory of Spontaneous Generation." *Phronesis* 7, no. 1 (1962): 91–104.

Baratay, Eric, and Elisabeth Hardouin-Fugier. *Zoo: A History of Zoological Gardens in the West*. Translated by Oliver Welsh. London: Reaktion Books, 2002.

Beagon, Mary. *Roman Nature: The Thought of Pliny the Elder*. Oxford: Clarendon Press, 1992.

———. "Wondrous Animals in Classical Antiquity." In *The Oxford Handbook of Animals in Classical Thought and Life*, edited by Gordon Campbell, 414–40. Oxford: Oxford University Press, 2014.

Bell, Robert E. *Women of Classical Mythology: A Biographical Dictionary*. New York: Oxford University Press, 1991.

Benedict, Barbara M. *Curiosity: A Cultural History of Early Modern Inquiry*. Chicago: University of Chicago Press, 2001.

Blair, Ann M. *Too Much to Know*. New Haven, CT: Yale University Press, 2010.

Bodéüs, Richard. "L'animal politique et l'animal économique." In *Aristotelica: Mélanges offerts à Marcel de Corte*, edited by André Motte and Christian Rutten, 65–81. Brussels: Presses Universitaire Liège, 1985.

Bodson, Liliane. "Motivations for Pet-Keeping in Ancient Greece and Rome: A Preliminary Survey." In *Companion Animals and Us: Exploring the Relationships between People and Pets*, edited by Anthony L. Podberscek, Elizabeth G. Paul, and James A. Serpell, 27–41. Cambridge: Cambridge University Press, 2000.

Boehrer, Bruce. *Animal Characters: Nonhuman Beings in Early Modern Literature*. Philadelphia: University of Pennsylvania Press, 2011.

———. "Introduction: The Animal Renaissance." In *A Cultural History of Animals in the Renaissance*, edited by Bruce Boehrer. Oxford: Berg, 2007.

Bolter, Jay David, and Richard Grusin. *Remediation: Understanding New Media*. Cambridge, MA: MIT Press, 2000.

Bolzoni, Lina. *The Gallery of Memory: Literary and Iconographic Models in the Age of the Printing Press*. Translated by Jeremy Parzen. Toronto: University of Toronto Press, 2001.

Bradley, Mark. *Colour and Meaning in Ancient Rome*. Cambridge: Cambridge University Press, 2009.

Braidotti, Rosi. "Animals, Anomalies, and Inorganic Others." *PMLA* 124 (2009): 526–32.

Browning Cole, Eve. "Theophrastus and Aristotle on Animal Intelligence." In *Theophrastus: His Psychological, Doxographical, and Scientific Writings*, edited by William Fortenbaugh and Dimitri Gutas, 5:44–62. New Brunswick, NJ: Transaction, 1992.

Brudzińska, Jagna. "Aisthesis." In *Handbook of Phenomenological Aesthetics*, edited by Hans Rainer Sepp and Lester Embree, 59:9–15. Dordrecht: Springer, 2009.

Burgess, Theodore C. *Epideictic Literature*. New York: Garland, 1987.

Burke, Kenneth. *Permanence and Change: An Anatomy of Purpose*. 3rd ed. Berkeley: University of California Press, 1984.

Campbell, Gordon Lindsay, ed. "Introduction." In *The Oxford Handbook of Animals in Classical Thought and Life*, edited by Gordon Lindsay Campbell, xv–xix. Oxford: Oxford University Press, 2014.

Carlson, Gregory I. "Fables Invite Perception." *Bestia: Yearbook of the Beast Fable Society* 5 (1993): 7–25.

Carruthers, Mary. *The Book of Memory: A Study of Memory in Medieval Culture*. 2nd ed. Cambridge: Cambridge University Press, 2008.

———. *The Craft of Thought: Meditation, Rhetoric, and the Making of Images, 400–1200*. Cambridge: Cambridge University Press, 1998.

———. "Rhetorical *Memoria* in Commentary and Practice." In *The Rhetoric of Cicero in Its*

Medieval and Early Renaissance Commentary Tradition, edited by Virginia Cox and John O. Ward, 209–37. Leiden: Brill, 2006.

———. "Sweetness." *Speculum* 81, no. 4 (October 2006): 999–1013.

Carruthers, Mary, and Jan Ziolkowski. "General Introduction." In *The Medieval Craft of Memory: An Anthology of Texts and Pictures*, edited by Mary Carruthers and Jan Ziolkowski, 1–31. Philadelphia: University of Pennsylvania Press, 2002.

Cavarero, Adriana. *For More Than One Voice: Toward a Philosophy of Vocal Expression*. Translated by Paul Kottman. Palo Alto, CA: Stanford University Press, 2005.

Cave, Terence. *The Cornucopian Text: Problems of Writing in the French Renaissance*. Oxford: Clarendon, 1979.

Charland, Maurice. "Constitutive Rhetoric: The Case of the Peuple Québécois." *Quarterly Journal of Speech* 73, no. 2 (1987): 133–50.

Chen, Chung-Hwan. "Different Meanings of the Term *Energeia* in the Philosophy of Aristotle." *Philosophy and Phenomenological Research* 17, no. 1 (September 1956): 56–65.

Clark, Donald Lemen. "The Rise and Fall of Progymnasmata in Sixteenth and Seventeenth Century Grammar Schools." *Speech Monographs* 19 (1952): 259–63.

Clark, Stuart. *Vanities of the Eye: Vision in Early Modern European Culture*. Oxford: Oxford University Press, 2007.

Clements, Robert J. "Emblem Books and the Revival of Learning." *Studies in Philology* 54, no. 2 (April 1957): 85–100.

Codognet, Philippe. "The Logic of Memory and the Memory of Logic: Relation with Emotion." In *Emotions of Animals and Humans: Comparative Perspectives*, edited by S. Watanabe and S. Kuczaj, 265–76. Tokyo: Springer Japan, 2013.

Cohen, Simona. *Animals as Disguised Symbols in Renaissance Art*. Leiden: Brill, 2008.

Colie, Rosalie L. *Paradoxia Epidemica*. Princeton, NJ: Princeton University Press, 1966.

Conley, Thomas. *Rhetoric in the European Tradition*. White Plains, NY: Longman, 1990.

Conte, Gian Biagio. *Genres and Readers: Lucretius, Love Elegy, Pliny's Encyclopedia*. Translated by Glenn W. Most. Baltimore: Johns Hopkins University Press, 1994.

Cooper, John M. "An Aristotelian Theory of the Emotions." In *Essays on Aristotle's* Rhetoric, edited by Amélie Oksenberg Rorty, 238–57. Berkeley: University of California Press, 1996.

———. "Political Animals and Civic Friendship." In *Aristotle's* Politics*: Critical Essays*, edited by Richard Kraut and Steven Skultety. Lanham, MD: Rowman and Littlefield, 2005.

———. "Rhetoric, Dialectic, and the Passion." *Oxford Studies in Ancient Philosophy* 11 (1993): 175–98.

Cope, E. M. *An Introduction to Aristotle's Rhetoric, with Analysis, Notes, and Appendices*. London: Macmillan, 1867.

Cox, Virginia. "Rhetoric and Humanism in Quattrocento Venice." *Renaissance Quarterly* 56, no. 3 (2003): 652–94.

Crane, Susan. *Animal Encounters: Contacts and Concepts in Medieval Britain*. Philadelphia: University of Pennsylvania Press, 2012.

Custodio, María Violeta Pérez. "Plinio el Viejo y los *progymnasmata*: La edición complutense de la *Naturalis historia* de 1569." *Humanismo y Pervivencia del Mundo Clásico* 4, no. 2 (2008): 973–96.

Cvetkovich, Anne. *Depression: A Public Feeling.* Durham, NC: Duke University Press, 2012.

Daly, Peter M. *The Emblem in Early Modern Europe.* Surrey, UK: Ashgate, 2014.

Daston, Lorraine, and Katharine Park. *Wonders and the Order of Nature, 1150–1750.* New York: Zone Books, 1998.

Davis, Diane. "Creaturely Rhetorics." *Philosophy and Rhetoric* 44, no. 1 (2011): 88–94.

De Jonge, Casper C. *Between Grammar and Rhetoric: Dionysius of Halicarnassus on Language, Linguistics, and Literature.* Leiden: Brill, 2008.

———. "Dionysius and Longinus on the Sublime: Rhetoric and Religious Language." *American Journal of Philology* 133, no. 2 (Summer 2012): 271–300.

DeKoven, Marianne. "Why Animals Now?" *PMLA* 124, no. 2 (2009): 361–69.

De la Fuente, Jorge Marcos. "El insecto como tema retórico y poético." *Minerva: Revista de Filologia Clasica* 17 (2004): 85–102.

Del Vaga, Perin. *An Allegory of Rhetoric Holding a Caduceus.* Painting. Accessed May 5, 2015. http://www.wikigallery.org/wiki/painting284875/Perino-del-Vaga-%28Pietro-Bonaccors %29/An-allegory-of-Rhetoric-holding-a-caduceus.

Depew, David J. "Humans and Other Political Animals in Aristotle's 'History of Animals.'" *Phronesis* 40, no. 2 (1995): 156–81.

Derrida, Jacques. *The Animal That Therefore I Am.* Edited by Marie-Louise Mallet. Translated by David Wills. New York: Fordham University Press, 2008.

———. *The Beast and the Sovereign.* Translated by Jeffrey Bennington. Chicago: University of Chicago Press, 2009.

Desmet, Christy. "Progymnasmata, Then and Now." In *Rhetorical Agendas: Political, Ethical, Spiritual,* edited by Patricia Bizzell, 185–91. Mahwah, NJ: Lawrence Erlbaum, 2006.

Detienne, Marcel, and Jean-Pierre Vernant. *Cunning Intelligence in Greek Culture and Society.* Translated by Janet Lloyd. Atlantic Highlands, NJ: Humanities Press, 1978.

Dolmage, Jay T. *Disability Rhetoric: Critical Perspectives on Disability.* Syracuse, NY: Syracuse University Press, 2013.

Doody, Aude. *Pliny's Encyclopedia: The Reception of the "Natural History."* Cambridge: Cambridge University Press, 2010.

Draaisma, Douwe. *Metaphors of Memory: A History of Ideas about the Mind.* Translated by Paul Vincent. Cambridge: Cambridge University Press, 2000.

Eagleton, Terry. *The Ideology of the Aesthetic.* Oxford: Blackwell, 1990.

Eden, Kathy. *The Renaissance Rediscovery of Intimacy.* Chicago: University of Chicago Press, 2012.

Egan, Rory. "Insects." In *The Oxford Handbook of Animals in Classical Thought and Life,* edited by Gordon Campbell, 180–91. Oxford: Oxford University Press, 2014.

Elden, Stuart. "Reading Logos as Speech: Heidegger, Aristotle and Rhetorical Politics." *Philosophy and Rhetoric* 38, no. 4 (2005): 281–301.

Enders, Jody. *Rhetoric, Memory, Violence: The Medieval Theater of Cruelty.* Ithaca, NY: Cornell University Press, 1999.

Enterline, Lynn. *Shakespeare's Schoolroom: Rhetoric, Discipline, Emotion.* Philadelphia: University of Pennsylvania Press, 2012.

Evans, Gillian R. "Two Aspects of Memoria in Eleventh and Twelfth Century Writings." *Classica et Mediaevalia* 32 (1971–80): 263–78.

Fahnestock, Jeanne. *Rhetorical Style*. New York: Oxford University Press, 2011.

Farrell, Thomas B. "Sizing Things Up: Colloquial Reflection as Practical Wisdom." *Argumentation* 12 (1998): 1–14.

———. "The Weight of Rhetoric: Studies in Cultural Delirium." *Philosophy and Rhetoric* 41, no. 4 (2008): 467–87.

Findlen, Paula. "Courting Nature." In *Cultures of Natural History*, edited by Nicholas Jardine and Emma Spary, 57–74. Cambridge: Cambridge University Press, 1996.

———. "Inventing Nature: Commerce, Art, and Science in the Early Modern Cabinet of Curiosities." In *Merchants and Marvels: Commerce, Science, and Art in Early Modern Europe*, edited by Paula Smith and Paula Findlen, 297–323. New York: Routledge, 2002.

———. *Possessing Nature: Museums, Collecting, and Scientific Culture in Early Modern Italy*. Berkeley: University of California Press, 1994.

Foerster, Richard, and Karl Münscher. "Libanios." In *Paulys Realencyclopädie der classischen Altertumswissenschaft*, vol. 12 (1925): 2485–2551.

Foley, Megan. "*Peitho* and *Bia*: The Force of Language." *Symploke* 20, no. 1–2 (2012): 81–89.

Frank, Jill. *A Democracy of Distinction: Aristotle and the Work of Politics*. Chicago: University of Chicago Press, 2005.

Fredborg, Karin M. "The Commentaries on Cicero's *De Inventione* and *Rhetorica ad Herennium* by William of Champeaux." *Cahiers de l'Institut du Moyen Âge Grec et Latin* 17 (1976): 1–39.

Frede, Dorothea. "Mixed Feelings in Aristotle's *Rhetoric*." In *Essays on Aristotle's "Rhetoric,"* edited by Amelie Rorty, 258–85. Berkeley: University of California Press, 1996.

Freese, John Henry. *Aristotle: Art of Rhetoric*. Cambridge, MA: Harvard University Press, 1991.

French, Roger. *Ancient Natural History: Histories of Nature*. New York: Routledge, 1994.

Freund, Lothar. "'Good Counsel': An Adaptation from Ripa." *Journal of the Warburg Institute* 2, no. 1 (1938): 81–82.

Fudge, Erica. *Brutal Reasoning: Animals, Rationality, and Humanity in Early Modern England*. Ithaca, NY: Cornell University Press, 2006.

———. *Perceiving Animals: Humans and Beasts in Early Modern English Culture*. New York: St. Martin's Press, 2000.

Garver, Eugene. *Aristotle's "Politics": Living Well and Living Together*. Chicago: University of Chicago Press, 2011.

———. *Aristotle's "Rhetoric": An Art of Character*. Chicago: University of Chicago Press, 1994.

Gianna Pomata, and Nancy G. Siraisi. "Introduction." In *Historia: Empiricism and Erudition in Early Modern Europe*, edited by Gianna Pomata and Nancy G. Siraisi, 1–38. Cambridge, MA: MIT Press, 2005.

Gibson, Craig A. "Introduction." In *Libanius's "Progymnasmata": Model Exercises in Greek Prose Composition and Rhetoric*, edited by Craig A. Gibson, xvii–xxv. Atlanta: Society of Biblical Literature, 2008.

Gladstone, W. E. "The Reply of Achilles to the Envoys of Agamemnon." *Contemporary Review* 23 (1874): 841–55.

Goldhill, Simon. "What Is Ekphrasis For?" *Classical Philology* 102, no. 1 (2007): 1–19.

Golden, Mark. *Children and Childhood in Classical Athens*. Baltimore: Johns Hopkins University Press, 1990.

Goldner, Rebecca Steiner. "Touch and Flesh in Aristotle's *De Anima*." *Epoché* 15, no. 2 (2011): 435–66.

Gombrich, E. H. "*Icones Symbolicae*: The Visual Image in Neo-Platonic Thought." *Journal of the Warburg and Courtauld Institutes* 11 (1948): 163–92.

———. *Symbolic Images: Studies in the Art of the Renaissance*. Vol. 1. Chicago: University of Chicago Press, 1985.

Gordon, Richard. "Serapis." *Oxford Classical Dictionary*. Oxford: Oxford University Press, 2012.

Gotthelf, Allan. "Teleology and Spontaneous Generation in Aristotle: A Discussion." *Apeiron* 22, no. 4 (December 1989): 181–93.

Greenblatt, Stephen. *Marvelous Possessions: The Wonder of the New World*. Chicago: University of Chicago Press, 1991.

Gudger, E. W. "Pliny's *Historia Naturalis*: The Most Popular Natural History Ever Published." *Isis* 6, no. 3 (1924): 269–81.

Gunn, Joshua. "Speech Is Dead; Long Live Speech." *Quarterly Journal of Speech* 94, no. 3 (August 1, 2008): 343–64.

Gunn, Joshua, and Mirko M. Hall. "Stick It in Your Ear: The Psychodynamics of iPod Enjoyment." *Communication and Critical/Cultural Studies* 5, no. 2 (2008): 135–57.

Gunn, Joshua, and Jenny Rice. "About Face/Stuttering Discipline." *Communication and Critical/Cultural Studies* 6 (2009): 215–19.

Habicht, Christian. *Athens from Alexander to Antony*. Cambridge, MA: Harvard University Press, 1997.

Halliwell, Stephen. *The Aesthetics of Mimesis: Ancient Texts and Modern Problems*. Princeton, NJ: Princeton University Press, 2002.

Hampton, Timothy. "'Turkish Dogs': Rabelais, Erasmus, and the Rhetoric of Alterity." *Representations* 41 (Winter 1993): 58–82.

Haraway, Donna J. *The Companion Species Manifesto*. Chicago: Prickly Paradigm Press, 2003.

———. "In the Beginning Was the Word: The Genesis of Biological Theory." *Signs* 6, no. 3 (1981): 469–81.

Hariman, Robert. "Theory without Modernity." In *Prudence: Classical Virtue, Postmodern Practice*, edited by Robert Hariman, 1–32. University Park, PA: Penn State Press, 2003.

Harriott, R. M. "The Argive Elders, the Discerning Shepherd and the Fawning Dog: Misleading Communication in the *Agamemnon*." *Classical Quarterly* 32, no. 1 (1982): 9–17.

Harris, Henry. *Things Come to Life: Spontaneous Generation Revisited*. Oxford: Oxford University Press, 2002.

Hart, Mary Louise. "Choral Dance in Archaic Athens." In *The Art of Ancient Greek Theater*, edited by Mary Louise Hart, 19–32. Los Angeles: J. Paul Getty Museum, 2010.

Hartog, François. *The Mirror of Herodotus: The Representation of the Other in the Writing of History*. Translated by Janet Lloyd. Berkeley: University of California Press, 1988.

Hassig, Debra. "Sex in the Bestiaries." In *The Mark of the Beast: The Medieval Bestiary in Art, Life, and Literature*, edited by Debra Hassig, 71–93. New York: Garland, 1999.

Hawhee, Debra. *Bodily Arts: Rhetoric and Athletics in Ancient Greece*. Austin: University of Texas Press, 2004.

——. "Kenneth Burke's Jungle Book." *Minnesota Review* 73/74 (2009): 171–82.

——. "Looking into Aristotle's Eyes: Toward a Theory of Rhetorical Vision." *Advances in the History of Rhetoric* 14 (2011): 139–65.

——. *Moving Bodies: Kenneth Burke at the Edges of Language*. Columbia: University of South Carolina Press, 2009.

——. "Rhetoric's Sensorium." *Quarterly Journal of Speech* 101, no. 1 (2015): 2–17.

——. "Toward a Bestial Rhetoric." *Philosophy and Rhetoric* 44, no. 1 (2011): 81–87.

Hawhee, Debra, and Christa Olson. "Pan-Historiography: The Challenges of Writing History across Time and Space." In *Theorizing Historiography in Rhetoric*, edited by Michelle Ballif, 90–105. Carbondale: Southern Illinois University Press, 2013.

Heath, John. *The Talking Greeks: Speech, Animals, and the Other in Homer, Aeschylus, and Plato*. Cambridge: Cambridge University Press, 2005.

Heath, Malcolm. "Cognition in Aristotle's Poetics." *Mnemosyne* 62, no. 1 (2009): 51–75.

——. "Longinus on Sublimity." *Proceedings of the Cambridge Philological Society* 45 (1999): 43–74.

——. "Theon and the History of the *Progymnasmata*." *Greek, Roman, and Byzantine Studies* 43 (March 2002/3): 129–60.

Heidegger, Martin. *Plato's "Sophist."* Translated by Richard Rojcewicz and André Schuwer. Bloomington: Indiana University Press, 1997.

Heller-Roazen, Daniel. *The Inner Touch: Archaeology of a Sensation*. New York: Zone Books, 2007.

Hobgood-Oster, Laura. *Holy Dogs and Asses: Animals in the Christian Tradition*. Urbana: University of Illinois Press, 2008.

Holsinger, Bruce. "Of Pigs and Parchment: Medieval Studies and the Coming of the Animal." *PMLA* 124, no. 2 (March 2009): 616–23.

Hornblower, Simon, and Antony Spawforth, eds. "Hermes." In *Oxford Classical Dictionary*. Oxford: Oxford University Press, 1996.

Howe, Timothy. "Domestication and Breeding of Livestock: Horses, Mules, Asses, Cattle, Sheep, Goats, and Swine." In *The Oxford Handbook of Animals in Classical Thought and Life*, edited by Gordon Lindsay Campbell, 99–108. Oxford: Oxford University Press, 2014.

Howey, M. Oldfield. *The Encircled Serpent: A Study of Serpent Symbolism in All Countries and Ages*. New York: Arthur Richmond, 1955.

Hunger, Herbert. *Die hochsprachliche profane Literatur der Byzantiner*. Munich: Beck, 1978.

Hyde, Michael. "Paradox: The Evolution of a Figure in Rhetoric." In *Rhetoric 78: Proceedings of Theory of Rhetoric, an Interdisciplinary Conference*, edited by Robert L. Brown and Martin Steinmann, 201–25. Minneapolis: Center for Advanced Studies in Language, Style, and Literary Theory, 1979.

Innes, Doreen C. "Introduction." In *Poetics. Aristotle in Twenty-Three Volumes*, 23:311–42. Loeb Classical Library 199. Cambridge, MA: Harvard University Press, 1995.

Isager, Signe. "Sacred Animals in Classical and Hellenistic Greece." In *Economics of Cult in the Ancient Greek World: Proceedings of the Uppsala Symposium, 1990,* ed. Tullia Linders and Brita Alroth, 15–20. Uppsala: Acta Universitatis Upsaliensis, 1992.

Jack, Jordynn. "A Pedagogy of Sight: Microscopic Vision in Robert Hooke's *Micrographia.*" *Quarterly Journal of Speech* 95, no. 2 (May 2009): 192–209.

Janko, Richard. *The Iliad: A Commentary.* Vol. 4. Cambridge: Cambridge University Press, 1992.

Jardine, Lisa. *Erasmus, Man of Letters: The Construction of Charisma in Print.* Princeton, NJ: Princeton University Press, 1993.

———. "Inventing Rudolph Agricola: Cultural Transmission, Renaissance Dialectic, and the Emerging Humanities." In *The Transmission of Culture in Early Modern Europe,* edited by Anthony Grafton and Ann Blair, 39–86. Philadelphia: University of Pennsylvania Press, 1990.

———. *Worldly Goods: A New History of the Renaissance.* New York: W. W. Norton, 1996.

Jasso, John. "Psychagogia: A Study in the Platonic Tradition of Rhetoric from Antiquity to the Middle Ages." PhD diss., University of Pittsburgh, 2014 (Proquest 3648034).

Johansen, Thomas Kjeller. "Parts in Aristotle's Definition of Soul: *De Anima* Books I and II." In *Partitioning the Soul: Debates from Plato to Leibniz,* ed. Klaus Corcilius and Dominik Perler, 39–61. Berlin: Walter de Gruyter, 2014.

———. *The Powers of Aristotle's Soul.* Oxford: Oxford University Press, 2012.

Johnson, Francis. "Two Renaissance Textbooks of Rhetoric: Aphthonius' 'Progymnasmata' and Rainolde's 'A Booke Called the Foundacion of Rhetorike.'" *Huntington Library Quarterly* 6, no. 4 (1943): 427–44.

Kahn, Charles. "Sensation and Consciousness in Aristotle's Psychology." *Archiv für Geschichte der Philosophie* 48, no. 1–3 (1966): 43–81.

Kahn, Victoria. *Rhetoric, Prudence, and Skepticism in the Renaissance.* Ithaca, NY: Cornell University Press, 1985.

Kaster, Robert A, ed. and trans. *Studies on the Text of Macrobius' "Saturnalia."* Oxford: Oxford University Press, 2010.

Kennedy, George A., trans. *Aristotle on Rhetoric: A Theory of Civic Discourse.* 2nd ed. Oxford: Oxford University Press, 2007.

———. *Classical Rhetoric and Its Christian and Secular Tradition from Ancient to Modern Times.* Chapel Hill: University of North Carolina Press, 1980.

———. "A Hoot in the Dark: The Evolution of General Rhetoric." *Philosophy and Rhetoric* 25, no. 1 (1992): 1–21.

———, ed. and trans. "Introduction." In *Progymnasmata: Greek Textbooks of Prose Composition and Rhetoric,* edited by George A. Kennedy, ix–xvi. Atlanta: Society of Biblical Literature, 2003.

Kennedy, Krista. "The Daw and the Honeybee: Situating Metaphors for Originality and Authorial Labor in the 1728 Chambers' *Cyclopaedia.*" *College English* 76, no. 1 (September 2013): 35–58.

Kennerly, Michele. "Getting Carried Away: How Rhetorical Transport Gets Judgment Going." *Rhetoric Society Quarterly* 40, no. 3 (2010): 269–91.

Kisling, Vernon N., Jr. "Ancient Collections and Menageries." In *Zoo and Aquarium History:*

Ancient Animal Collections to Zoological Gardens, edited by Vernon N. Kisling, 1–47. Boca Raton, FL: CRC Press, 2001.

———. "Preface." In *Zoo and Aquarium History: Ancient Animal Collections to Zoological Gardens*, ed. Vernon N. Kisling. Boca Raton, FL: CRC Press, 2001.

Konstan, David. *The Emotions of the Ancient Greeks: Studies in Aristotle and Classical Literature*. Toronto: University of Toronto Press, 2006.

Kowalska, Halina. "Anselmus Ephorinus of Freideberg, c. 1505-December 1566." In *Contemporaries of Erasmus: A Biographical Register of the Renaissance and Reformation*, edited by Peter G. Bietenholz, 1:436–37. Toronto: University of Toronto Press, 1985.

———. "Jan Boner of Cracow, 1516-12 September 1562." In *Contemporaries of Erasmus: A Biographical Register of the Renaissance and Reformation*, edited by Peter G. Bietenholz, 1:166–67. Toronto: University of Toronto Press, 1985.

Kraus, Manfred. "Aphthonius and the *Progymnasmata* in Rhetorical Theory and Practice." In *Sizing Up Rhetoric*, edited by David Zarefsky and Elizabeth Benacka, 52–67. Long Grove, IL: Waveland Press, 2008.

———. "Grammatical and Rhetorical Exercises in the Medieval Classroom." *New Medieval Literatures* 11 (2009): 63–89.

———. "Rehearsing the Other Sex: Impersonation of Women in Ancient Classroom Ethopoeia." In *Escuela y Literatura en Grecia Antigua: Actas del Simposio Internacional, Universidad de Salamanca, 17–19 Noviembre de 2004*, 455–68. Frosinone, Italy: Cassino, 2007.

Kullmann, Wolfgang. "Der Mensch als politisches Lebewesen bei Aristotleles." *Hermes* 108, no. 3 (1980): 419–33.

Kurke, Leslie. *Aesopic Conversations: Popular Tradition, Cultural Dialogue, and the Invention of Greek Prose*. Princeton, NJ: Princeton University Press, 2010.

Lamp, Kathleen S. *A City of Marble: The Rhetoric of Augustan Rome*. Columbia: University of South Carolina Press, 2013.

Lateiner, Donald. "Nonverbal Communication in the Histories of Herodotus." *Arethusa* 20 (1987): 83–119.

Lawler, Lillian B. "Zoologically Speaking." *Classical Journal* 25, no. 9 (1930): 671–82.

Lee, Richard A., and Christopher P. Long. "Nous and Logos in Aristotle." *Freiburger Zeitschrift für Philosophie und Theologie* 54, no. 3 (2007): 348–67.

Lefkowitz, Jeremy B. "Aesop and Animal Fable." In *The Oxford Handbook of Animals in Classical Thought and Life*, edited by Gordon Campbell, 1–23. Oxford: Oxford University Press, 2014.

Leighton, Stephen. "Aristotle and the Emotions." In *Essays on Aristotle's "Rhetoric,"* edited by Amélie Oksenberg Rorty, 206–37. Berkeley: University of California Press, 1996.

Lennox, James. "Teleology, Chance, and Aristotle's Theory of Spontaneous Generation." *Journal of the History of Philosophy* 20, no. 3 (1982): 219–38.

Lewis, Charleton T., and Charles Short. *A Latin Dictionary, Founded on Andrews' Edition of Freund's Latin Dictionary*. Oxford: Clarendon Press, 1980.

Liddell, Henry George, Robert Scott, and Sir Henry Stuart Jones. *Greek-English Lexicon*. 9th ed. Oxford: Oxford University Press, 1996.

Lilja, Saara. *Dogs in Ancient Greek Poetry*. Commentationes Humanarum Litterarum 56. Helsinki: Societas Scientiarum Fennica, 1976.

Lloyd, G. E. R. *Aristotelian Explorations*. Cambridge: Cambridge University Press, 1996.

——. *Science, Folklore, and Ideology: Studies in the Life Sciences in Ancient Greece*. Cambridge: Cambridge University Press, 1983.

Lonsdale, Steven H. *Creatures of Speech: Lion, Herding, and Hunting Similes in the "Iliad."* Stuttgart: Teubner, 1990.

Lord, Carnes. "Aristotle's Anthropology." In *Essays on the Foundations of Aristotelian Political Science*, edited by Carnes Lord and David K. O'Connor, 49–73. Berkeley: University of California Press, 1991.

Lunsford, Andrea, ed. *Reclaiming Rhetorica: Women in the Rhetorical Tradition*. Pittsburgh: University of Pittsburgh Press, 1995.

Mack, Peter. *A History of Renaissance Rhetoric, 1380–1620*. Oxford: Oxford University Press, 2011.

——. "Rhetoric, Ethics, and Reading in the Renaissance." *Renaissance Studies* 19, no. 1 (2005): 1–21.

MacKinnon, Michael. "Pets." In *The Oxford Handbook of Animals in Classical Thought and Life*, edited by Gordon Campbell, 270–74. Oxford: Oxford University Press, 2014.

Malloch, A. E. "The Techniques and Function of the Renaissance Paradox." *Studies in Philology* 53, no. 2 (April 1956): 191–203.

Martin, Richard P. *The Language of Heroes: Speech and Performance in the "Iliad."* Ithaca, NY: Cornell University Press, 1989.

Martin, Thomas. *Ancient Greece from Prehistoric to Hellenistic Times*. New Haven, CT: Yale University Press, 1996.

Maser, Edward. "Introduction." In *Cesare Ripa: Baroque and Rococo Pictorial Imagery; The 1758–60 Hertel Edition of Ripa's "Iconologia" with 200 Engraved Illustrations*, edited by Edward Maser, vii–xxi. New York: Dover, 1971.

Massumi, Brian. *Parables for the Virtual: Movement, Affect, Sensation*. Durham, NC: Duke University Press, 2002.

McCartney, Eugene S. "Spontaneous Generation and Kindred Notions in Antiquity." *Transactions and Proceedings of the American Philological Association* 51 (1920): 101–15.

McCulloch, Florence. *Mediaeval Latin and French Bestiaries*. Chapel Hill: University of North Carolina Press, 1960.

McGrath, Elizabeth. "Personifying Ideals." *Art History* 6, no. 3 (1983): 363–68.

McKinnon, Michael. "Pets." In *The Oxford Handbook of Animals in Classical Thought and Life*, edited by Gordon Campbell, 269–81. Oxford: Oxford University Press, 2014.

McPherson, Miller, Lynn Smith-Lovin, and James M. Cook. "Birds of a Feather: Homophily in Social Networks." *Annual Review of Sociology* 27 (2001): 415–44.

Mehta, Arti. "How Do Fables Teach? Reading the World of the Fable in Greek, Latin and Sanskrit Narratives." PhD diss., Indiana University, 2008 (Proquest AAI3297125).

Meier, Christian. "Historical Answers to Historical Questions: The Origins of History in Ancient Greece." *Arethusa* 20, no. 1/2 (1987): 41–57.

Merlen, R. H. A. *De Canibus: Dog and Hound in Antiquity*. London: J. A. Allen, 1971.

Mews, Constant J. "*Logica* in the Service of Philosophy: William of Champeaux and His

Influence." *Schrift, Schrieber, Schenker: Studeien zur Abtei Sankt Viktor in Paris und den Viktorinem* 2005:77–117.

Mifsud, Marilee. *Rhetoric and the Gift: Ancient Rhetorical Theory and Contemporary Communication*. Pittsburgh: Duquesne University Press, 2015.

Miller, Henry Knight. "The Paradoxical Encomium with Special Reference to Its Vogue in England, 1600–1800." *Modern Philology* 53, no. 3 (1956): 145–78.

Moore, Mark Paul. "Rhetoric and Paradox: Seeking Knowledge from 'Container and Thing Contained.'" *Rhetoric Society Quarterly* 18, no. 1 (1988): 15–30.

Morison, Stanley. *The Likeness of Thomas More: An Iconographical Survey of Three Centuries*. Edited by Nicolas Barker. New York: Fordham University Press, 1963.

Moss, Ann. *Printed Commonplace-Books and the Structuring of Renaissance Thought*. Oxford: Clarendon Press, 1996.

Moss, Jessica. *Aristotle on the Apparent Good: Perception, Phantasia, Thought, and Desire*. Oxford: Oxford University Press, 2012.

———. "Right Reason in Plato and Aristotle: On the Meaning of *Logos*." *Phronesis* 59 (2014): 181–230.

Muckelbauer, John. "Domesticating Animal Theory." *Philosophy and Rhetoric* 44, no. 1 (2011): 95–100.

Mulgan, R. G. "Aristotle's Doctrine That Man Is a Political Animal." *Hermes* 102, no. 3 (1974): 438–55.

Naddaf, Gerard. *The Greek Concept of Nature*. Albany: State University of New York Press, 2005.

Nagy, Gregory. *Poetry as Performance: Homer and Beyond*. Cambridge: Cambridge University Press, 1996.

Nauert, Charles, Jr. "Humanists, Scientists, and Pliny: Changing Approaches to a Classical Author." *American Historical Review* 84, no. 1 (February 1979): 72–85.

Neri, Janice. *The Insect and the Image: Visualizing Nature in Early Modern Europe, 1500–1700*. Minneapolis: University of Minnesota Press, 2011.

Nietzsche, Friedrich. "On Truth and Lying in the Extra-moral Sense." In *Friedrich Nietzsche on Rhetoric and Language*, translated by Carole Blair, Sander L. Gilman, and David J. Parent, 246–57. Oxford: Oxford University Press, 1989.

Norlin, George. "Introduction." In *Isocrates*, translated by George Norlin, 1:ix–lii. Cambridge, MA: Harvard University Press, 1928.

North, Helen F. "Emblems of Eloquence." *Proceedings of the American Philosophical Association* 137, no. 3 (1993): 406–30.

Nussbaum, Martha Craven. "The Role of *Phantasia* in Aristotle's Explanation of Action." In *Aristotle's "De Motu Animalium,"* edited by Martha Craven Nussbaum, 221–69. Princeton, NJ: Princeton University Press, 1985.

———. *Upheavals of Thought: The Intelligence of Emotion*. Cambridge: Cambridge University Press, 2001.

Ogilvie, Brian W. *The Science of Describing: Natural History in Renaissance Europe*. Chicago: University of Chicago Press, 2006.

O'Gorman, Ned. "Aristotle's *Phantasia* in the *Rhetoric*: *Lexis*, Appearance, and the Epideictic Function of Discourse." *Philosophy and Rhetoric* 38, no. 1 (2005): 16–40.

———. "Longinus's Sublime Rhetoric, or How Rhetoric Came into Its Own." *Rhetoric Society Quarterly* 34, no. 2 (2004): 71–89.

Ong, Walter J. *Ramus, Method, and the Decay of Dialogue*. Cambridge, MA: Harvard University Press, 1958.

———. "World as View and World as Event." *American Anthropologist* 71, no. 4 (1969): 634–47.

Osborn, Michael. "Rhetorical Depiction." In *Form, Genre, and the Study of Political Discourse*, edited by Herbert W. Simons and Aram A. Aghazanian, 79–107. Columbia: University of South Carolina Press, 1986.

Ott, Brian L. "The Visceral Politics of *V for Vendetta*: On Political Affect in Cinema." *Critical Studies in Media Communication* 27, no. 1 (2010): 39–54.

Ott, Brian, and Diane Marie Keeling. "Cinema and Choric Connection: Lost in Translation as Sensual Experience." *Quarterly Journal of Speech* 97, no. 4 (2011): 363–86.

Panagia, Davide. *The Political Life of Sensation*. Durham, NC: Duke University Press, 2009.

Panofsky, Erwin. *Meaning in the Visual Arts*. Chicago: University of Chicago Press, 1955.

Papaioannou, Stratis. "The Aesthetics of History: From Theophanes to Eustathios." In *History as Literature in Byzantium*, edited by Ruth Macrides. Surrey, UK: Ashgate, 2010.

Parrish, Alex. *Adaptive Rhetoric: Evolution, Culture, and the Art of Persuasion*. New York: Routledge, 2014.

Payne, Mark. *The Animal Part: Human and Other Animals in the Poetic Imagination*. Chicago: University of Chicago Press, 2010.

Pearce, Susan M. *On Collecting: An Investigation into Collecting in the European Tradition*. London: Routledge, 1995.

Pease, Arthur Stanley. "Things without Honor." *Classical Philology* 21, no. 1 (January 1926): 27–42.

Perelman, Chaïm, and Lucie Olbrechts-Tyteca. *The New Rhetoric: A Treatise on Argumentation*. Translated by John Wilkinson and Purcell Weaver. Notre Dame, IN: University of Notre Dame Press, 1969.

Pernot, Laurent. *Epideictic Rhetoric: Questioning the Stakes of Ancient Praise*. Austin: University of Texas Press, 2015.

Perry, Ben Edwin. "Appendix: An Analytical Survey of Greek and Latin Fables in the Aesopic Tradition." In *Babrius and Phaedrus*, edited by Ben Edwin Perry, 419–610. Cambridge, MA: Harvard University Press, 1965.

———. "Demetrius of Phalerum and the Aesopic Fables." *Transactions and Proceedings of the American Philological Association* 93 (1962): 287–346.

———. "Introduction." In *Babrius and Phaedrus*, edited by Ben Edwin Perry, xi–cii. Cambridge, MA: Harvard University Press, 1965.

Phillips, Margaret Mann. *The "Adages" of Erasmus: A Study with Translations*. Cambridge: Cambridge University Press, 1964.

Plett, Heinrich F. *Enargeia in Classical Antiquity and the Early Modern Age*. Leiden: Brill, 2012.

———. *Rhetoric and Renaissance Culture*. Berlin: Walter de Gruyter, 2004.

Poliquin, Rachel. *The Breathless Zoo: Taxidermy and the Cultures of Longing*. University Park: Pennsylvania State University Press, 2012.

Pollard, John. *Birds in Greek Life and Myth.* Boulder, CO: Westview Press, 1977.

Pope, Maurice. "Introductory Note to 'The Right Way of Speaking Latin and Greek: A Dialogue.'" In *The Collected Works of Erasmus*, edited by J. K Sowards, 26:348–62. Toronto: University of Toronto Press, 1985.

Porter, James I. *The Origins of Aesthetic Thought in Ancient Greece: Matter, Sensation, and Experience.* Cambridge: Cambridge University Press, 2010.

———. "Rhetoric, Aesthetics, and the Voice." In *The Cambridge Companion to Ancient Rhetoric*, edited by Erik Gunderson, 92–108. Cambridge: Cambridge University Press, 2009.

Poulakos, John. *Sophistical Rhetoric in Classical Greece.* Columbia: University of South Carolina Press, 1995.

Quinn, Arthur, and Lyon Rathbun. "Accumulatio." In *Encyclopedia of Rhetoric and Composition: Communication from Ancient Times to the Information Age*, edited by Theresa Enos. New York: Routledge, 1996.

Radcliff-Umstead, Douglas. "Giulio Camillo's Emblems of Memory." *Yale French Studies* 47 (1972): 47–56.

Rathbone, Dominic W. "Alexandria (1)." In *Oxford Classical Dictionary*. Oxford: Oxford University Press, 2012.

Redfield, James M. *Nature and Culture in the "Iliad": The Tragedy of Hector.* Durham, NC: Duke University Press, 1994.

Reece, Steve. "Homer's Winged and Wingless Words: ΠΤΕΡΟΕΙΣ/ΑΠΤΕΡΟΣ." *Classical Philology* 104, no. 3 (2009): 261–78.

Rice, Jenny. *Distant Publics: Development Rhetoric and the Subject of Crisis.* Pittsburgh: University of Pittsburgh Press, 2012.

Rickert, Thomas. *Ambient Rhetoric: The Attunements of Rhetorical Being.* Pittsburgh: University of Pittsburgh Press, 2013.

Rorty, Amélie Oksenberg. "Structuring Rhetoric." In *Essays on Aristotle's "Rhetoric,"* edited by Amélie Oksenberg Rorty, 1–33. Berkeley: University of California Press, 1996.

Rose, Gilbert P. "Odysseus' Barking Heart." *Transactions of the American Philological Association* 109 (1979): 215–30.

Rosen, S. H. "Thought and Touch: A Note on Aristotle's *De Anima*." *Phronesis* 6, no. 2 (1961): 127–37.

Rousselet, Gilles. *La Retorique (Rhetoric: A Young Woman Standing in a Decorated Interior with a Caduceus in Her Right Hand and a Closed Fan in Her Left Hand).* Engraving, 1635 1633. The Metropolitan Museum of Art, New York. http://www.metmuseum.org/collection/the-collection-online/search/399271.

Rowland, Beryl. "The Art of Memory and the Bestiary." In *Beasts and Birds of the Middle Ages: The Bestiary and Its Legacy*, edited by Willene B. Clark and Meradith T. McMunn, 12–25. Philadelphia: University of Pennsylvania Press, 1989.

Samuel, Raphael. *Theatres of Memory: Past and Present in Contemporary Culture.* Vol. 1. London: Verso, 1994.

Schnoor, Franziska. "Octopuses, Foxes and Hares: Animals in Early Modern Latin and German Proverbs." In *Early Modern Zoology: The Construction of Science, Literature and the Visual Arts*, edited by Karel A. E. Enenkel and Paul J. Smith, 2:529–45. Leiden: Brill, 2007.

Segal, Charles. "Kleos and Its Ironies in the *Odyssey.*" *L'Antiquité Classique* 52 (1983): 22–47.

Self, Lois S. "Rhetoric and Phronesis: The Aristotelian Ideal." *Philosophy and Rhetoric* 12, no. 2 (1979): 130–45.

Sergueenkova, Valeria Viatcheslavova. "Natural History in Herodotus' Histories." PhD diss., Harvard University, 2009 (Proquest 3385559).

Serjeantson, R. W. "The Passions and Animal Language, 1540–1700." *Journal of the History of Ideas* 62, no. 3 (2001): 425–44.

Shannon, Laurie. *The Accommodated Animal: Cosmopolity in Shakespearean Locales.* Chicago: University of Chicago Press, 2013.

Sherman, Nancy. *Making a Necessity of Virtue: Aristotle and Kant on Virtue.* Cambridge: Cambridge University Press, 1997.

Shouse, Eric. "Feeling, Emotion, Affect." *M/C Journal: A Journal of Media and Culture* 8, no. 6 (December 2005). http://journal.media-culture.org.au/0512/03-shouse.php.

Sihvola, Juha. "Emotional Animals: Do Aristotelian Emotions Require Beliefs?" *Apeiron* 29, no. 2 (1996): 105–44.

Sloane, Thomas O. *On the Contrary: The Protocol of Traditional Rhetoric.* Washington, DC: Catholic University Press of America, 1997.

———. "Schoolbooks and Rhetoric: Erasmus's *Copia.*" *Rhetorica: A Journal of the History of Rhetoric* 9, no. 2 (Spring 1991): 113–29.

Smyth, Herbert Weir. *A Greek Grammar for Colleges.* New York: American Book Company, 1920.

Sorabji, Richard. *Animal Minds and Human Morals: The Origins of the Western Debate.* Ithaca, NY: Cornell University Press, 1993.

———. *Aristotle on Memory.* 2nd ed. Chicago: University of Chicago Press, 2004.

———. "Esprits d'animaux." In *L'animal dans l'antiquité,* edited by Barbara Cassin and Jean-Louis Labarrière, 355–74. Paris: Vrin (Bibliothèque d'Histoire de la Philosophie), 1997.

———. "Body and Soul in Aristotle." *Philosophy* 187 (1974): 63–89.

Stallybrass, Peter. "Against Thinking." *PMLA* 122, no. 5 (October 2007): 1580–87.

Steel, Karl. *How to Make a Human: Animals and Violence in the Middle Ages.* Columbus: Ohio State University Press, 2011.

Stewart, Susan. *On Longing: Narratives of the Miniature, the Gigantic, the Souvenir, the Collection.* Baltimore: Johns Hopkins University Press, 1984.

Strick, James E. *Sparks of Life: Darwinism and the Victorian Debates over Spontaneous Generation.* Cambridge, MA: Harvard University Press, 2000.

Summit, Jennifer, and David Wallace. "Rethinking Periodization." *Journal of Medieval and Early Modern Studies* 37, no. 3 (2007): 447–51.

Sutton, Jane S., and Mari Lee Mifsud. *A Revolution in Tropes: Alloiostrophic Rhetoric.* Lanham, MD: Lexington Books, 2015.

Tatham, Edward H. R. "Erasmus in Italy." *English Historical Review* 10, no. 40 (October 1895): 642–62.

Taylor, C. C. W. "Aristippus." In *The Oxford Companion to Philosophy,* edited by Ted Honderich, 49–50. Oxford: Oxford University Press, 1995.

Thomas, Keith. *Man and the Natural World: Changing Attitudes in England, 1500–1800.* Oxford: Oxford University Press, 1983.

Thomas, Rosalind. *Herodotus in Context: Ethnography, Science, and the Art of Persuasion.* Cambridge: Cambridge University Press, 2000.

Tyler, Tom. *Cifarae: A Bestiary in Five Fingers.* Minneapolis: University of Minnesota Press, 2012.

Usher, Stephen. "Introduction." In *Dionysius of Halicarnassus: Critical Essays*, 2:3–12. Loeb Classical Library. Cambridge, MA: Harvard University Press, 1985.

van Dijk, Gert-Jan. *Ainoi, Logoi, Mythoi: Fables in Archaic, Classical, and Hellenistic Greek.* Leiden: Brill, 1997.

Vickers, Brian. "*King Lear* and Renaissance Paradoxes." *Modern Language Review* 63, no. 2 (April 1968): 305–14.

———. "'Words and Things'—or 'Words, Concepts, and Things'? Rhetorical and Linguistic Categories in the Renaissance." In *Res et Verba in der Renaissance*, edited by Eckhard Kessler and Ian Maclean, 287–335. Wiesbaden, Germany: Otto Harrassowitz, 2002.

Vivante, Paolo. "On Homer's Winged Words." *Classical Quarterly* 25, no. 1 (May 1975): 1–12.

Waddington, Raymond B. "Iconography." In *Encyclopedia of Rhetoric*, edited by Thomas O. Sloane, 367–75. Oxford: Oxford University Press, 2001.

Walker, Jeffrey. "The Body of Persuasion: A Theory of the Enthymeme." *College English* 56, no. 1 (1994): 46–65.

———. "Dionysius of Halicarnassus." In *Classical Rhetorics and Rhetoricians: Critical Studies and Sources*, edited by Michelle Ballif and Michael G. Moran, 137–41. Westport, CT: Greenwood, 2005.

———. *The Genuine Teachers of This Art: Rhetorical Education in Antiquity.* Columbia: University of South Carolina Press, 2011.

———. "Michael Psellos on Rhetoric: A Translation and Commentary on Psellos' Synopsis of Hermogenes." *Rhetoric Society Quarterly* 31, no. 1 (Winter 2001): 5–40.

———. *Rhetoric and Poetics in Antiquity.* New York: Oxford University Press, 2000.

Walter, Eugene Victor. *Placeways: A Theory of Human Environment.* Chapel Hill: University of North Carolina Press, 1988.

Walters, Shannon. *Rhetorical Touch: Disability, Identification, Haptics.* Columbia: University of South Carolina Press, 2014.

Ward, John O. "The Medieval and Early Renaissance Study of Cicero's *De Inventione* and the *Rhetorica ad Herennium*: Commentaries and Contexts." In *The Rhetoric of Cicero in Its Medieval and Early Renaissance Commentary Tradition*, edited by Virginia Cox and John O. Ward, 3–75. Leiden: Brill, 2006.

———. "Quintilian and the Rhetorical Revolution of the Middle Ages." *Rhetorica: A Journal of the History of Rhetoric* 13, no. 3 (1995): 231–84.

Webb, Ruth. *Ekphrasis, Imagination, and Persuasion in Ancient Rhetorical Theory and Practice.* Surrey, UK: Ashgate, 2009.

Weil, Kari. *Thinking Animals: Why Animal Studies Now?* New York: Columbia University Press, 2012.

Whitfield, B. G. "Virgil and the Bees: A Study in Ancient Apicultural Lore." *Greece and Rome* 3, no. 2 (1956): 99–117.

Wilson, Catherine. *The Invisible World: Early Modern Philosophy and the Invention of the Microscope.* Princeton, NJ: Princeton University Press, 1995.

Wilson, Elizabeth. *Psychosomatic: Feminism and the Neurological Body*. Durham, NC: Duke University Press, 2004.

Wolfe, Cary. "Flesh and Finitude: Thinking Animals in (Post)Humanist Philosophy." *SubStance* 37, no. 3 (2008): 8–36.

Wolfson, Harry. "The Internal Senses in Latin, Arabic, and Hebrew Philosophic Texts." *Harvard Theological Review* 28 (1935): 69–133.

Woods, Carly S., and Michele Kennerly. "Moving Rhetorica: Feminized Figures and Feminist Rhetorical Scholarship." Unpublished manuscript provided by authors.

Woods, Marjorie Curry. "Weeping for Dido: Epilogue on a Premodern Rhetorical Exercise in the Postmodern Classroom." In *Latin Grammar and Rhetoric: From Classical Theory to Medieval Practice*, edited by Carol Dana Lanham, 284–94. London: Continuum, 2002.

Woolfson, Jonathan. "The Renaissance of Bees." *Renaissance Studies* 24, no. 2 (2010): 281–300.

Wyatt, William F. *Iliad, Books 1–12*. Translated by A. T. Murray. Vol. 1 of 2. Loeb Classical Library. Cambridge, MA: Harvard University Press, 1999.

Yack, Bernard. *The Problems of a Political Animal: Community, Justice, and Conflict in Aristotelian Political Thought*. Berkeley: University of California Press, 1993.

Yates, Francis A. *The Art of Memory*. Chicago: University of Chicago Press, 1966.

———. "Paradox and Paradise." *New York Review of Books*, February 23, 1967. http://www.nybooks.com/articles/archives/1967/feb/23/paradox-and-paradise.

Zeitlin, Froma I. "Figure: Ekphrasis." *Greece and Rome* 60, no. 1 (2013): 17–31.

Zinn, Grover. "Hugh of Saint Victor and the Art of Memory." *Viator* 5 (1974): 211–34.

encomia, paradoxical, 89, 95, 99; and amplification, 99–101, 110; Aristotle on, 96–97;
on bedbug, 102–4; on bookworm, 111;
comparison in, 110; ekphrasis in, 103, 110;
on flea, 102, 103; on fly, 10, 89, 104, 106,
108, 109, 111; on gnat, 89, 109; on louse,
106–8, 111; nonhuman animals in, 95–97;
playfulness in, 109–10; in *progymnasmata*,
98; and science, 111; *synkrisis* in, 100, 101;
views of, 97; wonder in, 105–8. *See also*
"Fly, The"; Psellos, Michael
encomium, 10; connection with ekphrasis,
95, 99; in *progymnasmata*, 89–90, 98; and
wonder, 92
Encomium on Helen (Gorgias), 95, 108
Encomium on Helen (Isocrates), 97
Enders, Jody, 122
energeia, 10, 15, 34, 36, 38, 45; and animals,
46, 69; Demetrius's discussion of, 47;
in *Iliad*, 51; in *Rhetoric*, 33, 42; and
sound, 54
enthymeme, 78–79
Ephorinus, 153, 154
Erasmus, 11, 110; *Adages*, 134, 148, 154;
Adagiorum chileades, 148–50; "Amicitia,"
153; anthropocentrism of, 134; approach
to abundance, 137–43; attitude toward
nonhuman animals, 134, 148–52; *Ciceronianus*, 157; collections, 148–49; colloquy
on copiousness, 158; on description, 152;
"In Praise of Folly," 109–10; on maintaining order, 140–41; model of memory, 158;
on More's animal collection, 152; and
Natural History, 145, 147; natural history
in method of *copia*, 146; notion of *copia*,
139–40; on observation, 152–55; "On the
Method of Study," 142, 144; *Parabolae*,
150; *Parallels*, 148, 151, 156; on practice
necessary for developing *copia*, 138–39;
references to animals, 134; treatment of
describing people, 133; view of hunting,
159; views of life, 159. *See also accumulatio*; *De copia*
ēthopoeia, 87

Etsi cum Tullius, 122–24
Eupolis, 69
Euripides, 44, 45

fables, 10, 134; adaptability of, 76, 77; Aesop,
61, 69, 71, 76, 77, 79; as allegories, 168; in
ancient oratory, 72; apes in, 86–88; and
audience's ability to see likeness, 77–78;
and children, 82; comparison with historical events, 77; Crane on, 72; and deliberative *phantasia*, 73–75, 80; and deliberative
rhetoric, 71, 72, 76, 80; deliberative work
of, 74–79; Demetrius's discussion of, 61;
Derrida on, 71–72, 77; dog-wolf-sheep
triumvirate, 70, 71, 74, 79; efficiency of,
75–76; expanding, 87–88; invention of
speeches for, 86–88; linked to dreams, 84;
logic of comparison in, 71; Mehta on, 81;
and memory, 114; as method of provoking
laughter, 83; as mode of visualization, 81;
moral and rhetorical force, 80; pain in, 78,
84–85; and *phantasia*, 72–73; picturing
work of, 81, 84; plausibility in, 85–86; and
politics, 70, 71, 74; in *progymnasmata*,
73, 79–88; in *Rhetoric*, 74–79; views of
in animal studies, 71–72; wisdom in, 79;
witnessing performed by, 78–79
Fahnestock, Jeanne, 49, 137, 141, 142
Farrell, Thomas B., 56, 57
fear, in *Rhetoric*, 78
feeling, 7; transferral of, 28; use of term, 5, 6.
See also *pathē/pathos*
Findlen, Paula, 136, 146, 147
flea, encomium on, 102, 103
"Fly, The" (Lucian), 10, 89, 104, 106,
108, 109
force, 58
forcefulness, 66, 100
"foursquare," 33, 34
Frank, Jill, 17
Freese, J. H., 1
French, Roger, 145
friendship, 154–55
Furies, 44, 69

Philomela, 35
philosophy, relation to rhetoric, 3
phōnē/logos distinction, 16, 54
phronēsis, 21
phusis. See nature
picturing, 81, 84
pithanos principle, 86
Plato, 32
playfulness, 67–68, 109–10
pleasure, 22–23; in Aristotle, 29; and disturbing images, 118; and *mimēsis*, 57; and
wonder, 118
Plett, Heinrich, 162
Pliny the Elder, 11, 92, 124, 144–46, 148–
49, 153, 156, 158, 170. See also *Natural
History*
Plutarch, 70, 71, 150
Poetics (Aristotle), 56, 57
political behavior, 15–18
Politics (Aristotle), 16, 18; *aisthēsis* in, 30;
influence on animal studies, 8; *logos/
alogos* distinction in, 13, 15; *logos* in, 17;
magnitude in, 55–56; and role of *logos* in
polis, 25; voice vs. speech in, 54
politika, Aristotle's conception of, 18
pot, in Giarda's Rhetorica, 167
praise: of other animals, 22; and sight, 94. *See
also* encomium
principle of plenitude, 136
production, and accumulation, 155
progymnasmata, 3–4, 5, 7, 10, 171; and amplification, 100–101; ekphrasis in, 90, 91–94;
encomium in, 89–90, 97–99; exercise
sequence, 89–90; fables in, 73, 79–88;
legacy of, 113; in medieval period, 113; and
memory, 114, 128, 131, 132; paradoxical
encomia in, 98; role of nonhuman animals
in, 110; treatments of ekphrasis, 148
propriety, 35
prosōpa, 91
prudence, 166
Psellos, Michael, 10, 89, 101, 102–4, 106–8,
109

[pseudo-]Cicero, 114
Pseudo-Hermogenes, 85, 97

Quintilian, 8–9, 11, 39, 49, 83, 88, 99, 100,
115, 136, 140, 157, 158

recollection, 118, 119–22. *See also* memory
Renaissance, 101, 136
repetition, 55
reputation, 25
res, 141–42
retention. *See* memory
rhetoric, 27; and animal studies, 3–5; beyond
persuasion, 46–47; importance of to
understanding animal-human relations,
162; relation to literature, 3; relation to
philosophy, 3
Rhetoric (Aristotle), 15; account of delivery
in, 51–52; amplification in, 99; "bringing before the eyes" in, 33; clarity in, 35;
discussion of similes in, 32–33; dog in,
1–2, 4, 5; *energeia* in, 33, 42; fear in, 78;
influence of, 8; logic of likeness in, 32, 33;
magnitude in, 56; metaphor in, 33–34;
nonhuman animals in, 21–24; pain in,
22–23, 78; *pathē* in, 30; *phantasia* in, 19,
20, 117; pleasure in, 22–23; propriety in,
35; shame/honor in, 24–25, 27; on sound,
48; theory of deliberative work of fable in,
74–79; translation of, 166–67; treatment of
style in, 31–35; voice in, 54
rhetoric, transdisciplinary, 170–71
Rhetorica, emblems of, 160–63
Rhetorica ad Herennium, 11, 116, 118, 119–24,
126, 129, 136
rhetorical education. *See* education, rhetorical; *progymnasmata*
rhetorical energy, 2–3, 42
Ripa, Cesare, 162–66, 167, 168, 170
Roberts, W. Rhys, 64

Sarapis, 165
Satire (Horace), 149